Contemporary Poetics

AGM STUDIES

AVANT-GARDE & MODERNISM

Contemporary Poetics

EDITED BY

LOUIS ARMAND

Northwestern

University Press

Evanston

Illinois

Northwestern University Press
www.nupress.northwestern.edu

Printed in the United States of America

10 9 8 7 6 5 4 3 2 1

Library of Congress Cataloging-in-Publication Data

Contemporary poetics / edited by Louis Armand.
p. cm. — (AGM studies : avant-garde & modernism)
Includes bibliographical references.
ISBN-13: 978-0-8101-2359-5 (cloth : alk. paper)
ISBN-10: 0-8101-2359-2 (cloth : alk. paper)
ISBN-13: 978-0-8101-2360-1 (pbk. : alk. paper)
ISBN-10: 0-8101-2360-6 (pbk. : alk. paper)
1. Poetics. 2. Literature, Modern—20th century—History and criticism. 3. Literature, Modern—21st century—History and criticism. I. Armand, Louis, 1972– II. Series: Avant-garde and modernism studies.
PN1042.C5835 2007
809.911—dc22

2007023577

∞ The paper used in this publication meets the minimum requirements of the American National Standard for Information Sciences—Permanence of Paper for Printed Library Materials, ANSI Z39.48-1992.

Contents

Part Three. Conjunctions

Part Four. Cursors

Part Five. Transpositions

Illustrations

Acknowledgments

As with all projects of this nature, there are many people whose ideas, assistance, and encouragement were determining factors along the way. I would like to begin by thanking all the writers who were involved at various stages, either directly or indirectly—including Lucie Koutková, Véronique Vassiliou, Susan Schultz, Andrei Codrescu, David Antin, Bob Creeley, Laurent Milesi, Jean-Michel Espitallier, Derek Attridge, Karen Mac Cormack, Jed Rasula, David Seiter, Ron Silliman, Lou Rowan, Bill Berkson, John Kinsella, Kate Fagan, Larry Sawyer, Drew Milne, Aleš Debeljak, and Stephen Muecke. Marjorie Perloff was instrumental in encouraging me to pursue this project beyond its initial stages and see it through to completion. Martin Procházka, Ellen Berry, Carol Siegel, and Davin Heckmann generously made available the pages of their journals and provided editorial support. Clare Wallace gave unstinting moral support at all times, for which I am deeply grateful. Thanks are also due to Michel Delville and David Norris of the Centre Interdisciplinaire de Poétique Appliquée in Liège; Éric Giraud of the Centre International de Poésie Marseille; and Rod Mengham and Kevin Nolan of the Cambridge Conference of Contemporary Poetry. And last but not least, thanks to Susan Betz and Rachel Delaney at Northwestern for their support and encouragement of this project, and to Anne Gendler, Lori Meek Schuldt, and Joyce Petersen for their editorial efforts.

Editor's Introduction: Transversions of the Contemporary

"Contemporary poetics": these two terms, taken separately or together, signify a field of discourse which remains today both problematic and highly contested within the disciplines of philology, applied poetics, and literary studies—but also further afield, in debates concerning aesthetics, cultural theory, philosophy, and even cybernetics. Assumed as the title of a volume of writings, these terms require to be accounted for as naming a body of work that may at times seem only tangentially related to the subject of *poetics* and of the *contemporary,* and of what might broadly be considered as constituting "contemporary poetics." In any case, such a title would be of little value if it were not in some way provocative and thereby productive of further consideration as to what is at stake here.

Generally speaking, this volume does not purport to be *about* poetics, or about what Aristotle in the *Perì poietikés* ("On Poetic Art")—establishing the term—anticipated as a systematic theory or doctrine of poetry. Rather, this volume adopts a multifaceted structure in bringing together a body of critical, or poetico-critical, writings—none of which strictly purports to be a "poetics" as such but which, in relation, broadly delineate a possible poetics of the contemporary. A poetics, in other words, that both responds to and seeks to account for the particularly contemporary (and consequently *technological*) emplacement of language and the material basis of this emplacement as an "object" of poetic investigation, practice, and above all *technique*—from the historical advent of concrete poetry to the current technopoetics of cyberspace.

Neither is it the purpose of this volume to enter into a polemic as to the claims and counterclaims of various "schools of poetry," nor does it intend to suggest that there is any determinate aesthetic, formal, or philosophical dimension of "contemporary poetics" that could be taken as a legitimization of the views of one party over another. Moreover, it in no way seeks to report on what might be considered the current state of poetry or of poets writing "today." The sense of the term "contemporary poetics" as it is used in this volume rests neither in the delineations of a specific period or epoch nor in a *present* conceived in terms of it but rather of a "condition" of writing—of the poetic enterprise—which is both historical and attuned to the radical coimplication of poetics and the "present time of writing."

This *time of writing* is what distinguishes writing that is said to take place in the here and now from writing that is grounded in the here and now. This volume is therefore concerned with a poetics that extends beyond our own time, as a mere marker of present-day literary activity, to address the limits of a writing "practice"—beginning with Stéphane Mallarmé in the late nineteenth century—that engages concretely with what it means to be "contemporary." Consequently, it is in terms of this "contemporaneity" that the old antagonism between poetics and praxis obtains a renewed formulation in a generative technics of writing, wherein the two terms are no longer regarded as opposed but as inevitably intertwined.

The reasons for this renewal may best be clarified in historical terms, in particular the radical social, political, and technological changes that transformed the world during the later stages of the Industrial Revolution and which, arguably, gave rise to what we now understand by the term "contemporary" (it is worth remembering that New York, London, and Paris only became contemporary with one another, in any practical sense, with the opening of the transatlantic telegraph in the last decades of the nineteenth century). With the advent of telecommunications, automated production, mass media, rail, and aeronautics, the "present" as a genuinely global concept first came into being—a present conceived in relation to the quasi instantaneousness of an actual, technological condition and which may be considered as delineating the experience of modernity. Language, too, became globalized, and subject to a new temporality and a new materiality. The very substance of language underwent rapid transformation, a phenomenon Marshall McLuhan highlighted in his investigations of the twilight of "typographic man" and the advent of digital culture, and this transformation in turn began to increasingly affect the consciousness of artists disillusioned by antiquarianism, academicism, and the retrograde nature of "institutional" culture in Europe and elsewhere in the Western and New Worlds.

The contemporaneous emergence in the human and physical sciences of a nonlocal concept of the present (beyond the merely immediate and near at hand) also signaled the emergence of an increasingly global notion of the task of art and of writing in particular. The advent of an "avant-garde" not surprisingly coincided with an emergent "internationalism," as a reaction against nationalism and neoclassical ideas of timelessness in art as (in part) the basis for an ethical withdrawal from the world into the realm of metaphysics and statist ideology. (It is no accident that crises of aesthetic valuation—as an expression of the moral progress of civilization—have attended the advent of mechanized and, during the course of the twentieth century, increasingly globalized warfare in all of its constituent forms, but most notably perhaps in the forms and use of mass propaganda and its attendant "virtual realities.")

With the advent of the truly "novel," of information as *news* and fashion as *mode*—of what we might call "teleculture" (with its attendant condition of social amnesia)—the contest between so-called high and low art (the "good," the "beautiful," and the "vulgar"), previously defined along theological and moral grounds, began to assume its familiar form as a political contest between groups variously identified with traditionalism, laissez-faire, social realism, and so forth. In the majority of cases, these disputes have little to do with the question of "contemporary poetics," as their focus tends largely—as in the case of Jürgen Habermas's critique of postmodernity—toward the artifacts of mass culture and the institutions of established taste, or to other temporal manifestations of cultural hegemony.

It is important to appreciate that the sense of being "contemporary" that has emerged by way of social and technological change is not a superficial manifestation of zeitgeist or of an empirical science but rather of a *condition of possibilities* in which the very fabric of consciousness is affected. And that this fabric—language broadly conceived—avails itself as a *making* and a *bringing forth* (*poiēsis*) with or by means of the "time of writing" (*con-temporis*). And it is in this sense that we might most profitably understand Pound's dictum that *poetry is news that stays news.* In any case, "contemporary poetics" is not thereby constituted by any particular style or aesthetic but by a particular regard for those conditions under which language happens. For this reason, the present volume focuses both on poetics as critique and in terms of the historical record (the antecedence and ongoing "project" of modernity) while primarily concerning itself with addressing the notion of a "poetics of the contemporary" in which so-called theory is not divorced from praxis but rather hybrid forms provide *contours of emergence* of a "time of writing"—in other words, of a "contemporary poetics."

From Stéphane Mallarmé and continuing to the present time, the poetics of the "contemporary" has been entangled in controversy by those who stake claims to its foundational moments. This phenomenon is highly paradoxical given that, as with avant-garde practice in general, the emergence of discourses of the "contemporary," as an outgrowth of Anglo-European modernism, was the result of a complicated process of appropriation, synthesis, and rejection of antecedent forms and strategies beyond any straightforward temporal placement. Moreover, its relation to the "contemporary" as such situates those discourses surrounding it in an uneasy relationship with the assertions of literary historicity and with the deconstruction of concepts of "presence" and the "present." Claims for the clarity and purity of the foundations of contemporary poetics, therefore, should be considered with skepticism, since they are by and large projective, generalized, and often explicitly constructed in order to promote a particular tradition or a particular legacy.

A number of characteristics may nevertheless be identified as describing "antecedents" of contemporary poetics in the twentieth and twenty-first centuries. These characteristics would necessarily include the self-reflexivity of modernist writing and of modernist art in general, which systematically problematized and sought to dismantle integral elements of the traditional structure of the literary work and of literary production. Perhaps the most exemplary instance of this self-reflexivity is James Joyce's atomistic reduction of language in *Finnegans Wake,* demonstrating that there is no "degree zero" of signification; for as long as there is language, meaning or sense will consist even at the very limits of materiality. Consequently, one of the recurring characteristics of poetics that is referred to as contemporary has been a certain effect of material contiguity and the notion that the constituting elements of a text possess equal semantic value. For this reason there has been an increasing emphasis on the materiality of language and a broad equivocality across signifying structures, irrespective of discursive or rhetorical categories (trope, schema; genre; paronomasia, parataxis, etc.). In the process, the valuation of particular technical skills associated with classical or Renaissance poetics has been largely revised and to a certain degree set aside, along with prior notions of *claritas,* originality, cohesion, mimesis. In turn, serial and nonlinear structures have come to predominate, placing existing formal orthodoxies under duress and at the same time realizing other structural vocabularies, ranging from the Linotype errata of Etoian Srdlu to the *calligrammes* of Guillaume Apollinaire and cutups of Tristan Tzara, to John Cage's mesostics and the *lipogrammes* of Georges Perec; from Alan Turing's discursive "halting machines" to Theodor Nelson's "poetic" hypertext machines.

A second set of characteristics might include the reduction of the literary work, as envisaged by Roland Barthes in "From Work to Text" (1971), in which the conventional objecthood of the work is pushed toward a threshold of dematerialization. While at the same time as expanding the textual field, this movement of "reduction" has been accompanied by a radical exploration of materiality itself, most clearly exemplified in the later works of Joyce, Gertrude Stein, and Samuel Beckett. Accompanying this movement has been a parallel reduction of the object relation of signifying structures. Beginning with the work of Sigmund Freud, J. G. Frazer, and Ferdinand de Saussure and the early cybernetics of Hermann von Helmholtz, there has arisen a series of discourses which have broadened the concept of language across all fields of knowledge, production, and so on. One consequence of these developments has been a discrediting of utilitarian notions of language and the advent of what could be called a *technological* conceptualization. This conceptualization replaces the notion of language as a function or object of sociohistorical evolution with the idea of language as the medium and ultimately condition of such evolution. Consequently, language is not seen to be technologized, but rather to be technological, in a way which bears out the assertion of Martin Heidegger that "*technē* belongs to bringing-forth, to *poiēsis;* it is something poetic."[1]

The critique and, to a large extent, deconstruction of "aesthetic" content suggests a third set of characteristics. This suggestion should immediately be qualified by noting that this critique itself has been an outgrowth of developments within aesthetic discourse, from Immanuel Kant to Benedetto Croce, and forms a subtext to the erosion of those boundaries which had been established between "literary" criticism and practice following the increased professionalization of the former (after F. R. Leavis) as an academic discipline and its subsequent critique by Michel Foucault, Jacques Derrida, Pierre Bourdieu, and others. As a counterinstitutional tendency, the critique of aesthetics has often been traced back to a series of meditations throughout the twentieth century, beginning in the late nineteenth century with Mallarmé's *Crise de Vers* and proceeding in one sense or another through the writings of Apollinaire, Blaise Cendrars, Ezra Pound, Tristan Tzara, Wyndham Lewis, Antonin Artaud, Gertrude Stein, Marcel Duchamp, John Cage, Charles Olson, and Christine Brooke-Rose and reaching something of an apotheosis in journals such as *Aspen* and *Tel Quel,* and in the Art & Language, Oulipo (*Ouvroir de littérature potentielle*), and language movements of the 1970s and 1980s and the journal *L=A=N=G=U=A=G=E.* The outcome is that avant-garde practice has come to be seen as increasingly placing the poetics of the contemporary at the threshold of "information technology," as exemplified in the work of such present-day writers as Jeremy Prynne, Véronique Vassiliou, Allen

Fisher, Steve McCaffery, Susan Howe, ΠΟ, and the "procedural poetics" of Christian Bök and Caroline Bergvall.

A fourth set of characteristics might be one that overtly questions the logic and facticity of cultural, historical, or ethical *placement* according to the assumptions of any one of numerous given orthodoxies. Here the "poetic subject" has become both a reflection on the conventions that frame it or situate it and a self-questioning of how poetics is "communicated" or disseminated. Such questioning has often taken the form of a reevaluation of generic distinctions about what it is that determines the literary or poetic as such. One of the outcomes of this reevaluation has been to focus upon the "concrete" nature of language, as distinct from those otherwise arbitrary formal conventions which have sought to bind language to a system of mimetic ideality. Commencing at least with Mallarmé's *Un coup de dés* (*A Throw of the Dice;* or earlier, with Nietzsche's typewriter), this tendency extends by a transverse genealogy through the *Merzbau* of Kurt Schwitters, the readymades of Duchamp, the *zaum* texts of Velimir Khlebnikov, Hugo Ball's sound poems, Heiner Müller's theater machines, the *combines* of Robert Rauschenberg and chance-mediated assemblages of Cage, to the hypertextual genetics of Kenneth Goldsmith's *Fidget* and the performative cybernetics of Stellarc.

The consequences of this last trajectory have perhaps been most evident in the crossover between poetics and visual or verbal media, underwriting the work of a broad range of now canonical artists, from the cubists and constructivists to the Bauhaus and up to the present, including more recently Andy Warhol, Robert Smithson, Sol LeWitt, Martha Rosler, Joseph Kosuth, Fluxus, Bruce Nauman, Eva Hesse, Cy Twombly, and Jenny Holzer, among others. The invention of the World Wide Web in the early 1990s similarly expanded the field of contemporary poetics through what could be called a manifestly "technological" emplacement. Much of recent cyber art, such as Douglas Davis's *The World's First Collaborative Sentence* or Andruid Kerne's *CollageMachine,* integrates mechanical and chance procedures in the production of "textual objects" in "real time." The advent of such "interface ecologies" radicalizes and simultaneously banalizes the machine aesthetics of successive avant-gardes while at the same time evincing a poetics of the contemporary in its most literal and hence most excessive and "monstrous" formulations.

In *Virtual Geography: Living with Global Media Events,* McKenzie Wark—extending the psychogeographic investigations of Guy Debord and the Situationist International, Buckminster Fuller's geodesics, dymaxionism, and *Synergetics,* and Jean Baudrillard's neosimulationism—looks at how the contemporary manifests itself as a series of local-global vectors whose "textual" organization exceeds traditionally defined notions of literacy. Signaling an end point in the evolution of what McLuhan, in *The Gutenberg Galaxy,* called "typographic man," Wark's logistic conception of media as an interface between semantic and temporal coordinates nevertheless describes a form of *détournement* (deviation, diversion) in the discourse of a "posthuman condition" by reinstating to this "post-" its meaning in accordance with the logic of a "future advent" (à la Jean-François Lyotard's "postmodern"), that is to say, as a constellation of possibilities summoned forth in the figure of the program (as the anteriority of writing, or *pro-grammē*). The end-of-man hence describes an anteriority, ex post facto, of the human condition as such; the (paradoxical) nascency of a form of literacy or typographics that Wark, following Alan Sondheim, terms "codework."

The delimiting of textuality and its implications for contemporary poetics can again be traced, through Jorge Luis Borges's *Labyrinths* and Joyce's *Finnegans Wake,* back to Mallarmé's *Le Livre* and its conception of the ideal book. For Mallarmé, this was to be a type of *Signatura Rerum,* an "open totality" which would depend not on the relation of a divine Logos but upon the communication of material elements (the "meaning of format") posed against the "artificial unity that used to be based on the square measurements of the book." Necessarily, it presupposed a movement away from a symbolic function of language, toward a poetics of structure, in which the closed totality of the book would give way to "hesitation, disposition of parts, their alterations and relationships."[2] Mallarmé's exploration of typographics and syntactic recombination anticipates in many ways the inventions of an avant-garde poetics whose vocabulary of the "contemporary" was, arguably, first given formal expression in *Un coup de dés* (appropriately it was originally published in the journal *Cosmopolis* in 1897)—and which, somewhat paradoxically, also marks the belated realization of what McLuhan regarded as the legacy of the invention of movable type (Johannes Gutenberg, 1454) and the advent of print culture. Cuban poet Octavio Armand sums this up in what could almost stand for a manifesto of a contemporary poetics:

> The poem seems to evoke the theology and science of distant centuries and to anticipate twentieth-century physics. On the one hand it is impossible not to feel the ancient music of the spheres in the conjunction

of musical score and star chart embodied in the poem. On the other hand, the idea of spacing reading so as to accelerate or diminish movement . . . links the notions of space and time so closely that it fuses them, creating a space-time for poetry through the *simultaneous vision of the page.* Finally, *Un coup de dés* places thought in an orbit very close to Heisenberg's principle of uncertainty. Thought fits, or rather falls, in the cage of chance; it is impossible to escape chance, despite an heroic effort to place a limit on infinity. The fundamental phrase, which is the title, "A throw of dice will never abolish chance," continues until the very last line, "All thought is a roll of dice."

Typography underscores the idea that in essence we are reading a single, irrevocable, interminable, abysmal phrase. Scattered throughout the poem—on its only page—and mounted in the largest type used, the title is foregrounded continuously. The last verse, in the smallest type, occupies the background. This is doubly true in both instances: because of the order of reading and because of the spatial expansion or contraction implicit in working with different types. The throw of dice ends in another throw of dice that is the same one and the same as always. Dice, words, ideas, types run across the page until they are lost in the mind. Poem of blank spaces, music of silences. We see, read, hear the forms of absence. Verbal phrase and musical phrase tend towards extreme purity: they expand in silence and they express it. . . . The idea empties in an abyss of infinite possibilities, as does the poem. Poem? Drawing? Score? The poem seems to embody the uncertainty of the throw of dice. It is a genre of genres. *Un coup de dés* that combines and generates genres.[3]

In their joint statement, "Pilot Plan for Concrete Poetry," the *Noigandres* group (Augusto de Campos, Décio Pignatari, and Haroldo de Campos) made the claim in 1958 that "Assuming that the historical cycle of verse (as formal-rhythmical unit) is closed, concrete poetry begins by being aware of graphic space as a structural agent." The "Pilot Plan" points to Mallarmé's concept of "subdivisions prismatiques de l'idée" and the radical use of typographic devices as the first qualitative jump in the development of a poetics of the "concrete." A second jump is identified in the work of Apollinaire: "Il faut que notre intelligence s'habitue à comprendre synthético-idéographiquement au lieu de anylitico-discursivement." (It is necessary that our intelligence habituate itself to a synthetic-ideographic comprehension, in place of an analytic-discursive one.)[4] Concretion for

Augusto de Campos, as outlined in his 1956 manifesto, extends beyond mere typographics to a broadly material foundation of semantic systems, encompassing the "verbivocovisual" syntax of Joyce, the neoplasticism of Mondrian, and the tonal compositions of Webern, Boulez, and Stockhausen. This tendency towards a signifying materiality almost inevitably leads to an identification with the developments of cybernetics, and toward the end of the "Pilot Plan" concrete poetry is explained as "a mechanism regulating itself: feedback. Faster communication (problems of functionality and structure implied) endows the poem with a positive value and guides its own making. Concrete poetry: total responsibility before language" (see page 213 in this volume).

Writing in "After Language Poetry: Innovation and Its Theoretical Discontents," Marjorie Perloff in this volume discusses how this "visualisation of poetic text" and the development of a "differential poetics" of nomenalized, virtual media came to impact most heavily upon North American poetry from the 1970s onward. Perloff cites McCaffery, a prominent figure of the language movement, who wrote in 1977, "There is a group of writers today united in the feeling that literature has entered *a crisis of the sign* . . . and that the foremost task at hand—a more linguistic and philosophic than 'poetic' task—is to demystify the referential fallacy of language." As a synthesis of Olson's "field composition," the *simultanéisme* of Apollinaire and Cendrars, and various "poststructuralist" and "postmodernist" theories, language poetry in the late 1970s and early 1980s stood in direct communication both with the ideas of de Campos and the *Noigandres* group and with those of Cage, McLuhan, and the "primary structures" of Morris, Judd, and Carl Andre. And while Perloff is critical of the inflated assumptions inherent to discourses of the *new,* both as an avant-gardist stock-in-trade and as revisionist hype, her analysis of language poetry's legacy not only establishes a strong claim to the enduring significance of the concretist experiment but also delineates a contemporary poetics of intermedia as its necessary consequence: "the one revolution which really has occurred in our own time, namely, the habitation of cyberspace."

McKenzie Wark's essay, "From Hypertext to Codework," pursues this line of argument further, radicalizing Theodor Nelson's definition of hypertext in the 1960s as "non-sequential writing" beyond the reductivist application of this term to forms of electronic scripting. Likewise Darren Tofts, in "Epigrams, Particle Theory, and Hypertext," explores the ways in which hypertext emerges as an outgrowth of a particular "technological" concept of poetics (or "techno-poetics," as Donald Theall says) which antecedes its reduction as a term within contemporary media theory or as a set of computing protocols. Tofts cites Jorge Luis Borges, Italo Calvino, and Joyce's *Ulysses* as exemplary of hypertextuality in this respect, as an "extension" of the logic of the book, similar to Mallarmé's conception of *Le Livre.* Wark's notion of "codework," on the other hand, crosses directly into the field of programmatics, exploring ideas of permutation and feedback in linguistic and semantic relations, resembling in certain ways the differential poetics of *Finnegans Wake.*

Writing in his introduction to the October 2001 "Codework" issue of *American Book Review* (22:6), Alan Sondheim cites the term "codework" as a metaphor for a type of idealized mode of writing in which the terminological and formal aspects of computer programming assume an "aesthetic" function which is at the same time productive of semantic disturbance (or "information") within a conventionally defined field of signification. Codework in this sense is posed as a type of writing which detextualizes while at the same time exposing the materiality of text vis-à-vis the "pro-grammē," that is, "works using the syntactic interplay of surface language, with reference to computer language and engagement" and "works in which the submerged code has modified the surface language—with the possible representation of the code as well." In his essay "Codeworld" in this volume, Sondheim discusses "codework, codewriting" in terms of the "alterity of a substrate which supports, generates, and behaves as a catalyst in relation to its production." The relation of codework to computer programming operates on an analogy, here, of the British mathematician Alan Turing in the design of the first prototype electronic computer, or ACE (Automatic Computing Engine), in 1945. Following from his earlier work on the Universal Turing Machine in *Computable Numbers* (1936), Turing developed a concept of linking data to sets of instructions in such a way as to modify the existing instructions coded within the computer (a form of *détournement* between trope and schema; text and metatext). Such notions of autopoiesis bring contemporary poetics into proximity with current discourses in artificial intelligence, genetics, and bioinformatics.

Gregory Ulmer's essay "Image Heuretics" and J. Hillis Miller's "The Poetics of Cyberspace" likewise extend the discussion of literate technologies within the realm of contemporary technopoetics, while Steve McCaffery's "Parapoetics and the Architectural Leap" engages technopoiesis by way of architectonic metaphors of deconstruction (between Rem Koolhaas and Derridean *archi-écriture*). Charles Bernstein's address to Berkeley linguist

George Lakoff explores the structural logic of propositions and the technics of meaning formation by means of the seemingly fortuitous encounter between clichés (dead metaphors) reduced to phrasal units whose arbitrary character enforces rather than contradicts Wittgenstein's contention that all "logical" statements are tautological. Keston Sutherland's essay "Vagueness," on the other hand, addresses itself to the subjective experience of facticity and the limits of logical empiricism. Allen Fisher's "Traps or Tools and Damage" likewise addresses the means by which language and representation affect a vicarious habitation of other subjectivities—here directed at the figures of R. B. Kitaj and Josef Beuys. Engaging the notion of "utility," Fisher looks at how mechanisms of "sense" operate by means of a negative-regenerative grammar—both programmatically and strategically—arising at that point at which subjecthood and materiality become contiguous.

In the three-part dialogue "AND &" in this volume, the Textbase collective of D. J. Huppatz, Nicole Tomlinson, and Julian Savage explores the relationship between semantics and materiality in the way in which linguistic signs are coded and recoded within contexts that extend and exceed linguistic functions. As a group of "writers" working in and with art spaces, Textbase routinely engages with the physical limits of language and the generative possibilities that arise from exceeding the constraints of linguistic convention or "permissibility." At the same time, the work of Textbase resists affiliation to any particular genre, whether "visual art," "concrete poetry," "conceptualism," or any other determinate category of language-as-spectacle. D. J. Huppatz and Benjamin Brady's 1998 "soup can" installation (alphabet soup?)—with its echoes of Hannes Meyer's 1931 "Co-op" installations, 1960s Warhol, and 1970s Fluxus—plays with the formal dualism of "form and content," "tenor and vehicle," issuing from the proviso that these things are not merely the serial images of a linguistic consumer-fetishism, but they are also "real."

Simon Critchley's essay "Wallace Stevens and the Intricate Evasions of As" approaches the question of how poetic or discursive modes and the objects of poetic discourse segue into and interfere with one another, through an investigation of metaphor and simulationism. Commencing with a tacit critique of citation, paraphrase, and the relation of persona and "poetic voice," Critchley traces the echoes in Wallace Stevens's poetry of a shift from "is" to "as" in his poetico-philosophical engagement with metaphor and its doubles. Ricardo Nirenberg, on the other hand, in his essay "Metaphor: The Color of Being" explores the self-reflexive history of the metaphor of "metaphor-'as'-color-of-being," arguing for a removal from a purely speculative treatment of poetics to a materialist approach to metaphor as a function of the probable and the possible within language.

In "Discontinued Meditations," his second essay in this volume, Steve McCaffery explores "letters in dysfunctional relation" within a material poetics of ellipsis and deletion ("a fault line across congruence"). Returning again to Mallarmé, McCaffery's meditation explores a certain objecthood of signification, the "white spaces" of "a vast overdetermination of the blank." Kevin Nolan's essay "Getting Past Odradek" similarly investigates the object mechanisms of base signification, reading through the "tropic" figures of Kafka's *odradek* and Freud's *fort/da* game (with possible allusions to Harry Matthews's 1981 *Le Naufrage du stade Odradek*). For Nolan, these "fault lines across congruence" can be read as a chiasmus between the animate and inanimate. "For the modern epoch," Nolan argues, "the formal autonomy of literature was secured by a theory of language which decoupled the contingency of thinghood and language, replacing causal heterology with arbitrariness." As with McCaffery and Wark, Nolan's mechanisms of replacement suggest "a line that follows the discontinuous ends of all 'tropological' incorporation" as a type of interface technology, or cybernetic apparatus, between "arbitrary signs" and "arbitrary bodies."

Reprising the later work of Maurice Merleau-Ponty, D. J. Huppatz's essay on Kathy Acker elaborates a "corporeal poetics" as both topos and tropic apparatus, a "surface of inscription" defined by zones of semantic intensity. Repetition, chance procedures, narrative recursion, the absence of the original, plagiarism/*détournement*—each situates the "body" of Acker's writing as what Derrida, echoing Julia Kristeva and Hélène Cixous, elsewhere terms *écriture au corps.* Like the *fort/da* game of Freud's *Beyond the Pleasure Principle,* Acker's writing commits its bodies to an abyss of writing which in turn is made to produce them, or reproduce them, as specters of the unassimilable. This "body politic," punctured and punctuating the assumed discourses of power defined by the Western canon of literature, affects itself as a writing of a "present tense" in which the contemporary functions as hybrid, transgenic, in medias res.

In their essay "Frank Zappa, Captain Beefheart, and the Secret History of Maximalism," Michel Delville and Andrew Norris investigate the relationship between the "maximalist body" and metaphors of dentality/orality and the scatological effects of otherwise arbitrary linguistic and nonlinguistic patterns, as compared to the physicality of sound composition, sampling, and performance. In ways that echo, comment upon, and "inflate" the minimalist computer-mediated poetics of John Cage, Zappa's "maximalism" is held up as "typical of the contemporary avant-garde's attention to the material conditions of art production and the baroque's tendency to 'foreground matter.'" This play between contemporary avant-garde technoculture and the baroque preoccupation with fugue-form and topologically inspired architectural design is not so much intended as an ahistorical deviation by way of structural analogy but an investigation into the way in which parametric means of composition (i.e., the programmatic function of material constraints) lie at the heart of any properly *contemporary* poetics. In effect, Delville and Norris are concerned with tracing the contiguity between the "baroque" and the "technological" fold, and as with recent chaos theories this contiguity is seen to arise from an apparent structural paradox in the way in which figures of excessive complexity and unpredictability evolve from sets of highly constrained parameters. The consequent view that all forms of rigid designation must contain elements of instability, capable of giving rise to potentially "gratuitous" forms of autopoiesis, leads to the idea that language, too, operates by means of a correlative excess and unassimilability within the structure of meaning itself.

The project of a contemporary poetics is consequently seen to be situated between the unassimilable and the synthetic—as both the active and inevitable engagement with recursive, transgenred, "future anterior" forms of a writing "posed" in advance (and consequently in excess) of itself. Through the concretist experiments of the 1950s and 1960s, the linguistic poetics of the 1970s and 1980s, and the "international regionalism" of the 1990s, the "demystification of the referential fallacy of language," as McCaffery says, has followed a path of reduction and permutation, minimalism and expansive *discursus,* and through a series of *posts* (postmodernism, postcolonialism) has arrived in the era of digitization, with its proliferation of Internet publications, Web logs, and a general (malfunctional) condition of "archive fever." The technological placement that language has "attained" might indeed be thought of as a turning between these seemingly divergent tendencies—a tropic apparatus or "technopoetics," whose articulation as spatiotemporal difference can be seen to describe an "essence" of the contemporary. In so doing, it assigns to it a certain materiality and material expression—of which the habitation of cyberspace is not only the most recent and ubiquitous manifestation but also the most attenuated, reduced to a (mere) interval of light.

This—the maximalist paradox of the quasi-infinite devolving upon the infinitesimal—recalls Ezra Pound's definition of the poetic VORTEX: "a radiant node or cluster . . . from which, and through which, and into which, ideas are constantly flowing," describing a law, as Gilles Deleuze suggests, of *extremism of matter.* Accordingly, a broadly materialist conception of "contemporary poetics" tends, as various critics have proposed, "not to just *add to* existing views of the world, but to trace a path showing how we got to this position, and what is at stake."[5] At the same time, "contemporary" writing accelerates the production of "traces" to a point, as McLuhan might say, of light-speed data processing, verging upon a collapse into *instantaneousness* and a metaphysics of the sign (information as Platonic truth or *alētheia*)—a hypermnesic machine which, to reverse the usual formula, remembers by forgetting everything. Which is to say, a technics of archival inscription as prosthesis of memory, ex temporis. The mimetic "present" of representation is simultaneously collapsed and dilated, an aperture effect of reflexivity which takes the place of the subject illusion of "seeing oneself seeing oneself" as topology of the image placed en abyme, as it were, where to learn of the truth (*ek tēs alētheias,* as Plato says in the *Cratylus*) is to learn of the image (*ek tēs eikonos*).[6] It may be argued that the technological acceleration that took place in the twentieth century accompanied a form of "historical" acceleration in which not only representation of the past or of the present but also representation itself arrived at an excess of the quasi-instantaneous—no longer in the form of an interminable recurrence à la Nietzsche and Vico but of an event-driven seriality by which the unique blossoms forth from a mechanical "repetition" defined not by discrete or successive moments but by an event of continuity described by self-difference.

In the poetics of the contemporary, what is "at stake," then, is not so much the unpresentability of the present but rather those recursive forms which stand in place of it—no longer, perhaps, in terms of the Benjaminian notion of mechanical reproduction as an erosion or displacement of "aura" but rather of the Heideggerean concept of the essence of technology as emplacement. Those "critical inventions" which belong to the contemporary while deforming its limits. As Mallarmé says, "here anticipating, there recalling, in the future, in the past, *under the false appearance of a present.*"[7]

The purpose in gathering together the writings in this volume has thus been to attempt—while remaining open to the contingencies of the medium—to provide something like a coherent account of the implications that arise from thinking *contemporary poetics* in these terms, in particular of the way in which the structure of language itself—as differential and relational—can be seen to imply its own contemporaneity (what I term the "time of writing"). Meaning or intelligibility, conjured from syntactic, tropic, or schematic coincidence, affects a structural immediacy between events of language whose relatedness in conceptual, spatial, or temporal terms may otherwise be highly attenuated. Computerized hypertext is consequently one means of envisaging, in a practical way, the proximity, by way of linkage, of such radically dissimilar signifying entities or signifying events—in other words, allowing us, by way of the increasingly mobile, wireless computer interface, to envisage in concrete terms the structural contours of a fourth linguistic dimension, between the quasi-infinite and the infinitesimal, as a network of *instantaneity* between all signifying "moments."

Awareness of such possibilities has come more and more to inform the way in which such notions as the "present" and the "contemporary" are engaged, not only in terms of historiography or ontology (present Being) but as a commonplace "condition of language." As a direct outcome of this awareness, the concerns of poetics have broadened far beyond the task of elaborating poetic *technique* to the much more considerable task of accounting for the generative technics of language per se. Indeed, it is increasingly understood that for any "poetics" to obtain as a set of propositions or as a practice, its terms must be generalizable not only with regard to a closed system or body of written or verbal signs but also in its broadest possible sense. In any case, poetics as a "making" or "bringing forth" cannot credibly be regarded as bearing solely upon the use of language in (or for the purposes of) poetry as a literary genre. The uses arrived at by or through such so-called poetic language must be considered inherent to language in its broadest conception—to all means of signification—in order to be *possible* as such. It is for this reason not merely a caprice that Wittgenstein, in the *Tractatus,* notes that there is no such thing as "poetic language." There is only language. And language is what we make of it.

The arrangement of the present volume seeks, as much as possible, to realize the common concerns of the authors represented here in the way in which such *general, material conditions of language* (from the "concrete" to the cybernetic) thereby inform a *contemporary poetics.* The volume commences with the short part 1, entitled "Endgame," containing Charles Bernstein's Swiftian satire of generative poetics and the textual apparatus ("How Empty Is My Bread Pudding") and Marjorie Perloff's critical-historical treatment of "writing after" Bernstein, Bruce Andrews, Lyn Hejinian, Susan Howe, Steve McCaffery, and others ("After Language Poetry: Innovation and Its Theoretical Discontents"). The intention here is to provide, at the outset, something like an itinerary of contemporary poetics in terms of both theory and practice and also to establish the heterogeneity of the terms under which, and by means of which, contemporary poetics is to be effectively discussed.

The remainder of the volume is divided into four additional parts, and while they represent only one set of possible organizational schemes, they are nevertheless determined by a series of key topics or "thematic" designs. Part 2 is entitled "Precursors" and relates to the work of a number of recognizable figures within the histories or prehistories of contemporary poetics: Franz Kafka, James Joyce, William Carlos Williams, Wallace Stevens, Kathy Acker, and Frank Zappa. At the same time, each of the pieces included in this section constitutes a critical poetics "in and of itself." The two functions can be seen here as complementary—an idea made explicit in part 3, "Conjunctions," in which more strictly theoretical and poetic (poetico-critical) texts rest side by side in a concerted engagement with rhetoric, prosody, and the vicissitudes of "intelligibility."

Part 4, entitled "Cursors," develops the notion of antecedence ("Precursors") in terms of "pointers," focusing on the *forethrow of possibilities* that defines *contemporary* poetics as what remains in advance of the merely temporal, here and now, or the "belatedness" of a historical present upon which the "institution of literature" establishes its claim. From the concrete poetics of Augusto de Campos, to the codework of Alan Sondheim, a sense of open possibility, of "futurity," is maintained—in that we can continue to find here a matrix of invention, of *poiēsis.* The final part, "Transpositions," is likewise both projective and reflexive with regard to the limits of poetic invention, by way of technology—conceived in the broadest sense of the marriage of *technē* and *logos*—mechanism and discourse, architectonics and archi-text, tool and trap, analogical structures and digitality.

While this organizational scheme foregrounds a number of topics ahead of others, it in no way precludes reading the volume in other ways, pursuing different itineraries, or taking transverse trajectories. The thematics of cyberculture, of modernity, of poetic practice, of materiality—all place demands upon the reader, however consciously or unconsciously one seeks to adhere to a developmental or "linear" treatment of contemporary poetics. There is also the matter of the particular works not included in this volume and of authors not represented, as much as of the external affiliations of various contributors and their works beyond the scope allowed here—for practical or other, more contingent, reasons. From the very outset, however, there has been an attempt to ensure that the relationship between the individual works and the editorial project as a whole devolved upon a more substantial basis than simply the desire to illustrate a point or exemplify a tendency in "cultural evolution" within the Western literary tradition.

The present volume in this way came about as the outgrowth of several projects (between 2001 and 2004) focusing on contemporary poetics, hypermedia, and codework, published under my editorship as special issues of the journals *Litteraria Pragensia* 11, no. 22 (2001) and *Rhizomes* 6 (2002). A number of pieces, including those by Simon Critchley, Allen Fisher, Bob Perelman, Bruce Andrews, Michel Delville and Andrew Norris, Keston Sutherland, Charles Bernstein, and Marjorie Perloff, were published separately in the *PLR* (*Prague Literary Review*), again under my editorship, between June 2003 and May 2004. The essays by Ricardo Nirenberg and J. Hillis Miller were composed for the present volume.

No possible organization of this volume could ever mask the fact that it is in no way exhaustive or definitive, nor does it make claims to being so. As with all such attempts at anthologizing, the discourses represented here are "coordinated" in a tentative and provisional way. Nothing will have been concluded; rather it is anticipated, hoped, that instead new possibilities will continually emerge—that nothing will have been rendered static, a mere artifact, the documentary of an event that happened once and whose implications have already been exhausted in a final, rigidifying project of institutionalization. But as with all things, the present and future possibilities represented by this volume will ultimately devolve upon the "use" that it is put to—or merely that it is "used well," as the old expression goes. As Bill Viola says at the end of Marjorie Perloff's concluding essay, "Chopsticks can either be a simple eating utensil or a deadly weapon, depending on who uses them."

Notes

1. Martin Heidegger, "The Question Concerning Technology," in *Basic Writings: From Being and Time (1927) to The Task of Thinking (1964)*, rev. ed., ed. David Farrell Krell (London: Routledge, 1993), 308.

2. Cited by Jacques Scherer in *Le "Livre" de Mallarmé*, ed. Jacques Scherer

(Paris: Gallimard, 1957), 32; English translation by Barbara Johnson, in Jacques Derrida, "The Double Session," in *Dissemination,* trans. Barbara Johnson (Baltimore: Johns Hopkins University Press, 1981), 231 (emphasis in original).

3. Octavio Armand, *Refractions,* trans. Carol Maier (New York: Lumen, 1994), 187.

4. Augusto de Campos, Décio Pignatari, and Haroldo de Campos, *Teoria da Poesia Concreta: Textos Críticos e Manifestos 1950–1960* (São Paulo: Ediçãoes Invenção, 1965).

5. Stephen Muecke, "The Fall," *Litteraria Pragensia* vol. 11, no. 22 (2001): 106.

6. Plato, *Cratylus* 423a; 439a. Compare Derrida, "The Double Session," 188 n. 17.

7. Stéphane Mallarmé, "Mimique," cited in Derrida, "The Double Session," 175.

Contemporary Poetics

Part One : **Endgame**

How Empty Is My Bread Pudding

Charles Bernstein

for George Lakoff

The conceited poet believes the entire world to be his poem.

As if you could or could not, would or would not, were or were not; as if the day ended and a new one popped out of the imagination, free of shadows, hurtling to an end of hurt, beyond sorrow's gate; but could not nor can not, would not nor will not; as if promise were just make-believe and make-believe a veil behind a veil; as if the news were never told and ignorance took the place of this incessant, miserable rain.

All the signs say no passage; still, there must be a way.

Sometimes one has to shake off even the most sophisticated modes of self-presentation (or self-concealment) to find a sense of where you are.

Particulars and their constellation: mosaic, seriality. Imagination of the negotiation of democratic social space: the particular not consumed, not made into an abstraction nor into stone, not dominated.

The arrival of a station at the train.

Everyone is talking about memoir but I just want to forget. I want a poetry that helps me to forget what I never knew.

Show me the baloney and I will immerse myself in last season's mausoleums.

The new is never new but we make it new in order to keep it from becoming dead to us. The motto shouldn't be make it new but make it live, but necrophilia surrounds us and we take its stench as the perfume of our hip indifference to art as something that changes in time, shifts against the tides, hollers out in anguish and exasperation at the suffocating banalities that seem to call our name out loud, as if we were written by them.

Poetry is too important to be left to its own devices.

Show me a man with two feet firmly planted on the ground and I'll show you a man who can't get his pants on.

The questioning of the beautiful is always at least as important as the establishment of the beautiful.

Not the desert clarity of my lamp
But the blanched consequence of my intransigence
[from Mallarmé]

1848—Faraday: "A slight efflorescent appearance was seen on the broken edge."
Felix:
"Nothing to bite
but my tongue."

Free verse is not a type of poetry but an imperative to liberate verse from constraints no longer applicable for a new time and new circumstance.

The rich do live better and have the narcotic of money to help them forget how it was acquired.

Be thorough: leave no turn unstoned.

Poets can be more or less overlooked: known but not well known, like Willy Loman on a pipe fitter's holiday; known in their day but lost to us now; recovered or, if not, recovering. For every emerging poet a couple of others begin to fade; we even begin to fade to ourselves, if the truth be told. We know of the poet's poet and even hear from time to time of the poet's poet's poet, repeating, more in relief than disappointment, John Ashbery's famous quip that a famous poet is not famous. But poetry's "disappeared," as Ron Silliman once called them, haunt us, less from a fear for ourselves than a dread that the context that imparts meaning to our work is so fragile. *I* is not an *other* but many others, fellow travelers among the dead, near dead, and just about alive.

Digital poetry 2003: In 1975, everyone was worried about the idea that language is code; in 2003, everyone is worried that code is language.

To each his tone.

The truth of the poem is neither in the representation nor in the expression. Its truth dwells in what has never been and what will never be. Where possibility and impossibility collide, here the poem is forged.

Sometimes a sentence is just a sentence.

I've got difference, you've got the same.

Thought is more resourceful than reality; that is why reality repudiates thought.

The poem is not finished even when it is completed.

I embrace a poetics of bewilderment. I don't know where I am going and never have, just try to grapple as best as I can with where I am. The poetry that most engages me is not theoretically perspicacious, indeed it has a poetics and an aesthetics but not a predetermining theory; it is multiform and chaotic, always reformulating and regrouping. Competence is less important to me than responsiveness, mobility; ingenuity and invention more important than solutions to predefined problems.

You don't hear anything unless you first listen, just as you can't have truth without trust, or thirst without memory.

The translation of poetry is never more than an extension of the practice of poetry.

Traditional metrical verse in the twenty-first century is like having sex through a net.

"You ask me to throw you a bone & I throw you a bone & now you say you don't want a bone."

Everything is relative and if not relative it ought to be.

You can't get there from here
But you can pretend

Sometimes a cigar is just a symbol.

Clinging to the loss as if it would protect you against the loss.

A line of zeros totally nothing.

This is not a sentence.

Alexandar Becanovic, the editor of *Monitor,* a Montenegrin journal, asks me: "Can you find, in the massive plurality of recent American poetry, common reference points? Is there, in that 'cacophony,' some kind of harmony?" It is always possible to find points in common just as it is always possible to find differences. As to the points in common, the question for American poetry—and it has been a question for a long time—is: What are the terms of the common? Emerson imagines an America that is in process, where the commonness is an aspiration, not something that is a given social fact. Langston Hughes says we are a "people in transition." The "point" is not to hurry through this *going* because we never arrive. *Get used to it!* Perhaps this is what we have in common, the particularities that we cultivate within the same space: our simultaneous presence to, and difference from, one another. I worry that harmony would be too close to homogeneity. I go for a microtonal tuning where the music is discovered in the process of active (maybe activist?) listening, not given to, predetermined by, idealized scales. The sirens screeching in the night to take away the dead or wounded interrupt our quiet, refined meditations. I want a poetry that incorporates those interruptions without losing its own newly foundering rhythms.

The space between "is" and "as," "sigh" and "sight," is the infinity of finitude.

Morality vs. aesthetics: I don't want to make poems that tell you what to think but that show a different order of thinking.

Fragments not as discontinuous but as overlays, pleats, folds: a chordal poetics in which synchronic notes meld into diachronic tones.

Larry Eigner's *Another Time in Fragments:* another time—one that extends and deepens the always present present, created by the algebra of constellated (or multiplied) moments of perception; a kind of hyperperceptual poetry.

A criticism is responsible to the degree it is able to respond.

Reforming a famous remark of Rimbaud, I would say "I" is a question, poetry an exploration, poetics a foundering refounding.

Longing for nothing is often the only way to get anywhere.

I suppose I could equally say the foundation of language is empathy, that empathy is what allows us to get the sense of something, and that its absence puts us outside the possibilities for meaning. But I don't like my empathy solicited. Experience presented is one thing, but being directed toward how to feel about it, well, I'd rather take a walk. Problem is: Is it really possible for a poem not to tip its didactic hat? Poems can't just be, they always mean more than we might want to say or hear. Even the bracketing of experience leans toward a mode of experience.

I'm not telling you what you can't do but what you can do.

A sigh is the sword of a textual thing.

Angels are not just literary conceits or supernatural realities. The angelic might be a moment of grace in which the images we use to measure out, contain, or shield our suffering melt away. That would mean not using images to symbolize the real but rather letting the real pour in through the cracks between the words.

It is not the poets born in America that are native to our poetry but the ones who came here, in exile, and made America their home; for exile is a native, indeed founding, experience for American poetry.

Sticks and stones will break my bones
But names wound the soul

Two prosodies diverged in a striated field, and I—, I took the hand of the hired man, I took the hand of the hired man and did the polka in the dark, if polka governs in a thing so marked.

a world of misplaced desire in the aftermath of feeling's collusion with happenstance

Syntax is never what you thought it was; just when you think you've got it down, it bolts out of the corral into the high chaparral. The job of poetry is not to get syntax back in the corral but to follow its wild journey into the unclaimed.

When you're right you're right and even when you're wrong you're right, just not as right as when you're right.

Now you're cooking with salt pork.

> O, head, get me an ox
> an ox and toad
> to pay the toll
> till I get there
> with nary a care

In a recent poem, Leonard Schwartz asks: What can drive a nonviolent person to violence? My question would be what can drive a violent person to nonviolence, since that is the only hope when there is too much righteousness on all sides. Who's right (or who's been more wronged), who's got the rights (or who's got the wrongs), or when you date the right (or wrong) only feeds the fire, since there are so many factors, real and imaginary, that one or the other side chooses, as a matter of principle, to discount. While I am for counting all the factors. But then it's not poetry but violence that rules.

Don't confuse the puzzle for the solution, the poet for the poem.

If you can't say something nice it's better not to say anything at all. Yet being a parent, or teacher, gives a provisional license to be "frank," to be negative, even to be harsh. Provisional in that the license is given for good cause—to avert immanent harm or toward some necessary reflection. The license of a critic to be frank comes without provision, unless it be the good of the body politic, our collective aesthetic benefit.

Injustice in the pursuit of order is oppression.
Mendacity in the pursuit of security is tyranny.

From time to time, poets or editors suggest the value of reading poems anonymously, for example publishing a magazine without author attributions. It sounds democratic, as if this would allow us to read poems for themselves. But artworks, like people, are not self-sufficient but part of a series, embedded in contexts, that give them not only meaning but also resonance, depth; you might even say, life. Without some sense of the author, one cannot account for these other, often determining, factors. Prejudice may be avoided. But (poetic) justice is sorely checked.

I quote this from Rosmarie Waldrop, who is citing an embedded reference to Susan Howe, who is alluding to a line of Dickinson, who is echoing Emerson in a way that suggests Jabès, who is paraphrasing a remark of Waldrop's.

What you see is never what it is, just as what you don't see may forever remain invisible to you.

Hope is a thing with claws and a recently shorn mustache.

I long for a time when the longing will stop. This is the one anxiety that I have the power to overcome. Instead, I nourish it.

My saliva tastes like ash.

Régis Bonvincino asks about my remark in *With Strings* that "art is made not of essences but of husks," pointing out that this is exactly the contrary of Ezra Pound's dictum, "Great literature is simply language charged with meaning to the utmost possible degree." "I see your new book as a kind of songbook for 'sense remote,'" he writes, and goes on to wonder about *With Strings*'s sometimes comic dialogue with popular music.

—If poetry is a shell game it's because it's all about the shells not the peas. The peas have barely touched the spoon and already it's time to change the tablecloth. Once we got hold of the peas, the game would be over; whereas poetry never gets anywhere, it just makes you more present to where you are, or at least where you were when you were brushing up against it, rubbing closures. A husk is "the outer covering of an ear of maize"; mine was always that, enmazed, or, in other words, the inner lining of our outer aspirations. History is husk and eternity its other shore, its negation or, as they say in thrillers, neutralization. Pound's technique of collage is more weighted in husks than he believed; this is the secular redemption of *The Cantos.*

"Desafinado"—off-key—remains my motto. I love the intoxication but it doesn't trust me, and so I find myself always low and wet, humming another tune to taxi me to the next transit point. It's also that the tunes that are going through my head are remote, they remind me of being reminded. "Sense remote" is like "husks" in that way. As young Hamlet says early on, "too much in the sun." We seek the solace of shade. Discretion, indirection, sense remote leave a space for conversation, the gaps we will for one another, one after another. "The nearness of you" is also a measure of distance.

Reading the poems as about poetry is an inevitable fallout of the speculative nature of these imaginary songs, whose tune is maybe more res cogitans than res extensa, but then who said it was a race anyway? The motif of poetry is just a husk. When it falls away you don't get to essence but are drifting in time, like always, the strings maybe lifting you up (like a puppet?) or else playing alongside (Charlie Parker's "Everything Happens to Me" on *With Strings:* "But now I just can't fool / This head that thinks for me. / I've mortgaged all my castles in the air"). Deep in the middle of the everyday, which as you say is sometimes pretty comical (slipping on a banana peel, not the banana) and sometimes political (getting up).

The imaginary ride that actually works.

Bus me, baby, to the telltale tattle of invidious celebration.

The thought is always anterior to the reflection, even if the reflection averts resemblance.

Make love not unilateralism.

The cherry that is not in the garden has fallen under the canopy of the proposition.

The issue of availability is in many ways external to what I do as a poet (in contrast, for example, to what I do as a teacher). I do what I can, what I want, what I come up with, what appeals to me, what hasn't been done in this way before, what I don't understand, what holds my attention, what pushes me a little further than I have gone, what throws me back to ground I thought I knew so well but in which I can no longer find my way. Poetry is difficult in the sense that it is not easily consumed as a mass culture product, but that applies to a wide variety of poems. Writing poems that try to be available, by using familiar styles and subjects, or telling stories, or avoiding complication, doesn't necessarily make the work any more accessible. The genre of poetry is itself an unpopular one and is rarely (never say never) able to use such traditional principles as effectively (if the goal is accessibility to the greatest numbers) as films, pop music, TV, and the like. At the same time, actually existing readers of poetry will find quite available what would be considered inaccessible by mass culture criteria. So then the question is: Available to whom? People who have no sustained engagement with poetry?

> don't spell out what you can imply
> & never imply what you can't address
> for it's later than it once was

but early all the same
(earlier than it was once
but later just the same)

Let's just say that one day is completely different than the next, but they still connect and we call the pattern our lives.

Or how about: The storage you rent is equal to the mortgage you forgo.

Just because you think you can't change the world is not a reason to try any less.

No man is a peninsula entire unto himself.

Your desire for independence will ultimately be your slavery.

THE PEN IS TINIER THAN THE SWORD.

Not yet? When then?

The poetry is not in speaking to the dead but listening to the dead.

Even when it's over it's not over.

Are you sure, she asked, you're talking of ideas?

Dark, emptied of touch would be entire, null and void. Even on an island.

—Rosmarie Waldrop

After Language Poetry: Innovation and Its Theoretical Discontents

Marjorie Perloff

Innovate: from the Latin, *in + novare,* "to make new, to renew, alter." In our century, from Rimbaud's "Il faut être absolument moderne!" and Ezra Pound's "Make It New!" to Donald Allen's *New American Poetry* and Douglas Messerli's *From the Other Side of the Century: A New American Poetry 1960–1990,*[1] novelty has been the order of the day. Think of the (now old) New Criticism, the New Formalism, the New Historicism, the nouveau roman and nouvelle cuisine. As I was writing this essay, a message came over the Internet announcing the British poet-critic Robert Sheppard's *Poetics and Linguistically Innovative Poetry 1978–1997.*[2] And in recent years, two important anthologies of women's poetry—*Out of Everywhere: Linguistically Innovative Poetry by Women in North America & the UK,* edited by Maggie O'Sullivan; and Mary Margaret Sloan's *Moving Borders: Three Decades of Innovative Writing by Women*[3]—have made the case that, in O'Sullivan's words, "much of the most challenging, formally progressive and significant work over recent years, particularly, in the U.S. . . . is being made by women."[4]

It was not always thus. The *Oxford English Dictionary* reminds us that "innovation" was once synonymous with sedition and even treason. In 1561, Thomas Norton wrote in *Calvin's Institute,* "It is the duty of private men to obey, and not to make innovation of states after their own will." Richard Hooker in 1597 refers to a political pamphleteer as "an author of suspicious innovation." The great Jacobean dramatist John Webster in 1639 speaks of "the hydra-headed multitude / That only gape for innovation"; and in 1796, Edmund Burke refers to the French Revolution as "a revolt of innovation; and thereby, the very elements of society have been confounded and dissipated."[5]

Indeed, it was not until the late nineteenth century that "innovation" became perceived as something both good and necessary, the equivalent, in fact, of avant-garde, specifically of the great avant-gardes of the early century, from Russian and Italian futurism to Dada, surrealism, and beyond. I cannot here trace the vagaries of the term, but it is important to see that, so far as our own poetry is concerned, the call for Making It New was the watchword of the beats as of Black Mountain, of concrete poetry and Fluxus as of the New York School. At times in recent years, one wonders how long the drive to innovate can continue, especially when, as in the case of Sloan's *Moving Borders,* fifty contemporary American women poets are placed under the "innovative" umbrella. Given these numbers, one wonders, who *isn't* innovative? And how much longer can poets keep innovating without finding themselves inadvertently Making It Old?

The problem is compounded when we turn to the relationship of innovation to theory. When the various French poststructuralisms of the postwar period first became prominent, they were known as *la nouvelle critique.* But as time went on, *la nouvelle critique* became known as poststructuralism, just as the "new American poetry" was called, in Don Allen's revised version of 1982, *The Postmoderns.*[6] What, then, is the relation of "new" to "post"? The issue is complicated, but it's fair to say that, in the case of theory, "new" was an epithet applied from outside, for the theorists themselves were less concerned to Make It New than to establish certain truths, for example, to study the relation of literary to so-called ordinary language, to determine the respective role of author and reader in the interpretation of a given text, and to establish the ways in which individual texts speak for their culture. For Barthes and Derrida, as earlier for Benjamin and Adorno, Bataille and Blanchot, "innovation" as such was of little interest. Benjamin, for that matter, had no use for the Dadaists who were his contemporaries, dismissing them as instigators of little more than "a rather vehement distraction," designed "to outrage the public."[7] And Adorno regarded most of what passed for "new" fiction or poetry as little more than *Kitsch.*

Accordingly—and this is an important aspect of the language movement, which stands squarely behind so much of contemporary "innovative" poetry—the "new" rapprochement between poetry and theory that we find in the first issues of *L=A=N=G=U=A=G=E* and in such equally important journals as the San Francisco-based *This* and *Hills* and the Canadian *Open Letter*, all now a quarter century old,[8] had less to do with innovation per se than with the conviction on the part of a group of poets, themselves keenly interested in philosophy and poststructuralist theory, that poetics was an intellectual enterprise, deserving a larger place than it had in the Creative Writing classroom of the 1970s.

Consider the symposium work edited by Steve McCaffery, published in the Canadian journal *Open Letter* in 1977 and reprinted by Andrews and Bernstein as *L=A=N=G=U=A=G=E Supplement Number One* in June 1980. The symposium was called "The Politics of the Referent"; it includes McCaffery's "The Death of the Subject: The Implications of Counter-Communication in Recent Language-Centred Writing," Bruce Andrews's "Text and Context," Ray DiPalma's "Crystals," Ron Silliman's "For Open Letter," and Charles Bernstein's "Stray Straws and Straw Men." Although three of these presentations were to be reprinted in their authors' own books on poetics,[9] these early versions are revealing. For so quickly did their authors soften their stance that the 1980 *Supplement* begins with the editorial disclaimer: "It seems worth remembering, in looking back on these essays, that the tendencies in writing McCaffery is talking about under such headings as 'language-centered' are as open to the entrapments of stylistic fixation as any other tendency in recent poetry."[10] And when McCaffery came to revise "The Death of the Subject" for his collection *North of Intention* (1986), he declared, "I was never happy with the title and both it and much of the content have been revised. The essay, whose original thoughts and materials were gathered through the mid-seventies, concentrates on a partial aspect of language writing: a concern primarily with the morphological and sub-lexemic relations present and obtainable in language. A decade later I can safely speak of this concern as an historic phase with attention having shifted . . . to a larger aspect—especially to the critical status of the sentence as the minimal unit of social utterance and hence, the foundation of discourse."[11]

McCaffery's original version begins dramatically with this declaration: "There is a group of writers today united in the feeling that literature has entered *a crisis of the sign* . . . and that the foremost task at hand—a more linguistic and philosophic than 'poetic' task—is to demystify the referential fallacy of language." "Reference," he adds, "is that kind of blindness a window makes of the pane it is, that motoric thrust of the word which takes you out of language into a tenuous world of the other and so prevents you seeing what it is you see."[12] Such a thrust—the removal of what McCaffery calls later in the essay "the arrow of reference"—is essential because "language is above all else a system of signs and . . . writing must stress its semiotic nature through modes of investigation and probe, rather than mimetic, instrumental indications" (Supplement 1).

Here, in a nutshell, is the animating principle of the movement: poetic language is not a window, to be seen through, a transparent glass pointing to something outside it, but a system of signs with its own semiologic "interconnectedness." To put it another way, "Language is material and primary and what's experienced is the tension and relationship of letters and lettristic clusters, simultaneously struggling towards, yet refusing to become, significations" (Supplement 2). McCaffery himself points to the Russian formalists and to Wittgenstein, Barthes, Lacan, and Derrida as the sources for his theory, and indeed language poetics, in this first stage, owes its greatest debt to French poststructuralism, although Charles Bernstein, for one, was much closer to Wittgenstein, whom he had studied with Stanley Cavell at Harvard, than to Derrida, whose analysis of signification he distrusted, even as Silliman and Andrews were drawn to a more politicized Frankfurt school poetics. But McCaffery himself sounds a Derridean note when he declares that "the empirical experience of a grapheme replaces what the signifier in a word will always try to discharge: its signified and referent." Indeed, in poetry the signifier is always "superfluous," overloaded with potential meanings and hence more properly a *cipher* (Supplement 4).

There are two corollaries, one Barthean, one Marxist-Althusserian. "Language-centred writing," McCaffery tells us, "involves a major alteration in textual roles: of the socially defined functions of writer and reader as the productive and consumptive poles respectively of a commodital axis."[13] And again: "The text becomes the communal space of a labour, initiated by the writer and extended by the second writer (the reader). . . . The old duality of reader-writer collapses into the one compound function, and the two actions are permitted to become a simultaneous experience within the activity of the engager."[14] "Reading" is thus "an alternative or additional writing of the text." Indeed—and here the Marxist motif kicks in—"Linguistic reference is a displacement of human relationships and as such is fetishistic in the Marxian sense. Reference, like commodity, has no connection with the physical property and material relations of the word as a grapheme."[15] Direct communication, on this count, is the hallmark of the commodity fetish. Thus, "to remove the arrow of reference," to "short-circuit the semiotic loop"[16] becomes a political rather than a merely aesthetic act. In his "Text and Context," Bruce Andrews reinforces this notion, dismissing referentiality as the misguided "search for the pot at the end of the rainbow, the commodity or ideology that brings fulfilment."[17]

As the utopian manifesto of a twenty-eight-year-old poet, "The Death of the Subject" inevitably overstated its case. The call for "unreadability" and "non-communication," for example, was largely exemplified by sequences of disconnected word fragments and isolated morphemes, as in the citations from Andrews, Clark Coolidge, and Barbara Baracks, the latter giving us a two-column poem such as

stint	grits
darts	file
gratis	ways to fit tins
dapper	angle
ill	apple

McCaffery calls on us to "produce one's own reading among the polysemous routes that the text offers,"[18] a challenging invitation, even though, as soon became apparent, less-stringent readers than McCaffery himself took him to mean that one reading would be just as good as another. Moreover, the rejection of all "instrumental" language as commodity fetish in favor of a poetic paradigm that, if we are to trust McCaffery's examples, includes only the most extreme form of wordplay, fragmentation, decomposition of words, and absence of all connectives, as in Andrews's "mob cuspid / welch / eyelet / go lavender / futurible,"[19] could be seen as excessively dismissive of alternate ways of composing poetry.

But despite McCaffery's Ubu-esque iconoclasm, his basic premises—and this is the irony—were by no means as extreme or as new as both the proponents and opponents of language poetics would have had us think. What McCaffery and Andrews[20] call the "referential fallacy" takes us right back to Roman Jakobson's central thesis that in poetry the sign is never equivalent to its referent and the corollary notion that poetry is language that is somehow extraordinary.[21] The case against transparency, against instrumental value and straightforward readability, was the cornerstone of Russian formalist theory as well as of Bakhtin's theory of dialogism and heteroglossia. In *The Noise of Culture,* William Paulson has shown that the concept of poetry as "noise," as blockage of the normal (transparent) channels of communication, is a notion that was already central, if intuitively so, for romantic theorists.[22] As for Wittgenstein, who refused to distinguish between ordinary and extraordinary language, finding "ordinary" language quite "strange" enough, the basic tenet that there are no meanings outside language gave McCaffery and his fellow symposiasts license to denounce what Bernstein called, in "Stray Straws and Straw Men," the "natural look" as itself a construction with particular implications. Poetry, Bernstein argued, is never really "natural" (e.g., "I look straight into my heart & write the exact words that come from within"); rather, "it emphasises its medium as being, constructed, rule governed, everywhere circumscribed by grammar & syntax, chosen vocabulary: designed, manipulated, picked, programmed, organised, & so an artifice."[23]

Twenty years after its appearance, we can read "The Politics of the Referent" symposium as an important intervention, reminding readers, on the one hand, that poetry has always been "an artifice" and, on the other hand, that poetry cannot be too far out of step with the other discourses—philosophical, political, cultural—of its own time. By the mid-1970s, let's recall, these discourses, as studied on every campus across the United States, had produced a highly sophisticated and challenging body of texts about the nature and function of *écriture,* or "writing," whether "writing the body" (Cixous and Irigaray), the position of subjects in particular discourses (Kristeva), or the relationship of truth to fiction (Todorov, Bahktin). I remember clearly, in those years, walking into St. Mark's Bookshop in the Bowery and seeing, on the central table, the stacks of Barthes's *The Empire of Signs,* Derrida's *Of Grammatology* in the Gayatri Spivak translation, and Foucault's *The Order of Things,* which was published not by a university press but by Random House in 1970. These books were selling as if they were popular novels. At the same time poetry, insofar as it had become the domain of the Creative Writing workshop, was no longer the contested site it had been in the days of Pound, Eliot, and Williams, or even of the "raw versus cooked" debates of the early 1960s. In the 1970s, for reasons too complex to go into here,[24] the production of poetry had become a kind of bland cottage industry, designed for those whose intellect was not up to reading Barthes or Foucault or Kristeva. The feeling-versus-intellect split had probably never been wider. For even as students were absorbing Barthes's "The Death of the Author" and Benjamin's "Work of Art in the Age of Mechanical Reproduction," official verse culture, as Bernstein called it, was spawning poems like "Hollandaise," from *The Morrow Anthology of Younger American Poets,* edited by Dave Smith and David Bottoms (1985), which begins:

> The sauce thickens. I add more butter,
> slowly. Sometimes we drank the best wine
> while we cooked for friends,
> knowing nothing could go wrong,
> the soufflé would rise, the custard set,
> the cheese be ripe.[25]

Here McCaffery's arrow of reference is flying straight into the saucepan, ready to curdle that hollandaise. The lasting contribution of language poetics, I would posit, is that at a moment when workshop poetry all across the United States was wedded to a kind of neoconfessionalist, neorealist poetic discourse, a discourse committed to drawing pretentious metaphors about failed relationships from hollandaise recipes, language theory reminded us that poetry is a *making* [*poien*], a construction using language, rhythm, sound, and visual image, that the subject, far from being simply the poet speaking in his or her natural "voice," was itself a complex construction, and that—most important—there was actually something at stake in producing a body of poems, and that poetic discourse belonged to the same universe as philosophical and political discourse.

None of this, of course, was all that new, but it was new within the particular context of *Naked Poetry,* as an important anthology edited by Robert Mezey and Steven Berg was called,[26] or vis-à-vis Allen Ginsberg's insistence on "First thought, best thought"—a precept Ginsberg fortunately didn't put into practice, at least not in his best poetry.[27] By the 1990s, in any case, all three of the language principles that McCaffery put forward had been subtly transformed even as their force remains implicitly operative today. The referential fallacy, to begin with, has given way to a more nuanced emphasis on the *how* of poetic language rather than the *what.* The dismissal of instrumental language as the commodity fetish has come under criticism from both Left and Right, as readers have realized that so-called innovative writing—writing that is fragmented, asyntactic, nonsensical, etc.—can be just as fetishized as anything else. And the emphasis on readerly construction, an article of faith in the semiotic theories of Barthes, Foucault, and Eco, and, in the United States, of reader response theory, has given way to a renewed perception that the alleged authority of the reader is, as Ron Silliman has remarked in a recent essay, merely a transfer of power whereby, in ways Barthes could not have foreseen, "the idealised, absent author of the New Critical canon has [merely] been replaced by an equally idealised, absent reader."[28]

Language poetics, let's remember, had a strong political thrust: it was essentially a Marxist poetics that focused, in important ways, on issues of ideology and class.[29] But it was less attuned to questions of gender and race: indeed, in the case of *L=A=N=G=U=A=G=E,* although one senses that every effort was made to include "innovative" women poets—for example, Rae Armantrout, Barbara Baracks, Abigail Child, Lynne Dreyer, Johanna Drucker, Barbara Einzig, Carla Harryman, Lyn Hejinian, Susan Howe, Bernadette Mayer, Leslie Scalapino, Rosmarie Waldrop, Diane Ward, and Hannah Weiner—the more overt theorizing itself was left, with rare exceptions,[30] to the men in the movement. Thus students in the 1980s were usually introduced to language poetry by such "reference books" as Barrett Watten's *Total Syntax,* Charles Bernstein's *Content's Dream,* Steve McCaffery's *North of Intention,* and Ron Silliman's *The New Sentence,* all published between 1985 and 1987. The dominance of these "founding fathers" can be seen in the British reception of language poetics, a reception coming largely from the Left, which was keenly interested in but also highly critical of the doctrines put forward in "The New Sentence," "Artifice of Absorption," and "The Death of the Subject" but had little to say about specific poems.[31]

What, then, of the women poets in the original movement? Interestingly, their background was more literary and artistic than that of, say, Andrews and Bernstein, who had studied political science and philosophy, respectively. Susan Howe began her career as an artist and was very much influenced by concrete poetry, especially the work of Ian Hamilton Finlay and Tom Phillips. Johanna Drucker was trained as a printmaker and visual poet and wrote her PhD thesis at Berkeley on the Russian avant-gardist Iliazd. Rosmarie Waldrop was a student of modernism and of concrete poetry and a translator of Edmund Jabès, Maurice Blanchot, and many Austrian and German avant-gardists. Kathleen Fraser had studied with the New York poets, especially Kenneth Koch. And so on.

The increasing recognition of the women poets associated with *L=A=N=G=U=A=G=E* was made evident in Lee Hickman's superb journal *Temblor,* which began publication in 1985 and ceased, with issue number 10, in 1989 because its editor was dying of AIDS and could no longer sustain the operation. Hickman is to my mind one of the great unsung heroes of the so-called innovative poetry scene. Unaffiliated with a university or even a specific movement, he published *Temblor* from his home on Cahuenga Boulevard in the much-despised San Fernando Valley above Hollywood. *Temblor* had no editorial board, no mission statement, and, until the last few issues, no grant money. Hickman simply published the poetry that interested him—a good chunk of it "language poetry" but also the related poetries coming out of the Olson-Duncan school, the objectivists, and the "ethnopoeticists" associated with Jerome Rothenberg: for example, Clayton Eshleman, Armand Schwerner, Rochelle Owens, Kenneth Irby, Robert Kelly, Jed Rasula, Gustaf Sobin, and John Taggart. *Temblor* was a portfolio with a nine-by-twelve-inch page which allowed for visual design, as for example in Leslie Scalapino's "Delay Series" (*Temblor* 4) and a long (twenty-eight-page) section from Susan Howe's *Eikon Basilike* (*Temblor* 9). The journal published Rosmarie Waldrop's *A Form of Taking It All* in its entirety (*Temblor* 6), Kathleen Fraser's sequence "In Commemoration of the Visit of Foreign Commercial Representatives to Japan, 1947" (*Temblor* 9), nine poems from Hejinian's "The Person" (*Temblor* 4), Fanny Howe's "Heliopathy" (*Temblor* 4), sections of Rachel Blau DuPlessis's long sequence *Drafts,* and work by Barbara Guest, Rae Armantrout, Carla Harriman, Mei Mei Bersenbrugge, Johanna Drucker, Norma Cole, and Martha (Ronk) Lifson. The magazine introduced the work of poets from other countries and cultures: Anthony Barnett, Paul Buck, and Peter Middleton from Britain; Anne-Maria Albiac, Michel Deguy, Edmond Jabès, and Jacqueline Risset, from France; Saúl Yurkievich and Tomás Guido Lavalle from Argentina; Minoru Yashioka from Japan; and so on. And finally, unlike the various "language" journals, *Temblor* focused on poetry rather than theory, although it did include critical prose, especially on or by its own poets.

Here, then, was an opening of the field that nevertheless avoided the merely eclectic. Like any editor, Hickman had his idiosyncrasies (a number of poets, no doubt, were published simply because they were Los Angeles friends), yet, with rare exceptions,[32] no effort was made to recruit the mainstream. Hickman never published Derek Walcott or Galway Kinnell, Adrienne Rich or Rita Dove. Why not? We cannot, alas, ask Hickman himself, and there is no mission statement to guide us. But I suspect there were three reasons. First, I imagine the editor felt these other poets got enough of a hearing in the mainstream press and, if he was to edit and produce a journal, he might as well introduce lesser-known poets. Second, publication of the established poets would have been too expensive. And third, although there is no *Temblor* manifesto, the journal's unstated aesthetic remained true to what was the cornerstone of language aesthetics, namely, that poetry is more than the direct voicing of personal feeling and/or didactic statement, that poetry, far from being transparent, demands rereading rather than reading, that it is News that Stays News.

Consider, in this connection, Lyn Hejinian's "Two Stein Talks" in *Temblor* 3 (1986). Hejinian makes a strong case for Stein's brand of "realism" as "the discovery that language is an order of reality itself and not a mediating medium—that it is possible and even likely that one can have a confrontation with a phrase that is as significant as a confrontation with a tree, chair, cone, dog, bishop, piano, vineyard, door, or penny."[33] In the course of her talks, Hejinian shows us how one can analyze such poetic language; how, for example, in the first of the *Tender Buttons,* "A Carafe, That Is A Blind Glass," the first phrase "A kind in glass and a cousin" binds "carafe" with "blind" phonically. As for "blind," Hejinian states, "A carafe is a container, a glass one, which, if filled with a thick liquid, that is a coloured one, might be, so to speak, blind, opaque." "A blind glass," she adds, "might also be a blank mirror, or a draped window—as my aunt would say, 'Draw the blinds, it's dinner time.' "[34]

The poet's offhand phrase "as my aunt would say" shows that reading semiotically rather than referentially, "in" rather than "for," need not be as impersonal an activity as it may have looked in its first incarnation. On the contrary, after citing Stein's sentence, "A gap what is a gap when there is not any meaning in a slice with a hole in it," Hejinian decides "to quote myself," in a stanza that begins "going / by the usual criteria for knowledge / I vowed not to laugh / but to scatter things."[35] Elsewhere in this issue we have Susan Howe's "12 Poems from a Work in Progress," which begins with a play on "sitt" / "site" / "cite" in keeping with McCaffery's account of the *cipheral* text and ends with an oblique prayer to "Keep and comfort come / unhook my father / his nest is in thick of my / work."[36] How does one "unhook" a father, and why? We never know for sure any more than we can paraphrase Fanny Howe's observation, in her "Scattered Light," that "Some patios won't allow the shadow of a maid / It's where I want to go with my tray / Sea heat unbearably white / Each book must fall, a scholar's mind."[37]

Here pun ("Sea heat unbearably white") and burlesque, as in the last line's play on "Into each life, a little rain must fall," complicate the story of this "shadow of a maid" carrying her tray on the forbidden patio.

Throughout *Temblor* 4 (which contains the complete *Conduit* by Barrett Watten and *Demo* by Ron Silliman), the language program is operative even if—and here we come to Hickman's own predilection—emotion, if by no means personal confession, is brought back into the equation. Further along in Fanny Howe's "Scattered Light" we read the following fragment:

> It was a night to be left alone
> To dig out fifteen pounds of pumpkin guts
> Stick in a candle and water the curtains
> I phoned a friend with What do you want
> Money and luck they said
> When I asked the angel in the bottle
> She fluttered and cried
> I want to die!
> Sex, too, squeezes out a lot of pleasure
> Till nothing is left but the neck[38]

Failed domesticity probably looms as large here as it did in "Hollandaise," but the relationship between the pumpkin carving of the opening, the allusion to the Cumaean Sybil trapped eternally in her bottle, and the image of the sex act hollowing out the body like an empty pumpkin cannot be transformed into any sort of coherent narrative. "Till nothing is left but the neck" is especially graphic. The neck of the bottle? The neck of the woman as external to the emptied-out body? The neck as all one has without money or luck? Oddly, my own image, if I am to follow McCaffery and become a coconstructor of the poem's meaning, is that of a chicken neck: the hard ugly piece of flesh (rather like a distorted penis or "stick in a candle") that remains when one has hollowed out the chicken, as opposed to the pumpkin, guts—the liver, heart, and other giblets, the fat along the inside chicken wall. Phonemically, in any case, the monosyllabic "neck" in final position connotes an unpleasant cut of some sort.

Howe's "Scattered Light" happens to be followed, a few pages later, by Nathaniel Mackey's "Uninhabited Angel," which begins:

> Sat up sleepless   in the Long Night Long, love
>   Stood me up. Stayed away though its
> Doing so stirred me. Wine on my shirtsleeve,
>   Wind on my neck.[39]

Again, love standing the poet up, again that ugly word "neck" in final position. But here in Mackey's jazz-inspired lyric, rhythm is quite other—an allusion to the Dogon myth of the Andoumboulou fusing with the "attempt to sing the blues," as in the drumbeat of:

> Tilted sky, turned earth.   Bent wheel, burnt
>   we.
>   Bound I. Insubordinate
>   us

where "we" is what's left when the wheel is bent and "I," bound to the wheel, becomes part of that "we" or "Insubordinate / us."

Nathaniel Mackey's poem serves as a reminder that even as women poets who were associated with poststructuralist experimentation were gaining recognition, persons of color had rarely been included. And here we come to a major shift in the 1990s, when what could loosely be called a language poetics has come into contact with one of color. A signal example is the poetry of Harryette Mullen, to which I now turn.

Musing and Drudging

In a 1997 interview for the first issue of *Combo,* Harryette Mullen recalls her own initiation into poetry:

> I had come from Texas to Northern California. I was in graduate school at Santa Cruz. I was reading all of this theory as a student in Literature at UC-Santa Cruz. So, at that point when I would . . . be taken to these talks and readings . . . I had a context for it . . . although of course no one at the university was dealing with the work of the [language] poets. But [they] read the same theory that my professors did—in fact they probably read twice as much, and had read the same theory earlier than a lot of my professors had, and they were highly intellectual poets . . . and they were saying interesting things . . . for instance the idea of problematizing the subject.[40]

And Mullen jokes about her fellow minority graduate students at Santa Cruz, who used the argument that it was all very well for white male poets to renounce "voice" but that "We *need* our subjectivity." Either extreme, she decided, seemed unsatisfactory. In her drive to problematize her own subjectivity, she began to incorporate into the language poetics that animated *Trimmings,* her book of prose poems based on Stein's *Tender Buttons,* the actual verbal games of her own culture—the childhood jump rope rhymes and "pseudo-courtship, formulaic exchanges" of preadolescence, like the male "What's cookin' good lookin'?" with its female response, "Ain't nothin' cookin' but the beans in the pot, and they wouldn't be if the water wasn't hot."

Trimmings is a wonderful example of the new fusion of language poetics and a renewed "Personism," to use Frank O'Hara's phrase. In an interview with Barbara Henning, Mullen remarks that "*Tender Buttons* appeals to me because it so thoroughly defamiliarises the domestic, making familiar 'objects, rooms, food' seem strange and new, as does the simple, everyday language used to describe common things."[41] But Mullen's own version of *Tender Buttons* also becomes, as she puts it, "a reflection on the feminisation and marginalisation of poetry: a whole poem composed of a list of women's garments, undergarments, & accessories certainly seems marginal & minor, perhaps even frivolous & trivial."[42] Consider the following:

> Tender white kid, off-white tan. Snug black leather, second skin. Fits like a love, an utter other uttered. Bag of tricks, slight hand preserved, a dainty. A solid color covers while rubber is protection. Tight is tender, softness cured. Alive and warm, some animal hides. Ghosts wear fingers, delicate wrists.[43]

This glove poem takes its inspiration from Stein but is really quite different. Mullen keeps her eye more firmly on the object than does Stein, whose cushions, umbrellas, and hats quickly give way to other related items, often quite abstract. Mullen's poem immediately raises the issue of color with the punning of "Tender white kid," and "off-white tan." For the poet, the "snug black leather" is in fact "second skin," and so it "fits like a love" even as it is "utter other," with its play on "udder"—the female body—and the need to speak, to give poetic voice to what has been voiceless. Further: the emphasis on "utter other" leads to classification: rubber gloves, leather gloves, gloves that are too tight, gloves that fit. But also an unease as to the source of leather gloves that is quite un-Steinian: "Alive and warm, some animal hides," where the pun on "hides" (as of "softness cured") leads directly to the image of ghosts known by their large white fingers in the dark. Do those ghost fingers belong to the predominantly white glove wearers? Mullen doesn't press the point: gloves are "tender" and "dainty": they make the wrists look "delicate."

The *Trimmings* poems thus have a complicated derivation. On the one hand, one could read this particular playful prose poem in conjunction with the short paragrammatic pieces cited by McCaffery in his essay for "The Politics of the Referent"—poems by Bruce Andrews, bpNichol, and McCaffery himself. On the other, Mullen's piece is more overtly political and engaged in the contemporary discourse about gender and race. Indeed, Mullen internalizes the theoretical paradigm of language poetics so as to refigure the relationship between the various ethnicities and communities to which she belongs.

In a 1993 lecture called "Visionary Literacy: Art, Literature and Indigenous African Writing Systems," for example, Mullen uses the deconstructionist analysis of *écriture* to call into question the standard explanatory models of African American vernacular orality.

> That black literary traditions privilege orality . . . has become something of a commonplace, in part because it's based upon what seems to be a reasonable and accurate observation. . . . Presumably, for the African-American writer there is no alternative to production of this authentic black voice but silence. This speech-based and racially inflected aesthetic that produces a black poetic diction requires that the writer acknowledge and reproduce in the text a significant difference between the spoken and written language of African Americans and that of other Americans.[44]

As Aldon Nielsen, who discusses this lecture in his *Black Chant,* points out, Mullen's proposed study of African *signage,* as the background for understanding the relationship of oral to written, "has much to tell us about the falsity of the assumed opposition between singing and signing in both Africa and America." And he cites her statement:

> The larger question I am asking is this: How has the Western view of writing as a rational technology historically been received and transformed by African Americans whose primary means of cultural transmission are oral and visual, rather than written, and for whom graphic systems are associated not with instrumental human communication but with techniques of spiritual power and spirit possession. . . . In

> order to construct a cultural and material history of African-America's embrace and transformation of writing technologies one might ask how writing and text functioned in a folk milieu that valued a script for its cryptographic incomprehensibility and uniqueness rather than its legibility or reproducibility.[45]

Here is a theoretical project that has very real poetic implications, involving, as it does, the struggle against the received idea that one is either "black or innovative." "*Muse & Drudge,* Mullen explains, really was my attempt to show that I can do both at the same time."

Muse & Drudge is written, seemingly against the "language" grain, in irregularly rhyming and heavily syncopated ballad quatrains. Its eighty pages have four quatrains per page, with no stops or indeed any punctuation except for the capitalization of proper nouns and apostrophes marking the possessive, as in "galleys upstart crow's nest." Each page, as Kate Pearcy points out in an excellent essay on the book,[46] seems to be a discrete unit, unbroken during oral performance. Accordingly, the lines of contiguity—that is, the network of metonymic associations—are offset by an oral paradigm that insures temporal reception of a given four-quatrain unit. Consider the following:

> Sapphire's lyre styles
> plucked eyebrows
> bow lips and legs
> whose lives are lonely too
> my last nerve's lucid music
> sure chewed up the juicy fruit
> you must don't like my peaches
> there's some left on the tree
>
> you've had my thrills
> a reefer a tub of gin
> don't mess me I'm evil
> I'm in your sin
>
> clipped bird eclipsed moon
> soon no memory of you
> no drive or desire survives
> you flutter invisible still[47]

Of this pseudoballad, we might say, in Steve McCaffery's words, "a reading activates certain relational pathways, a flow of parts, and . . . a structural 'infolding' of the textual elements."[48] In the first stanza, each of the fourteen words functions paragrammatically. "Sapphire's lyre" (the play on Sappho places Mullen's own blues singer in a rich poetic tradition)[49] "styles" (or is "styles" a noun, designating Sapphire's lyric styles?) "plucked eyebrows," where "plucked" can also be a verb, as can the "bow" in "bow lips." "Bow lips and legs" is a witty false parallel: it refers to being "bow-legged," but "bow lips" are the Cupid's mouth, a lovely rounded form. Or do the "lips and legs" bow down? Most important: "lyre styles" sounds like "lifestyles," and, lo and behold, the last line reads, "whose lives are lonely too."

Now consider the role sound plays—the rhyming of "Sapphire's" / "lyre" / "styles," the consonance of "lyre," "lives," the alliteration of *l*'s in seven of the fourteen words, the eye rhyme of "brows" / "bow." We can hear "Sapphire" playing the blues in this poignant and droll love song. What's more, in the second stanza, the "lucid music" comes to incorporate the southern black idiolect of "you must don't like my peaches / there's some left on the tree."[50] Individual morphemes create tension: "chewed up the juicy fruit" refers to a common brand of chewing gum, but "chewed up" relates that "juicy fruit" to those rejected peaches. Again, "you've had my thrills" is a brilliant send-up of the expected "I've had my thrills / a reefer a tub of gin / don't mess with me I'm evil." And "I'm in your sin," with its allusion to the Bessie Smith song "A Pig Foot and a Bottle of Gin," undercuts self-recrimination (e.g., "I'm full of sin") by putting the blame squarely on the lover. Then again, "you've had my thrills" can be read as, "you've had my best moments; I've given it all to you!" Finally, the semantic and phonemic conjunction of "clipped bird" and "eclipsed moon" plays on the standard romantic clichés about love. Is the poet herself the "clipped bird"? Or is she getting rid of the lover? The poem's last line, "you flutter invisible still" makes for a comic rhyme with the "thrills" of line 9; it also echoes the image of the swans who glide through the water "Unwearied still" in Yeats's "Wild Swans at Coole." The substitution of "invisible" could hardly be more deflating: if "you" (the lover) has been reduced to no more than an invisible flutter, it is surely time to move on. And in the penultimate line, "drive" rhymes with the second syllable of "survives," the chiming of "drive"—"desire"—"survives" underscoring the poet's case for survival.

"Despite random, arbitrary, even nonsensical elements," Mullen has remarked of *Muse & Drudge*, "the poem . . . is saturated with the intentionality of the writer." "I intend," she insists, "the poem to be meaningful: to allow, or suggest, to open up, or insinuate possible meanings, even in those places where the poem drifts between intentional utterance and improvisational wordplay." And she talks of the poem's amalgam of "topical references to subculture and mass culture, its shredded, embedded, and buried allusions, its drift between meaning and sound, as well as its abrupt shifts in tone or emotional affect."[51] Metonymy and pun, already much in evidence in the earlier *Trimmings*, are the key tropes, but they function in a traditional lyric form that ironizes their mode of operation, and is itself ironized by these figures. In the words of a later stanza:

down there shuffling coal
humble materials hold
vestiges of toil
the original cutting tool[52]

where the paragram "coal"—"hold"—"toil"—"tool" contradicts the ballad account of the miner's dreary work routine. Lyric and linguistic play combine to create a vision at once detached and yet oddly "personal."

Caveat Lector

I come back now to the question of "innovation." To call *Muse & Drudge* "innovative" is not especially helpful because it would be just as accurate to say that—as the very title, with its nominal/verbal collocation of inspiration and hard work, suggests—the book is quite traditional in its respect for the lyric contract, the emphasis on sound structure, the personal signature, and the mimetic grounding of experience. What matters more than "innovation," I think, is that *Muse & Drudge* is a book that speaks very much to its own time, that taps into various writings and speech formations in ways that are compelling. If Mullen's is a "theoretical" poetry, it is one that has deftly internalized the theories in question.

But—and this is where the situation has become problematic—such internalization is hard earned. Like any mode, the production of "text without walls," as McCaffery called it, can become a mere tick. And so can the theory that ostensibly animates it. One of the most problematic manifestations of what we might call postlanguage poetics is that, in the wake of the foundational theory that filled the pages of avant-garde little magazines of the 1980s, poets—and this has been especially true of women poets, perhaps because they have felt, quite rightly, excluded from the earlier formulations of poetics (a situation that can be traced back to the homage paid to Charles Olson's "Projective Verse")—have engaged in a good bit of "soft" theorizing. Indeed, exploring such venues as the "Women / Writing / Theory" symposium for *Raddle Moon* (nos. 11 and 13), *Poetics Journal* (no. 10, June 1998), or the "Poetics and Exposition" section of *Moving Borders,* I find myself wishing that the poets in question would engage in more hands-on explication and critique of one another's work—something very much needed today—rather than producing so much "theoretical" prose.

In an essay for the "Poetics" section of *Moving Borders,* for example, I came across the following sentence: "Mimesis can partner metonymy, another obstruction to either/or."[53] What can this mean? Metonymy is the trope that relates one image or phrase to another along the axis of contiguity, as in "hut," "hovel," "poor little house," "shack" (Jakobson's example). The discussion of *mimēsis* or representation is perhaps the cornerstone of literary theory from Plato on down, but, however we construe *mimēsis,* the word refers to the mode of the verbal construct itself and its relation (or nonrelation) to an external reality. Metonymy, on the other hand, is a trope and hence exists, if it does exist, *within* the *mimēsis,* not side by side with it. Tolstoy's *Anna Karenina,* for example, is considered a highly mimetic novel, and one of its main verbal devices is metonymy, as when Anna sees her husband at the train station after she has already fallen in love with Vronsky and notes that Karenin's ears stick out underneath his hat in a peculiar (and unpleasant) fashion, the protruding ears becoming a synecdoche (the most common form of metonymy) by which Karenin is known throughout the novel. Not only can't mimesis partner metonymy, there being no equivalence between the two ("another obstruction to either/or"), but metonymy is in fact one of the key features *of* the mimetic text.

Further down on the same page we read, "Can the rational accommodate the irrational? Can forms exist which truly allow for the accidental, absurd, grotesque, horrific, incommensurate—is this what Adorno meant?" The answer is quite simply no, for Adorno never equated "form" with the "rational"; he knew it was quite possible to have complex and subtle forms that are by no means "rational"; moreover, he did not conceive of form as the container of the thing contained. Again, in an essay called "In 'Re Person,'" there is a statement that reads, "The *value* of perspective to nascent capitalism was that it eventually aided in the creation of a new reality, a rationalised objectified space which could then be opened to exploitation."[54] What artist can this author have in mind? Perugino? Raphael? Leonardo? Giorgione? All those wonderful Italian painters who used perspective to create the most amazing sense of palpability of nearness and distance, of mysterious background events that complicate what is seen in the foreground? Was theirs a "rationalised objective space"—a space of nascent capitalism?

Such theory buzz, like the current spate of what I call Big Name Collage—the large theoretical essay or even poem that is no more than a collage of nuggets by Big Names (Agamben and Heidegger, Cixous and Wittgenstein, Deleuze and Adorno) without any real analysis of what the philosophers in question are actually arguing—is problematic because this particular form of "innovative" writing may well alienate the very readership it hopes to capture. That readership is, I think, more attuned to specific issues, as when Mullen tries to navigate the minefield among the particular idiolects or, as Jeff Derksen has called them, "communolects"[55] of our increasingly multilingual society. For those "communolects" now have everything to do with the one revolution that really has occurred in our own time, namely, the habitation of cyberspace. I don't have time here to discuss the poetic experiments—and many of them really are experiments in that they fail as often as they succeed and are replaced by more adequate models—on sites such as Kenneth Goldsmith's *UbuWeb: Visual/Concrete/Sound Poetry*,[56] but clearly, two important things are happening. The first is the visualization of poetic text—a visualization which is again a time-honored mode, as in George Herbert's *The Temple* or Mallarmé's *Un coup de dés* (*A Throw of the Dice*), but reconfigured in important semantic ways in Johanna Drucker's *The Word Made Flesh* or Susan Howe's *Eikon Basilike.* The second is a form which I call, for want of a better name, "differential poetry," that is, poetry that does not exist in a single fixed state but can vary according to the medium of presentation: printed book, cyberspace, installation, or oral rendition.

In the performative work of Laurie Anderson and Suzan-Lori Parks, Joan Retallack and Caroline Bergvall, for example, the issue is less the referential fallacy, as it was for McCaffery in the mid-1970s, than the semiosis of the verbal/visual field itself, where words and phrases can be moved around, reconfigured, and assigned to different slots, so that the "poem" has a variety of different forms. In a piece called "RUSH (a long way from H)," for example, Caroline Bergvall has designed a text you can access and activate on the Electronic Poetry Centre Web site or read in book form, but it can also be seen and heard as performed and videotaped, in which case temporality becomes an important determinant of meaning. As a barstool monologue cum brawl, interrupted and qualified by visual diagrams, media argot, and verbal breakdown, Bergvall's puts an ingenious spin on such pub monologues as that of Lil's "friend" in *The Waste Land.*

Is it "innovative"? Is it in Bergvall's words, "kindajazz or excitingly passée"? Well, there are surely Dada precedents for this performance model, and "RUSH (a long way from H)" recalls the work of John Cage and Fluxus. So, to rephrase the question, is Bergvall's an *interesting* rendition of a lonely, anxious, and hilarious conversation, presumably between two women, in the neighborhood pub? A close look at the work's linguistic deformations and repetitions lays bare the complex layering that defines "this gigantic submarined trancehall" as it takes shape on the cyberpage. And the next step, one we find taken in Kenneth Goldsmith's Java Applet called "Fidget," is to have the words themselves put in motion, touch one another, and vary according to what time of day one accesses the site.

Would Adorno, with his distaste for kitsch and his revulsion of the consciousness industries (of which the Internet is surely a prime instance) be the right guide for reading this text? Or would a better frame be provided by a critic such as N. Katherine Hayles, whose new study, subtitled "Virtual Bodies in Cybernetics, Literature, and Informatics," raises the issues which poets, like the rest of us, are now facing? It is less a question of novelty as such than of coming to terms with specificity and *difference.* As Gertrude Stein put it so nicely in "An Acquaintance with Description":

> What is the difference between three and two in furniture. Three is the third of three and two is the second of two. This makes it as true as a description. And not satisfied. And what is the difference between being on the road and waiting very likely being very likely waiting, a road is connecting and as it is connecting it is intended to be keeping going and waiting everybody can understand puzzling.[57]

Notes

Opening quotation from Rosmarie Waldrop, "Association," in *Split Infinitives* (Philadelphia: Singing Horse Press, 1998).

1. Donald Allen, ed., *New American Poetry* (New York: Grove Press, 1960); Douglas Messerli, ed., *From the Other Side of the Century: A New American Poetry 1960–1990* (Los Angeles: Sun and Moon, 1994).

2. Robert Sheppard, *Poetics and Linguistically Innovative Poetry 1978–1997* (Exeter, UK: Stride, 1999). I wrote a blurb for this excellent book, as I did for Sloan's *Moving Borders.*

3. Maggie O'Sullivan, ed., *Out of Everywhere: Linguistically Innovative Poetry by Women in North America & the UK* (London: Reality Street Editions, 1996); Mary Margaret Sloan, ed., *Moving Borders: Three Decades of Innovative Writing by Women* (Jersey City: Talisman Publishers, 1998).

4. O'Sullivan, *Out of Everywhere,* 9.

5. *Oxford English Dictionary* (Oxford: Clarendon Press, 1961), vol. 5, 314.

6. Donald Allen, ed., *The Postmoderns* (New York: Grove Press, 1982).

7. Walter Benjamin, "The Work of Art in the Age of Mechanical Reproduction," in *Illuminations,* ed. Hannah Arendt (New York: Schocken Books, 1969), 238.

8. *L=A=N=G=U=A=G=E,* edited by Bruce Andrews and Charles Bernstein, was a mimeograph magazine, the first issue of which appeared in the spring of 1978. *This,* edited by Robert Grenier, began publication in 1971; *Hills,* edited by Bob Perelman, started in 1973. Frank Davey's *Open Letter,* published in Toronto, was established in 1972. These foundational journals as well as such projects as Lyn Hejinian's Tuumba Chapbook series were thus in place by the mid-1970s.

9. See Steve McCaffery, "Diminished Reference and the Model Reader," in *North of Intention: Critical Writings 1973–1986* (New York: Roof Books, 1986), 13–29; Bruce Andrews, "Text and Context," *Paradise & Method* (Evanston, Ill.: Northwestern University Press, 1996), 6–16; Charles Bernstein, "Stray Straws and Straw Men," *Content's Dream: Essays 1975–1984* (Los Angeles: Sun and Moon Press, 1986), 40–49.

10. *L=A=N=G=U=A=G=E Supplement Number One* (June 1980), front page, unpaginated. For convenience sake, I shall supply page numbers.

11. McCaffery, "Diminished Reference," 13.

12. McCaffery, "The Death of the Subject," *L=A=N=G=U=A=G=E Supplement Number One,* 4.

13. Ibid., 3.

14. Ibid., 8.

15. Ibid., 3.

16. Ibid., 9.

17. Andrews, "Text and Context," *L=A=N=G=U=A=G=E Supplement Number One*, 20.

18. McCaffery, "The Death of the Subject," *L=A=N=G=U=A=G=E Supplement Number One,* 4.

19. Ibid., 5.

20. Ibid., 19.

21. See especially Roman Jakobson, "Linguistics and Poetics," in *Language*

in Literature, ed. Krystyna Pomorska and Stephen Rudy (Cambridge, Mass.: Harvard University Press, 1987), 62–94. Many of the essays in this collection are relevant to the topic: for example, "The Dominant," "Problems in the Study of Language and Literature," and "Two Aspects of Language and Two Types of Aphasic Disturbances."

22. See William R. Paulson, *The Noise of Culture: Literary Texts in a World of Information* (Ithaca, N.Y.: Cornell University Press, 1988), chap. 2.

23. Bernstein, "Stray Straws and Straw Men," 40–41.

24. In his essay "1973," Peter Middleton begins to engage the thorny issue of 1970s poetry. He relates the demise of Clayton Eshleman's *Caterpillar,* the last issue of which was published in 1973, and the founding of *American Poetry Review* in 1972 to post-Vietnam, Watergate politics and the new distrust of public speech and the increasing separation of the white avant-garde from black writing. Middleton takes into account such important poetic developments as Jerome Rothenberg's projects to place cultural difference and the recognition of non-Western poetries on the agenda, David Antin's turn toward improvisation, and Michael Palmer's incorporation of French avant-garde poetics into his work. But he notes that at the moment when Barrett Watten's *This* was devoting a whole issue to Clark Coolidge (1973), the dominant poetic discourse valorized such poets as Robert Lowell, Maxine Kumin, and William Stafford. Middleton's essay may be found in Christine Pagnoulle and Michel Delville, eds., *Postwar American Poetry: The Mechanics of the Mirage* (Liège, Belgium: Liège Language and Literature, 2000), 49–66.

25. Sharon Bryan, "Hollandaise," in *The Morrow Anthology of Younger American Poets,* ed. Dave Smith and David Bottoms (New York: William Morrow, 1985), 107–8. The author, born in 1943, holds an MFA from the University of Iowa and has published a book called *Salt Air* from Wesleyan. In their introduction, Smith and Bottoms describe the typical Morrow Younger Poet as one whose "knowledge, while eclectic, seems focused on the psychological and mythical resonances in the local surface, event, or subject. . . . He seems to jog more than to write literary criticism" (19).

26. Stephen Berg and Robert Mezey, eds., *Naked Poetry: Recent American Poetry in Open Forms* (New York: Bobbs-Merrill, 1969).

27. Allen Ginsberg, "First Thought, Best Thought," in Allen Ginsberg, *Composed on the Tongue,* ed. Donald Allen (Bolinas, Calif.: Grey Fox, 1980), 106–17. The piece was originally published in 1975 in *Loka: A Journal from Naropa Institute.* Again and again Ginsberg speaks of "natural" speech, spontaneity, the breath as guide to measure, and so on.

28. See Ron Silliman, "Who Speaks: Ventriloquism and the Self in the Poetry Reading," in *Close Listening: Poetry and the Performed World,* ed. Charles Bernstein (New York: Oxford, 1998), 365. Silliman's is a seminal essay for understanding the limitations of reader response theory.

29. See, on this point, George Hartley's *Textual Politics and the Language Poets* (Bloomington: Indiana University Press, 1989). This first book-length study of language poetry was largely devoted to the movement's politics, drawing heavily on Ron Silliman, Bob Perelman, and Barrett Watten.

30. The most notable exception is Lyn Hejinian, who contributed essays and manifestos to the early issues of *L=A=N=G=U=A=G=E*, for example, "If Written is Writing," and was coeditor, with Barrett Watten, of *Poetics Journal*. Another very different exception is Susan Howe, who combined not poetry and theory so much as poetry and historical scholarship, negotiating in fascinating ways between the two in *My Emily Dickinson*. A key volume that includes a number of women poets writing as theorists is Bob Perelman's *Writing/Talks* (Carbondale: Southern Illinois University Press, 1985). The book contains Rae Armantrout's "Poetic Silence," Beverly Dahlen's "A Reading: a Reading," Carla Harryman's "The Middle," Fanny Howe's "Artobiography," and Lyn Hejinian's now well-known "The Rejection of Closure."

31. See, for example, Rod Mengham, *Textual Practice* 3, no. 1 (Spring 1989): 115–24; D. S. Marriott, "Signs Taken for Signifiers: Language Writing, Fetishism and Disavowal," *fragmente* 6 (1995): 73–83; Anthony Mellors, "Out of the American Tree: Language Writing and the Politics of Form," *fragmente* 6 (1995): 84–91. Marriott's essay, for example, begins with the sentence, "It will be the argument of this paper that language writing, in its systematic attempt to empty the linguistic sign of its referential function, replaces representation with a fetishistic substitute, that of the signifier" (73), the reference being to essays by McCaffery, Bernstein, Silliman, and Andrews.

32. Ashbery's "The Ice Storm" is in *Temblor* 5 (1987), as are extracts from *Conversing with Cage*, ed. Richard Kostelanetz.

33. Lyn Hejinian, "Two Stein Talks," *Temblor* 3 (1986): 129.

34. Ibid., 132.

35. Ibid., 133.

36. Susan Howe, "12 Poems from a Work in Progress," *Temblor* 3 (1986): 27.

37. Fanny Howe, "Scattered Light," *Temblor* 4 (1986): 51.

38. Ibid., 52.

39. Nathaniel Mackey, "Uninhabited Angel," *Temblor* 4 (1986): 36.

40. Farrah Griffin, Michael Magee, and Kirsten Gallagher, "A Conversation with Harryette Mullen," ed. Michael Magee, *Combo* 1 (Summer 1998), as reprinted on the Harryette Mullen Web site, Electronic Poetry Centre, SUNY Buffalo, http://wings.buffalo/edu/epc.authors/mullen, 1–2.

41. Barbara Henning, "In Interview with Harryette Mullen," *Poetry Project Newsletter* (1999): 2. As read online on the Poetry Project Web site: www.poetryproject.com/mullen.html.

42. Henning, "In Interview," 2.

43. Harryette Mullen, *Trimmings* (Providence: Tender Buttons Press, 1994), 9.

44. Haryette Mullen (lecture, Intersection for the Arts, San Francisco, May 24, 1993). I owe my knowledge of it to Aldon Lynn Nielsen's important study *Black Chant: Languages of African-American Postmodernism* (Cambridge, Mass.: Cambridge University Press, 1997), 35–37.

45. Nielsen, *Black Chant,* 36.

46. Kate Pearcy, "A Poetics of Opposition: Race and the Avant-Garde" (paper presented at the Poetry and the Public Sphere Conference on Contemporary Poetry, April 24–27, 1997).

47. Harryette Mullen, *Muse & Drudge* (Philadelphia: Singing Horse Press, 1995), 1.

48. *L=A=N=G=U=A=G=E Supplement One,* 11.

49. Juliana Spahr points out that *Sappho's Lyre* is the title of Diane J. Rayor's translations of archaic lyric and women poets of Ancient Greece, and adds, "Only here Sappho is marked as the African-American Sapphire. Resonating here is Hortense Spillers's beginning of 'Mama's Baby, Papa's Maybe: An American Grammar Book': 'Let's face it. I am a marked woman, but everybody knows my name. "Peaches" and "Brown Sugar," "sapphire" and "Earth Mother."'" See Juliana Spahr, "'What Stray Companion': Harryette Mullen and the Politics of Reading's Communities," *Everybody's Autonomy: Connective Reading and Collective Identity (Tuscaloosa: University of Alabama Press, 2001).*

50. Spahr cites the Steve Miller Band's "The Joker" as a source of this image: "No don't worry mama. / Cause I'm right here at home. / You're the cutest thing / That I ever did see / Really love your peaches / Wanna shake your tree." And there are related songs by Blind Lemon Jefferson and Ma Rainey that stand behind the peach image as well as the "juicy fruit" that follows.

51. Ann Lauterbach, "Pragmatic Examples: The Nonce," in Mullen, *Muse & Drudge,* 660.

52. Mullen, *Muse & Drudge,* 11.

53. As cited by Mullen, www.poetryproject.com/mullen.html, 2.

54. Beverly Dahlen, "In 'Re Person,'" in Mullen, *Muse & Drudge,* 664.

55. As cited by Mullen, www.poetryproject.com/mullen.html, 2.

56. The site is located at www.ubu.com.

57. Gertrude Stein, "An Acquaintance with Description" (1929), in *A Stein Reader,* ed. Ulla E. Dydo (Evanston, Ill.: Northwestern University Press, 1993), 507.

Part Two : **Precursors**

to restore silence is the role of an object

—Beckett, *Molloy*

Getting Past Odradek

Kevin Nolan

I want to follow a thread along certain well-known lines in order to advance an argument which occasionally benefits from restatement. The thread begins with a short fable written in 1917 by Kafka, "Die Sorge des Hausvaters" (variously translated as "Cares of a Family Man," "Problems of a Housekeeper," or, as in J. A. Underwood's translation, "The Householder's Concern"). In this inconclusive story there are two ends: Odradek, a "star shaped cotton reel" trailing "old, broken-off bits of thread, knotted and tangled together," and the narrator, a father and family man, in whom mortal doubts are aroused by the presence in his house of the little stranger:

> I ask myself to no purpose, what is likely to happen to him? Can he possibly die? Anything that dies has had some kind of aim in life, some kind of activity, which has worn out; but that does not apply to Odradek. Am I to suppose, then, that he will always be rolling down the stairs, with ends of thread trailing after him, right before the feet of my children, and my children's children? He does no harm to anyone that one can see; but the idea that he is likely to survive me I find almost painful.[1]

We feel we know this Kafkaesque figure with the full force of a déjà vu; solitary and houseless, of *no fixed abode,* the ur-form of Brod's "homeless stranger" or the orphan figures of the longer tales, "the form which things assume in oblivion," as Walter Benjamin notes in his long essay of 1934. Of Odradek in particular, Benjamin observes that this "oblivion" has a double face; his liminal status places the little reel not en abyme but in direct relation to the juridical spaces he seems to elude. Since he is found in attics, staircases, and corridors and hallways, he "prefers the same places as the court of law which investigates guilt."[2]

Perhaps this aspect, of "guilt" or a "certain tone of resignation," was what irritated Bertolt Brecht when he discussed Kafka's story with Benjamin in Berlin that year: "Kafka's outlook is that of a man caught under the wheels. Odradek is characteristic of this outlook."[3] In correspondence with Benjamin the following year, Theodor Adorno came to a complementary conclusion, seeing the reel not as an emblem of abulia or critical paratonia but as the means to an "overcoming of the creaturely state of guilt—truly a case of Heidegger put right side up—the secret key, indeed the most indubitable promise of *hope,* precisely through the overcomings of the house itself. Certainly as the other face of the world of things Odradek is a sign of distortion, but as such he is also a motif of transcendence, namely of the ultimate limit and reconciliation of the organic and inorganic, or of the overcoming of death: Odradek lives on. . . . Odradek is indeed so dialectical that it can also properly be said of him that almost nothing has made everything well again."[4]

For Adorno the task of a renewed dialectic involved "thinking so that the thought form will no longer turn its objects into immutable ones, into objects that remain the same." But staying the *same* is not the same as *living on.* For Adorno ideas were themselves liminal; they lived "in the cavities between what things claim to be and what they are."[5] Thus the fables of Kafka are allowed to serve as exemplars of negative ideation:

> Nowhere in Kafka does there glimmer the aura of the "infinite idea," nowhere does the horizon open. Each sentence is literal and each signifies. The two moments are not merged, as the symbol would have it, but yawn apart, and out of the abyss between them blinds the glaring ray of *fascination.* Here too, in its striving not for symbol but for allegory, Kafka's prose sides with the outcasts. Each sentence says interpret me and none will permit it. Each compels the reaction "that's the way it is" and without the question "where have I seen that before": the déjà vu is declared permanent.[6]

Between "immortality without hope" and a permanent sense of déjà vu is one definition of what the fascinated *Hausvater* means by being outlived, and it is tempting to view Odradek anthropologically, as the embodiment of whatever is culturally abject or avulsible, *oder dreck*. But for all his objecthood, Odradek is disturbingly anthropocentric: talkative, mobile, *transitional*—this is his paradoxical status. He is a common thing, a reel of thread, but as all commentators since Emrich have implied, the *singularity* of Odradek counts against his commonness. Baptized with a Czech name in a German text, one of the few Czech words to appear anywhere in Kafka and derived from *odraditi* (to dissuade, dishearten), he is "the little dissuader," also perhaps *od-rad-ek*, "the little creature cut off from order." In this way, "Odradek" becomes heterological; his name is not self-descriptive (he is the cause of dissuasion in others), and so right from the start all literal recognition is compromised by the uncertainty of interpretation:

> Some say the word Odradek is of Slavonic origin, and try to account for it on that basis, others believe it to be of German origin. . . . No-one would occupy themselves with such studies if there were not a being (*wesen*) called Odradek.[7]

Anthony Thorlby counters the problems implied by Adorno's reading of the "literal" with an appeal to traditional anthropomorphism:

> There is . . . a kind of negative agreement between the language and the reality of Kafka's fiction. Furthermore, this negative basis of agreement is altogether unlike the positive correspondence between words and the world which a realist view of language (or a mimetic view of art) leads us to expect. . . . In Russell's jargon, Kafka's fictional vocabulary is homological, that is, it is an instance of the incomprehensibility it represents, and thereby escapes the nonsense of the heterological paradox. Put less technically, we may say that Kafka enables us to see that words refer to nothing beyond themselves; they are entirely embedded in a reality which they themselves sustain and perpetrate.[8]

It may be that many of Kafka's "words" (and sentences, paragraphs, etc.) by corroding transcendental perspectives seek to persuade us of the kind of phenomenalism that Thorlby favors. Kafka stressed the literal aspects of his writing on many occasions and in conversation with Janouch compared himself to a "bungling copyist."[9] But if the traditional paradox of heterology is that something may not apply to itself if and only it does apply to itself, then Odradek's exceptional status, or Kafka's, cannot prove any rule that leans for support on the law of appearances. Following Thorlby a little way back toward Kant, we might say that since experience is constituted by appearances which are *of* something that cannot be known "in itself," then in certain encounters reason may not prove its power to itself in any way, is in fact obliged to lean upon language for the perpetuation of appearances. The more intense the need for symbolization, the more the metasystemic resistance to meaning. Thus the unnameable-as-*Ding-an-sich* evinces the *odranec* (the ragged figure) of Pure Reason by recursive anticipation.

Heidegger saw a close nexus between this the naming-relation and a contemporary nihilism located at the very essence of *Das Ding* (the Thing):

> The Roman word "res" designates that which concerns somebody, an affair, a contested matter, a case at law. The Roman word "res" denotes what pertains to man, concerns him and his interests in any way or manner. That which concerns man is what is real in "res." But the Romans never properly thought through the nature of what they thus experienced.[10]

Gadamer amplifies: "the concept of the thing reflects more than the Roman legal concept of Res, *sache* permeated by *causa* (disputed matter)." The legal idea of the nature of things does not mean a disputed issue but "the limits that are set to the arbitrary will of the legislator in a judicial interpretation of law. The appeal to the nature of things refers to an order removed from human wishes." For Heidegger the thing is a "gathering" (*Versammlung*) but again, "only what conjoins itself out of world becomes a thing." No "World," no Thing; but world means more than the totalizing aggregate of systemic *laws.* Odradek does not "conjoin," "gather," suture, or mend—he trails loose threads and the textual (textural) abyss of "fascination" that Adorno identifies as Odradek's unfixed abode is the other side of legislation, "*sache* permeated by *causa.*"[11]

But before the hermeneutical abyss yawns too rapidly, we need to look at some further threads. In 1853 Herman Melville published in *Putnam's Monthly* his tale "Bartleby the Scrivener." The narrator is a "rather elderly" man, a lawyer convinced that "the easiest way of life is the best" who hires as legal copyist in his office the "motionless young man" Bartleby, who gradually refuses most exhortations to work with the laconic, "I would prefer not to." This state of things continues to the consternation of the lawyer, since "nothing so aggravates an earnest person as a passive resistance." Bartleby has no home and refuses to leave when told, saying, "I would prefer not to quit you."[12]

It is interesting to compare the lawyer's reactions with those of the *Hausvater.* Both are confronted by a "passive resistance," frequently mute when questioned. The family man condescends, treating Odradek "rather like a child" and speculates about his "aim in life." The New York lawyer also attempts "charity" but comes to feel that "these troubles of mine touching the scrivener, had all been predestined from eternity." And what vexes him also is the nagging fear of being outlived: "the idea came to me again of his possibly turning out a long lived man, and keep occupying my chambers, and denying my authority, and in the end perhaps outlive me." The lawyer moves offices but Bartleby will not quit his former office, and so follows their penultimate encounter, before Bartleby's imprisonment and death from starvation "there was Bartleby, silently insisting upon the banister at the landing."[13]

Two stairwell encounters: in Prague, with a *thing,* disturbingly anthropomorphic; in New York, with a *person,* uncannily demotivated. Odradek lives, Bartleby dies. Both are liminal creatures, moving between domesticity and law. The thing speaks, has movement and volition; the person has little of either. The thing will outlive his "father"; Bartleby is outlived by the narrator. Odradek begins with etymology and ends with angst, the inability to discover an aim, purpose, or origin. Bartleby (another trisyllabic rune) is discovered to have formerly been a clerk in a dead-letter office, dealing with lost correspondence, the pathos of which situation, on "errands of life, these letters speed to death" provokes the narrator's final susurration: "Ah Bartleby, Ah Humanity."[14]

Did Kafka know Melville's story? Almost certainly not, though many symmetries might lead us to think so. There are numerous hints of the Kafkaesque psychomachia in Melville: Bartleby's inanition, his "I would prefer not to," anticipates the Hunger Artist's reason for starving, just as Melville's "Confidence Man" anticipates Kafka's. Kafka's own legal training would have made him appreciate the Prufrockian self-regard of Melville's narrator, an enlarged version of his *Hausvater*'s vexed prudentialism.

And there is the same recursion—object, subject, *thing;* all alien to the concerns of a *person* awaiting the invasion of his *house* like the coming of an inevitable destiny. But in what form?

In the same year that Odradek made his appearance, Freud published his study "Das Unheimliche" ("The Uncanny," 1919) in which "that class of the terrifying which leads back to something long known to us" is the occasion for some extensive revaluation of metapsychological principle. For "among its different shades of meaning the word heimlich exhibits one which is identical with its opposite, unheimlich." The uncanny is not a return of the repressed but the uneasy recognition that one is confronted by "the idea of something fateful or inescapable when otherwise we should have spoken only of 'chance.'"[15]

What the uncanny demonstrates is a chiasmus between the worlds of persons and of things, the animate and the inanimate, but only insofar as that is the product of denial, "of castration or other infantile phobias." To Freud, the *unheimlich* would constitute an infinite repetition unless it were possible to get past that nexus, by the resolution of Oedipal drama, "until which one does not see others as other, know and acknowledge their (separate, animate, opposed) human existence." Stanley Cavell sees this to mean that the *unheimlich* ultimately imparts "a version of the skeptical problem concerning the existence of other minds." Kafka's loose threads of the literal may be an example of irresolution, then, but in Cavell's terms are also a "standing philosophical threat": something that may not be got past simply by an act of will.[16]

The problems of otherness and its possible resolutions become an important stage in Freud's more dramatic restructuring of the ego in his paper also begun in 1919, "Beyond the Pleasure Principle," in which a cotton reel also plays a central part. Here Freud tells how his grandchild Ernst had the "occasional disturbing habit of taking any small objects he could get hold of and throwing them away from him into a corner, under the bed. As he did this he gave vent to a long drawn out 'o-o-o-oo' accompanied by an expression of interest and satisfaction. His mother and the writer of the present account were agreed in thinking that this was not a mere interjection but represented the German word 'fort' (gone). I eventually realized that it was a game, and that the only use he made of his toys was to play 'gone' with them. . . . The child had a wooden reel with a piece of string tied round it. . . . What he did was to hold the reel by the string and very skillfully throw it over the edge of his curtained cot, so that it disappeared into it, at the same time uttering the expression 'Oo-o.' He then pulled the reel out of the cot by its string and hailed its reappearance with a joyful 'da' (there). This then was the complete game, disappearance and return."[17]

Freud continues that the "game" was "the child's great cultural achievement"—a way of achieving some control over the anxiety he felt whenever his mother left him. For every departure then, the prospect of a "joyful return": *oooo–da.* Thus time is allayed by the arts of preemptive forestallment, through a kind of regulated acceptance which only underlines the ultimate essence of instinctual life according to Freud: that "the aim of all life is death." The instinct of a living organism is inherently conservative; only the modifications of external stimuli oblige it "to diverge ever more widely from its original course of life and to make ever more complicated detours before reaching its aim of death" (*und zu immer komplizierteren Umwegen bis zur Erreichung des todeszieles nötigten*). For every *o,* then, here and present, a *fort:* absence, disappearance, detour. Or if there is no return, if the game is interrupted or overplayed, if accident supervenes over the imaginary, we are better prepared for the unexpected by the incomplete mastery which the rehearsal of departures prepares us for.[18]

Did Freud, writing in 1919, know Kafka's story, published the same year? Might Kafka have furnished Freud with important contraindications to the development of his own theory of the uncanny, and then the pleasure principle, through an image of the *uncontrolled* return of a cotton reel? Freud might have been amused by the idea of an expulsion never fully accomplished, returning to haunt the patriarch, lawyer, analyst; coming to obstruct the passageways and exits of his mansion like a systemic overload, "ein freudigen Da" (a joyful return). The German meaning of "reel," after all, is chiefly "solid respectable," even a little earnest, "eminently safe," like Bartleby's employer.

The view of literary criticism (the present resting place of psychoanalysis) has for some while now been that all symbolization, whether systemic or individual, is voluntaristic, therefore that object choices are purely symptomatic and arbitrary. Maud Ellmann is too anxious to sacrifice the reel when she writes that "the *drama* fascinates the child rather than the toy itself, for the bobbin belongs to a series of objects which he substitutes indifferently for one another."[19] Yet it may be that in this drama of fascination the baby (or the critic) is more "indifferent" to the objects of experience than Freud. For if the play is to be more than a set of substitutions, then it must of course reach its own form of peripeteia and recognition. The bobbin is the precondition for the Freudian *da,* but the compound estrangements of the object itself must also be a precondition for the uncanny: "The awareness of a fissure in reality making it appear superreal is the sense of fascination," wrote Wyndham Lewis in an essay of 1917. To Lewis also, a route through depersonalizing estrangement was a principal technique for renewed encounter, so as to "introduce my puppets, and the Wild Body, the generic puppet of all. . . . These intricately moving bobbins are all subject to a set of objects or one in particular."[20] If the "set" does not simply involve replacing a thing with a system (or its operant substitutions) what might that particular law involve?

The law which regulated the wild body of Lewis was the law of irony in traditional Kantian form: the reification of an empirical self overseen by a reflexive awareness, sentient but powerless, from which condition Lewis propounds no escape save for the changeless glint of analytic clarity. For Freud the instinct to life, though geared to the anterior, concedes the inevitability of time and change through darker ironies by which pleasure from postponement is a necessary approach to the end. Peter Brooks notes acutely that "repetition can take us both forward and backward because these terms have become reversible: the end is a time before the beginning."[21] This already suggests an alteration in that reciprocity of person and thing which Heidegger, gesturing to Hölderlin and Rilke for support throughout the 1920s, still invoked. The Durkheimian view that a social order regulates the world of things on the pattern of the structure that prevails in the world of persons gives way to the new literalism, "a set of objects" that constrains both these worlds simultaneously, constructing things as it constructs people, to the very limits of translatable cultural intelligence.

What is this newer condition, which seems so bound up with the fascination of Odradek, "who can never be laid hold of," tied up in his world by his noncoincidence with another whom he constantly threatens to destabilize? Agamben views him as a "nachleben of the emblematic form," yet he is also close to the Marxian commodity which "as soon as it begins to function as such, changes into something at once accessible and inaccessible to sense, something transcendent (sinnlich ubersinnliches). It not only stands with its feet on the ground, but in relation to all other commodities it puts itself on its head," which for Agamben means that techniques of aesthetic estrangement (*ostranenie*) can never be other than symptomatic: "the discomfort of man with respect to the objects that he has himself reduced to 'appearances of things' is translated into the suspicion of a possible 'animation of the inorganic, and into the placing in doubt of the bond that unites everything to its own form, each creature to its familiar environment.' "[22] But if there is, now, a "logic of the commodity," is that an unchanging state awaiting all object relations like an eternal destiny? Traditional critical theory sought to show the interpenetration of persons and things in a "creaturely state of guilt": has any version of the new literalism offering "language" as the subject matter of poetry ever managed to go beyond heterology, or even wanted to?

One final filament. The Bukovinian exile Paul Celan receives a prize in Darmstadt in 1967, where unfamiliar environments are among the things he maps in his speech of acceptance, "Der Meridian." His family name (Ancel) chimes with Kafka's Hebraic name Amschel (blackbird), and, with Kafka much in mind, Odradek too, he is thinking of conditions of return, to and from the poem, to a mother country that might exist no longer and from an art which might not be vulnerable to, or complicit with, the violence of history.

He is not seeking to dissuade. Thinking of Kafka, Celan calls art a "childless being"—"shall we say eternal." And because of Kafka, art is also a form of estrangement; one of its synthetic forms is "something marionette-like, iambic-five-footed, childless." Childless, even if productive; thus Benjamin (who called Odradek a "bastard") is corrected by Celan: since art is more than a temporary appearance it must endure, yet if it were merely fecund it would revert to the pathos of an endlessly deconstructive anthropomorphism.

So that when thinking of the manner in which art "lives," Celan points to Siegfried Lenz in Büchner's account, remembering Marx's commodity also: "He who walks on his head, Ladies and Gentleman, has the sky as a precipice below him." Nietzsche was not the first to recognize the profound comforts of the abyss, the condition of an aesthetics of "rupture," after all, being simply an unlimited textual productivity, a thread with no end to it but also no density beyond the hypothetical limits of language itself. But to Celan "poetry runs ahead" and attempts to see this figure in its direction, "*We know whereto he lives, as he lives on.*" In the mystery of the "encounter" Celan sees not chiasmus of thinghood and personification but a primordial otherness. "Ich bin . . . mir selbst begegnet" ("It was . . . myself I encountered"), he declares toward the close of the speech, with a memory perhaps of Spencer Brydon's "I was to have known myself" after his own stairwell encounter in *The Jolly Corner.* Despite all indirection, then ("Sind diese Wege nur Um-Wege, Umwege vondir zu dir" [Are these paths only detours, detours from *thee* to *thee*]), "every thing, every human is for the poem which is directed towards this other, an appearance of this other."[23]

Did Celan know Melville's story? And Kafka's? And James's? And Freud's? Why should such questioning seem, after a certain date, almost superfluous? Perhaps for the same reason that a *Nachleben* (afterlife) of the emblematic form ought not to be a transcendental emblem of the emblem? For the same reason that not every mise en abyme is an encounter; for the same reason that the fascination of romantic irony guarantees no otherness at all? In the same year as the Meridian speech, Celan wrote in an uncollected poem:

ST
Ein Vau, pf, in der That,
schlägt, mps
ein Sieben-Rad;

o
oo
ooo
O

Bruns sees the "O" of this text as "the basic unit of Celan's poetry," a "cry" of limitation, as of the "corporeality and exteriority of poetic language"; but here too, "these letters speed towards death."[24] For here, where no further turn is possible, is one last echo of little Ernst Freud's "great cultural achievement," the looping gesture of the *fort,* the whine of a spinning top, whirr of a cotton reel. There is no *da,* since even the cautious protectiveness of parent or *Hausvater* has been eliminated. Of Celan's mother, Jean Bollack writes in his new book that "elle avait rejoint pour lui cet au-dela de la parole" (for him, she was able to reconnect the beyondness of language). This was, perhaps, Celan's own "great cultural achievement," a *fort-da* in no way confirmatory: "L'acte poétique fondateur de Celan fut de se retourner contre une tradition culturelle" (The constitutive poetic act for Celan was an act of self-ricochet against a tradition determined by culture).[25] Therefore art is "childless," because its own condition is orphan, "defamilialized." But the structure of action is altered: Faust's "im anfang war die That" is rearticulated. This was the place from which no return was assured, the place after which no poem was completely possible, where nothing is left to chance because the arbitrariness of indirection itself reflects starker determinations.

From here the *Umweg* holds sway over all. For what is Celan's O, the dark star of unredeemed transience, if not a memory of Odradek, *ein sieben rad?* Where Benjamin could precede his reflections on the little "star-shaped" reel, with a memory a few lines earlier of Rosenzweig's *Stern der Erlösung,* now there is no homeland old or new to offer as sanctum of closure. What is Celan's "five footed creature" if not the pathos of lyric, the unwinding radial of Odradek, "caught up in the wheels," "*sache* permeated with *causa*"? Is he not the figure of the poem, "in itself," never quite expelled, the disjointed remainder on porch and stair, the reminder that there is no *heimlich,* ever, without a corresponding *unheimlich,* and that this "standing threat" to psychoanalysis—the iconicity of the object—is itself "incapable of self support" beyond the relativity of contextual dependence articulated a fortiori by the laws which then seek to entail it?

For the modern epoch the formal autonomy of literature was secured by a theory of language which decoupled the contingency of thinghood and language (sign and signified, if you prefer), replacing causal heterology with arbitrariness. Inside the enclosure of language now conceived as a *Form und Systemhaus* (now conceived as systemic form) the dialectics of inside and outsided eternalized interiority into another version of "that infinite regress of reflection" which Benjamin (in *Central Park*) had seen to be central to romanticism, "simultaneously expanding living space in ever expanding circles and reducing it within ever more narrowly defined boundaries."

Since nature no longer followed its own logic but was governed by necessity, its powers to arbitrate in matters of dogma had mostly disappeared. Now the synthetic activities of *persons* alone prescribed laws to nature and norms of freedom, which then face the juridical countermand that objects of experience attest to the rule of *appearances.* Once systemic interiority has been established by the concept of an arbitrary relation, categories of person and thing may be conflated *ad libidinem.* The pathos of autonomy is essentially the pathos associated with the indefinite substitution which constitutes that process; any *particular* object will arrest it only long enough to become itself a creature of fascination, the *da* returning to the fortress of the ego which of course it helps assail.

The loss of density implied by the autonomization of art meant for Hegel its expropriation; for another version of modernism, its reanimation as the pure potentiality of negation. Rather than the confirmation of a journey traveled, aesthetic instances disconnect by recursive obviation, so many detours on the way to death. Or they are articulated by substitutive metaphors that comprise language in a dialectical movement that "closes when it returns to its beginning point." If one version of that process is survival (the simple desire to live on), then it is purchased at the cost of an unequal exchange. The arbitrary sign replaces the arbitrary body: language becomes the causality of fate. But if poetry is not an error of language, mesmerized by the esprit de l'escalier, just as language is not an errancy of life, just as an exteriority *to* language is not the same thing as an exteriority *of* language or an exteriority *within* language, then the assumption of an irreducible element of *readability* in the poem (*not* irreducible unreadability) is the extent to which poetry is not disfigurative before it can be lived and even acted upon. The organism "trying to die in its own fashion," on "errands of life towards death" may also be capable of reversal, and even changes in direction, Celan's *Toposforschung.*

The earliest injunctions of industrial modernism exhorted a *return:* to "things themselves," in which there were no ideas but. Or else they urged "direct treatment of the thing," or parodied the appetite for "things as they are." The use value of the poetic "ob-ject," embodied like Odradek and depersonalized like Bartleby, transitional, uncanny, the metaphor of metaphor, argues a crucial linkage between ontology and morality: what constitutes an object, its objectivity (*enstand: gegenstand: widerstand*), may not be a pure product of will, may then be a primary determinant of what we assume as right and liberty. For Celan language is not a system of errancies, an *Umweg,* because poetry is not merely a process of indefinite substitution. But between the return to a homeland that no longer exists, Ithaka or Czernowitz, and the acceptance of change by continuous indirection, is a fine line ever narrowing.

In an intellectual climate now widely characterized as "posttheoretical" and which in fact is mostly precritical, the intent resistance of any object or person to juridical integration can always be seen as an aspect of a larger cultural detotalization. One paradoxical name for this experience was poetry, the art of disentangling in order to weave together. The present hypostasis of resistance as a cultural term fulfills exactly the opposite criterion, just as the present displacement of poetics by rhetoric will not be reversed by appeals to "the unmediated constellation" or any other shibboleth of negative transcendence. Between mechanical repetition and mechanized pathos is a filiation measured by the slenderest of threads.

No "heimlich" without an "unheimlich" is not much to ask; no *unheimlich* without a primordial self-encounter, reckoning at its true cost the amount of *willkür* (willfulness) left not merely to continue (live on) but to act on (*in anfang war der That*) is slightly more disturbing. How many poems ask as much? Or as little? It may not be enough to live on, and in many cases now may even be the matrix of morbid inanition. It is at the same time a line that follows the discontinuous ends of all "tropological" incorporation, the unwritten law behind each and any resolution we might care to outlive.

Notes

This essay is the revised text of a paper presented in the Department of English and American Studies, Charles University, in November 2000. With thanks to Professors Martin Hilský and Louis Armand for their comments. The epigraph is taken from Samuel Beckett, *Molloy* (1950).

1. Franz Kafka, "Die Sorge des Hausvaters," *Die Erzählungen* (Schocken Verlag: Berlin and New York, 1935, reprinted 1953), published in English as "The Cares of a Family Man," in Franz Kafka, *The Complete Stories* (New York: Schocken Books, 1971), 427–28.

2. Walter Benjamin, *Franz Kafka, on the Tenth Anniversary of His Death.* This essay was first published in the *Judische Rundschau* in 1934 and is collected in Michael Jennings et al., *Walter Benjamin Selected Writings,* vol. 2 (Cambridge and London: Harvard University Press, 1999), 794–818.

3. Bertolt Brecht, quoted in Walter Benjamin, "Versuche über Brecht" (1966), translated as *Conversations with Brecht* (London: Verso, 1998), 105.

4. Theodor W. Adorno [in a letter to Walter Benjamin], in Walter Benjamin, *Gesammelte Schriften* (Frankfurt am Main: Suhrkamp, 1978), vol. I.3, 1000–6. Adorno's comments on the essay in his letter of December 17, 1934, are printed in Theodor W. Adorno and Walter Benjamin, *The Complete Correspondence 1928–1940,* ed. Henri Lonitz, trans. Nicholas Walker (Cambridge, Mass.: Harvard University Press, 1999), 66–67.

5. Theodor Adorno, *Negative Dialectics,* trans. E. B. Ashton (London: Seabury, 1973), see especially part 2, Concept and Categories, 134–66.

6. Theodor Adorno, "Notes on Kafka," *Prisms,* trans. Samuel and Shierry Weber (Cambridge, Mass.: MIT Press, 1967), 245–71.

7. Franz Kafka, "The Cares of a Family Man," 427.

8. Anthony Thorlby, "Anti-Mimesis: Wittgenstein and Kafka," in *On Kafka: Semi-Centenary Perspectives,* ed. Franz Kuno (New York: Harper and Row, 1976). The "Slavonic origin" of the name Odradek discussed in the first lines of Kafka's story compasses a wide territory, including the concept of speculation itself, since

odrazit means "reflection" (*teorie odrazu:* reflection theory) and *odrazet* means "to mirror" (*odraz:* rebound, reflection). *Odranec* means "in tatters." All err to the saturnine, though, so it is worth remembering another Slavonic course, through Polish, where *odrazac* means the opposite: "to revitalize." Perhaps also the final resting place of speculation should be mentioned, since Russian *smertnom odre* means "on one's deathbed." Some useful scholia are in Gertrude Durusoy, *L'incidence de la litterature et de la langue tcheques sur les nouvelles de Franz Kafka* (Berne, 1981). Ulrich Holbein's *Samthase und Odradek* (Frankfurt, 1990) traces the verbal and pictorial morphology of Odradek back to the figure of Hydra and forward through the imagery of Klee to some twentieth-century children's books.

9. Compare Gustav Janouch, *Gespräche mit Kafka. Aufzeichnungen und Erinnerungen* (Frankfurt am Main: Fischer, 1961). Kafka's remark is taken from Max Brod's biography and also from Brod's conversations with Kafka.

10. Martin Heidegger, *Das Ding,* a lecture of 1950, translated by Albert Hoftsadter as "The Thing" in *Poetry, Language and Thought* (New York: Harper & Row, 1971), 175.

11. Hans-Georg Gadamer's essay *Die Nature der Sache und die Sprache der Dinge* is translated by David E. Linge as "The Nature of Language and the Nature of Things" in *Philosophical Hermeneutics* (Berkeley and Los Angeles: University of California Press, 1976), see especially 70–71. See also Heidegger, "The Thing," and Adorno, "Notes on Kafka."

12. Herman Melville, "Bartelby the Scrivener," *Billy Budd, Sailor: And Other Stories,* intro. Frederick Busch (New York: Viking, 1986), 17.

13. Ibid.

14. Ibid.

15. Sigmund Freud, *Das Unheimlich* (*The Uncanny,* 1919) in the *Standard Edition of the Complete Psychological Works of Sigmund Freud,* trans. James Strachey (London: Hogarth Press), vol. XVII, 219–52. *Jenseits der Lustprinzips* (*Beyond the Pleasure Principle,* 1920), standard edition, vol XVIII, 1–65. Peter Brooks comments extensively on *Beyond the Pleasure Principle* in *Reading for the Plot: Design and Intention in Narrative* (Oxford, 1994). Stanley Cavell's interesting observations on "Die Unheimlich" are from a lecture, *The Uncanniness of the Ordinary* (1986) reprinted in *In Quest of the Ordinary: Lines of Skepticism and Romanticism* (Chicago: University of Chicago Press, 1988), see especially pages 155–56.

16. Freud, *Das Unheimlich;* Cavell, *In Quest of the Ordinary.*

17. Sigmund Freud, *Beyond the Pleasure Principle,* 15.

18. Freud, *Beyond the Pleasure Principle,* 38; Maud Ellmann, "Eliot's Abjection," in *Abjection, Melancholia and Love,* ed. John Fletcher and Andrew Benjamin (London: Routledge, 1990). In a footnote concerning Ernst a page later, Freud quietly notes that "when this child was five and three quarters, his mother

died. Now that she was really gone (o-o-o), the little boy showed no signs of grief." The "mother" was Freud's beloved daughter Sophie, and his interest in the cotton reel also perhaps derived as much from the filiations of the father-daughter bond as well as from the more savage antiphony of *Spule* (the innocuous cotton reel—thread innocently paid out) and the violent recoil of its related verb form spülen (to remove, flush away). In a letter written to Oscar Pfister two days after her sudden death on January 18, 1920, the bitter restraint of Freud's language is notable: "unsere liebe Sophie in Hamburg von einer Grippe-Lungenentzündung hinweg-gerafft worden ist, so weggerafft aus blühender Gesundheit . . . in vier oder fünf Tagen als wäre sie nie da gewesen" (our dear Sophie in Hamburg was snatched away from us by a flu-pneumonia, snatched away as if she had never lived). "Snatched away as if she had never lived": the savage contradiction of *Umweg* (deviation, circuit, detour) by *weggerafft* (snatched away) is the precise amount of contingency that *Jenseits des Lustprinzips* (Beyond the Pleasure Principle), with its exclusive focus on the inner drives of the human organism, cannot account for. This in turn suggests a more haunted matrix of absence and return in Freud's late work and a more uncanny origin to the theory of repetition.

19. Ellmann, "Eliot's Abjection."

20. Wyndham Lewis's remarks on his bobbins are from *The Little Review* version of his essay "Inferior Religions" (1917) reprinted in *The Complete Wild Body,* ed. Bernard Lafourcade (Santa Barbara: Black Sparrow Press, 1991).

21. Peter Brooks, *Reading for the Plot* (New York: Random House, 1985), 103.

22. Georgio Agamben, "In the World of Odradek: The Work of Art Confronted with the Commodity" from *Stanzas: Word and Phantasm in Western Culture,* trans. Ronald L. Martinez (Minneapolis: University of Minnesota Press, 1993), see also chap. 18, "The Proper and the Improper" (143–51). Agamben's highly interesting essay of 1993, "*Bartleby,* or On Contingency," which sees the scrivener as "the extreme figure of the Nothing from which all creation derives," constituting at the same time "the most implacable vindication of this Nothing as pure, absolute potentiality" is collected in *potentialities* (Stanford: Stanford University Press, 1999). A powerful account of the aesthetic as the pure potentiality of *negation* is Christopher Menke's *The Sovereignty of Art: Aesthetic Negativity in Adorno and Derrida* (Cambridge, Mass.: MIT Press, 1998). Agamben is notably uninterested in the figure of the lawyer in Melville's story and consequently has nothing to say on the dialectical relation of *potentia* to *voluntas* which is one of the tale's main concerns. The lawyer consults Jonathan Edwards and Joseph Priestley for advice on how to proceed in the case of Bartleby, and that is perhaps because he, like the hausvater, is suffering from *akrasia,* variously defined by Aristotle in the *Nichomachean Ethics* as a form of incontinence, that is "action against choice," as for example, in the case of being "convinced that one ought to do one thing and nevertheless doing the other" (1151a). In his classic essay

"How Is Weakness of the Will Possible?" Donald Davidson sees incontinence as a paradigm case of the difficulty of reading reason into behavior. "What is special in incontinence is that the actor cannot understand himself; he recognises, in his own intentional behaviour, something essentially surd" (Davidson, *Essays on Actions and Events,* Oxford: Oxford University Press, 1980). Davidson in his turn has little to say on the unconscious motivations of any behavioral sequence, since for him "an action is an event that is caused by the agent's reasons for performing the action."

23. Paul Celan, "Der Meridian," in *Paul Celan: Gesammelte Werke in Funf Banden* (Dritter Band), ed. Beda Allemann and Stefan Reichert (Frankfurt: Suhrkamp, 1983), 187–202. Brydon's "apparition" is midway between Melville and Kafka, not someone or something wholly other but again familiar, "the virtual screen of a figure," both objectified and personified: "it was something, it was somebody, the prodigy of a personal appearance." Brydon is of course another "exile" seeking home, but the domestic estrangements of James's technique here belong precisely to the realms of fascination that Celan wishes to dismantle.

24. Gerald Bruns's comment on Celan's "O" is in his introduction to Hans-Georg Gadamer's *"Who Am I and Who Are You?" and Other Essays* (Albany: SUNY Press, 1997), 18. The relation of Odradek to the circle of meaning around the word "Rad" is discussed in Wilhelm Emrich's *Franz Kafka* (Frankfurt am Main: Athenäum Verlag, 1958); published in English as *Franz Kafka: A Critical Study of His Writings,* trans. Sheema Zeben Buehne (New York: Ungar, 1968).

25. Jean Bollack, *Poésie contre poésie: Celan et la littérature* (Paris: PUF, 2001), 94.

The Avant-Garde and the Wake of Radical Modernism

Donald F. Theall

New media, digiculture, and virtuality have become hot topics in the interface between academia and the media. The talk is related to the difference between the world prior to 1950 and that at the beginning of the twenty-first century. Most of the hype emphasizes radical change, while deliberately or inadvertently dissociating it from past history. Yet the visions of the contemporary magic of virtuality, as well as much else involved in the new digiculture, were present throughout history in the percepts and concepts of the arts. Certainly there is a short-range prehistory which begins with the impact of mathematics, electricity, photography, thermodynamics, and linguistics on the poets and artists of the nineteenth and early twentieth century. Simultaneously these artists and poets knew of the long-term prehistory behind their experimental works that began in the Lascaux caves, ancient Egypt, and Greek mysteries and rituals. There has been some recognition of this complex history, notably in such books as Daren Tofts's *Memory Trade* and the essays in *Prefiguring Cyberspace,* and Victor Grau's *Virtual Art,* as well as various publications on the new media such as the anthology *Multimedia* edited by Randall Packer and Ken Jordan, or the MIT reader, *The New Media.*

Today I would like to explore a particular historical moment to see how these ideas crystalized around artistic perceptions of the machine, of the postelectric universe, of mathematics which explored a "chaosmos," and of major concerns involved in the debate over the new concept of space-time. All of these ideas permeated the avant-garde arts from around the turn of the nineteenth century and particularly those of the early twentieth until the onset of the Second World War. In a brief presentation it is useful to focus on a particular moment in which this interplay of science, technology, and art produced a crucial literary vision. The year, 1939, on the eve of the war, also marked a moment by which the particular intuitions of symbolist, modernist, and avant-garde poets and artists achieved a momentary vision of what would become digiculture and of the move toward a computerized virtual reality that was about to emerge—an emergence that would be accelerated by that war's research needs. The year 1939 marked the closing of the decade which had opened with Ezra Pound exploring the relation of mathematics, mechanics, and music and in 1930 publishing his "Machine Art."

In 1939 James Joyce's *Finnegans Wake* appeared, bringing to completion his "Work in Progress" which began in 1922. The *Wake* is a work that involves a "designed" language, which Joyce declares is not English, because as it noted, "in the Nichtian glossery which purveys aprioric roots for aposteriorious tongues this is nat language at any sinse of the world."[1] The uniqueness of Joyce's last two productions—*Ulysses* and the *Wake*—is their post-Viconian fusion of history embracing aspects of the history of the most ancient times, the history of the liberal arts and drama from Greece to Augustan England, and the recent history of the arts and poetry from Blake and Poe to the 1930s. Joyce's "new science" in *Finnegans Wake* weaves such themes as the contemporary space-time debate and its relation to dream and virtuality together with such artistic motifs as Proust's remembrance, Wyndham Lewis, and the vorticist's artistic concerns with space-time that become the subject of a satiric section of twenty pages (148 to 168) in the *Wake.* Earlier in the 1920s other artists such as Paul Valéry, Laszlo Moholy-Nagy, and Antheil had explored extensively this more recent history. On the literary side, Valéry covered most of it, with the possible exception of Blake. T. S. Eliot produced his essay "From Poe to Valéry."

Poe had thought of the artist as an engineer; Joyce sees himself as a technoscientist and engineer—in fact, the greatest engineer as designer of the *Wake,* and thus declares in his book "sifted science would do your arts good" (*FW* 440.19). Meanwhile Valéry had argued that the role of the contemporary poet or artist is to be "a cool scientist, almost an algebrist, in the service of a subtle dreamer."[2] Valéry's view of the "poet," which occurs in a discussion about Poe and Baudelaire, easily includes a wide range of contemporary artists: Duchamp, Klee, Schoenberg, Hans Richter, Cage, Borges, and Joyce as well as numerous other musicians, artists, and poets of the first two thirds of the twentieth century.[3] The technoscientific poetic vision of all these artists comes to a particular focus in their anticipation of the integration of the arts in an approximation of the total work through the impact of science, mathematics, and technology on their practice.

Laszlo Moholy-Nagy's *Vision in Motion* placed Joyce's work, and particularly the *Wake,* as the then high point in this process—and he paralleled his claim that Pascal with his juncture of philosophy, science, and mathematics launched a tradition that spawned Faraday, Maxwell, Rutherford, and Einstein with a tradition in the arts beginning with Poe that culminated in Joyce's *Wake.*[4] Moholy-Nagy pointed out that this had partly to do with the mechanics of Joyce's manipulation of language in compounds such as "wavyavyheavyeavyevyevy hair,"[5] a nuts-and-bolts compound, or as in "immarginable," the result of fusion. This approach parallels the interest of Pound in "machine art" and its relation to Antheil's *Ballet Mécanique* as well as the machine-oriented experimentation of Léger, Duchamp, Richter, or Moholy-Nagy himself.

Joyce's *Wake* was further highlighted by the resurrection in the late 1980s and 1990s of Marshall McLuhan through the efforts of Stuart Brand in *The Media Lab,* of *Mondo 2000,* and later of *Wired* magazine, which consecrated him as the patron saint of the new media of digiculture. The visions of Saint Marshall were built from the poetic and artistic work that inspired his major writings—Duchamp, Klee, Moholy-Nagy, Antheil, Schoenberg, Baudelaire, Laforgue, Mallarmé, Valéry, the mainline Anglo modernists (Yeats, Pound, Eliot, and Wyndham Lewis), and most particularly Joyce, as well as historians and critics such as Sigfried Giedion, Lewis Mumford, I. A. Richards, and C. K. Ogden. McLuhan, like Moholy-Nagy, had given a nod to the fundamental importance of Joyce when just prior to the publication of *The Gutenberg Galaxy,* he dubbed it "The Road to *Finnegans Wake.*" This along with the approbation of Cage, Cunningham, and Rauschenberg (music, dance, and visual arts) mark the *Wake* as a major climactic moment in the prehistory of cyberspace in which percepts and insights from the interaction of music, visual art, cinema, and the poetic arts are woven together, arising from the arts interface with the technoscientific world as reflected in such passages as:

> his dectroscophonious photosensition under suprasonic light control may be logged for by our none too distant futures as soon astone values can be turned out from Chromophilomos, Limited at a millicentime the microamp. (*FW,* 123.12–15)

Echoes of scientific and technological interests of many major artists from Blake and Poe to Valéry and Duchamp permeate the *Wake.* In achieving a comprehensiveness of encyclopedic inclusion of the contemporary technoscientific world, Joyce's interests ranged from remote historical perspectives in the classical world, the Middle Ages, and the Renaissance to cryptography and mathematics, Whitehead and Russell's mathematical logic, atomic physics, Riemannian and other contemporary geometries, relativity theory, post-Einsteinian understandings of relativity and quanta, Gödel's "Incompleteness Theorem," the physicochemical properties of light, and the various technologies arising from post-Enlightenment sciences. In the process there are references in the text to Pascal, Berkeley, Rutherford, Maxwell, Poincaré, Helmholtz, Whitehead, and Einstein, among others. Joyce combined a particular balance of traditional science and mathematics with recent contemporary developments and transformations as well as with esoteric and alchemical speculation and ancient philosophy, as I have shown at length in my book, *James Joyce's Techno-Poetics.*[6]

It is well known that Poe as scientist-algebraist was a cryptographer and intuited language itself as a code, which is partly linked to his writing in the period when electrification and photochemical reproduction of information were becoming possible. While Poe's fascination with codes is a function of his interests as an amateur cryptographer, it is also connected with his living in the period when the beginnings of the remote transmission of language by electricity necessitated the quasi-mathematical codification of language—ultimately in Morse code. Joyce clearly recognizes this in speaking of the *Wake* as a "new book of Morses" (*FW,* 123.35) in which "what can't be coded can be decorded, if an ear eye seize what no eye ere grieved for" (482.34–36). Joyce's playful punning nevertheless ties together a complex of issues associated with the hypertextual and virtual transformation of the book and the arts as well as with communication and information. The synesthesia and orchestration of the arts implied in the interplay of eye and ear in the dechording and decoding of the transformation of the text from the book of Moses to the electronic writing of Morse appeared earlier (heavily under Poe's influence) in Baudelaire's *Fleurs du Mal,* beginning with his poem "Correspondences."

As already noted, the *Wake,* picking up a theme from Poe promulgated by the symbolists, emphasizes the fundamental link between the algebraist (the mathematical logician), the code, and the poet. In so doing Joyce can link the emerging scientific linguistics of de Saussure and the semiotics of the pragmatists, Ogden and Richards, with the way in which mathematics both permeates contemporary art and has always permeated art from Egyptian times. For in Egyptian times, while the building of the pyramids represented an intuitive understanding of complex geometry, their hieroglyphics demonstrated an intuitive understanding of language as involved with codes. Consequently, Joyce could speak of the Holy Spirit as their "homely codes" (*FW,* 614.32) and see the focus of his contemporary evolution of his hyperpoem as a return to the "highpriest's hieroglyph[s]" (122.7)—a production of "engined Egypsians" (355.23).

Technoscientific connections that interrelate with the future cyberspace are present throughout the *Wake.* Complementing the interest with and in codes and harking back to Baudelaire and Apollinaire as well as visual artists such as Duchamp is the Joyce engrossed in allegory—an involvement which became central in *Ulysses* but which continues and permeates the entirety of the *Wake* where his very use of sigla for the main characters becomes a way of indicating they stand for a variety of multiple meanings. This links code to allegory and imparts to allegory a status as a kind of hyperlinguistic or semiotic algebra. The initials of his heroine ALP become the vertex points on a triangle (a diagram of Euclid's first proposition) in a discussion of the "rhythmatick of our Eternal Geomater" within which he intermingles throughout the creations of the poet with the inventiveness of the mathematician. His very title "rhythmatick" ties mathematics to music in a chapter of the *Wake* which explores insights of such figures as Poincaré, Kronecker, Russell, Carnot, Pythagoras, and Euclid, among others. But mathematics is directed toward understanding the relationships between mathematics and the range of arts.

Like Lewis Carroll, who plays a major role in the *Wake* and who had previously established how logic and mathematics could be utilized in shaping a dreamworld where nonsense holds sway, it is not surprising that through a knowledge of Bertrand Russell, Sir Arthur Eddington, Poincaré, J. W. N. Sullivan, and others, he would also come to realize the affinity of modern mathematics and the new physics with the world of dream and as perceiving in the process an intuitive prophecy of future virtual realities. Sensing that the poet as engineer constructs his poetic machines as an applied mathematician and scientist, Joyce in his most overtly mathematical chapter 2.2, the schoolroom ("Triv and Quad") explored the bridge between 2.1 ("The Mime"), the ludic, dramatic learning of the small child, and 2.3 ("The Pub"), the mediated storytelling and broadcasting (gossip, rumor, news, radio, TV) of adults. The interesting thing about "Triv and Quad," which Joyce describes as "the muddest thick that was ever heard dump since Eggsmather got smothered in the plap of the pfan" (296.20–21), is that it treats the evolution of the "hieroglyphs of engined egypsians" as encompassing numeracy as well as literacy, arithmetic as well as language, mathematics as well as linguistics.

In this section he thus constructs a sensory-physiological, a philosophical, and an "educational" relation among literacy, numeracy, and *technē* as the means by which people develop from childhood through adolescence to maturation. More specifically, the modern outgrowths of the seven liberal arts, the trivium and quadrivium, are seen to be a function of an all-encompassing, if rather "ambiviolent" and "chaosmotic," semiotic machine, which disperses itself from time to time through the "sound sense sympol" into the full range of artistic hieroglyphics or signs, for as the *Wake* puts it: "After sound, light and heat, memory, will and understanding. Here (the memories framed from walls are minding" (*FW,* 266.18–21). Joyce treats the mathematical world of such things as common denominators, as a "comedy nominator" (*FW,* 283.7), for the episode immediately preceding "Triv and Quad" ends with the invocation "Loud heap miseries upon us yet entwine our arts with laughters low" (*FW,* 259.7–8).

In harmony with the tactics of but much more complex than Lewis Carroll's writings, Joyce's *Wake* continues that "mathematical doodling," since Joyce's use of algebra, arithmetic, and geometry, which is "analytical plausible" (*FW,* 299.27–28), will be "a lozenge to me all my lauffe" (299.28–29) [lozenge = lesson, lauffe = laugh + life), because a blending of comedy and logic is the key to his treatment of the family of the Innkeeper in the *Wake*—the "Doodles family" (299.F4), which is represented throughout the *Wake* by sigla as well as names. The intellectual as mathematician can be described as "laying him long on his laughside" (*FW,* 301.28). As Gilles Deleuze demonstrates in *Logic of Sense,* in the machinic universe there is a fantastic sense embedded in its nonsense, and so Joyce plays with and on arithmetic, geometry, and other aspects of mathematics while simultaneously describing the mechanics and dynamics of his book and its dreamworld. If the avant-garde visual artists and radical modernist symbolist poets all envisioned an integration of the arts, for Joyce it arose out of Poe's algebraist fascination with code, Baudelaire's understanding of the importance of allegory in that process, Rimbaud's and Valéry's treatment of "synaesthesia," and Mallarmé's and Duchamp's play with chance, ambivalence, and potential chaos. Chance, ambivalence, and chaos appear in the *Wake* in such crucial phrases as the following: (chance) "chanching letters for them vice o'verse to bronze mottes and blending tschemes for em in tropadores and doublecressing twofold thruths and devising tingling tailwords too whilest, cunctant that another would finish his sentence for him" (*FW,* 288.1–5); (ambivalence) "Language this allsfare for the loathe of Marses ambiviolent about it" (518.2–3); (chaos) "every person, place and thing in the chaosmos of Alle anyway connected with the gobblydumped turkery was moving and changing every part of the time" (118.21–23).

Yet Joyce, seeing the dream of a codified, allegorical, ambivalent, chance-oriented dreamworld in keeping with the emerging physics of a "chaosmos" (orderly disorderliness worthy of Dada) could shape his dream and its language which is "nat language in any sinse of the world" into a hypermnesic, hyperlinguistic, virtual vision of a world that wishes to integrate performance, music, film, visual art, pop art, architecture, and poetry—a total work as he notes in the *Wake:*

> Of all the stranger things that ever not even in the hundrund and badst pageans of unthowsent and wonst nice or in eddas and oddes bokes of tomb, dyke and hollow to be have happened! The untireties of livesliving being the one substrance of a streamsbecoming. Totalled in toldteld and teldtold in tittle-tell tattle. Why? Because, graced be Gad and all giddy gadgets, in whose words were the beginnings, there are two signs to turn to, the yest and the ist, the wright side and the wronged side, feeling aslip and wauking up, so an, so farth. (*FW,* 597.4–12)

The play with space-time in the phrase "the untirities of the livesliving" is linked to the dream as "totalled in toldteld"—a total work (or at least the hyperverbal mimesis of a total work), the *Gesamtkunstwerk* as noted by Wagner and the baroque but also implicit in Greek theory. Toward the end of the *Wake,* leading up to the concluding virtual vision, Joyce reveals that from one allegorical perspective the husband, HCE, and the wife,

ALP, are "Father Times and Mother Spacies" (*FW,* 600.3) with ALP also as the river that flows through "the space of the time being" (109.22). As Joyce learned from Sigfried Giedion and indirectly from Moholy-Nagy, time and space combine in the movement of the machine, so the world of the *Wake* is a dreamworld in which "we are recurrently meeting em, par Mahun Mesme, in cycloannalism, from space to space, time after time, in various phases of scripture as in various poses of sepulture" (*FW,* 254.25–27).

This passage about "streamsbecoming" (*FW,* 597.8) introduces the closing chapter in which the *Wake*'s climactic virtual dream vision occurs. (It is important to note that this vision is one of the earliest passages Joyce drafted as he began composing his work in 1923). This vignette of a debate about the nature of light and its impact on the real and the virtual takes place between the philosopher-scientist, Bishop Berkeley, and Saint Patrick—allegorically: the archdruid and the saint; but also the man of learning and the down-to-earth, everyday man. To underline its involvement with the orchestration and synthesis of the arts, this vignette is introduced within the context of references to media and spectacle, for example, film—"Shoot. / Rhythm and colour at park mooting" (*FW,* 611.33–34); spectacle—"Peredos Last in the Grand Natural" (611.34–35); TV—"velivison victor" (611.35); theatrical drama and newspaper with a nod toward comic strips—"Dubs newstage oldtime turftussle, recalling Winny Willy Widger. Two draws" (611.35–36); and a radio news broadcast—"And here are the details" (611.3). The heliotropic (*FW,* 610.36), heptachromatic (611.6) presentation of the debate about the nature of light and optical theories clearly situates it in an ambivalent, technoscientific, utopian dream vision of multimedia or "new" media.

This final debate, which is dealt with in the penultimate chapter of my book *James Joyce's Techno-Poetics,* is too complex to explore in detail now. It brings into focus most of the major science and technology themes from the early decades of the twentieth century. It is as well known a debate about the nature of light and the spectrum with their associations with contemporary theories of physics and optics counterpointed with the Berkeleian and Newtonian accounts of vision. Essentially, this debate situates the whole of Joyce's book as a postverbal reconstruction of the coalescence of the dreamworld and the new media through the mediation of technology and science. This position is confirmed by its being followed by a passage in which the book becomes a "millwheeling vicociclometer, a tetradomational gazebocroticon," which is in and of itself a virtual reality bringing together the visual, the written, the aural, and the iconic through history and memory.

If new modes of electronic communication and other technologies (e.g., the railroad, the automobile, film, and the airplane) complemented by Riemann's discovery of descriptive geometry partly transformed the nature of space and time, artists explored these new altered perceptions in poetry, mobiles, montage, and the exercise of the imaginary. Valéry celebrates the engineer and the mathematician; Proust explores the changing face of time, duration, speed, and transformation; the younger Eliot is a monist who stresses the importance of Russell, Whitehead, and Einstein more than Husserl. In the visual arts, Léger stresses engineering; Duchamp, mechanical assemblages and mass-produced culture; the futurists, speed, power, and movement; Picasso, the relativization of perspective and its social impact. Léger and Picasso's cubist vision reintegrated people with a space that was rapidly transforming under the impact of time (as well as under the impact of cinematic motion on time and space); while the futurists explored the metamorphosis of distance with changing concepts of speed. Early theories of psychoanalysis that deeply influenced cultural production also borrowed some concepts from machinery, electricity, and other technological assemblages.

Living within this context, Joyce organized this network of intuitions and linked them to the longer-term prehistory of the newly emerging media world which many of his fellow artists had also intuited, thus providing an even greater irony to his statement, "Wait till Finnegan wakes," for that waking would be both the transformation of dream into virtual reality and the transformation of the participants (the audience) through their understanding of the media effects. What T. S. Eliot had announced as Joyce's introducing with *Ulysses* "the death of the book" becomes in the *Wake* a representation in print of the *transformation of the book* into a multimedia virtual reality by playing with the malleability of oral and written language as code.

Notes

1. James Joyce, *Finnegans Wake* (New York: Viking, 1958), 83: line 12. Hereafter cited in text as *FW* followed by page and line numbers.

2. Paul Valéry, "On Literary Technique," in *The Art of Poetry* (introd. T. S. Eliot), trans. Denise Foliot (New York: Random House, 1958), vol. 7 of *Collected Works* (Bollingen Foundation), 315.

3. T. S. Eliot, "From Poe to Valéry," *Hudson Review* 2 (autumn, 1949).

4. Laszlo Moholy-Nagy, *Vision in Motion* (Chicago: Theobald, 1947), 61, 350.

5. James Joyce, *Ulysses (The Corrected Text)*, eds. Hans Walter Gabler et al. (Harmondsworth, Middlesex: Penguin, 1986), 228, line 809.

6. Donald F. Theall, *James Joyce's Techno-Poetics* (Toronto: University of Toronto Press, 1997).

My heart rouses
thinking to bring you news
of something
that concerns you
and concerns many men. Look at
what passes for the new.
You will not find it there but in
despised poems.
It is difficult
to get the news from poems
yet men die miserably every day
for lack
of what is found there.
Hear me out
for I too am concerned
and every man
who wants to die at peace in his bed
besides.

—William Carlos Williams

Doctor Williams's Position, Updated

Bob Perelman

Trivia

In the early 1950s when William Carlos Williams wrote "Asphodel, That Greeny Flower,"[1] poetry had recently been pushed to the unfamiliar precincts of the American front pages by the crescendoing public drama of Ezra Pound: his raving but clearly profascist radio speeches during the war; the aborted treason trial at the war's end; and the long firestorm over his being awarded the Bollingen Prize in 1949. Williams's forced withdrawal from consideration for the position of poetry consultant to the Library of Congress in 1952 had been something of a public event, too, though in this, as with most everything else, he was overshadowed by Pound. One factor contributing to Williams's defeat was his lifelong association with Pound. In "Asphodel," after decades of absorbing, chafing against, and seconding Pound's lessons, Williams offers a correction, more socially nuanced and ethically capacious, to Pound's absolutist "Literature is news that STAYS news."[2] Pound grants writing (only the best writing, of course) extraordinary powers and brooks no personal, spatial, or temporal obstacle to legibility: it *is,* and it *stays,* news. For Williams, news is equally valuable, but its reception is more specific. The body is the locus of poetry's claimed effects: an embodied reader either gets the news and can die in bed at peace or does not receive the blessing and dies miserably. Williams's claim, unlike Pound's, recognizes failure as one of the structuring possibilities of valid poetry.

Such senses of contingency have mostly fallen away, however, as for many readers the passage has come to stand as a proclamation of poetry's virtues with any possibility of failure omitted. The title for Adrienne Rich's essays, *What Is Found There,* quarries out a positive assertion from lines where Williams only names a lack; more recently, as controversies over Amiri Baraka's "Somebody Blew Up America" and the cancellation of Laura Bush's poetic soiree have again put poetry on the front page,[3] "the news from poems" has become something of a commonplace, a basic justification of poetry or simply a synonym for it. A letter writer to the *New York Times* quotes the lines and then comments, "What people find in poetry is a deeper, more creative and moral way of looking at the world";[4] a review of an anthology of international poetry is entitled "The News from Poetry"—in both cases the difficulties and absence at the heart of Williams's claim have been erased. While its appearances on op-ed pages and the like could in some sense be a vindication for Williams, it is hard to avoid the sense that it is precisely the vagueness of these lines that is latched onto, making them say something like, "Poetry is wonderful, but *they* just don't get it," a sense that reinforces the standoff between individual and community that the passage is addressing in the first place.

I remain intrigued by the confident, oddly blank promise of Williams's claim. I realize how conveniently comforting it can be and, when it is quoted in defense of poetry I don't particularly respect, how it can sound like the stiffest cultural ideology. But I am not willing, finally, to resign myself to writing in a world without such a promise. The lines are a commonsense riddle which both points out the modernist endgame that has pinched poetry into specialist niches and at the same time promises that, in some unspecified way, poetry's social dilemma is capable of being solved.

Williams's current centrality in American poetry is an obvious but nevertheless odd fact of literary history. When his poetry is read closely, there are repeated oddnesses that can't be resolved by appeals to voice, theory, or history. These oddnesses point to what I am interested in here: qualities I call social and poetic candor, terms I will discuss in the final section. For now, I don't want to be misunderstood as intending to sweep away all prior readings. The useful and, at best, inspiring achievements of the poetry are there, as many readers have found; but, as many readers are also undoubtedly aware, Williams's work is full of problematic moments. I have come to see them not simply as blemishes, miscalculations, or carelessness, which, if we like Williams, are to be overlooked or forgiven or, if we don't, serve to prove that he's second-rate. Rather, they are a fundamental part of his writing. This doesn't redeem them. What, in the "Eumaeus" chapter of *Ulysses,* may look at first like terrible writing becomes yet another example of Joyce's mastery: nothing like that happens with Williams. Nor is it a matter of Williams the democratic modernist exemplifying a proletarian agenda and writing unrefined work to yank elite readers down to the real world. For all of its use of everyday language and events around him, Williams's poetry can no more be mistaken for ordinary language than can Dickinson's or Zukofsky's. For all its legibility, it guards its news jealously. "The Clouds" contains an apt emblem of this. His initial description of the clouds ends:

> a rank confusion of the imagination still uncured,
> a rule, piebald under the streetlamps, reluctant
> to be torn from its hold.[5]

By writing the word "rule," Williams posits its existence, but he is unable to articulate it, to tear it loose from the imagination; he has no cure (either medically or in the sense of proper aging) for its confusions. The same unresolved struggle is present in his sense of news. The still-prevalent received idea makes the modernist poet the one who knows and who challenges readers to overcome their own ignorance. But Williams's pronouncement "It is difficult to get the news from poems" applies to him as much as to those who die miserably without it: their condition is part of his—and our—difficulty.

When pressed, the sentence itself is quite slippery—an odd thing to say, since the language couldn't be simpler or more direct. It's not hard to place it in poetic history: the stakes are obvious. This is the American idiom that Williams supported in the face of Pound's and Eliot's Euro-historical erudition. But even though "news" and "get" are the most basic American words, they are not simple or clear.

Why is it difficult to get the news from poems? Is it a lack of literary expertise? "People don't get how to read poetry; they read for plot or imagery and don't get what really makes a poem news." Is it a problem of circulation? "It's hard to get the crucial poetry books in local libraries and bookstores." Or, using "get" in its most untranslatable sense, is it that pedantic imaginations, inflexible libidos, and tin ears are impervious to poetic inspiration? "They just don't get it." This last sense makes news quasi-transcendental, something like the "good news" of the Gospel.

Is this the "imprecision" that both Pound and Eliot abhor? Their poetics are distinct from one another, but both supply criteria that Williams's poetry fails to meet. For Pound, poetry had to be clear; for Eliot, it has to embody hieratic power. Though Pound consistently gave Williams himself a ration of praise for his "opacity,"[6] it was not a quality he praised elsewhere. In *ABC of Reading* he admitted logopoeia, "the dance of the intellect among the words,"[7] which allows the words to dance as well, but by midcentury, words had to dance in their prescribed places: the necessity for an unwobbling pivot made the mot juste the only acceptable poetic currency. What we now so often and easily call polysemy was taboo. Eliot's distaste for the contemporary vulgate was spelled out in carefully conventional terms in "Burnt Norton": "Words strain / . . . / Under the tension, slip, slide, perish, / Decay with imprecision." Williams's language is imprecise; "polysemous" is a bit grand to apply to it, though "socially polysemous" is not inaccurate. A paradoxical praise-adjective would be "trivial," in the ancient sense of *tri-via:* where three roads meet. There is tremendous traffic in words there, jammed in contradiction, zealous, lost, wandering, purposeful, mired in the boredom of blockage. It's where we still live.

Inspiration: Williams and Ion

My heart rouses
thinking to bring you news
of something
that concerns you
and concerns many men.

Thinking to bring you my sense of the news from "Asphodel," my heart rouses, but not without qualms. Rouses because I am continually struck by the claim these lines make; familiarity does not flatten it. At times, I can find it inspiring, to use that most suspect word. It is not simply saying that poetry can enrich any life—an easy enough proposition to agree with, especially for those enriched lives already committed to poetry. The claim here intends a wider reach, out beyond any established audience to society at large, and thus it is harder to believe. The news from poems can answer to the sharpest personal and the largest social demands? What kind of answer would that be? Would wars stop, to allow for harmonious lives and happy deathbed scenes on a universal scale?

Like the audience listening to Homer in the *Ion,* is my feeling of inspiration simply a link of contagious excitement, attached to nothing more substantial than what I read to be Williams's feeling of excitement?

Despite being 2,300 years old and despite the fact that the poetry it discusses is oral,[8] the *Ion* offers an interesting frame in which to consider "Asphodel." This is not because of the poem's references to the *Iliad.* Such references are either vacuous ("The sea! The sea! / Always / when I think of the sea / there comes to mind / the *Iliad*") or almost comically inappropriate in a poem that, among other things, is meant as an apology for the poet's infidelities ("there comes to mind / the *Iliad* / and Helen's public fault / that bred it").[9] But comparing Williams to the rhapsodist Ion does bring out an interesting implications for both poet and reader.

Coming into dialogue with Socrates, Ion is certain of poetry's emotional power and epistemological plenitude. Its power is undeniable: the evidence is there in his body and the bodies of others: when the poem is pitiful, he weeps, the audience weeps; when it is horrific, his hair stands on end, their hair stands on end. He also believes that his prize-winning recitations of Homer give him access to all the skills and knowledge represented in the poems, until Socrates shows him (and us) that what he considers to be his knowledge is neither his nor knowledge, that his words are shaped "not by art or science . . . but by . . . divine possession."[10] In the *Ion* Plato does not have Socrates spell out the conclusions that are so emphatic in the *Republic,* but they are implicit here: poetry's unwieldy power makes people dangerous; Ion and his audience become emotional automatons following the feelings scripted by the poems; and these scripts sprawl promiscuously across ethical boundaries.[11]

In "Asphodel" poetry arrives in much the same way as it does for Ion, despite a different poetic technology: Williams speaks elegiacally of "the words / made solely of air / or less, / that came to me / out of the air / and insisted / on being written down."[12] While there is no Socrates in "Asphodel" nor any magnetized audience, there is that initial poetic enthusiasm: "My heart rouses / thinking to bring you news." But what is the news?

"News / of something." A cynical reading could parse this as a variant (in the American idiom) of Lear's substanceless fulmination: "I will do such things— / What they are, yet I know not; but they shall be / The terrors of the earth."[13] Or, in a harsher reading, one could inflect it into a naive version of the "drumroll . . . pratfall" trope that Eliot dramatizes in "Prufrock," where the initial stanza leads up to the portentous "overwhelming question" only to dissolve into light verse: "Oh, do not ask, 'What is it?' / Let us go and make our visit." Such an inflection would read like so: "I bring you [the most crucial] news of [. . . um, well . . .] something."

This is too harsh. But whether one reads it harshly or forgivingly, the news remains unspecified: it fills Williams with enthusiasm, but ultimately he does not know what this news is and cannot translate it out of the medium of his enthusiasm. Possibly the news *is* nothing but his enthusiasm. This lack of specific content can be a virtue since breadth of address seems the point. The news concerns "you"—Williams's wife Flossie—and "many men," a universality which is then amplified: "every day" men suffer the want of this news; it concerns "every man." However, if poetic news should be construed as purely a function of personal and universal address without its content mattering, what happens next in "Asphodel" isn't all that encouraging: just a few lines after announcing that he has crucial news for her, the poet has to beg Flossie to keep listening, "Hear me out," a refrain which is varied throughout the poem. Perhaps she tunes out because the news seems only addressed to a male public ("all men"), with the additional, singular, aggrieved wife singled out privately in hopes of restoring domestic tranquillity.

Location, Location, Location

Thinking to transmit the news from "Asphodel" via critical prose written at the beginning of the twenty-first century, I am filled with qualms, which are not helped by my having used, straightaway and without any saving irony or contextual specificity, "inspiring," a word which marks criticism as bellelettristic and poetry as naive cape-wielding. The problem with Williams, to miscite John Ashbery, is there is not enough of a problem. At this point, it's not easy to think of his work as news, especially "Asphodel," a late poem where his avant-garde antagonisms have all but evaporated and where the language—sometimes eloquent, sometimes sloppy or banal—is never difficult in a modernist sense.

"Asphodel" is not a critically fashionable poem nor a poetically fashionable one. While it is celebrated for the lines I've been discussing, and praised (and sometimes panned) for its depth of sentiment, it is not a particularly modernist poem nor a forward-looking poem in terms of technique. It is obviously the poem of an old man. Old age, memory, and approaching death are predominant subject matter: in Greek myth, asphodel grows next to the Elysian fields. Stylistically, the poem shows what is known as "slackening of the artist's power": it can be prolix, words are repeated carelessly, the rhetoric is clumsy in places. Its many moments when Williams addresses his wife Flossie can be strained and mawkish: "You have forgiven me," the poet asserts at one particularly unconvincing moment.

The poem has its strengths, too, amid these problems. But whatever one's aesthetic verdict, "Asphodel" is situated to offer a useful perspective on modernist poetry: Does midcentury mark its conclusion, or, as Marjorie Perloff and I and others have argued, its midpoint? (Midpoint in a noncontinuous historical trajectory, that is.) A major retrospection of Williams's career, the poem can stand out as one of the more visible conclusive points of American modernist poetry. It's less easy to imagine it as a midpoint, since, as I've said, it seems stylistically retrogressive (for example, in its unpainterly, crudely symbolic flower imagery, or its nonironic allusions from Spenser, using the same phrases that Eliot had, one thought, made permanently ironic thirty years earlier in *The Waste Land*). However, "Asphodel" 's odd mix of genre and subject remains quite germane. It is a love poem, aggressively intimate (emotionally, not bodily) and confessional, poetic territory that Williams explored quite a bit before Ginsberg, O'Hara, Lowell, Rich, or Plath. It is an ars poetica written from a personally situated, noninstitutional perspective.

Williams is now a central figure in American poetry history. But the center is a bland place to be, at best. Williams scores points as a modernist, but in terms of critical cachet he's not in the first rank. The basic elements of his poetics are easy to domesticate: the American idiom, "no ideas but in things," "a poem is a machine made of words," the variable foot. That poetry should use the contemporary idiom has long been poetic common sense; "no ideas but in things" can be taken as a slogan gesturing rather abstractly toward the here and now,[14] "a poem is a machine of words" as a slogan aligning the poet with modernity; the variable foot might encode Williams's dynamic intuitions behind his own poetic practice, but the only point on which readers agree is that it's a vague formulation. It does not take much reading outside the critical demonstration-pieces to find that many of Williams's poems don't stay within the confines of any of these notions.

His work is hard to characterize or evaluate. He has become an honored predecessor for an uncomfortably wide range of contemporary poets. Heterogeneous in itself, his work has had unmistakable influence on a contradictory set of heirs, leading to the polemical plainness of Levine and Rich as much as to O'Hara's erotic wit, Ginsberg's prophetic politics, and the textual activism of Language writing. Just about any poem not in regular meter could claim Williams as a precursor.

His work points to the future in contradictory ways. For Charles Bernstein, Williams's poetic iconoclasm remains an unfinished project. Bernstein sees the academy and other gatekeeping institutions allowing only a tamed Williams to circulate: "As Williams passes through the narrow and well-guarded gates of official verse culture, it likely will be at the expense of so decontextualizing and neutralizing his work that it will be unrecognizable on his own terms . . . official verse culture is no more hospitable to Williams's literary politics now than it was fifty years ago."[15] For Robert Pinsky, it is the democratic Williams who awaits acknowledgment: Williams's "influence has been immense, but his model has yet to be completely realized"; his work aspired to put poetic innovation at the service of cultural legibility: "originality of technique and the ambition to write a poetry of American life, in language based on the American idiom, embodied a single, unified project."[16]

Logically, both positions value the range of Williams's address and the vividness of his language; but when placed in a Bourdieuvian literary field, the poet-critics represent starkly polarized positions: poet laureate versus Language writer, official verse culture versus oppositional poetries.[17] It is striking that it is possible for Williams to be claimed as a central figure by both positions, something that is far less likely in the cases of Stein, Olson, Zukofsky, Riding, or Pound.

Poetic principalities guard their borders fiercely, while at the same time claiming right of unimpeded passage from the poetic sphere to the world at large. Two factors lie behind these contradictory attitudes toward boundaries: one is the current state of the poetic field, which is crowded as never before; the other is the powerful momentum of a modernist legacy. For close to a century we have been living and writing under its dispensation in which the news and the new have been synonymous, both standing for the central value organizing all battles for poetic position. "Make It New" describes the impulse governing significant writing. How to determine what is significant? "Literature is news that STAYS news." In other words, the new is news that stays news. Inside this circle the problem of poetry's social authority is solved: poetic knowledge ceases to be merely specialized; poetry (particular, eccentric) is united with history (universal).

Recent developments have made this tight certainty brittle. Poetry, in its most general sense, has become a social fact to a fairly wide extent. It may not play an authoritative role in the culture—its niche in the entertainment industry is minor, as is its presence in the curriculum at all levels—nevertheless, more people in more situations write, hear, and study more different kinds of poetry than ever before. Innovative poetry is not totally excluded from this modest success. There are now more innovative publications, venues, paper and electronic archives, Listservs and blogs, more reviews of innovative work, more critical articles and books, more slots in syllabi than ever before. To be sure, innovation is still almost always given the cold shoulder when it comes to jobs, awards, grants, and standard anthologies; and senses of embattlement are widespread. But-what is the social objective of the battle? To supplant the mainstream? Doubtful. What, then? To defend the circle where New = News?

Poetic innovation and news have become unspecific, formally and factually. There is little way of determining, strictly from internal evidence, whether a poem is innovative. Few results appearing under the right name in the right place could be excluded: chance procedures; improvisation; collaboration; Steinian meditation involving syntactic fracture, repetition, or rhythmic play; allusive literary collage; antiliterary pastiche; plain denotation à la Reznikoff; highly worked or slack verbal surfaces—the list could go on. As for news, it is becoming more obvious by the minute that it is extraordinarily difficult to separate it from ideology, from propaganda, from weaponry. Both the new and the news have become something like Freud's primal words except that they don't point to some originary condition but to an unfathomable terminus improbably called the present. There are other key words in the "Asphodel" passage: "every man," "you," "bed." Here I'll confine myself to that quarrelsome pair—don't call them twins—new and news.

A Fable

When it comes to poetry, the present, the cumbersome obvious present, plays the most uncanny trick on the new.

After some period of coalescence, the new emerges into the present.

There must have been some fortunate hours or it wouldn't have emerged at all. But the hours were fortunate and the new does emerge, energetically. Having done so, it fortifies its identity by focusing its aim, which is to progress directly and unambiguously toward the future. It streamlines its modes to get there more quickly and to separate itself from its compromised, conservative, mildewed rivals. After intense stretches of invention, self-presentation, polemic, self-correction, gathering articulation, and further invention all happening more or less simultaneously, a time comes to take stock of how far it has progressed.

Now the present is no nimble magician; there is no sudden revelation from behind a flashing cape. But it happens every time: the new has not reached the future; for all its ferocious velocity, it finds itself stuck fast in the past. Nostalgia becomes an occupational hazard at this point . . .

The New and Its Reproductive Practices

If time is a one-way, irreversible continuum, the past will always resolve into a receding vista of terms denoting periodization: Postlanguage, Language writing, New American poetry, Objectivism, high Modernism, Romanticism. For some, the avant-garde is visible right behind high Modernism; others place it in front; others see it everywhere; still others don't see it at all. Many reproductions of the vista are sold each year; most omit the avant-garde. All versions of the vista ironize vanguard aspirations; iconoclasm always becomes "The New is Dead, Long Live the New!" a salute to the unchanging reign of Continuity.

For those of us temporarily enmeshed in the present, however, things are not so clear. Rather than the steady hand of chronology smoothly adding to the shelves, there's a chronic battle of the books. Behind makeshift barricades, partisans hurl small magazines, chapbooks, Listservs, and blogs like cobblestones against the uncomprehending but irritated enemy; they heap up regressive prizewinning volumes, careers, academies, and entire centuries to feed the bonfires. Powerful currents of comradeship unite the partisans, but they are subject to disruption, with accusations of double-dealing not uncommon. It's not surprising: the enemy has control over a great deal of institutional recognition, so that without the constant support from other members of the group behind the barricade, an individual career can fade rapidly.

The partisans' place in the synchronous literary field is tight and embattled; but their temporal claims are secure and immense. Breathing space in the present may be circumscribed, but the present opens securely onto the future, and the past is under control as well. It can be destroyed, as with the futurists, or shaped by definition and identification: either way it's under control. A list of some representative stances: Stendhal enlists past writers into his partisan fight for an emergent romanticism: "Molière was romantic in 1670, because the court was full of Orontes and the châteaux in the provinces were full of very discontented Alcestes. Actually, ALL GREAT WRITERS WERE THE ROMANTICS OF THEIR DAY."[18] Baudelaire sets up a two-state solution, granting autonomy to both the present and eternity: "By 'modernity' I mean the ephemeral, the fugitive, the contingent, the half of art whose other half is the eternal and the immutable."[19] Zukofsky's capsule poetics in section 6 of "A" unites the past; an observed, multiform present; and the future as he asks for writing that is "objectively perfect / Inextricably the direction of historic and contemporary particulars."[20] The salient aspect of this formula is the assertion of control: the artwork is objectively perfect and coincides exactly with the direction of history. In this regard, Zukofsky is quite like Eliot: "The existing monuments form an ideal order among themselves, which is modified by the introduction of the new (the really new) work of art among them."[21] In asserting his power to enter and to change the past ideal order, Eliot idealizes his own power under the name of the new; Zukofsky's claim of perfection does the same, although the power is put in history's name.

It's awkward to yoke Eliot with Zukofsky or with any partisans of innovation. The strain is evident in the single word "monuments" Eliot uses to designate literary works. This gesture of protoinstitutionalization anticipates his full conversion to exaggerated respectability and assiduous genuflection to the triumphant theological literariness he invented. He never acknowledged the invention nor the triumph, instead acting out a pious self-extinction in the service of tradition: "We shall often find that not only the best, but the most individual parts of his work may be those in which the dead poets, his ancestors, assert their immortality most vigorously. And I do not mean the impressionable period of adolescence, but the period of full maturity."[22] To reach full maturity is also to enlist in the ranks of the dead. As for mere living, that's for "impressionable adolescence."

If Eliot's dead ventriloquizing poets are subtracted, the 1988 quasi manifesto by six Language writers makes a claim on tradition that is structurally similar to Eliot's in one way. For us the avant-garde tradition was as crucial and established a fact as Eliot's tradition. Language writing's emergence was not "an unusual narrative. Developments of such collective activity have characterized the history of the avant-garde" such as "the Black Mountain, San Francisco Renaissance, and New York schools of poetry." In a move that, again, has surprising similarities to Eliot, we assumed a position of normative mature knowledge as we called those who repressed or were ignorant of our tradition parochial: "On analogy with the visual arts, where the 'avant-garde' is felt to be a virtual commonplace, the situation of poetry is as if the entire history of radical modernism . . . had been replaced by a league of suburban landscape painters."[23] Unlike Eliot, we emphasized community: our basic principle was "not the 'self-sufficiency of language' or the 'materiality of the sign' but *the reciprocity of practice implied by a community of writers who read each other's work.*"[24] But it was our community, defined solely by the activity of reading and writing, temporarily free from larger social striations and antagonisms.

The general pattern, where power over history is wielded to solidify an embattled position in the present literary field, is maintained in Steve Evans's recent castigation of the journal *Fence.* The ferocity of the charge of apostasy against the avant-garde is clear from the title, "The Resistible Rise of Fence Enterprises"—change "Fence Enterprises" to "Arturo Ui" and you have the title of Brecht's allegory of Hitler's rise. Evans draws a fiery line between the avant-garde and writing that is merely "linguistically innovative," "indeterminate," or "experimental."[25] The avant-garde is distinguished less by any formal distinctions than its set toward the social and toward history in the present. The avant-garde is "collective and contentious";[26] its core values are "solidarity, integrity and generosity." But without the "imaginative work of connecting [its] expressions back to the social forces, contradictions, and struggles that animate contemporary life," the avant-garde falls into "formalism."[27] For Evans, this is the fate of *Fence,* which supports, in its editor's words, "a distinguished grey area," taking care to "exclude no one . . . in the name of an academic purity, or a pre-ordained set of obscurities." Evans calls this a "facile pluralism," which selectively appropriates "radical poetic techniques, shorn of their contexts and motivating commitments."[28] Borrowing Adorno's description of compromised atonal composers, Evans predicts that such a "despicable artistic credo" will only produce "a respectably routined neo-academicism"; "self-flattery" that mistakes "linguistic for social structures," it has no future and is merely a "spent poetics . . . the radical imagination has already left . . . behind."[29] Despite Evans's eloquent evocation of outward, synchronic social context as fundamental to the avant-garde, the coup de grâce that defines it and condemns *Fence* is temporal. Because of its desire for social generality, *Fence* is expelled from history.

My section heading promised an account of reproductive practices of the new, but there's been precious little in evidence. If it occurs at all, reproduction takes place not in the secure realm of history but in the embattled social spaces of the present, with the inevitable danger of becoming reproducible, routine doxa, some "respectably routined neo-academicism." Schematically, a pessimistic logician could say: if the new reproduces, it's not new. Existence itself, if continued, is problematic: How can extending across the temporal boundary of the present moment be distinguished from extending across spatial, institutional boundaries that separate a *Fence* magazine from the genuine avant-garde? If the continuous and the contiguous aren't fenced off, they will dissolve the avant-garde community. Controlling extension is basic to avant-garde self-fashioning, thus Spicer's insistence that his books not leave the Bay Area or his comment that poetry means nothing to nonpoets[30] and Olson's valorization of "a nation of nothing but poetry."[31]

The motley, ersatz, Delphic territories of the new encompass the hard-to-read historical demands that are basic to interesting poetry, but it's my sense that a different syntax is needed to direct these demands outward toward the heteronymous present rather than toward the goal of a purely autonomous future. Seen in this light, Williams's poetic messiness is a sign of his continually making contact with the present, where his poems faced dissolution. Mess—not the transgressive waste of Bataille's general economy, but just plain mess—sloppiness, compromise, common sense: these qualities can attend the best of Williams's poems. To be sure, Williams always proclaims a desire for breakthrough, freshness, the word cleaned of all common gunk, but his writing gives evidence of a more interesting lack of rigor. To recall his nemesis Eliot's phrase, it half-enacts a kind of poetic "self-extinction": rather than poetic autonomy, contact with the outside.

But the basic question of value obtrudes here. I don't mean to be valorizing mess, per se. Isn't there a bad infinity of messy, compromised, commonsense, uninteresting poetry? How is value authenticated in poetry?

Expertise, Witness, Authentication

Intellectual hoaxes dramatize the boundaries of authenticity. Unlike plagiarism and forgeries, which are meant to stay concealed, these hoaxes are constructed to be revealed and then reveal incompetence. It takes an expert to construct a hoax; a hoax targets would-be experts (though others may be fooled); it takes an expert to reveal a hoax. More than a simple lie like a bomb hoax, an intellectual hoax is a guerrilla weapon in a battle of possession of knowledge.

But in poetry, where knowledge and imagination have been fencing for millennia, knowledge and expertise remain elemental Gordian knots. Thus, while there have been poetry hoaxes, at least in some empirical sense, it's an awkward point that the poetry produced in these hoaxes is as legible as any other poetry. In fact, in the case of "Ern Malley," where the poetry was meant to be nonsense, the resulting poems now seem more interesting than the serious poetry of the poets who constructed the hoax.[32] Reading Ern Malley no longer elicits the hoax-cry: "Can you believe someone took this seriously?" A hoax poem is a highly unstable form. There have been hoax poets, but it seems there can't ultimately be hoax poems. Then again, if hoax poetry can't be differentiated from other poetry, doesn't that imply that all poetry is something of a hoax? Sidney's defense of poetry, that the poet "nothing affirms, and therefore never lieth," could easily be cited in support of such a dismissal of poetry's claims to authenticity.

Here I want to consider an interesting recent (1997) example: the Yasusada affair, or hoax, depending on how you want to parse it. It is in marked contrast with two closely contemporaneous events: the debates over the Smithsonian's Enola Gay presentation and Alan Sokal's pseudoscientific essay, "Transgressing the Boundaries: Toward a Transformative Hermeneutics of Quantum Gravity," that hoaxed the editors of *Social Text*.[33] Tapping into widespread anger and angst over perceived postmodern assaults on certainty, the Sokal hoax reverberated through academia and beyond to the op-ed pages of the *New York Times;* Yasusada reached the front page of the Japanese equivalent, *Asahi Shimbun*. But the parallel stops there: the Sokal hoax stayed a hoax while for many critics and poets the Yasusada poems mutated into something at least semiauthentic. In the Smithsonian/Enola Gay wrangles the politics of history was clear, with the strength of different constituencies measurable by what could or couldn't be included in an exhibition marking the fiftieth anniversary of Hiroshima. In contrast, the question of the historical validity of a Yasusada poem dispersed into questions of imaginative sympathy and poetic license.

A basic polemical joke of Sokal's "Transgressing the Boundaries" is that time and space are no longer binding categories: "The key point is that this invariance group [involving the Einstein field equation $G\mu\nu = 8\pi GT\mu\nu$] 'acts transitively': . . . any space-time point, if it exists at all, can be transformed into any other. . . . The infinite-dimensional invariance group erodes the distinction between observer and observed; the *p* of Euclid and the *G* of Newton, formerly thought to be constant and universal, are now perceived in their ineluctable historicity." Later we learn that "the key property of quantum mechanics is precisely its *non-locality.*"

This is the first half of a polemical pedagogy addressing two groups: a coterie, the targets of the hoax; and general readers. At first, the coterie is the advanced group: they may not be able to make much of $G\mu\nu = 8\pi GT\mu\nu$, but they do know that it's interesting when long-accepted constants are shown "in their ineluctable historicity." After the second step—Sokal's revelation that the science was bogus—the general readers have become the advanced group, with the coterie now the remedial class. Common sense has been confirmed: the general reader has already ("always already," as the saying goes) passed the test. The incomprehension provoked by "$G\mu\nu = 8\pi GT\mu\nu$" and by the equally strange "ineluctable historicity" is the correct answer. The lesson for the coterie is less pleasant: transgressing the boundaries of your discipline is wrong, using words outside your training is foolish. It is akin to the bitter precept presented to the Poky Little Puppy: if you dig under the fence, you won't get back in time for strawberry shortcake. Time and space, especially social time and social space, are quite real: you belong inside the fence, not outside; dessert occurs uniquely in time and space, so once you miss it, it's gone.

The hoax's teaching stops at this point. It does not teach topology or quantum mechanics, only that these concepts are out of the reach of mere citation. A sphere of specialized knowledge is defended against illegitimate experts, with common sense the ultimate court of appeal. Sokal worked both sides of the expertise boundary: as a physicist, his scientific howlers were real howlers; but getting his nonexpert theory-babble published also scored hoax points. Physics was knowledge, requiring an expert to draw the line between significance and nonsense; but apparently anyone could pretend to write theory.

No experts were dethroned nor were any lines sharply drawn by the ambiguous rhetorical address of the Yasusada affair. To give a quick synopsis of the story: notebooks of a hitherto-unknown and now deceased poet, Araki Yasusada, surfaced in 1996, translated into idiomatic English but containing many indications of Japanese provenance. The work was accompanied by an unusual narrative, provided by the translators: Yasusada was a *hibakusha,* a survivor of the A-bomb at Hiroshima; but his disjunctive poems were unlike those of other survivors. Late in life he had enthusiastically discovered Roland Barthes and Jack Spicer, displaying an appetite for poetic experiment and theory that placed him on the innovative side of the divide between language and self (or text and experience; or defamiliarization and communication). Such tension goes back at least to Mallarmé and Swinburne, but the emergence of the language movement in the 1970s had re-promoted it into a basic polemic structuring the English-speaking poetic field. After almost three decades, the binary still has enough inertia to be self-replicating, having less to do with specific poems or poets than with creating differentiated areas. A critic still needn't have read any Language writing to decry it as theory-driven, mechanistic, antipoetic.[34] But as a *hibakusha* Yasusada had full rights on either side of the divide. His poetry was innovative, but it was also the quintessential "poetry of witness," to use Carolyn Forché's term for work produced by "significant poets who endured conditions of historical and social extremity during the twentieth century."[35] Poems of witness themselves bear "the trace of extremity within them, and . . . are, as such, evidence of what occurred."[36] If Hiroshima wasn't a historical extreme, what was? Yasusada's wife and one daughter were killed instantly, according to the translators' notes; another daughter died from radiation four years later; Yasusada himself died of cancer in 1972.

Mad Daughter and Big-Bang
December 25, 1945*

Walking in the vegetable patch
late at night, I was startled to find
the severed head of my
mad daughter lying on the ground.

Her eyes were upturned, gazing at me, ecstatic-like . . .

(From a distance it had appeared
to be a stone, haloed with light,
as if cast there by the Big-Bang).

What on earth are you doing, I said,
you look ridiculous.

Some boys buried me here,
she said sullenly.

Her dark hair, comet-like, trailed behind . . .

Squatting, I pulled the
turnip up by the root.

* [*In the aftermath of the bombing, many survivors moved into the foothills of the Chugoku mountains surrounding Hiroshima. This was the case with Yasusada and his daughter.*][37]

The translators' note, its bureaucratic prose undergirding the extremity of Hiroshima, is a crucial frame. Forché's introduction to *Against Forgetting,* her anthology of poetry of witness, begins with a similar gesture, quoting "the coroner's report for corpse #12": "Cause of death: shot in the nape. In the back pocket of the trousers a small notebook was found soaked in the fluids of the body and blackened by wet earth. This was cleaned and dried in the sun."[38] The notebook contained the last poems of the Hungarian poet Miklós Radnóti. His death, unlike Yasusada's, was real, but the same rhetorical structure governs both accounts. The poetry of witness involves two witnesses: the prose historian, bureaucrat, attesting to the authenticity of the poet-witness. Read without its note, the Yasusada poem could be a dream, or a small narrative meditation inflected toward surrealism, tinged with astronomical imagery; the note reframes it as tragedy. (In any case, the final line break, "the / turnip," is pure Williams.)

Yasusada's amalgamation of poetic antagonisms was interesting to many, and his poems were accepted by a wider range of magazines than was usually open to one poet. What followed was more interesting: rumors that there was no Yasusada. A consensus soon emerged that the author was Kent Johnson, a contemporary American translator and poet. Wesleyan University Press quickly dropped publication plans; but the results of Yasusada's nonexistence were quite publishable, and within a year Roof Books issued *Doubled Flowering.* This volume gathered the now-pseudographic writing; some initial reaction (for the editor Arthur Vogelsang, it was "essentially a criminal act";[39] for John Solt, translator of Japanese poetry, it was "Japanesed crap"[40]); and an overview by Marjorie Perloff, who showed how careful reading might easily have revealed some of the historical impossibilities involved: there were no scuba divers before World War II; in 1925 there was no Hiroshima University for Yasusada to have attended, and so on.[41]

Ron Silliman's prehoax comments on Yasusada are those of an expert: "There's an elevation in tone . . . that reminds me more of Michael Palmer than Spicer, perhaps because the translators are all Hiroshima poets (one of whom seems to spend half of each year in Sebastopol. . . . These works kept me up last night and probably will again."[42] The contrast with the Sokal hoax is marked: far from having his authority diminished by having placed his detailed poetic knowledge in enthusiastic service of the supposedly Japanese poems, Silliman furnishes a posthoax blurb for *Doubled Flowering* in which he agrees with Perloff: "The 'scandal' of these poems lies not in the problematics of authorship, identity, persona, race or history. . . . This book makes the argument for anti-essentialism. That it has done it so well infuriates folks with a proprietary interest in categories. Thank you, Araki Yasusada!"

In one sense there are no boundaries to transgress here: at least the boundaries of time, place, and identity are fully porous. But within the literary field the boundary separating innovative from noninnovative was monitored carefully. Transgressing the boundaries of identity, narration, and emotional scripting was fully consonant with staying within the territory of innovative poetry.

What has happened to the notion of hoax? The issues of expertise and knowledge, so sharply bounded in the Sokal hoax, are fuzzy here. Knowledge of Japanese poetry, not to mention the experiences of a *hibakusha,* don't seem crucial. Nor are there are simple criteria of contemporary poetic mastery: they can only be judged in poetic context. Gestures an untrained reader might find outrageously incompetent often occur in the work of the sophisticated writers. Two examples from celebrated innovative poets:

The goop / is like mulberry soup

*

The Great Wall of China is really a thrill
It cleaves through the air like a silver pill

It was built by the hand of man for good or ill
Showing what he can do when he decides not to kill

The fact of authorship, of innovative provenance, is crucial in literary judgment. To one who knows Jack Spicer's work, "goop" sounds its despairing, jokey chord. Ashbery's readers know that the clunkiness of these lines is just another example of his wide formal repertoire. By authenticating Johnson's authorship, Perloff and Silliman grant him a place within the anti-mainstream arena where judgments such as Solt's "Japanesed crap" are no longer relevant. Either this now is textbook antiessentialism or, viewed as an act of "imaginative sympathy" (which is how Kent Johnson characterized *Doubled Flowering* at a panel, without acknowledging authorship), "Yasusada" becomes a poetic device associated with the tradition (going back at least to Whistler) of American innovative artists not letting lack of knowledge derail their enthusiastic engagement with Asia. Pound's *Cathay* and Noh translations are notable positive results.

Another piece, which I'll now say was written by Johnson, not Yasusada, runs as follows:

> [*undated*]*
>
> two daikons
>
> three rice cakes
>
> one [*blotted by crease. eds.*] seaweed packet
>
> 4 crane eggs
>
> empress oil chrysanthemum root best rice
>
> *Bear yourself with a serious air through the labyrinth of the market. Feign to ignore the* [*blotted by crease, eds.*] *spirit medium of plum-coloured lips*
>
> American cologne
>
> * [*Despite the curious interjection, this appears to be a shopping list. It was found in one of the notebooks, folded into an origami bird.*][43]

Read inside the innovative frame, the translators' fictional authentication that this page is witness to Hiroshima becomes an authentic poetic element in a context where fragmented poetic utterance and shopping lists are both poetry. Such poetic intention is very clear at the end of the book, as *Doubled Flowering* ends with a slightly modified pastiche of the ending of Spicer's *After Lorca:* The penultimate "Yasusada" piece begins, "Dear Spicer, This is the last letter";[44] the last letter in Spicer's *After Lorca,* "Dear Lorca, This is the last letter."[45] Such literariness makes it easier to hear in this excerpt an echo of Williams's interview with Mike Wallace in book 5 of *Paterson:*

> Q: . . . here's part of a poem you yourself have written: . . . "2 partridges / 2 mallard ducks / a Dungeness crab / 24 hours out / of the Pacific / and 2 live-frozen / trout/ from Denmark . . . " Now, that sounds just like a fashionable grocery list!
>
> A: It is a fashionable grocery list.
>
> Q: Well—is it poetry?[46]

Poetic News

It is poetry. Why? Because it's in a poem, and the interviews, letters, and historical documents in *Paterson* are also poetry, as is the asterisk-ringed SODA transfixing "The Attic Which Is Desire." No list of poetic innovation can be at all fashionable if it doesn't include the pastiche we find in countless passages in *The Cantos,* just about any line in a Moore poem, Ginsberg's citations of newspapers and radio in "Wichita Vortex Sutra." As Williams says to Mike Wallace, "Poetry can be made out of anything." He cites the musical verve of speech, which lifts it out of the quotidian: "If you treat [it] rhythmically, ignoring the practical sense it forms a jagged pattern. It is, to my mind, poetry." Modernist framing easily incorporates social noise and historical marks. But when poetry moves outside its frame, the result is impropriety if not scandal: from Pound's broadcasts and Bollingen upsets to the recent flaps over Baraka's poem and Laura Bush's poetry tea. A basic reaction of supporters or critics is to put a poetic frame back around the whole mess, which, to simplify, is basically what happened with Pound. It has been a constant strategy for over half a century: the former president of Students for a Democratic Society, Bill Ayres, uses it to defend Baraka: "Spreading myths and printing falsehoods may violate the standards of a decent newspaper, but they are the very stuff of poetry, and that's why no one with an ounce of sense goes to Homer or . . . Bob Dylan for the facts."[47]

But "Asphodel" does attempt to incorporate fact, most notably the atomic bomb. However, it does so by reducing it to a rumor of cataclysm, which is then made "poetic" with clumsy, poeticized sleight of hand as Williams splits the actual devastation caused by the bomb into "heat" and "light":

> in an eternity
>   the heat will not overtake the light.
>   That's sure.
> That gelds the bomb,
>   permitting
>   that the mind contain it.
> This is that interval,
>   that sweetest interval,
>   when love will blossom,
> come early, come late
>   and give itself to the lover.
>   Only the imagination is real![48]

Decades earlier, the author of *Spring and All* had warned against such stale metaphors: "Crude symbolism is to associate emotions with natural phenomena such as anger with lightning, flowers with love."[49] One of the myriad descriptions of imagination in *Spring* is apropos:

> Imagination is not to avoid reality, nor is it description nor an evocation of objects or situations, it is to say that poetry does not tamper with the world but moves it—It affirms reality most powerfully and therefore, since reality needs no personal support but exists free from human action, as proven by science in the indestructibility of matter and of force, it creates a new object, play, a dance which is not a mirror up to nature, but—[50]

In "Asphodel" the unscriptable force of the bomb flattens this to a brittle assertion: "Only the imagination is real!"

I realize that in criticizing "Asphodel" for its handling of the bomb, I'm sliding from poetic to historical news, and thus I could be said to frame the issue in Zhdanovian terms, where the utterly superstructural poem must be judged by how well it matches a prescribed real world. Such show trials are not of the slightest use. But an opposite conclusion where the poem is detached from referential demands employs a similar Zhdanovian binary, separating the spheres instead of forcing them together. Nor will splitting the difference between these two positions find some semireferential middle ground where the structures of news and poetry can be durably reconciled: they're incommensurate.

The news, both external and poetic, in Williams's own poems is often contradictory, garbled, or imaginary—here, for instance, the "sweetest interval" in "Asphodel" merely names aesthetic autonomy.

Candor

But the social and poetic candor of Williams's writing as a whole remains something to learn from. The word *candor* comes from Allen Ginsberg, who used it increasingly in his last years as a capsule description of his poetics, ethics, and politics—three aspects of what he intended as a unified activity. For him, candor revealed the unfallen body; enacted the healthy, spontaneous mind; and, by extension, would eventually reveal and enact world liberation, political, spiritual, sexual. He wasn't naive about the difficulties involved, but he was optimistic.

Williams's candor is more contradictory, revealing his limited and often problematic social personhood (doctor; husband; philanderer; father; atheist; more or less avant-garde poet, privately enthusiastic, publicly obscure and frustrated), his subject position (male; American; white but non-WASP; heterosexual; middle-class), his place in history (the Model T; the telephone; the typewriter; world wars), and in space (hometown; Nowheresville, New Jersey, but with New York City nearby). A real person is writing: "real" and "person" in all their theoretical clumsiness and shame. But this does not make Williams himself the privileged core of the poetry: knowing the life is not a prerequisite for reading the poems, nor is what the poems reveal the life of the person Williams.

Williams's social candor means simply that his writing never hides any of his social coordinates. These coordinates are not static; they intersect ceaselessly with the positions of many others. Williams's hourly social mobility as a doctor was clearly a benefit here; and the poems present a much more focused and interactive social existence than is the case with Whitman's enthusiastic spectating: "I behold the picturesque giant and love him"—society and nature were equally picturesque for Whitman. Compare Williams:

> Doc, listen—fiftyish, a grimy hand
> pushing back the cap: In gold—
> Volunteers of America
>
> I got
> a woman outside I want to marry, will
> you give her a blood test?[51]

But accuracy of registration is something of an intermittent by-product of Williams's poetic candor.

Again, a contrast with Ginsberg will be useful. Ginsberg's candor meant fidelity to the body at the moment of composition: "first thought, best thought." Since, as another of his slogans has it, "mind is shapely," such discipline would ensure that the poem would be shapely as well. Williams's compositional methods are not completely different, to be sure, since improvisation marks much of his work; but his attention is given primarily to the poem, which neither is an unaltered record of process nor does it preexist as any kind of template or received form. Poetic candor means that Williams is constantly working on, witnessing, and adjusting the form of the poem as he writes it. Such is the case whether the time of writing is a single period of two minutes between patients or a series of stops and starts over years as with *Paterson.* The results are valuable beyond conventional standards of articulation and coherence or innovative standards of unpredictable language. They are a bit out of focus from either perspective, which is why Williams is so widely acknowledged but not all that deeply respected. His work, even in *Spring and All,* was never purely new. The sheen of newness was always scuffed by the poems' contact with social space. A small poem from the early 1940s, "Details for Patterson," can illustrate. This poem seems to have been cobbled together from Williams's manuscript *Detail and Parody for the Poem Paterson* (1939), where versions of the first two stanzas comprise a poem, and the third and fifth stanzas stand as two separate poems. These pieces, less interesting when separated, combine into an odd whole.

"I just saw two boys." Not a very prepossessing opening. It seems unexceptional to think that the "I" represents the poet. "One of them gets paid for distributing circulars": a scrap of realism; but adding "and he throws it down the sewer," with the singular "it" not matching the plural "circulars," reframes this as a quoted voice, not Williams's. But it won't help to take Williams's suggestion in the Mike Wallace interview and treat this rhythmically, ignoring the practical sense so that it becomes "poetry." This is leaden language which the described action mimes. Printed matter, circulars, are waste. They might be the newsprint Pound so loathes in the Hell Cantos; they might be small press books: print on paper—dreck. But speech is not the answer here; it is certainly not presented as the valorized solution.

The speaker continues with the tiny story: "I said, Are you a Boy Scout? / He said, no. / The other one was." For me the salient feature of this is the glacial clumsiness, capped off with the bizarreness of a received idea decayed into unfamiliarity. "I have implicit faith in / the Boy Scouts."

"If you talk about it / long enough / you'll finally write it— / If you get by the stage / when nothing / can make you write—If you don't die first." With no transition, this new voice has a querulous urgency, which I take as the poet berating himself. But the boundaries of person are oddly fluid. It wasn't the poet who was talking, but the Boy Scout admirer. But then again it wasn't the Boy Scout admirer who was working up the courage to finally write. I can't keep the speakers of these first two parts completely separate; but the poet's melodramatic consideration of death at the end of the stanza feels like some overblown but not utterly false reaction to the linguistic gloom of the opening stanza. If *those* are your social materials, do you really want to write? But then again, what better to do with such stuff than to try to make a poem, active and unpredictable, of it?

"I keep those bests that love / has given me / Nothing of them escapes—" Out in Paterson spoken and printed words go down the sewer. In the poet's mind, the gifts of love are held onto tightly, too tightly to permit any retroactive description of them. The next lines continue the passionate tautness, but what are they saying? "I have proved it"—proved what? That none of love's bests have escaped you? Who did you have to prove this to? The voice insists further, "proven once more in your eyes." The vocabulary and tone are self-consistent in the stanza, but the rhetorical, emotional, situational dynamics are as mysterious as anything in Ashbery, at least to me. "Proven once more," as if another emotional test has been passed, but what test? What was the first one? "Your eyes" belong to the beloved, presumably; though they could also be the reader's.[53] In either case, the relation is odd: the lover keeps the ecstasy of love locked tightly away inside and yet asks for confirmation from the beloved.

I don't sense any attempt here to construct a mystery or a Rube Goldberg machine. What is so incommensurate and irresolvable here has to do with candid verbal registration and a kind of free-floating flickering negative capability that's closer to Jameson's cognitive mapping than Keats's beautiful empathy. Here speech, mimetic depiction of banality, internal didactic rant, and stumbling approaches to more illuminated states of mind are all granted equal access to the page.

There is also compositional force making the best of these materials. As the stanzas follow one another, each makes something different and a little more active out of what has come before.

In the last stanza, who says "Go marry!" to whom? Is the poet speaking to himself? "Go marry! your son will have / blue eyes and still / there'll be no answer / you have not found a cure."

This is one of the ways that Williams insists on the value of what emerges in successive stanzas moment by moment. The poem is made of "historic and contemporary particulars," but they're not "objectively perfect," nor are they moving inextricably in the single proper historical direction. This is not the new in the midst of some mysterious virgin auto-reproduction. It is [underline "is"] a new poem, made out of materials heavy with the inertia of an unredeemed history. It cures nothing. The blue-eyed son is not a poem; nor is the poem some miraculous offspring.

The last lines start with an odd simulacrum of conversation, although the you and the I seem to refer to the same person: "No more have I for that enormous / wedged flower, my mind / miraculously upon / the dead stick of night."

The American idiom? I suppose, but it's stirred around so much that most of this can't be called idiomatic. Williams the materialist, no ideas but in things? With that miraculous, socially wedged flower for a writing mind? Hardly. Then what? If we try to paraphrase what is being said—and paraphrase often remains a usefully heretical act—then the question is: What is the problem for this "I," i.e., Williams? What is he failing to find a cure for?

Apparently, it's his writing mind: "for that enormous / wedged flower, my mind / miraculously upon / the dead stick of night." Having the writing mind be something that needs a cure is admitting a powerfully traumatic defeat.

In a complex twist, however, Williams is admitting defeat precisely when his process of composition—which seems to have stretched intermittently over a period of years—finally reflects a little inspiration.

The motion of the poem is various, unpredictable; and the more closely it's read, the more surprising it is.

Notes

1. William Carlos Williams, "Asphodel, That Greeny Flower," in *The Collected Poems of William Carlos Williams,* 2 vols.; vol. 1, ed. A. Walton Litz and Christopher MacGowan; vol. 2, ed. Christopher MacGowan (New York: New Directions, 1988), 2:318.

2. Ezra Pound, *ABC of Reading* (New York: New Directions, 1960), 29.

3. As I write, the events are familiar to those in the United States, but as the half-life of any public memory is getting shorter and shorter, I include them here. In the fall of 2002, Amiri Baraka's "Somebody Blew Up America" caused a storm when he read it publicly. Among its many pungent polemical thrusts, the item that caused the outcry was the suggestion that the Israeli government had had advance knowledge of the September 11, 2001, terrorist attacks on the United States. The problem, commentators and politicians kept repeating, was not the poem—they all granted Baraka freedom of expression—but that he read it in his capacity as poet laureate of New Jersey: taxpayers mustn't be forced to finance such poems. In the spring of 2003, Laura Bush's poetry afternoon at the White House was canceled due to administration worries over the possibility of the invited poets making leftist political statements. The cancellation created much more publicity, of course, which helped create Web sites, readings, and anthologies of poems protesting the Iraq war.

4. Kate Farrell, letter to the editor, *New York Times,* February 12, 2003, A36; Margo Jefferson, "The News from Poetry," *New York Times Book Review,* May 11, 2003, 27.

5. Williams, "The Clouds," in *Collected Poems,* 2:171.

6. Pound to Williams in 1917: "You thank your bloomin gawd you've got enough Spanish blood to muddy up your mind. . . . The thing that saves your work is *opacity,* and don't you forget it" (*Selected Letters of Ezra Pound and William Carlos Williams,* ed. Hugh Witemeyer [New York: New Directions, 1996], 124). In his 1928 review, "Dr. Williams's Position," *Dial* 85, no. 5 (November 1928): 395–404, Pound describes Williams's work as "opaque, obscure, obfuscated, confused, truncated," qualities which become signs of intellectual honesty given the situation confronting the writer in the United States. While "art" may be "the supreme achievement," Williams's work furnishes "the other satisfactory effect, that of a man hurling himself at an indomitable chaos, and yanking and hauling as much of it as possible into some sort of order (or beauty), aware of it both as chaos and as potential" (*The Selected Letters of William Carlos Williams,* ed. John C. Thirlwall [New York: New Directions, 1957], 394–96).

7. Pound, *ABC of Reading,* 37.

8. It is generally agreed that the Homeric poems coalesced out of oral performance and that by the latter sixth century B.C. they had been transcribed in a form that resembles what we read today. (Details of the transition from oral to written are far from settled.) But although the Homeric poems had existed in written form for over a century by the time Plato wrote the *Ion,* they and other poems functioned orally. "Homer may, for convenience, be taken as the last representative of the purely oral composition. . . . It is certain that all his poet successors were writers. But it is equally certain that they always wrote for recitation and for listeners." Eric Havelock, *Preface to Plato* (Cambridge, Mass.: Harvard University Press, 1982), 46.

9. Williams, "Asphodel," in *Collected Poems,* 2:315.

10. Plato, *Ion,* trans. Lane Cooper, in *Plato: The Collected Dialogues,* ed. Edith Hamilton and Huntington Cairns, Bollingen Series 71 (Princeton, N.J.: Princeton University Press, 1963), 536c.

11. Plato, *Ion,* 222.

12. Williams, "Asphodel," in *Collected Poems,* 2:325.

13. *King Lear,* ed. Jay L. Halio (Cambridge: Cambridge University Press, 1992), act 2, scene 4, lines 273–74.

14. Geoff Ward, *Statutes of Liberty: The New York School of Poets* (London: Palgrave, 1993), 55: "To Williams, the task . . . was to demystify, to purge writing of metaphysics, and celebrate what actually impinges on the senses as the sum total of what is. To enable the reader to see as if for the first time becomes the aim, but Williams failed to see (or did see, and didn't care) that such a recourse to origin, to a primary moment of authentic perception, is nothing if not metaphysical."

15. Charles Bernstein, *Content's Dream* (Los Angeles: Sun and Moon Press, 1986), 247–48: "The Academy in Peril: William Carlos Williams Meets the MLA." This is the first place that Bernstein articulates the influential concept of "official verse culture": "the poetry publishing and reviewing practices" of magazines such as *Parnassus,* the *New Yorker, American Poetry Review,* etc., and academic presses; the hiring practices of university writing and literature programs; "the interlocking accreditation" of judges giving each other awards; and "the self-appointed keepers of the gate who actively put forward biased . . . accounts of American poetry, while claiming, like all disinformation propaganda, to be giving . . . non-partisan views."

16. Robert Pinsky, *Poetry and the World* (Hopewell, N.J.: Ecco Press, 1988), 18–19.

17. For three decades, this boundary has been the site of charged debate. More recently, the rise of identity poetries has established perspectives from which Pinsky and Bernstein would seem quite close: both are white, male, hetero, somewhat Jewish-identified, intellectual spokesmen for poetry. For discussion of "official verse culture," see Bernstein, *Content's Dream,* 247–51.

18. Stendhal, *Racine and Shakespeare,* trans. Guy Daniels (New York: Crowell-Collier Press, 1962), 145.

19. Charles Baudelaire, "The Painter of Modern Life," in *Art in Theory, 1815–1900,* ed. Charles Harrison and Paul Wood with Jason Gaiger (London: Blackwell, 1998), 497.

20. Louis Zukofsky, *"A"* (Berkeley and Los Angeles: University of California Press, 1978), 24.

21. T. S. Eliot, *The Complete Poems and Plays 1909–1950* (New York: Harcourt Brace Jovanovich, 1971), 5.

22. Ibid., 4.

23. Steve Benson, Carla Harryman, Lyn Hejinian, Bob Perelman, Ron Silliman, and Barrett Watten, "Aesthetic Tendency and the Politics of Poetry: A Manifesto," *Social Text* 19/20 (Fall 1988): 261–75.

24. Ibid., 271. Though the piece was printed as "Aesthetic Tendency and the Politics of Poetry: A Manifesto," the magazine's editors added the designation "Manifesto" without consulting us.

25. Steve Evans, "The Resistible Rise of Fence Enterprises," http://third-factory.net/resistible.html, 8.

26. Ibid., 1.

27. Ibid., 8.

28. Ibid., 1–3.

29. Ibid., 6–9.

30. Jack Spicer, *The House That Jack Built: The Collected Lectures of Jack Spicer,* ed. Peter Gizzi (Middletown, Conn.: Wesleyan University Press, 1998), 167.

31. "It is a nation of nothing but poetry . . ." in *The Collected Poems of Charles Olson,* ed. George F. Butterick (Berkeley and Los Angeles: University of California Press, 1987), 562.

32. See Michael Heyward, *The Ern Malley Affair* (London: Faber and Faber, 1993).

33. Alan Sokal, "Transgressing the Boundaries: Toward a Transformative Hermeneutics of Quantum Gravity," in *Fashionable Nonsense: Postmodern Intellectuals' Abuse of Science,* by Alan Sokal and Jean Bricmont (New York: Picador USA, 1998).

34. There are still numerous instances of this opposition. For instance, in an interview with Robert Pinsky in the Winter 2002 issue of *Barrow Street,* Daniela Gioseffi observes, "The language school of poetry seems to be about art for art's sake; and the abstract or action poetry schools, or the1New York School, a sort of laid-back observation on the poet's experience" (77; cited in a post from Tom Fink to Ron Silliman's Web log: http://ronsilliman.blogspot.com/2003_02_01_ronsilliman_archive.html). The designations may seem quite blurry, but the basic choice between Art and Life remains constant.

35. Carolyn Forché, introduction to *Against Forgetting: Twentieth-Century Poetry of Witness,* ed. Carolyn Forché (New York: Norton, 1993), 29.

36. Ibid., 30.

37. Ariki Yasusada, *Doubled Flowering: From The Notebooks of Ariki Yasusada* (New York: Roof Press, 1997), 11.

38. Forché, *Against Forgetting,* 29.

39. Yasusada, *Doubled Flowering,* 130.

40. Ibid., 131.

41. Marjorie Perloff, "In Search of the Authentic Other: The Poetry of Araki Yasusada," in Yasusada, *Doubled Flowering,* 148–68.

42. Ibid., 149.

43. Yasusada, *Doubled Flowering,* 26.

44. Ibid., 117.

45. Jack Spicer, *The House That Jack Built,* 51.

46. William Carlos Williams, *Paterson,* rev. ed. prepared by Christopher MacGowan (New York: New Directions, 1992), 222.

47. *New York Times,* October 5, 2002, A26.

48. Williams, *Collected Poems,* 2:334.

49. Ibid., 1:188.

50. Ibid., 234–35.

51. Williams, *Paterson,* 103.

52. Williams, *Collected Poems,* 2:24.

53. Elsewhere, Williams does address the reader erotically, with an indeterminate amount of irony: "In the imagination, we are henceforth (so long as you read) locked in a fraternal embrace, the classic caress of author and reader. We are one. Whenever I say 'I' I mean also 'you.' And so, together, as one, we shall begin" (*Collected Poems,* 1:78).

Wallace Stevens and the Intricate Evasions of As

Simon Critchley

1. Poetry is the description of a particular thing—a tin plate, the loaf of bread on it, the wine that I drink, clear water in a brilliant bowl, a small rock in the palm of my hand, the leafless stubby tree that I see from my kitchen window, the moon in a clear winter's sky.

2. The poet describes those things in the radiant atmosphere produced by the imagination. Poetic acts are thus acts of the mind, which describe recognizable things, real things, *really* real things, but which vary the appearance of those things, changing the aspect under which they are seen. Poetry brings about *felt* variations in the appearance of things. What is most miraculous is that poetry does so simply by the sound of words:

> This city now doth, like a garment wear,
> The beauty of the morning, silent, bare . . .

3. Poetry imaginatively transfigures a common reality, a morning walk in London, for example. But that common reality can press in on the self, the city becomes oppressive and the self depressive. The world becomes a deafening, violent place dominated by an ever-enlarging incoherence of information and the constant presence of war. Such is arguably our pres-

ent. This feels to me a leaden time, a time of dearth, a world that cannot move for the weight of its own heaviness.

4. What, then, are poets for? In a time of dearth, they resist the pressure of reality, they press back against this oppressiveness with the power of imagination, producing felt variations in the appearance of things. Poetry enables us to feel differently, to see differently. It leavens a leaden time. This is poetry's nobility, which is also a violence, an imaginative violence from within that protects us from the violence from without—violence against violence, then.

5. The poetic act, the act of the mind, illuminates the surface of things with imagination's beam. This act is part of the thing and not about it. Through it, we detect what we might call *the movement of the self* in those things: plate, bread, wine, water, rock, tree, moon. In poetry, the makings of things are makings of the self. Poets are the artificers of the world in which they sing and, singing, make.

6. Words of the world are the life of the world. Or so we say.

7. That which is, is for a self who declares it to be. Philosophically expressed, all poetry is idealistic, at least in ambition. But the *materia poetica,* the raw stuff out of which poetry makes its radiant atmospheres, is the real, real particulars, actual stuff. Poetry is the imagination touching reality.

8. To introduce my first "as," and it's quite an "as," poetry allows us to see things *as* they are. But, and this is its peculiarity, poetry lets us see things as they are anew, under a new aspect, transfigured, subject to a felt variation. The poet sings a song that is both beyond us yet ourselves. Things change when the poet sings them, but they are still our things: recognizable, common, near. We hear the poet sing and press back against the pressure of reality.

9. It is easily said that the poet makes the ordinary extraordinary. Yet, the extraordinary is only extraordinary if it refers back to the ordinary, otherwise it would be empty. This is another way of drawing the distinction between imagination and fancy: the poetic imagination imagines things

as they are, but beyond us, turned about, whereas fancy simply fantasizes about things that are not.

10. We find an order in things. When I look at the boats at anchor in the harbor there, as night descends, their lights tilting in the air, they seem to master the night and portion out the sea, arranging the harbor and fixing the surrounding village. When I place a jar on a hill, the slovenly wilderness that surrounded that hill rises up to that jar and is no longer wild. We find an order in things. Poetry reorders the order we find in things. It gives us things as they are, but beyond us. Poetry, it might be said, gives us an *idea* of order.

11. Think of truth as troth (that's another "as"), as an act of betrothal, of wedding, of pledging oneself to things. *Dichtung und Wahrheit,* poetry and truth, poetry is truthful as trothful. It speaks the truth of things, it speaks the truth out of things, a truth that is something we both recognize and something new, something beyond us yet ourselves.

12. Poetry describes life as (there's another) it is, in all the intricate evasions of as. It gives us the world as it is—common, near, recognizable—but imagined, turned about. It is a world both seen and unseen until seen with the poet's eyes.

13. Poetry momentarily focuses the *bewilderment* to which we are attached and which passes for our inner life.

14. Poetry is an elevation, an enlargement of life. At its noblest, poetry helps people live their lives.

15. What is essential is that poetry should produce this elevation, this enlargement, in words free from mysticism, that is, free from any intellectual intuition of a transcendent reality. There is no such intuition. I have no reason to believe that there is any such transcendent reality. Poetry might ennoble, but it is acutely mundane.

16. The climate of our world is not that of gods, monsters, and heroes, or the winged soul taking flight into the silent ether, but that of the near, the low, the common, the imperfect. The imperfect is and can be our only paradise. A poet might write poems appropriate to that climate, to the

things we find scattered around: to cities, towns, and villages; to buildings and houses; to birds, plants, and trees; to transport systems, the subtleties of trade, and the speed of commerce; to weather, heavy weather and slight, to the movement that clouds make over a wet landscape on an afternoon in late November; to a time of war and what passes for peace; to wine, water, and the sensation of eating oysters; to air, light, and the joy of having a body; to your mother and your lovers, who should not be confused; to the sea: cold, salt, dark, clear, utterly free; to quail, sweet berries, and casual flocks of pigeons; to your pet cat Jeoffrey who can detect electricity; to the whole voluptuousness of looking.

17. The poet finds words for these things which are not the revelations of religious belief but the more precious portents of our powers, of imagination's beam reordering the order we find in the world.

18. If I bang my head on the door, I do not cry out "Oh God" or "Sweet warm blood of Jesus," but "door," "head," and, most probably, "ouch." Poetry can teach this.

19. God is dead, therefore I am. Such is poetry's proposition. Yet, how *is* one? Such is poetry's question.

*

Let me try to explain myself a little further.

I want to address the topic of poetry as philosophy by considering the work of Wallace Stevens, in my view the *philosophically* most interesting poet to have written in English in the twentieth century. Some of the words I have just used are his, some are mine, and some are borrowed from others. As a philosopher (another "as"), what it is about Stevens that interests me is the fact that he found a manner, one that is wholly poetic, of developing full thoughts, theses, hypotheses, conjectures, ruminations, and aphorisms that one should call philosophical. As his work developed, Stevens created a unique meditative form, most often in the late work, the blank verse triplet, often grouped into units of six or seven stanzas, as you will see.

A fine example of this meditative form can be seen in the important long, late poem, "An Ordinary Evening in New Haven." It shows Stevens poetically capable not just of stating a proposition, exploring a line of thought, or initiating a hypothesis—"If" is a very common word in

Stevens's lexicon, "as if" is even more common, and Stevens's is a philosophy of the "as if," of qualified assertions. He will also suddenly change tack, introducing new personae and topoi, or simply let the poetry slide into comic bathos or very often into the bathos of sheer sound, "the micmac of mocking birds"[1] or "the mickey mockers and plated pairs" (*PEM,* 114). Toward the end of the poem, Stevens writes:

> If it should be true that reality exists
> In the mind: the tin plate, the loaf of bread on it,
> The long-bladed knife, the little to drink and her
>
> Misericordia, it follows that
> Real and unreal are two in one: New Haven
> Before and after one arrives or, say,
>
> Bergamo in a postcard, Rome after dark,
> Sweden described, Salzburg with shaded eyes
> Or Paris in conversation at a café.
>
> This endlessly elaborating poem
> Displays the theory of poetry,
> As the life of poetry. A more severe,
>
> More harassing master would extemporise
> Subtler, more urgent proof that the theory
> Of poetry is the theory of life,
>
> As it is, in the intricate evasions of as,
> In things seen and unseen, created from nothingness,
> The heavens, the hells, the worlds, the longed-for lands.
> (*PEM,* 349)

Stevens's language moves from a hypothesis, "if it should be true," to concrete particulars, "the tin plate, the loaf of bread on it," to syllogistic conclusions, "it follows that," to propositions of the most general import, "the theory of poetry is the theory of life"—with a possible allusion to Coleridge's *Theory of Life.* The proposition is then pursued in the most finely ambiguous manner, where it is a question of life "as it is, in the intricate evasions of as." Poetry is ambiguous. This is what appalls some philosophers and attracts others. Poetic language is a matter of what he calls

> the edgings and inchings of final form,
> The swarming activities of the formulae
> Of statement, directly and indirectly getting at . . .
> (*PEM,* 351)

Yet, Stevens's qualified assertions, his "ifs" and "as ifs," deploy ambiguity to get at the evasiveness of poetry's matter, which is reality:

> We seek
> Nothing beyond reality. Within it,
> Everything, the spirit's alchemicana
> Included . . .
> (*PEM,* 336)

But that is not all. Going back to the previous passage, we move instantly from grand propositions about the real and unreal into the almost comic, touristic particularity of "Sweden described, Salzburg with shaded eyes," and from there into moments of visionary lyrical rapture, "the heavens, the hells, the worlds, the longed-for lands." The curious and distinctive thing about Stevens, it seems to me, is that all these aspects occur concurrently within the meditative form of the poem: metaphysics, a little casuistry, lyricism, bathos, and pathos. It is this combination of normally distinct properties that gives the verse its movement and edge. We feel illuminated, deepened, amused, and perplexed, turn and turn about.

Furthermore, what is enacted in the poem, for Stevens, is the very nature of poetry itself. The poem is the enactment of poetry's essence. What this means is that *this* very poem, "This endlessly elaborating poem / Displays the theory of poetry, / As the life of poetry." In Stevens's verse, the frontier between poetry and poetics is constantly being crisscrossed *in* and *as* the work of the poem itself. As he writes in "The Man with the Blue Guitar,"

> Poetry is the subject of the poem,
> From this the poem issues and

To this returns. Between the two,
Between issue and return, there is

An absence in reality,
Things as they are. Or so we say.
(*PEM,* 143)

The nature of poetry is elicited through the poetic act itself, through "the naked poem, the imagination manifesting itself in its domination of words."[2] The theory of poetry—poetics—which a more harassing Coleridgean master would view as the theory of life, is performed in the specific poem insofar as that poem concerns itself with some real particular, with some object, thing, or fact.

. . . Or so we say. A final qualification necessitated by both the evasiveness of what is being elicited by Stevens and its banality: things as they are only are in the act that says they are.

*

To forestall a possible misunderstanding, by "philosophy" I do not mean religious brooding. Although there are important religious concerns in Stevens, as when he says in a late poem that "God and imagination are one" (*PEM,* 368), he is not a religious poet in the same way as, say, the later T. S. Eliot. Stevens fondly describes Eliot as "an upright ascetic in an exceedingly floppy world." Stevens is a somewhat floppier, worldly poet writing in the wake and complex crosscurrents of romanticism. The latter can arguably be reduced to the belief that art is the supreme medium for attaining the fundamental ground of life and that the problems of the modern world can be addressed and even reconciled in the production of a critically self-conscious artwork. This is what Friedrich Schlegel saw as the great novel of the modern world, a secular bible. Poetry written in the wake of romanticism—and I think that all poetry has to be in romanticism's failure, but that's another story—is animated by the belief that poetry should take onto itself the existential burden of religious belief without the guarantee of religious belief. As Stevens expresses it at the beginning of his longest and most ambitious poem, "Notes Toward a Supreme Fiction," "The death of one god is the death of all" (*PEM,* 207).

Poetry has to be vitalized by the question of the ultimate meaning and value of life without claiming to know the metaphysical or theological answer to that question. Stevens makes this assertion crystal clear in one of his *Adagia,* which were notebooks he kept in the 1930s and 1940s:

> After one has abandoned a belief in god, poetry is that essence which takes its place as life's redemption.[3]

Poetry takes the place of religion as that medium which offers the possibility, or at least pursues the question, of life's redemption. It does so by producing fictions that return us to the sense of the world; and it goes without saying that there is no sense in claiming, for Stevens, that there is anything that transcends the world. In "The Man with the Blue Guitar," he writes:

> Poetry
> Exceeding music must take the place
> Of empty heaven and its hymns,
>
> Ourselves in poetry must take their place,
> Even in the chattering of your guitar.[4]

Philosophy is atheism, but an anxious atheism, a restlessness with a religious memory and within a religious archive.

*

Stevens was self-consciously philosophical in his interests and much of his reading. He read widely in philosophy, and his criticism abounds with references to classical texts, such as Plato, and authors closer to his own time, including Bergson, William James, Russell, his teacher Santayana, and his friend Jean Wahl. He was evidently a highly cultivated man. So what, you might exclaim.

Much more significantly, his entire work might be viewed as an extended elaboration of the guiding question of epistemology: the relation between thought and things or words and world. In the history of philosophy, this question has been posed in different ways in successive epochs. For the Pre-Socratic Parmenides, it is the question of the sameness between thought and Being, or between thinking and that which is. For Plato, it is the correspondence between the intellect and the forms, where knowledge of a thing is knowledge of the form of that thing. For Aquinas, it is the *adaequatio* between the intellect and things, where both persons and things are creatures created by a God himself uncreated. For Descartes and modern philosophy, it becomes the basic question of the theory of knowledge, namely, what is the relation between a thinking self or subject and the objects that appear to the subject?

The basic advance of Kant's epistemology is that it does not suppose, as is supposed by both Plato and Descartes in quite different ways, that in order for knowledge to be possible, there must be a correspondence between thoughts or mental representations and things-in-themselves, whether the realm of forms, the metaphysical realities of the soul, God and material substance, or simply a belief in the radical independence of reality from the mind, what Wilfrid Sellars calls "the Myth of the Given."[5] After Kant, that which is true is that which is *taken* to be true, that is, that which appears to a subject or self. Now, that which so appears might indeed refer to a thing in itself, but we can never be in a position to *know* this fact independently of how that fact *appears* to us. On Kant's picture, the realm of sensibility is our access to a world that is indeed real for us, but that world is always already shot through with conceptual content; it is articulated as such through the categories of the understanding and is dependent upon the spontaneity of the subject. That is why, as Kant says, "the transcendental idealist is, therefore, an empirical realist."[6]

It is in this Kantian lineage that Stevens has to be placed. After all, what could be more Kantian than the thought that "If it should be true that reality exists / In the mind . . . it follows that real and unreal are two in one." Stevens can be said to be offering a poetic transposition of the thesis of transcendental idealism, where the relation between thought and things and words and world is redescribed as the relation between *imagination* and *reality,* the two master concepts of Stevens's poetics.[7] Imagination is that activity or, better, *power,* of forming concepts beyond those derived from external objects. Understood in this way, the imagination is a power over external objects, or the transformation of the external into the internal through the work of subjective creation, a creation that is given sensuous form and is therefore rendered external in the work of art, the poem. I take it that this is what Hegel means when he speaks of art being born of the spirit and then reborn in being aesthetically regarded.[8] In "An Ordinary Evening in New Haven" Stevens writes: "Misericordia, it follows that / Real and unreal are two in one: New Haven / Before and after one arrives or, say / Bergamo on a postcard, Rome after dark, / Sweden described, Salzburg with shaded eyes / Or Paris in conversation at a café."

In one of his Athenaeum fragments, Friedrich Schlegel writes, "No poetry, no reality."[9] We should keep this in mind when reading Stevens, particularly as he places himself within a romantic tradition with its vast premise that the world might be transformed in and through a great artwork. So, no poetry, no reality, that is, our experience of the real is dependent upon the work of the poetic imagination. Yet, If there is no reality without poetry, then the inversion of Schlegel's remark would also seem to be true for Stevens, that is, "No reality, no poetry." For Stevens, the poet must not lead us away from the real, where the solitary work of the imagination would result in fantasy or *fancy*. In Stevens's terminology, Coleridge's famous distinction between imagination and fancy might be redrawn in the following way: the poetic imagination must adhere to reality, whereas fancy works without reference to reality. As Stevens puts it, "The real is only the base. But it is the base" (*OP*, 87). So, the real is the base, it is the basis from which poetry begins, what Stevens calls the *materia poetica*, the matter of poetry, but it is only the base. One might say that reality is the necessary but not the sufficient condition for poetry, but it is absolutely necessary.

I am not saying that Stevens is simply a Kantian, but rather that he begins from Kantian premises read through romantic spectacles. That is, he begins from a perceived failure of Kantianism, from what might be called a *dejected transcendental idealism*. The shape of the thought I am after here can be found in Coleridge's 1802 "Dejection: An Ode," whose melancholy mood laments the abyssal distance between nature and the self, or between things-in-themselves and things-as-they-are-for-us. Coleridge famously writes:

> Though I should gaze for ever
> On that green light that lingers in the west:
> I may not hope from outward forms to win
> The passion and the life; whose fountains are within

Therefore, the only meaning that we find in nature is that which we give to it,

> O Lady! we receive but what we give
> And in our life alone does Nature live.[10]

Nature in itself is that which resists the "shaping spirit of imagination." Thus, if transcendental idealism is true, it is only so faute de mieux and inspires dejection in us. I pursue this question of dejection in relation to the experience of nature elsewhere in relation to Stevens's very last poems.

Stevens's poetic deepening of the thought of transcendental idealism might be said to lead him toward a more *phenomenological* sense of the real.[11] Phenomenology is a description of things as they are that seeks to elicit or make explicit the sense of our practical involvement with the world. Again, more paradoxically stated, phenomenology brings out the meaning of the fact that, in Merleau-Ponty's words, "we are condemned to meaning." Phenomenology gives us the meaning of meaning. Phenomenological descriptions, if felicitous, foreground things as they are experienced in the everyday world we inhabit, the real world in which we move and have our being, the world which fascinates and benumbs us. From this phenomenological perspective, the problem with Kant's approach is that it presupposes two things: first, a conception of the subject as what Kant calls the "I think" that has, at the very least, a family resemblance to Descartes' res cogitans, even if it is a cogito without an ergo sum. Second, that the subject's relation to the objective world is mediated through representations, what Hegel calls "picture thinking," Kant's and Fichte's *Vorstellungen*. If we place in question these two presuppositions, then it might lead us to abandon the entire epistemological construal of the relation of thought to things, words to world. The world does not first and foremost show itself as an "object" contemplatively and disinterestedly viewed by a "subject." Rather, the world shows itself as a place in which we are completely immersed and from which we do not radically distinguish ourselves: "Real and unreal are two in one."[12]

Stevens's working assumption, which he owes once again to romanticism, is that the "two in oneness" of the world is phenomenologically disclosed or reflectively transfigured not in philosophy but through a poetic act, that is to say, in an artwork. It is the task of poetry to elicit the sense of the world as it is, in the intricate evasions of as, directly and indirectly getting at the real in the edgings and inchings of final form.

*

So, in my view, Stevens is philosophically significant because his verse recasts the basic problem of epistemology in a way that perhaps allows this problem to be cast away. What we might call his "poetic epistemology" can be said to place in question the assumptions behind the traditional epistemological construal of the world. This is what I think is at stake in approaching poetry as philosophy.

Let me close with an example from Stevens's 1943 lecture, "The Figure of the Youth as Virile Poet," which is his finest piece of criticism and which, in some passages, bears comparison with his verse. Stevens is broaching the question of poetic truth. Poetry is truthful when it is in agreement with the world, that is, an agreement between imagination and reality. Such agreement is *emotional* for Stevens—it is *felt* agreement. Poetic truth is an agreement with reality in what Stevens calls, in one of his favorite nicknames, a *mundo.* The latter is the environment created by the poet, what Stevens often describes in this lecture and his poetry as the *radiant* atmosphere of the poet. What the poet does is to create a *mundo,* a specific habitat with an identifiable voice, personae, climate, and set of objects. Such an imagining elevates and liberates both the poet and the reader who finds vitality in this world, who finds in it some affluence of the planet they inhabit.

There then follows an extraordinary passage, where Stevens asks us to enter into a thought experiment, to enter the *mundo* of the poet, that radiant atmosphere. How do things look when we inhabit the world of the poet? At the end of a rather unhelpful brief discussion of metaphysics, Stevens asks an extremely long and tortuous question:

> And having ceased to be metaphysicians, even though we have acquired something from them as from all men, and standing in the radiant and productive atmosphere, and examining first one detail of that world, one particular, and then another, as we find them by chance, and observing many things that seem to be poetry without any intervention on our part, as, for example, the blue sky, and noting, in any case, that the imagination never brings anything into the world but that, on the contrary, like the personality of the poet in the act of creating, it is no more than a process, and desiring with all the power of our desire not to write falsely, do we not begin to think of the possibility that poetry is only reality, after all, and that poetic truth is a factual truth, seen, it may be, by those whose range in the perception of fact—that is, whose sensibility—is greater than our own? (*NA,* 159)

What we see when we take on board the poet's *mundo* is that the things around us that make up the world seem to be poetry without any intervention on our part. For example, the blue sky: the blue sky is poetry, but it is also the blue sky as it is. That is, the power of the poetic imagination produces a world that we recognize as our world, which is not a fantasy world or thing of fancy. If the poet's world is true, then this is because it attempts to be true to the perceived contours of the world we actually inhabit: this place, this blue sky, this clear water in a brilliant bowl, this green grass, this leafless tree, these sweet berries, my cat Jeoffrey. It is only by agreeing with reality that the imagination has vitality. As Stevens succinctly puts it in the *Adagia,* the task of poetry is "to touch with the imagination in respect to reality" (*OP,* 287).

Stevens then asks us that if we indeed accept that we stand within the radiant *mundo* of the poet (and everything hangs on that "if"; you can't force someone to take on board a poetic vision, and there is no accounting for taste), then are we not obliged to accept "the possibility that poetic truth is a factual truth"? Namely, that true poetry, the work of the imagination that touches reality, is a poetry of fact, of fact created in a fiction. If we take the small leap of faith implied in that "if," then we are no longer inhabiting our ordinary world but the *mundo* of the poet, namely, someone "whose range in the perception of fact—that is, whose sensibility—is greater than our own." The consequence of Stevens's argumentation is that the truth that we experience when the poet's fictive imaginings are in agreement with reality is a truth of fact. But it is an *enlarged* world of fact: things as they are, but beyond us.

*

The world that we inhabit is neither a bubble of subjective fancy nor an epiphenomenon to an alien, subject-independent realm. Epistemologically speaking, both antirealism and transcendental realism are wrong. Poetry touches reality, a solid, shared realm of real particulars, but it is a reality shot through with conceptual content, a world in words. This poeticized version of transcendental idealism is hypothesized in the following terms:

> It comes to this, that poetry is part of the structure of reality. If this has been demonstrated, it pretty much amounts to saying that the structure of poetry and the structure of reality are one or, in effect, that poetry and reality are one, or should be. This may be less thesis than hypothesis. (*NA,* 81)

Despite this coy qualification, we are here being brought close to what Stevens calls his *intimidating thesis.* What is this thesis? He writes, "poetry is the imagination of life" (*NA,* 65). This thesis entails that there is no such thing as bare alien fact, what Stevens calls "absolute fact." Rather, "absolute fact includes everything that the imagination includes. This is our intimidating thesis" (*NA*, 61).

Absolute fact is not absolute, it is simply the *arrière-pays* of the imagination and therefore relative to its power. Stevens illustrates this in a disarmingly prosaic and charming manner:

> One sees demonstrations of this everywhere. For example, if we close our eyes and think of a place where it would be pleasant to spend a holiday, and if there slide across the black eyes, like a setting on a stage, a rock that sparkles, a blue sea that lashes, and hemlocks in which the sun can merely fumble, this inevitably demonstrates, since the rock and sea, the wood and sun are those that have been familiar to us in Maine, that much of the world of fact is the equivalent of the world of the imagination, because it looks like it. (*NA*, 61)

Poetry is the imagination of life. That is, it is the imagination of life as it is, the coastline of Maine or Essex or wherever. The imagined coastline is true to the factual coastline simply "because it looks like it." Yet, it is life elevated, a world of fact enlarged and rendered radiant through the sound of words. Poetry is life as it is, ourselves yet beyond us.

Words of the world are the life of the world, and poetry is the highest use of those words. Without poetry we are diminished, we become mere "castratos of moon-mash" (*PEM*, 281). Poetry is like the light which illuminates objects in the world, it is the unseen condition for seeing, unseen until seen with the poet's eyes and then seen anew. Like light, it adds nothing but itself. Close to the heat of that light, we live more intensely. Or so we say.

Notes

1. Wallace Stevens, *The Palm at the End of the Mind*, ed. Holly Stevens (New York: Vintage, 1971), 349. Hereafter cited in text as *PEM*.

2. Wallace Stevens, *The Necessary Angel: Essays on Reality and the Imagination* (London: Faber, 1960), viii. Hereafter cited in text as *NA*.

3. Wallace Stevens, *Opus Posthumous*, rev., enl., and corr. ed.; ed. Milton J. Bates (London: Faber, 1990), 185. Hereafter cited as *OP*.

4. Wallace Stevens, *Collected Poems* (London: Faber, 1955), 44–45.

5. Wilfrid Sellars, *Empiricism and the Philosophy of Mind*, intro. Richard Rorty (Cambridge, Mass.: Harvard University Press, 1997).

6. Immanuel Kant, *Critique of Pure Reason,* trans. Norman Kemp Smith (London: Macmillan, 1952), 194 [A371].

7. See Sebastian Gardner, "Wallace Stevens and Metaphysics: The Plain Sense of Things," *European Journal of Philosophy* 2, no. 3 (1994): 322–44.

8. G. W. F. Hegel, *Introductory Lectures on Aesthetics,* trans. B. Bosanquet (Harmondsworth, Eng.: Penguin, 1993), 4.

9. Friedrich Schlegel, *Philosophical Fragments,* trans. Peter Firchow (Minneapolis: University of Minnesota Press, 1991), 70.

10. Samuel Taylor Coleridge, *The Complete Poems,* ed. William Keach (London: Penguin, 1997), 308.

11. Stevens dabbled—but no more than that—in phenomenology. Some evidence of this can be seen in the passing reference to Husserl in the 1951 lecture, "A Collect of Philosophy," although Stevens is merely citing his correspondence with Jean Wahl (*OP,* 275).

12. Maurice Merleau-Ponty, *Basic Writings,* ed. Thomas Baldwin (London: Routledge, 2004), 76.

Corporeal Poetics: Kathy Acker's Writing

D. J. Huppatz

Kathy Acker's oeuvre maps the interaction of forces of power, tracing the overflow of primal drives and the circulation of myths which continue to endure, even in a supposedly disenchanted and rational world. Without a clear narrative or stable characters, it's easy to get lost in her dense network of competing theoretical references, from feminism, politics, psychoanalysis, and literary theory to art history, while the excessive sex and violence make her work instantly appealing to would-be bohemians and censors alike.[1] The limits of nineteenth-century realist narratives, although challenged continually during the course of the twentieth century, seem completely surpassed when confronted with an Acker text. Her work constructs spaces and presents possibilities for a corporeal poetics that subverts patriarchal authority, a poetics that pushes excessively toward failure, a poetics both of and in the material body. In the following analysis of Acker's oeuvre, I am not attempting to cover the myriad possibilities suggested by her writing but instead concentrating on the development of this corporeal poetics.

Possessing Bodies

The whore visits a fortune-teller: "O no, O. This card says that you're a dead person who's still alive. You're a zombie."[2] Acker's writing is populated by zombies, corpses revived by magic or witchcraft, soulless bodies that lack human sensations. Her city is devoid of living beings, the remaining population are a few stray ghosts. Acker's ensemble of characters includes ghostly figures reanimated from other writings—novels, diaries, biographies, pornography, films, newspapers, and fairy tales. Now death has been taken from them, they are without an end point. Reanimated on flows of desire, these spectral figures inhabit the spaces of Acker's novels, reappearing in different contexts, coming into existence and dissolving again into words. Her writing invests these soulless bodies with sensations, notably pleasure and pain, in a theater that intimately involves the reader.

In her first trilogy, *The Childlike Life of the Black Tarantula by the Black Tarantula* (1973), *I Dreamt I Was a Nymphomaniac: Imagining* (1974), and *The Adult Life of Toulouse Lautrec by Henri Toulouse Lautrec* (1975), Acker embarked upon a poetics founded on appropriation. Like the artists of New York's downtown scene in the 1970s (including Sherrie Levine, Barbara Kruger, Jenny Holtzer, and Richard Prince), the use of appropriation for Acker was not simply a formal exercise but a strategy—first, as a means of exploring subjectivity, and second, as a critique of power relations in contemporary American society.[3] If American institutions such as the government, the church, and the school were creating a society of lobotomized zombies possessed by capitalist and patriarchal ideology, Acker was animating her own zombies—whores, criminals, terrorists, sailors, pirates—moving nomadlike through the twilight spaces between life and death, overflowing with corporeal desires.

Her 1970s trilogy analyzes the centralized narrative "I" of autobiography. In an interview, Acker revealed her motives for this analysis: "In *Tarantula* I was trying to see if, rather than to integrate the 'I,' if you could *dis*-integrate it and find a more comfortable way of being."[4] Her first novel, *The Childlike Life of the Black Tarantula by the Black Tarantula,* begins in a pseudoautobiographical mode, playing with the notion of the centralized "I":

> I become a murderess.
> I'm born in the late autumn or winter of 1827.
> Troy, New York.
> . . . My name at this time is Charlotte Wood.[5]

Acker then proceeds to juxtapose accounts of Victorian murderesses with "real" autobiography, inhabiting in turn the voices of Charlotte Wood, Henrietta Robinson, Sophie Dawes, and Laura Lane within the first fifteen pages of the book. In a confessional tone, Acker mixes her own memories and experiences with historical accounts of nineteenth-century murderous women, creating a schizophrenic mode of autobiography in which the voices are brought back to life in a contemporary context.

Following Jacques Lacan's "Mirror Stage" theory, Acker affirms a fundamental split in Western subjectivity: "I look at myself in the mirror. I don't understand whether I'm beautiful or ugly I have to use what I see as an object make it as attractive as possible to other people. Now I'm two people."[6] However, Lacan's "Mirror Stage" (and much subsequent psychoanalytic theory and practice) posits the primary mirror identification with a fundamental lack, as the subject constantly seeks to affirm his (in Lacan's case) wholeness by seeking unity with the objectified self in the mirror.[7] Acker goes beyond this fundamental lack, taking the objectification of the self (particularly the female self) as a positive and productive trait. Rather than lament a lack of wholeness, she uses this split as the opportunity for fluid movement between multiple selves, inhabiting a number of identities in her animation of past murderesses. While Lacan's subject appropriates the objectified self in order to feel like a whole subject, appropriation is a tactic used paradoxically by Acker in order to feel less complete.

The "I" in Acker's early trilogy becomes a textual effect, an unstable identity constituted *in* and *by* writing. In *I Dreamt I Was a Nymphomaniac: Imagining,* she mixes many possible autobiographies, including sex show stories which may be "real" (given Acker's often-cited work in a sex show in the 1970s) next to obviously appropriated material: "My identity at any time depends on (my) lacks of stabilities."[8] This refusal to maintain a stable identity entails a rejection of the fundamental identity of Western patriarchal culture, the centralized "I" (also God, father, authority figures).[9] The fluid model of subjectivity Acker develops in the trilogy is that of a subject that is continually coming into being, constantly threatening to dissolve in an ecstasy of becoming:

> I'm completely pleasure. At this moment. (1) I'm opening enough to contain all identities, things, change everything to energy, a volcano. (2) I'm constant energy and I can never be anything else. (3) I have no emotions; I sense textures of everything against textures; I'm completely part of and aware of the object world. I don't exist.[10]

In Acker's writing, the line between possessing (an active appropriation of identity) and being possessed (a passive being appropriated) blurs.

This fluid movement is contrary to conventional accounts of subjectivity (including Lacan's mirror stage model cited earlier) whereby appropriation is used actively as means of binding together subject and object into a stable, unified self. At times, Acker's streams of words, unedited in accordance with conventional grammar or narrative, lose all sense of authorial control. Her early trilogy operates with the tense dialectic of yielding and control whereby there is an oscillation between the "opening enough to contain all identities" and a reinforcing of stable (if fleeting) characters. In a later short work, "The End of the World of White Men," Acker theorizes this more clearly in her identification with the tarot card of the Hanged Man: "The Hanged Man card represents the slight possibility that this intolerable society (in which identity depends on possessing rather than on being possessed), this society in which I'm living, could change."[11] The idea of "being possessed" occurs throughout her early writing with the rush of characters inhabiting the autobiographical "I" suggesting the loss of authorial control over the zombies she has animated.

The author of the final work of Acker's early trilogy, *The Adult Life of Toulouse Lautrec by Henri Toulouse Lautrec,* with its mix of detective stories, pornography, film synopses, economic theory, political theory, and art history, is possessed by an eclectic array of texts. This type of collage poetics reaches its climax in her infamous *Blood and Guts in High School* (1978), where she completes the shift from subjective possession to textual possession. While the nineteenth-century romantics were possessed by spirit, inspiration, or "the muse" from within (a trend which might also include the surrealists' automatic writing), Acker as author and as autobiographical character is possessed by a kaleidoscope of fragmentary characters coming from outside, usually from already existing texts. Acker's dialectic of being possessed and possession works against the stable unity of an autobiographical author but, more important, challenges the author's authority as master of the narrative. By allowing herself to be possessed by "outlaw" characters such as murderesses, terrorists, and pirates and by appropriating "outlaw" genres such as pornography, Acker's poetics oscillates between yielding and control, the yielding constantly undermining efforts on the part of both the author and the reader to control the flow of texts.

Acker's accumulation and disintegration of characters parallels the continual flow of contemporary media culture, particularly the fantasy constructions of advertising. Advertising seeks to both create a lack in its viewers and fulfill that lack, providing a solution to unstable identity with images of wholeness, while at the same time offering a utopian promise of community. Acker's novels, on the contrary, offer little promise of wholeness for her readers, and her sense of community is a complex one. As with the ideal subject of advertising, Nicola Pitchford argues that the participatory role of the reader in Acker's pastiche is crucial. What Pitchford refers to as the "freak reader" in Acker's work is called into being with her appeals to "we." The confessional tone of her narratives and the dialogue implicate the reader in a position of both voyeur and participant in the ensuing action. In both pornography and Acker's texts, "one is haunted by the awareness of arousal taking place elsewhere, in the previous lives or original intentions of these words."[12] Pitchford argues that the sexual texts are haunted by the male masturbator, on the one hand, and the antiporn feminist, on the other. At their intersection she locates Acker's community of "freak readers." As an audience plays an active part in creating the unified images of advertising, so Acker's readers participate in creating and participating in this community of "freaks."

In advertising, so the cliché goes, sex sells. Part of Acker's project is trying to recuperate sex from the orgy of consumerism. By utilizing the emptiness of pornography, Acker's texts reveal its fundamentally conservative nature, while at the same time staging sexuality in her own terms. In his response to Acker's *My Mother, Demonology,* Steven Shaviro writes of Bataille's staging of sexuality in a way that might also apply to Acker: "It's more the sense we get that all these transgressions have somehow been staged; that the guilt and dread have been assumed by Bataille, for the sake of emotional effect. It's roleplaying, or performance, very much in the spirit of s&m."[13] The staging of sexuality in Acker's writing, particularly in the early work, is always tied to economic realities: "Having any sex in the world is having to have sex with capitalism."[14] In her endless repetition of sexual scenes, Acker pushes pornographic language to excess so that it empties its content to become a rhythm pulse. From Bataille, Acker also extends the idea of excess expenditure that cannot be appropriated into useful production or knowledge, difference that cannot be appropriated into identity, or, importantly, consumer desire. Following Freud in a twisted way, desire for Acker comes before reason, perversion comes before regulated sexuality.

Mythical Bodies

Rather than operate on a narrative model whereby the reader traces the progress of a single character or group of characters through a text, Acker's novels form a network of character references. After reading several of her works, characters accumulate and become familiar to the reader through repetition—a father becomes a schoolteacher becomes a male artist becomes the president, while Kathy becomes Charlotte becomes Janey. This mythical approach to writing, where familiar characters are repeated in several narratives, becomes more apparent in Acker's middle-period novels, which include *Great Expectations* (1982), *My Death, My Life, By Pier Paolo Pasolini* (1983), and *Don Quixote* (1986). Within this series, the focus of her poetics shifts from appropriation of characters and stories to a more overt plagiarism of well-known fiction. Acker's plagiarism of classic "high" literature becomes clearer in this middle trilogy, certainly in *Don Quixote,* which Acker described as "my version of a Sherrie Levine painting."[15] Like Levine's interventions into the canon of high art, Acker recontextualizes high literature by re-presenting it in relation to porn, theoretical texts, and her own autobiographical fragments. Her use of plagiarism entails a shift from possession by characters to possession by texts, with Acker inhabiting narratives in order to reveal the mythologies they produce and reinforce.

In his *Suburban Ambush: Downtown Writing and the Fiction of Insurgency,* Robert Siegel describes Acker's practice as "an attempt to regain for narrative a voice and form that are commensurate with our information age but capable of performing, against that age's colonisation of its 'processors,' the novel's quite traditional function of renewing the possibility for fresh subjectivity."[16] He links Acker's writing directly to Irigaray and Cixous's calls for a "new insurgent writing" which utilizes guerrilla tactics to challenge the rule of patriarchy. In a poetics similar to Irigaray's method of "inhabiting" the texts of Freud, Lacan, Plato, Descartes, and Nietzsche, Acker uses the texts of the Western literary canon against themselves to expose how patriarchy is maintained through culture, "inhabiting" Dickens, Cervantes, and de Sade, among others, and reanimating their work by juxtaposing it with pornography, feminist theory, and philosophy.[17]

Her plagiarism is both destructive and deconstructive, she stated in an interview: "My main reason for writing *Great Expectations* and *Don Quixote* was to see how texts that had already established themselves within our societal matrix worked—or I wanted to destroy them, or do something else with them."[18] Beyond the identity politics of her earlier works, in the middle trilogy Acker explores the idea that language itself has been appropriated (possessed) by patriarchy, while patriarchy's reason and order are structured by narrative. Her poetics aims to repossess language, developing a feminine language which could undermine patriarchy's stable unity and reveal multiple meanings rather than the singular linear reading emanating from a God/father/authority figure. In this way, her plagiarized texts are as much exercises in reading as they are in writing, exposing the rips, flaws, and excesses in the literary canon, tears that might open productive spaces for a feminist intervention.

In the shift from challenging the authority of the central subjective "I" to the authority of a single stable reading, Acker's plagiarism goes further to challenge the authority of narrative structure itself. If the central "I" reproduces the authority of a unified (patriarchal) subject, narrative reproduces the phantom of a whole articulated system—from the formation of identity through to patriarchal and capitalist ideology, which are reinforced as unified visions through narrative. Narrative is both the means and the space in which systems such as patriarchy or capitalism are rendered "natural," even to the point of naturalizing heterosexual reproduction and capitalist production. For Acker (following the work of Gertrude Stein), narrative is a form of continuity which legitimates established forms of order and produces bodies ("I"s) within that order:

> A narrative is an emotional moving.
> It's a common belief that something exists when it's part of a narrative.
> Self-reflective consciousness is narrational.[19]

In Acker's rewriting of canonical works, narrative conventions such as chronology, character development, and geographic locations are disrupted as characters, times, and spaces slide into one another. With her "perverse" tactics of gender-bending and extreme language, Acker exposes the sexual dynamics of narrative and, more particularly, the "grand narratives" of Western culture. Sexualities become confused as the binary logic of male-female and hetero-homo are challenged, undermining the power structure of the bourgeois family as capitalism's (re)productive unit. The mythical bourgeois family which contains and controls perversion is constantly called into question by Acker's writing. Even formally, her writing is "perverse," not disciplined into a traditional novel form but fragmented, repetitive, and incomplete, making it difficult to translate into productive "information" or useful "knowledge."

One of Acker's sustained challenges is her reworking of one of the fundamental myths of Western culture, the Oedipal myth. Oedipal dramas are played out again and again in Acker's texts, but hers are not the romantic Hollywood "happy ending" version nor the mythological family of advertising (the key unit of consumerism) but a dysfunctional family constantly erupting into incest (rape by the father) and violence (including the mother's suicide). Within the mainstream nuclear family, the production of desire is cut off and caught under the authority of the Father/Law/Capitalist Boss/President so that Oedipal narratives establish and reinforce the law of the father, as well as channel desires into consumerism. Beyond their incestuous and "perverse" family relations, Acker's narratives short-circuit, they frustrate reproduction because there is no pleasurable end to master, no sense of wholeness to consume nor any pleasurable orgasm of a happy family at the end.

While the Oedipal myth (central to both Freud and to Lévi-Strauss's structuralism) is the narrative that distributes genders, it is also profoundly heterosexual. In mainstream culture, the Oedipal father-son struggle becomes universalized as *the* defining cultural narrative that links identity to masculinity and a movement toward completion, wholeness, and stability. The daughter, largely absent from the Oedipal myth, recurs in Acker's version as the father's lover/whore/sexual object, displacing the son as the productive future. In her constant play with familial characters, from Janey of *Blood and Guts in High School,* who "depended on her father for everything and regarded her father as boyfriend, brother, sister, money, amusement and father,"[20] to her mother committing suicide at the beginning of *Great Expectations* (a scene repeated several times in Acker's books), Acker's "perverse" Oedipal dramas reformulate a myth fundamental to Western culture in such a way that the daughter becomes a powerful key figure.

If desire is either repressed or channeled into (re)productive activities by the Oedipal schema, Acker releases this desire, allowing it to freely proliferate across her writings. Deleuze and Guattari, in their assault on Oedipal structures in *Anti-Oedipus,* use language in a similar way to Acker, interrupting conventional narrative flows and utilizing montage techniques. For them, desire has the potential to be revolutionary as it "cuts across the interest of the dominated, exploited classes, and causes flows to move that are capable of breaking apart both the segregations and their Oedipal applications-flows capable of hallucinating history, of reanimating the races in delirium, of setting continents ablaze. No, I am not of your kind, I am the outsider and the deterritorialised, 'I am of a race inferior for all eternity . . . I am a beast, a Negro.' "[21] In Deleuze and Guattari's terms, Acker's writing is "De-oedipalising, undoing the daddy-mommy spider web, undoing the beliefs so as to attain the production of desiring-machines."[22] That is, if Oedipal logic is the logic of both patriarchal and capitalist discourse, Acker's impersonal flows of desire decode this logic, releasing the flows of desire back into language and through language until language itself short-circuits and stalls.

Both Acker's middle trilogy and Deleuze and Guattari's *Anti-Oedipus* project are attempts to develop a politics that is not founded on an authoritative "I." Siegel argues that Acker attempts to create an alternative community in her *Quixote,* a "language community forged by the novel,"[23] a community inclusive of Pitchford's "freak reader." Acker's Quixote character explains poetry to dogs: "Language is community. Dogs, I'm now inventing a community for you and me."[24] This is a community of outsiders who do not function within the mainstream Oedipal matrix, molded instead by the "perversions" or gaps inherent in canonical works of literature. Quixote's community of dogs is also Acker's community of criminals, sailors, and pirates (in a similar spirit to William Burroughs's pirate communities of *The Port of Saints* and *Cities of the Red Night*), communities formed via new modes of writing that push narrative to its limits. The changes in both American and British politics during the 1980s (Acker spent much of the 1980s in Britain), particularly Reagan and Thatcher's "family values," represented a new Oedipal fundamentalism, challenged by "wild" writing such as Acker's. Beyond Oedipus, Acker's poetics of plagiarism opened the possibility for an alternative community forged through rewritten mythologies where desire is released from its mainstream moorings.

Marked Bodies, Excessive Bodies

In Acker's final book, *Pussy, King of the Pirates,* Antonin Artaud writes to O:

> *I have found this language, which is why I can write this letter to you, O. You see, Gérard, who was naked like you are, gave me a language that doesn't lie, for it spurted out of the hole of his body . . . When Gérard cut off his head, he made all that was interior in him exterior: today all that's interior is becoming exterior and this is what I call* revolution, *and those humans who are holes are the leaders of this revolution.*[25]

Here, the decapitation of Gérard de Nerval brings about a change in language—release from the language of authority (centralized "I") and the language of the father (Oedipal narratives) opens the possibility for a subversive corporeal poetics. Paralleling Acker's interest in tattooing and bodybuilding, her later works, including *Empire of the Senseless* (1988), *In Memoriam to Identity* (1990), *My Mother, Demonology* (1993), and *Pussy, King of the Pirates* (1996), explore this corporeal poetics more explicitly. In his analysis of the tattooing sections of *Empire of the Senseless,* Robert Siegel notes, "Acker's tactile sense of individuality is one modeled on the body rather than, as traditionally, upon conceptual abstraction."[26] Although he does not develop this idea further, Acker's focus on the physical body becomes a key theme of her later work.

Acker's bodies are excessive. Bodily fluids flow freely, discharges of menstrual blood, streams of vomit, and spouts of semen—excessive bodies overflowing the limits of individual subjectivity. For many commentators, such as Richard Walsh, Acker's portrayal of women is linked to "Irigaray's analysis of the concept of woman defined by men as an absence or void—and of the commodification of women as sexual objects."[27] According to Walsh, strategies Acker uses in *Don Quixote* against the dominant sexual power structure end in frustration. Her corporeal poetics, particularly in her later works, offers a way out of this impasse of frustrated desire (which also became the impasse of plagiarism in her middle trilogy). In her later work, Acker continues to challenge the domestication of desire but leaves behind the overt deconstruction of canonical texts. The female body, disciplined by patriarchy into a position aligned with nature (to be possessed in heterosexual sex or colonized in reproduction), is repositioned by Acker into a surface extended through writing and into writing, an active and productive body.

Elizabeth Grosz writes of the body as a "surface of inscription." She develops this concept out of a tradition including Nietzsche, Kafka, Foucault, and Deleuze, against which she contrasts the psychological tradition of the "lived body" that takes an imaginary body-schema as its object (as in the Lacanian model discussed earlier). Rather than an imaginary autonomous body, the "surface of inscription" tradition "conceives the body as a surface on which social law, morality, and values are inscribed."[28] In the latter, each body is inscribed in a particular way, while the "lived body" tradition conceives particular bodies in terms of universal, ahistorical, and abstract categories. Concern for how the body is written upon and constrained by various regimes of power is common to the work of both Acker and Grosz. Grosz's description of the body might well serve as an analysis of Acker's later interest in tattooing (which occurs in several of her later books as well as in her "real" life): "Inscriptions mark the surface of the body, dividing it into zones of intensified or de-intensified sensation, spreading a libidinal concentration unevenly over the written-and-erotic living surface."[29]

This body is singular and particular. While Grosz notes the erotics of inscription onto the body's surface, the art is not necessarily a pleasurable experience. Acker writes: "Cruel Romans had used tattoos to mark and identify mercenaries, slaves, criminals, and heretics. For the first time, the sailor felt he had sailed home . . . today a tattoo is considered both a defamatory brand and a symbol of a tribe or of a dream."[30] Here, tattoo is identified with the fringe dwellers who inhabit Acker's later works—sailors, criminals, bikers, pirates. Her interest in tattooing might also be linked to her interest in punk, specifically punk's use of the body as a site of resistance to mainstream conformity (from brightly dyed hair to piercings). As well as a mark of the outsider, tattooing in Acker's texts becomes a mode of writing that is not controlled by regimes of external power but a self-inflicted process that generates both pain and pleasure.

In her analysis of *Don Quixote,* Linda Kauffman notes Acker's interest in the pleasure/pain theater of masochism: "Masochism becomes a means of rebellion for Acker's Don, daily assaulted by the disciplinary mechanisms of family, school, nation."[31] While sadism is defined by possession of or power over the other, masochism is defined by a contract with the other, as Deleuze points out: "The sadist thinks in terms of institutionalised possession, the masochist in terms of contracted alliance. Possession is the sadist's particular form of madness just as the pact is the masochist's."[32] The famous masochist O, the main character of Pauline Réage's classic French novel *The Story of O,* appears as a character in several of Acker's texts. Paralleling Acker's earlier challenge to the unified and authoritative author through "being possessed," Acker's masochism challenges the disciplinary mechanisms of the state and family which seek to regulate and control the body and domesticate desire. For Arthur Redding, "Masochism is a play whereby the semantic as well as the somatic range of suffering eludes the proprietorship of domination."[33] That is, the theater of masochism brings together Acker's critique of both sexual and textual power relations.

In Michel Foucault's *Discipline and Punish,* discourse "frames" and "forms" the body—the figure of the prisoner is both produced and regulated by discourse. The body of the prisoner is invaded and regulated by the institution, a notion feminist theorists have taken up in relation to the disciplinary production of gender. In Foucault's *History of Sexuality*, power not only produces the subject's boundaries but also invades the subject. A subject only remains a subject through reiteration of itself, but inherent in this repetition is also the possibility of redirecting the norm. Judith Butler argues, "For Foucault . . . the disciplinary apparatus produces subjects, but, as a consequence of that production, it brings into discourse the conditions for the subversion of that apparatus itself."[34] Acker seizes upon this disciplinary apparatus, transforming it into a masochism which operates counter to the universal and essentializing tendencies of the modern state's institutions. She initiates this transformation through suggesting a disciplined approach to pain which links the subject to a wider utopian vision: "Like the edges of a dream during the waking state, tattooing showed the sailor that dreams are made actual through pain. Humans make themselves and're made through pain plus dreams."[35]

Furthering her exploration of masochism, Acker's interest in bodybuilding, particularly in *My Mother, Demonology*, extends her corporeal poetics in a slightly different direction. In the theater of bodybuilding, the body is self-disciplined and transformed without a particular end, attaining psychic power for aesthetic rather than functional reasons. There is also, in the repetitive stretching and tearing of muscles, a sense of the self displaced onto the body. For the bodybuilder, according to Alphonso Lingis, "existence, for the self, no longer means inwardness, visceral or cerebral involution, but exposure. This self is a movement to extend itself across contours and forms, and not to maintain a point of view, a repair in space. As the ego surfaces, distends and exposes itself, it depersonalises."[36] In both its exposure and its depersonalization, bodybuilding and a corporeal poetics seem a logical trajectory from Acker's earlier concerns with subjectivity. In her later work, instead of being possessed by different selves or texts, there is an extension of the material body's boundaries through the marking of tattoos and bodybuilding's excessive transformations.

Acker writes in *My Mother, Demonology:* "STORYTELLING METHOD: THE ACT OF BODYBUILDING PRESUPPOSES THE ACT OF MOVING TOWARD THE BODY OR THAT WHICH IS SO MATERIAL THAT IT BECOMES IMMATERIAL."[37] The excessive pumped-up body becomes immaterial as it becomes exposed, becoming a surface that extends so that the body's psychic interior is also exposed, displacing socially inscribed markings. While bodies are coded by sexual desire and regulated by regimes of power, Acker's corporeal poetics suggests a writing that can produce erotogenic zones. Indeed, there is a clear sense of corporeal production in reading Acker's texts (or listening to her perform); the predominance of dialogue and multiplicity of voices take on another dimension when read aloud. While the sense of sight when reading functions by doubling and dividing, hearing functions through resonance. Like poetry, Acker's writing works on the body of the reader. While visual possession of characters is difficult and the complicity of sight and speech in conventional narrative is undermined, when heard aloud, Acker's excessive writing attains a rhythm; the repetitive scenes and speed of changes become cinematic ebbs and flows of desire.

Pushing beyond the body organized by the centralized "I" and structured by the Oedipal nuclear family, Acker's bodies are constantly re-formed by flows of desire. The bodies of her later work are also exposed to the outside, as is evident both in the tattooed surfaces of inscription and in the excessive bodies of bodybuilding. In this exposure, her corporeal poetics attains an almost spiritual dimension, exposing oneself to the unknown. Her later works suggest a poetics beyond the utopian vision of a community of outsiders in a more radical push toward the limits of both the body and writing. Acker writes of tattoo in *Empire of the Senseless:* "Beginning as abstract maps of spiritual visions, records of the 'other' world, tattoos were originally icons of power and mystery designating realms beyond normal land-dweller's experience."[38] Her writing constantly pushes to the edge of meaning, approaching failure—from the depersonalization of her early works to her fragmentary characters who inhabit dilapidated narratives. Bodybuilding is also about pushing the body toward failure, and in the same way as in bodybuilding, her corporeal poetics, through tearing apart the "I," ripping up literary texts, and reworking of Oedipal themes, exposes the reader to the outside or the unknown, which is, ultimately, death.

Notes

1. On Acker's bohemian appeal and marketing of both her work and her image, see Joe Moran, "A Star of Bohemia: Kathy Acker," in *Star Authors: Literary Celebrity in America* (London: Pluto Press, 2000).
2. Kathy Acker, *Pussy, King of the Pirates* (Sydney: Picador, 1996), 10.
3. Robert Siegel provides a good reading of Acker's links to the New York

downtown art scene of the 1970s. See Robert Siegel, "Kathy Acker: The Blood and Guts of Guerrilla Warfare," in *Suburban Ambush: Downtown Writing and the Fiction of Insurgency* (Baltimore: Johns Hopkins University Press, 1989).

4. Quoted in Larry McCaffery, "The Path of Abjection: An Interview with Kathy Acker," in *Some Other Frequency: Interviews with Innovative American Authors* (Philadelphia: University of Pennsylvania Press, 1996), 23.

5. Kathy Acker, *The Childlike Life of the Black Tarantula by the Black Tarantula*, in *Portrait of an Eye* (New York: Grove Press, 1998), 3.

6. Ibid.

7. See Jacques Lacan, "The Mirror Stage as Formative of the Function of the *I* in Psychoanalytical Experience," in *Écrits: A Selection,* trans. Alan Sheridan (New York: W. W. Norton, 1977).

8. Kathy Acker, *I Dreamt I Was a Nymphomaniac: Imagining,* in *Portrait of an Eye,* 118.

9. By her later work, this "I" is more particularly defined as *the* patriarchal leader of the 1990s: "'*I,* this country's Supreme Dictator,' Bush spoke clearly into his Dictaphone, 'otherwise known only as *I* . . . '" Kathy Acker, *My Mother, Demonology, a novel* (New York: Pantheon Books, 1993), 180.

10. Acker, *Childlike Life,* 60.

11. Kathy Acker, "The End of the World of White Men," in *Posthuman Bodies,* ed. Judith Halberstam and Ira Livingston (Bloomington: Indiana University Press, 1995), 66.

12. Nicola Pitchford, "Flogging a Dead Language: Identity Politics, Sex, and the Freak Reader in Acker's Don Quixote," *Postmodern Culture* 11, no. 1 (2000): paragraph 29, http://muse.jhu.edu/journals/pmc/v011/11.1pitchford.html.

13. Steven Shaviro, *Doom Patrols,* chap. 8, http://www.dhalgren.com/Doom/ch08.html.

14. Kathy Acker, *Blood and Guts in High School, plus two* (London: Pan Books, 1984), 204.

15. Quoted in McCaffery, "Path of Abjection," 29.

16. Siegel, "Kathy Acker," 101.

17. Through undermining academic language (ignoring citation rules, stressing typographic figures), Irigaray's texts work to point to patriarchal modes of repression and oppression. Acker performs similar "disruptions" to the conventions of novel writing. See especially Luce Irigaray, *This Sex Which Is Not One* (Ithaca, N.Y.: Cornell University Press, 1985); and her "writing through" Nietzsche book, *Marine Lover of Friedrich Nietzsche,* trans. Gillian C. Gill (New York: Columbia University Press, 1991).

18. Quoted in McCaffery, "Path of Abjection," 29.

19. Kathy Acker, *Great Expectations,* in *Blood and Guts in High School, plus two* (London: Pan Books, 1984), 204.

20. Acker, *Blood and Guts*, 7.

21. Gilles Deleuze and Félix Guattari, *Anti-Oedipus: Capitalism and Schizophrenia*, trans. Robert Hurley, Mark Seem, and Helen R. Lane (Minneapolis: University of Minnesota Press, 1983), 105.

22. Ibid., 112.

23. Siegel, "Kathy Acker," 107.

24. Kathy Acker, *Don Quixote* (London: Paladin, 1986), 191.

25. Acker, *Pussy*, 20.

26. Siegel, "Kathy Acker," 123.

27. Richard Walsh, "The Quest for Love and the Writing of Female Desire in Kathy Acker's *Don Quixote*," in *Novel Arguments: Reading Innovative American Fiction* (Cambridge: Cambridge University Press, 1995), 147.

28. Elizabeth Grosz, *Space, Time and Perversion: The Politics of Bodies* (London: Routledge, 1995), 33.

29. Ibid., 34.

30. Kathy Acker, *Empire of the Senseless* (London: Picador, 1988), 130.

31. Linda S. Kauffman, "New Inquisitions: Kathy Acker and William Vollman," in *Bad Girls and Sick Boys: Fantasies in Contemporary Art and Culture* (Berkeley and Los Angeles: University of California Press, 1998), 211.

32. Gilles Deleuze, "Coldness and Cruelty," trans. Jean McNeil, in *Masochism* (New York: Zone Books, 1989), 20.

33. Arthur F. Redding, "Bruises, Roses: Masochism and the Writing of Kathy Acker," *Contemporary Literature* 35, no. 2 (1994): 284.

34. Judith Butler, "Subjection, Resistance, Resignification: Between Freud and Foucault," in *The Identity in Question*, ed. John Rajchman (New York: Routledge, 1995), 242.

35. Acker, *Empire of the Senseless*, 138.

36. Alphonso Lingis, "Orchids and Muscles," in *Exceedingly Nietzsche: Aspects of Contemporary Nietzsche Interpretation*, ed. David Farrell Krell and David Wood (London: Routledge, 1998), 114.

37. Acker, *My Mother, Demonology*, 110.

38. Acker, *Empire of the Senseless*, 140.

There are the minimalist pleasures of Emily Dickinson—"Zero at the Bone"—and the maximalist ones of Walt Whitman.

—John Barth

There's no single ideal listener out there who likes my orchestral music, my guitar albums and songs like "Dyna-Moe-Humm." It's all one big note. Ladies and gentlemen . . .

—Frank Zappa

Frank Zappa, Captain Beefheart, and the Secret History of Maximalism

Michel Delville and Andrew Norris

Like Mozart's *The Marriage of Figaro,* Zappa's music has often been accused of being far too noisy and of containing too many notes. Because of their density and complexity, his sound sculptures have alternately enthused and alienated several generations of critics and listeners. With more than sixty albums (including no less than twenty-one double albums and two triple albums) released over a period of twenty-eight years and fifteen "official bootlegs," Zappa stands out as one of the most prolific artists of the twentieth century, a composer whose sheer musical output could stand accused of maximalist excess. His attempts to embrace different genres and creative practices (rock, jazz, blues, orchestral music, film, opera, etc.) have often been interpreted as a bulimic desire to explore the totality of past and present modes and styles in order to create strongly contrasting musical collages and establish his reputation as an outsider in both the rock and the art music communities.

Certainly one of the difficulties in dealing with Frank Zappa's (or anybody else's) maximalist art arises from the lack of serious attention to the development of maximalist aesthetics itself. That the history of maximalism in the arts is the poor relation of contemporary criticism is already indicated by the fact that the term is systematically absent from all lexicons of literary terms and, indeed, most discussions of contemporary music except when it refers to Milton Babbitt's "maximal" extension of Schoenberg's ideas of serial composition or, more rarely and even more loosely, to the New Complexity school of Brian Ferneyhough and Michael Finnissy. One of the rare exceptions to the rule comes from the American novelist John Barth, who, in an article first published in the *New York Times* in 1986, offers the following definition of literary maximalism:

> The medieval Roman Catholic Church recognized two opposite roads to grace: the *via negativa* of the monk's cell and the hermit's cave, and the *via affirmativa* of immersion in human affairs, of being in the world whether or not one is of it. Critics have aptly borrowed those terms to characterize the difference between Mr. Beckett, for example, and his erstwhile master James Joyce, himself a maximalist except in his early works. Other than bone-deep disposition, which is no doubt the great determinant, what inclines a writer—sometimes almost a cultural generation of writers—to the Negational Path?[1]

For Barth, the distance that separates Joyce from Beckett (or Whitman from Dickinson, or Faulkner from Hemingway) cannot be reduced to an aesthetic option (the desire to embrace richness and completeness, on the one hand, or aim for a narrative of precision and brevity, on the other) but is immediately translated into social terms. Barth opposes maximalist fiction to the so-called New American Short Story of the early 1980s, a tendency represented by Ann Beattie, Raymond Carver, Bobbie Ann Mason, and others who are "both praised and damned under such labels as 'K-Mart realism,' 'hick chic,' 'Diet-Pepsi minimalism,' and 'post-Vietnam, post-literary, postmodernist blue-collar neo-early-Hemingwayism.'"[2] The collusion of style and politics in minimalist fiction echoes a number of similar accusations made against postmodern art in general, whose success story has been linked with the expansion of capitalist hegemony. For Fredric Jameson, for example, this tendency reaches a climax in Andy Warhol's work, which, far from parodying commercial culture in a "modernist" (e.g., Joycean) fashion, incorporates it into its very substance, thereby abolishing the critical distance that separates artists from their socioeconomic environment. The total interpenetration of aesthetic and commodity production is indeed the logical result of the gradual process of "immersion in human affairs" brought about by Barth's *via affirmativa*. Another critic of postmodernism, Takayoshi Ishiwari, believes that the "style which is broadly called maximalism" is characterized not only by a tendency to embrace the time's modes and conventions but also by a typically postmodernist attitude to the notion of the "authentic":

> Under this label come such writers as, among others, Thomas Pynchon and Barth himself, whose bulky books are in marked contrast with Barthelme's relatively thin novels and collections of short stories. These maximalists are called by such an epithet because they, situated in the age of epistemological uncertainty and therefore knowing that they can never know what is authentic and inauthentic, attempt to include in their fiction everything belonging to that age, to take these authentic and inauthentic things as they are with all their uncertainty and inauthenticity included; their work intends to contain the maximum of the age, in other words, to be the age itself, and because of this their novels are often encyclopedic. As Tom LeClair argues in *The Art of Excess,* the authors of these "masterworks" even "gather, represent, and reform the time's excesses into fictions that exceed the time's literary conventions and thereby master the time, the methods of fiction, and the reader."[3]

Zappa's ambition "to be the age itself" clearly manifests itself in his penchant for works that seek to incorporate—albeit in a frequently ironic fashion—nearly all existing musical genres and modes, from straight blues-rock and doo-wop to musique concrète, free jazz, and symphonic orchestral works. And Tom LeClair's definition of maximalism as an art that exceeds its own historical context and represents more than the sum of all past and present compositional styles would seem perfectly suited to the development of Zappa's aesthetics. But we will see that the impact of maximalism on contemporary art cannot be reduced to the decision of what to include or exclude in a literary text or musical score or even the rather dubious notion that such a decision should be dictated by a Baudrillardian sense of "epistemological uncertainty." For Zappa's disdain for accepted distinctions between the "authentic" and the "inauthentic," high and low art, as well as other aesthetic and generic hierarchies, is only one aspect of his commitment to the *via affirmativa* of contemporary music, one which allies him with other musical eccentrics such as Charles Ives—who was among the first to integrate elements of low music (gospel hymns, jazz, fanfare) into classical/orchestral music—and Zappa's self-confessed master Edgar Varèse, with whom he shares not only an interest in bruitism, tape music, and percussion-based orchestral pieces but also a penchant for gigantic compositional structures that exceed traditional performance formats.[4]

According to David Jaffe, one of the very few composers to address the development of a "maximalist" *musical* style, the maximalist approach in contemporary music "embraces heterogeneity and allows for complex systems of juxtapositions and collisions, in which all outside influences are viewed as potential raw material."[5] The example of Charles Ives once again comes to mind, and Zappa's tribute to Ives in the fifth box set of the *You Can't Do That On Stage Anymore* series confirms his early interest in his predecessor's use of "multiple colliding themes"[6] and fragments of (sometimes distorted) melodies, a technique emulated in Zappa's "Call Any Vegetable," which, like many of Ives's compositions, seeks to convey "the musical illusion of several marching bands marching through each other":

> In our low-rent version, the band splits into three parts, playing "The Star-Spangled Banner," "God Bless America" and "America the Beautiful" all at the same time, yielding an amateur version of an Ives collision.[7]

Ben Watson rightly underlines the historical significance of Ives's "simultaneous musics" as probably one of the first instances of predigital "xenochrony" (a term coined by Zappa to describe the art of connecting apparently unrelated musical objects and live idiosyncrasies which are liable to be fitted together and synchronized into further studio constructions) and points out that "while a boy [Ives] would sing one hymn while his father played the accompaniment to a different one."[8] For readers familiar with the aural collages of Zappa's *Freak Out* and *Absolutely Free,* Zappa's delight in merging fundamentally incompatible materials and rhythms cannot be considered as a simple manifestation of the modernist cult of irony or its hypothetical extension into postmodern eclecticism, quotation, and pastiche. Rather, the satirical spirit of Zappa's xenochronic experiments originates in what Amiri Baraka describes as jazz saxophonist John Coltrane's decision to "murder the popular song" and "do away with weak Western forms."[9] Nowhere is this more apparent than in the doo-wop send-ups collected in *Cruising with Ruben and the Jets* (1968), which Zappa claimed to have conceived "along the same lines as Stravinsky's neoclassical period" ("If he could take the forms and clichés of the classical era and pervert them, why not do the same thing with the rules and regulations that applied to doo-wop in the fifties?").[10]

As indicated by both Baraka's comments on Coltrane and Barth's description of the "K-Mart" aesthetics of the New American Short Story, the maximalist-versus-minimalist axis inevitably invites a political reading. In another chapter of his *Negative Dialectics of Poodle Play,* Ben Watson discusses the work of the feminist critic Susan McClary, for whom Schoenberg's twelve-tone technique is the expression of an "asexual" musical language that puts an end to the binarisms (major/minor, masculine/feminine) around which sexism articulates itself. McClary claims that minimalist music, being based on repetition-with-variation and therefore deprived of the sexual climaxes of, say, Beethoven's Ninth or Bizet's *Carmen,* simultaneously undermines the supremacy of the male models of phallic telos and verticality that characterizes a sexist culture. Compared with the soothing sounds of Brian Eno's *Music for Airports,* Zappa's "The Torture Never Stops" would no doubt be condemned by McClary as too sensual and orgasmic to qualify as anything other than an expression of the male libidinal self. Whatever one makes of McClary's suggestion that female sexuality is fundamentally anticlimactic, it would be pointless to try to defend Zappa from accusations of sexism or even deny that his music and lyrics derive much of their energy from the representation (or shameless endorsement) of popular archetypes of masculine domination, rawness, and obscenity. But Zappa's own remarks about minimalism indicate his desire to shift the debate from the domain of sexual politics to more largely political and economic matters. Reflecting on the popularity of minimalist music with established critics and foundations, Zappa suggests that minimalism arose out of the necessity of being cost-effective (in the same way as, for instance, the success story of the "theater of the absurd" format is at least in part due to the fact that it lends itself to low-budget productions requiring only two or three actors and very few additional staging costs):

> It used to be that they would fund *only boob-beep stuff* (serial and/or electronic composition). Now they're funding *only minimalism* (simplistic, repetitive composition, easy to rehearse and, therefore, *cost-effective*). So what gets taught in school? *Minimalism.* Why? Because it can be FUNDED. Net cultural result? Monochromonotony.[11]

Maximalism and the Baroque Fold

> Matter that reveals its texture becomes raw material, just as form that reveals its folds becomes force. In the Baroque, the coupling of material-force is what replaced matter and form.
>
> —Gilles Deleuze

> La vie dans les plis
>
> —Henri Michaux

As suggested at the beginning of this essay, one of the most visible contemporary avatars of musical maximalism is the New Complexity school of contemporary British music (a term which was itself coined against the "new simplicity" of the minimalists), a style shared by composers who sought to push the limits of instrumental virtuosity, rhythmic structure, and polyphonic models. To some extent, Zappa's taste for extremes of register, his penchant for density and abstraction, and his increased performance demands (as well as his constant search for methodological and technological procedures devised to cope with problems traditional performance could not fulfill) ally his work with that of Brian Ferneyhough and Michael Finnissy, to name but two of the godfathers of the New Complexity style. There is no reason to believe, however, that Zappa had any specific interest in the works of these composers. By contrast, his admiration for Pierre Boulez, which culminated in his collaboration with the French composer on *The Perfect Stranger* (1984), points to his affinities with an art which would be more aptly described as neobaroque rather than as merely promoting various forms of "density" and "complexity." In *The Fold: Leibniz and the Baroque,* Gilles Deleuze cites Boulez, the author of the Mallarmé-inspired *Pli selon pli,* as a continuator of the baroque style, with its emphasis on virtuosity and eccentricity and its tendency to create a mass of curves, convolutions, and folds that, according to Deleuze, "[unfurl] all the way to infinity."[12] By citing Boulez as an example of a neobaroque tendency in modern music—one which signals the birth of an "extended chromatism" and a "polyphony of polyphonies"[13]—Deleuze invokes a major interface between Zappa and the realm of "official culture." But perhaps the best way to do justice to the infinite compositional foldings of Zappa's works is to resort to an architectural model. According to Yago Conde, the effect produced in architecture by folding is "the ability to integrate unrelated elements within a new continuous mixture."[14] While it would be a mistake to reduce the maximalist quality of Zappa's oeuvre to his penchant for density and exuberance, it is the fluid, seamless character of his later transgeneric experiments (which began after the merz-inspired, "collagist" period that ended more or less with *Weasels Ripped My Flesh* in 1970) that allies him with the efforts of other neobaroque artists who attempt to discover "new ways of folding, akin to new envelopments"[15] that reflect the composer's desire to privilege process and mobility over juxtaposition and rupture.

This tendency is most apparent in the Synclavier compositions, whose entry into the Zappa catalog was marked by the publication of *The Perfect Stranger,* in 1984. The album contains three orchestral pieces conducted by Pierre Boulez and four electronic pieces including "The Girl in the Magnesium Dress," a piece adapted eight years later by Ali N. Askin for the Ensemble Modern's *Yellow Shark* concert and which was originally based on the rhythms indicated by the "dust particles" resulting from guitar notes recorded by the Synclavier and which Zappa subsequently converted into pitched sounds.[16] (In the mid-1980s, Zappa discovered that the Synclavier's G page, which contains the machine's inaudible inner codes and numbers, could be used to generate "G numbers" that never surface at the level of the "user-friendly" part of the machine.) On a more thematic level, the liner notes to *The Perfect Stranger* suggest that the light, ductile, silver-white metal dress is only the prelude to a bizarre *dance fatale* whose outcome will be the death of the lover, who is destined to be impaled upon the lethal pike that adorns the girl's plate armor:

> "The Girl in the Magnesium Dress" is about a girl who hates men and kills them with her special dress. Its lightweight metal construction features a lethally pointed sort of micro-Wagnerian breastplate. When they die from dancing with her, she laughs at them and wipes it off.

But if we dare to look up the girl's deadly dress and try to make sense of the inner dynamics of the piece, the conversion of digital "dust" into audible pitched rhythms appears as yet another manifestation of Zappa's maximalist fold, one which delights in blurring the boundaries between matter and sound, the literal and the figurative, the real and the virtual. The seemingly infinite polyphonies of the piece, the irregular rhythmic groupings and the overall absence of symmetry, combined with the strange phrasing of the lead melody all help to blur the outer limits of the piece as well as those of the girl's body. Typically, the function of the baroque fold—in Zappa's music, Bernini's sculptures, and elsewhere—is to relay and prolong traditional mimesis when the latter has reached its limits. Here, Zappa's maximalist dress once again returns us to the body (and to the folds and circonvolutions of the skin) only to disrupt our most ingrained assumptions about how to deal with the opposition of inside and outside, both of which are subsumed into a reversible plication which comprises an "inside as the operation of the outside."[17]

In the same way as the true subject of Zappa's piece becomes not the girl itself but the dress she is wearing, the unfinished body, eventually confronted with its own absence of limits, gives way to the aesthetics of the baroque garment, which detaches itself from its instrumental destiny and is no longer subordinated to the body that wears it.[18] The baroque costume ceases to translate or even prolong the shapes and movements of the body and becomes its own movement, "wrapping the body with its autonomous, always multipliable folds."[19] The baroque fold and its sculptural extension in, say, Bernini's Saint Theresa is in turn interpreted as a body of infinite folds, curved lines and surfaces that twist and weave through the changing conditions of time and space. Whereas Bernini's goal was to give three-dimensional expression to the body possessed by religious ecstasy (and in a state of abandonment often interpreted as a form of eroticized suffering), Zappa's "Girl in the Magnesium Dress" is an example of a secular baroque art that seeks to conquer formlessness by allowing a profusion of matter to overflow the frame.[20]

For Deleuze, the baroque embodies "the law of extremum of matter, that is, a maximum of matter for a minimum of space." In a footnote to the closing chapter of his study, he claims that there are therefore a lot of affinities between the baroque and certain kinds of minimal art where "form no longer limits itself to volume, but embraces an unlimited space in all directions."[21] Deleuze cites Robert Morris's felt folds and Christo's wrapped buildings as examples of minimalism's "constant confrontation with the baroque." The complex and often paradoxical dialectics of minimalism and maximalism in their relationship to time are beyond the scope of this essay. One must nonetheless point out that Zappa's Dionysian aesthetics, which constantly returns us to the carnivalesque body, remains radically opposed to the more austere, Apollonian landscapes of architectural minimalism. Zappa's performance of John Cage's *4′33″* in which he let the composition sheets fall from the piano, once again allows the body to interrupt the illusion of absolute silence and timelessness created by

Cage's blank intervals.[22] Ultimately, however, as Yves Bonnefoy remarks, the baroque is "neither illusion nor insight"; instead, it "puts illusion to the service of being" where illusion is converted into "a space of hallucinatory presence,"[23] a tendency reflected in Zappa's interest in the physicality of sound and the creation of material musical objects. Like Bonnefoy's baroque, which exists at the paradoxical conjunction of maximum presence and extreme absence, Zappa's magnesium dress can be seen as so many interacting prototonal microevents that signify both the absence of matter and the essence of immateriality. They are, to quote Deleuze on Leibniz, very similar to the musical monad, "an eternal object of pure Virtuality which actualises itself in the [sound] sources . . . pure Possibilities which realize themselves in vibrations and fluxes."[24]

Zappa's eagerness, in "The Girl in the Magnesium Dress," to let the hardware of the computer generate the basic parameters of his compositions, in particular, is as typical of the contemporary avant-garde's attention to the material conditions of art production as it is characteristic of the baroque's tendency to "foreground matter"[25] to the detriment of (traditional) form. But the technological fold affected by Zappa's electronic compositions also raises the question of the contributions the Synclavier made to Zappa's maximalist art. Was Zappa using the Synclavier as a maximalist "desiring machine" liable to multiply the conceptual vectors of his oeuvre ad infinitum by combining "various elements and forces of all types"?[26] And should Zappa's work then be regarded as a late modernist collage or a postmodern "rhizomatic" assemblage of heterogeneous genres and styles (which would therefore exemplify what Deleuze and Guattari have described as a reworking of traditional notions of subjectivity into a network of multiplicities, a heterogeneous aggregate of parts functioning in "social and natural machines")? These considerations seem less important than the suggestion that Zappa's investment in Synclavier technology was a necessary stage in the folding and unfolding trajectories of a transmorphic art which has confounded several generations of listeners and left them speculating about the origins, influences, and limits of his work. The next logical stage in the construction of the Project/Object (a formulation meant to describe "the overall concept of [his] work in various mediums")[27] was the creation of music that coalesced the technical infallibility of the machine and the personalities of live musicians. In this respect, the coexistence of Synclavier pieces and works written and executed by Boulez's Ensemble InterContemporain on *The Perfect Stranger* (1984) anticipates Zappa's later mixed experiments, which typically hesitate between the gestural and the mechanical, the "authenticity" of "organic" execution and the necessities of accurate performance (in the liner notes, Zappa thanks Boulez for "having the patience to demand accurate performance of the *killer triplets* on page eight").

An example of Zappa's commitment to the materiality of sound and the physicality of performance, Zappa's "Girl in the Magnesium Dress" also establishes the body as the supreme maximalist receiver and generator of meaning, rhythm, and being.[28] The profusion of grotesque and abstract(ed) bodies and body parts in the works of Frank Zappa and his old friend and occasional collaborator Don Van Vliet (aka Captain Beefheart)—from the latter's *Trout Mask Replica,* with its horrific fishy prosthesis, to the exaggerated, phallic noses that appear on the cover of Zappa's *Ruben and the Jets*—represents what Bakhtin described as "the epitome of incompleteness,"[29] an unfinished unit transgressing its own limits, often through eating, excretion, and sexuality, as exemplified by Zappa's penchant for sexually and scatologically charged lyrics. The stress, therefore, is on the excesses and potentialities of the body's folds and orifices, "on the apertures or the convexities, or on various ramifications and offshoots: the open mouth, the genital organs, the breasts, the phallus, the potbelly, the nose." This "unfinished and open body (dying, bringing forth and being born)," Bahktin adds, "is not separated from the world by clearly defined boundaries; it is blended with the world, with animals, with objects."[30] Zappa's and Beefheart's lyrics are full of similar images of bodies coming out of themselves to meet the world of animal and objectivist reality. The point where body and things enter each other (literally or figuratively) is where the unfinished chain of growth, proliferation, and metamorphosis comes to represent the whole potential of the integrated body, the body emptying itself to become like nothing and preparing itself to go out and m-eat the world again, devouring the universe and being devoured by it.

Subject, Meaning, Pleasure, Body

Like the human body, criticism is pervious to its objects, and just as maximalist art develops out of and contributes to a sense of the body as a point at which subject and object interpenetrate and reconfigure each other, so any bid to write about maximalism can only accept a similar suspension of its traditional limits and certitudes. The maximalist body-in-progress, then, in its occupation of the libidinized liminalities of the edge (between discourses, ideas, styles, genres, bodies, objects, bodies and objects, genres and styles, ideas and discourses) opens a space in which the neglected (and sometimes repressed) question of pleasure may again be asked of poetics.

When in 1977 Roland Barthes announced the death of the author, the basis for his extrapolation was a sentence in a short story by Balzac. Writing, for Barthes, is "that neutral, composite, oblique space where our subject slips away, the negative where all identity is lost, starting with the very identity of the body writing."[31] Neutral, bodiless, oblique, emptied of subject and identity, the death of the author would seem to render moribund the entire textual scene. Before Barthes resurrects the body of the author in that of the reader at the very end of his text, it is impossible to see in his vision how the literary exchange could be a source of pleasure, or of anything else for that matter. Critical premises are never innocent, of course, and the panache with which Barthes deconstructs the authorial subject seems in retrospect directly proportional to the crassly ideological sentence he cites from Balzac:

> This was woman herself, with her sudden fears, her irrational whims, her instinctive worries, her impetuous boldness, her fussings, and her delicious sensibility.[32]

If ever there was an attempt to write determinately, this must be it; and one can only sympathize with the desire to save this sentence as writing by expunging any traces it may harbor of an authorial subject. Suitably dehistoricized by the time Barthes has finished with it, the sentence-formerly-written-by-Balzac is ripe for repossession by the newly nascent reader. Now, if such a procedure makes satisfying sense in relation to a particularly strident example of nineteenth-century "realism," how would it fare in the maximalist context, when confronted, for example, with something from *Finnegans Wake* or, to skip media, something from Zappa? And how would the transference of agency from author to reader work in such a context to impinge on the problem of pleasure? We have been arguing that, as a maximalist paradigm, the body is immanent (and sometimes exorbitant) in maximalism. Without trying to say *whose* body is present *where,* such an assumption immediately seems to put us at odds with Barthes's vision of writing as disincarnate. Conversely, to accept the death of the author as implicitly true of maximalism would, we suggest, imply an inconceivable mastery of such art on the part of its audience.

Or it would simply imply a neutrality of nonresponse equally difficult to conceive of in relation to the sublime irritant of maximalism. In the face of its excess, the reader of the maximalist text (whether literary or musical) *needs* a body, and this is the short explanation for why Zappa as author is ever-present in his work, while Joyce the author, with his bad eyes and perforating ulcer, is a cult among readers of Joyce.[33] This need, of course, is a double bind: while the presence of the body in maximalist art may help the audience take pleasure in the work, creating at the same time a sense of political agency, it may also contribute to the deferral of such pleasure. There is sometimes a feeling that our pleasure must wait until the body in the work has finished taking its own; that the work is a tireless body determined to pleasure itself endlessly. For Barthes, the death of the author would seem to precipitate a deferral of meaning and the pleasure which is traditionally contingent upon it:

> In the multiplicity of writing, everything is to be disentangled, nothing deciphered; the structure can be followed, "run" (like the thread of a stocking) at every point and at every level, but there is nothing beneath: the space of writing is to be ranged over, not pierced; writing ceaselessly posits meaning ceaselessly to evaporate it, carrying out a systematic exemption of meaning.[34]

This sounds suspiciously like the postmodern sprawl which may offer us a mild and strangely technical amusement even as it teaches us indifference. Maximalism is a much more confused and urgent situation, where it is no longer certain whether pleasure is contingent on meaning or the other way around. Under such conditions, nothing is exempted, everything accumulates. It is as if maximalism had taken root during the interval between the death of the author and the birth of the reader as Barthes conceives of them; the body of maximalism is heavily pregnant with a meaningful pleasure that is also a pleasurable meaning, and it is with this unwieldy body that the audience must grapple.

Barthes attacks the author as a final signifier which caps meaning; the demise of this authorial subject, however, does not in the first instance produce a wild expansion of sense; rather it unravels meaning to its degree zero, the point at which it has been rendered "systematically exempt." While one formulation of this particular emptiness might be the depthless surface of the postmodernist text, another might be something much closer to classical minimalism as articulated in the 1960s by figures such as Frank Stella, Donald Judd, Steve Reich, or Terry Riley, where unraveling is to be viewed as reduction, and the author is just one more element to be forced out of the text (once again, to be understood as literary, musical, or visual). One of the fascinations of minimalism is its determination, against all the philosophical odds, to make nothing, an aesthetic strategy which pits art against death. And one of the key discoveries of minimalism is that dead art doesn't exist: one can only reduce up to a point. If we think of this point as a Barthesian degree zero of meaning, it is very difficult to answer the question: What limits reduction? One would need to consider how it is exactly that a code is wrested from a subject. If, however, we think of the minimalist point of maximal reduction as coincident with the maximalist double contingency (the point at which the etiology of meaning and pleasure becomes impossibly ambiguous), one can indeed posit an answer. Just as the last redoubt of subjective experience is the body, so the degree zero of meaning is also the body; somehow a transference is affected between the symbolic links in the signifying chain and the somatic significance of the body. One can kill an author, but a text (that is *something* rather than nothing) will always have a body.

The minimalist body residing at the point of double contingency is, as we have suggested earlier, pregnant with its own maxima. The maximalist anatomization of the body produces a body-in-progress to set alongside the "Work in Progress" of Joyce and Zappa's Project Object. Even though it was intended as an act of revolution, Barthes's execution of the author, as we have seen, runs the risk of installing a neutral territory empty of meaning and thus void of political discourse. The maximalist body-in-progress, by contrast, functions as a guarantor of political content. It is clear, for example, in reviewing Zappa's work that its political content has always depended on its physicality and that this has much more to do with its maximalist credentials than a few references to blow jobs, noses, and feet. Maximalism is politically embodied and thus stands as a vital check on the bodiless ideology conjured up by Barthes and translated into the antipractice of political quietude by certain strains of postmodernism.

The degree zero of meaning lies beyond the body in an unimaginable nothing, it is bodilessness, and in the light of this discovery, the author may begin to look like something of an Aunt Sally. With this in mind, perhaps, we should consider a later essay by Barthes, on the French painter Bernard Réquichot, which goes a long way toward acknowledging this body beyond the author and its crucial location at the crossover point between the impossible zero of minimalism and the inconceivable everything of maximalism.

Minimalism into Maximalism Will Go

William Blake articulated the coincidence of minima and maxima with his famous quatrain:

To see a world in a grain of sand
And heaven in a wild flower,
Hold infinity in the palm of your hand
And eternity in an hour.[35]

And, as a child, Salvador Dalí would press on his eyeballs to make the angels come, imitating the gesture of the human fetus and countering his fear of the dark with benign intrauterine hallucinations. That we are all relatively myopic is clear from the paranoid imaginings which begin where the penetration of our senses tapers off, when one sight, sound, smell, taste, or touch fails to suggest another, thus creating a maximalist concentration of focus and endurance, which is also a nexus of pleasure and pain.

Minimalism in painting and the minimalist use of repetition in music seek to restrict our sensory receptions and test our aesthetic tolerance. How can one go on listening to or looking at the same thing? For Vico and Nietzsche and any other philosopher of eternal return, repetition does not pose a problem, since its pulse is so infinitesimally slow; in the absence of an enduring observer, objects and events can pass themselves off as unique. History itself would be a minimalist work if its pulse were accelerated to a rate which allowed us to experience it again and again, if we could be outside it and eternal. Since we are within it and finite, history for us is too full and must remain for the time being a maximalist paradigm. Music, painting, literature, however, are there to be endured.

In his essay on Bernard Réquichot, Barthes argues that "quite often in a single painter [there is] a whole history of painting";[36] by changing the levels of perception, for example, with the aid of a magnifying glass, "Nicholas de Staël is in three square centimetres of Cézanne."[37] What determines our experience of a work is the level at which we perceive it:

"isolate, enlarge, and treat a detail, you create a new work."[38] Minimalist music, according to Jonathan Bernard, can induce its listeners to effect a similar perceptual shift:

> The small number of events over time tends to focus the listener's attention intensely on each event, in all its particularity, thus resulting, from the minimalist point of view, in a music of parts rather than a whole.[39]

This is not pointillism, where each constituent dot remains a functional part of the whole, submissive and superficial; minimalism (an)atomizes its material, distilling particles which have *different* properties, which *depart from* the original unity. In this way, each particle may be a composition, or something else. The minimalist cell is a new maximalist body.

With typical raw intuition, Don Van Vliet may have stumbled across this process and formulated it for the amusement of his musicians in what he called his "exploding note theory." When learning "Flavour Bud Living" prior to the recording of the album *Doc at the Radar Station,* Captain Beefheart guitarist Gary Lucas took for his model an earlier version of the piece performed by John French on the *Bat Chain Puller* tapes. Van Vliet wasn't pleased and sent Lucas back to relearn it according to his new theory: "You play every note as if it has only a tangential relationship to the preceding note and the note that follows."[40] Each constituent part of the piece becomes semi-autonomous, it may detach itself from its syntagmatic functionality and become a tiny but expanding center of new experience—a paradigm. Our argument at this point trespasses on one of the classical dichotomies of formal philosophy which pitted Spinoza's monism against the monadology of Leibniz. Each note in "Flavour Bud Living" if played according to Van Vliet's exigencies would perhaps be a monad, not "windowless," as Leibniz suggested, but separated from its neighbors by a translucent veil, rendering relations oblique at best. Spinoza's monism admits only one substance: God. Everything else is merely a mode of this oneness: "Whatever is, is in God, and nothing can either be or be conceived without God."[41] In our musical model, God would be the unified work which imposes modality on its parts and arrogates to itself the exclusive right to exist. In critical parlance, this may be what we mean when we say that a work is "self-contained." In Leibniz's "best of all possible worlds," by contrast, God has created a maximum of independent substances; the world is exemplary precisely because it has been created on maximalist principles. In criticizing John French's performance as "too religious," Van Vliet may have thought that it made his composition sound too monistic (or even monastic), too much like a substantial God who is ineluctable essence and cannot be subdivided. He must have heard too much veneration in French's playing, a worshipful submission to a single spirit in the piece which checks its capacity to stimulate the ear in and into detail.

This theological cleavage is again audible in "Peon," which was performed by Bill Harkleroad and Mark Boston for the album *Lick My Decals Off, Baby* from 1970 and then rerecorded by the same duo in 1976 for the debut album of the group Mallard. In the *Decals* version, one of the first things we notice is how loud the bass is in relation to the guitar; they are not playing on the same dynamic level, and this discrepancy tends to emphasize both inexactitudes of timing and the piece's asymmetrical intervals, opening up a space for the ear to engage in creative decomposition. It would be interesting to know how deliberate this mixing strategy was and at whose insistence it was allowed to stand. The guitar itself sounds excessively dry and treble, with a lot of muting to cut off its resonance. There is a staccato sinfulness about the unison bends which appear after a definite pause about three-quarters of the way through the piece; and when Harkleroad plays the final descent, each of its eight notes sounds as if it has something separate to say. The Mallard version, by contrast, is ushered in with a few seconds of twittering birdsong. This pastoral backing track continues throughout, filling in the gaps between the notes, rounding off the edges, assuaging its peristaltic crises. The guitar and the bass are mixed together now, and the former has a mellow jazz tone traceable to the soft-stroking fingertip rather than the nit-picking nail. The reverb is up and those unison bends are played with a tasteful tremolo. Glissandi are introduced to spread the notes into the gaps with a mollified attack, most notably on the fourth of those last eight notes, which slips self-effacingly into its neighbor, executing the self-sacrifice of melody, an offering to the oneness of the whole. Don Van Vliet said that French's "Flavour Bud Living" "put the whole thing in heavy syrup,"[42] and with the Mallard "Peon" we have a second helping of the sticky.

If the mechanical aid to the shift of perceptual level in painting is the magnifying glass, in music it is the tape recorder, which not only records sequences of sound, but allows them to be played back at different speeds, helping the ear focus differently.[43] Don Van Vliet's assessment of *Decals* pinpoints the link between its aesthetics and the speed at which it is perceived:

> What the music is going at is complete absence. That's the way we did it. You can't think about that music. That music is moving so fast that if you think about it it's like watching a train go by and counting the cars.[44]

Here there is no danger of minimalist endurance, and the consequent effect is one of "total absence." Except it isn't, of course, Van Vliet is indulging in hyperbole; though there is an accelerated rate of event in the music, which certainly runs ahead of our ability to concentrate on any one moment. It is like the scary succession of ideas during insomnia, which defeats our efforts to pin down a single thought or image and endure it long enough to enter the expanded realm of dream, to count sheep, for example, rather than those impossibly speeding railway cars. It is very difficult to shift the level of our perception of *Decals,* perhaps even more so than was the case with its predecessor, *Trout Mask Replica.* This music is antithetical to minimalism, and it is therefore very intriguing that Van Vliet should associate it with an experience of emptiness, "total absence." If slowed down maybe it would begin to provoke those minimalist moments of escape into new multitudes, or at least some odd points of access for the ear's proactive penetrations. Or perhaps we should think of it rather as fairy music, that is to say, the kind of thing we might hear after shifting our level of perception of something which has been pressing on our eardrums, a minimalist piece, for example. Could Captain Beefheart be a sonic equivalent of Dalí's angels? Perhaps it is *coming from* as well as "going at" absence, reveling in what Samuel Beckett has called the "cyclic dynamism of the intermediate,"[45] a phrase which might be usefully set alongside Van Vliet's definition of painting as "fulfilling the absence of space between the opposite meanings,"[46] and which also suggests the technical phenomenon of interference, caused by the intersection of two or more wave systems. In any case, we begin to see here the logic of repetition within the minimalist aesthetic, for what better way is there to slow down the rate of progression of a piece of music than to begin to repeat its parts?[47]

The close scrutiny of minimalist repetition invites the listener to rehear music. After a certain number of habitual expectations are confounded, the listener and the music arrive at a point of double contingency where it is impossible to decide whether pleasure is a concomitant of meaning or vice versa, where art is reduced to art matter and incorporated into the body-in-progress. Moving from Vico to Bruno the Nolan and still concerning himself with the poetics of *Finnegans Wake,* Beckett reminded us that "the maxima and minima of particular contraries are one and indifferent."[48] Joyce's writing, like *Lick My Decals Off, Baby,* moves too fast whereas minimalism moves too slow, but both are maximalist in that they tap into frequencies beyond the normal perceptual range, at the low end or at the high end, where extremes of contraries meet and structured response collapses into an urgency of matter. Blake's fairies, Dalí's angels, and the dreamer of *Finnegans Wake* are all avatars of the body-beyond-the-author which presides over this point of double contingency, plying its excruciating pleasures. They are not metaphors, since they inhere at a point of concentration, equivalent to Zappa's Big Note, where the space and time necessary to see one thing in terms of another is no longer available. The shift of the level of perception is now revealed to be a rematerialization of the language, of the music, in which what you hear is what you hear *and* everything else, miraculously disrobed of the acculturated vestment designed to fast-track pleasure at the expense of its painful other. It is the "special art [made] in an environment hostile to dreamers" announced by Zappa in the communiqué published by the *International Times* in 1971, and its dreamer, along with everything else, is to be taken as literally as possible.

The Last Laugh

Responding to a question about his ability to combine emotion, political commentary, beauty, and humor, Zappa replied, "You can reduce it to this—you can ask this question: Is it possible to laugh while fucking? I think yes."[49] And this image of the coordinated pleasures of mirth and sex recenters alienated pleasure as a self-present maxima of joy. Zappa's key aesthetic question—"Does humor belong in music?" (to cite the title of a live album released in 1986)—may be taken, then, as an enquiry into the capacity of the maximalist body to pass from its melancholy hysteria into a state of coordinated pleasure, a self-perpetuating jouissance of sex-laughs.

In his first four albums Zappa was determined to establish a distinction between freaks and hippies. By June 1967 and the release of the Beatles'

Sergeant Pepper, the hippie ethic had reduced the body to an instrument of self-transcendence, sex had become peace and love, and the immediacy of humor had been displaced by a drug-fueled quest for spiritual "truth." *Freak Out* (1966), *Absolutely Free* (1967), *Lumpy Gravy* (1967), and particularly *We're Only In It for the Money* (1968) reintroduced sex and laughter in the form of satire. The musical laugh became an act of sociological aggression in "The Chrome-Plated Megaphone of Destiny," *Money*'s extraordinary finale. After two minutes of musique concrète and abstract piano, the track degenerates into a cacophony of forced hilarity which is not laughter but the *sound of* laughter. This burst of antihilarity sums up the condition of the body in hippie ideology, which imposes an ethic of enjoyment. Staged laughter, like choreographed applause, is a sure sign of political subjection. Zappa's satire attempts a subtle reversal of this situation by turning laughter into a joke. Henri Bergson observed that

> Les attitudes, gestes et mouvements du corps humain sont risibles dans l'exact mesure où ce corps nous fait penser à une simple mécanique.[50]

and the body laughing at laughter updates Bergson's image of the ridiculous body as dysfunctional machine into a body enjoying its own social trauma. It hystericizes hippiedom by reintroducing the principle of pain. Similarly, Zappa's sex satire might be seen as a reintroduction of sexual suffering into the ideology of universal love, which was and remains a nightmare of social conformism. Without pain, which is to say real pain and not just its theoretical possibility, pleasure is not pleasurable. In the light of this rediscovery, Zappa's coordinated sex-laugh appears as a jouissance of pain, hysteria brought to orgasm. Is this, in the end, what the maximalist body-in-progress is progressing toward?

The most disturbing laughs in "The Chrome-Plated Megaphone of Destiny" are those which seem to return to their point of departure after playing out a permutated series of pitches and intonations. Since self-accomplishment requires the bliss of selective ignorance, these serial laughs express deep skepticism in the ability of the body-in-progress to ever bring itself off. Maximalism, these laughs suggest, obsessionalizes the subject at the same time as it hystericizes it, undercutting the laugh which laughs at the forced laugh until it in turn becomes laughable. The very circularity of this reverberating laughter precludes the coordination upon which orgasm depends. Zappa's work, in defiance of postmodernist pastiche, insists that every act of satire it performs may become the subject of a similar act. In such a system the height of gratification becomes the successful avoidance of pain, characterized by the obsessional's delaying of orgasm until exactly the right moment. The prime moment to come is, of course, under constant revision, which is to say that orgasm is constantly deferred. The maximalist diffusion of significance across an ever-broadening mass of apparently significant detail creates the perfect context for these delaying tactics. While hysteria might be defined as a repossession of the body carried too far, the obsessional body must be held in abeyance, hovering somewhere between presence and absence; its pleasures can only be provisional. The psychosomatic symptom is held in check by something which might be called "symptomatic thought,"[51] or bodiless anxiety, where the obsessional's need to delay the last laugh of hysterical orgasm encounters its powerlessness and enters a crisis. And this chaotic interplay of neurotic structures, where the laughing body slugs it out with the bodiless laugh, typifies the dialectical instability of maximalism and further differentiates it from the indifferent quietudes of postmodernism. The maximalist is like a gambler whose gains and losses follow each other so incontinently that they blur into an undifferentiated medium where the euphoria of victory coexists with the misery of defeat driven by the double charge of excitement and anxiety. It is this overreaching wager of hysterico-obsessional creativity that the receiver of maximalist art plays out for real in his or her body.

The self-conscious humor of the Mothers of Invention fed and concealed Zappa's real interest in the aesthetic potential of the dysfunctional or hysterical laugh. The low-highpoint of this high-lowness was probably the "Uncle Meat" film where Zappa presides over a succession of insanely unfunny scenarios played out in large part by Don Preston and Phyllis Altenhouse. The film inaugurates an aesthetic category—maximalist boredom—which works by spinning out the impossibly inane and pointless through a technique of deferred gratification. Titillation is raised to the power of hysteria and then labored obsessively. As Zappa pushes his juxtapositions through tedium, hysteria, and beyond, one loses the will to recuperate detail, and still the film continues. "Uncle Meat" is a collage which raises key questions about that particular mode of composition. As handled by Zappa, it becomes incipient sprawl, and its maximalism emerges as precisely a failure to determine content, an aesthetic white-out played to a sound track of sonic irritants. The refusal to develop key phrases such as "using the chicken to measure it" and "it makes me hot" contribute to the effect of wastage, as if Zappa is squandering a whole aesthetic form in his pursuit of the epically unfunny. The feeling is that instead of composing in time, Zappa has thrown things together in an improvised arrangement designed to last forever, a procedure that seems to belie the minute accumulation of conceptual continuity in the Project Object while mocking the transtemporal concentration of the Big Note.

The inside-outside on the edge laugh in Zappa, which encapsulates the maximalist body, represents the rhythm of response we have described in this essay, with its vertiginous plunge from miraculous gain to catastrophic loss and back again, while at the same time mocking it with an audaciously recessive form of metafiction. In the light of this phenomenal laugh one might even be tempted to risk a universalizing statement and suggest that the origin of maximalist art is the antisocial impulse to go on joking regardless of the potential for real or feigned amusement.

Notes

1. John Barth, "A Few Words About Minimalism," *New York Times Book Review,* December 28, 1986, 1.

2. Ibid, 1.

3. Takayoshi Ishiwari, "The Body That Speaks: Donald Barthelme's *The Dead Father* as Installation," (master's thesis, Osaka University, 1996), http://www.asahi-net.or.jp/~KP7T-ISWR/.

4. Varèse used four hundred loudspeakers to perform his "Poème électronique" at the 1958 Brussels World's Fair.

5. David Jaffe, "Orchestrating the Chimera—Musical Hybrids, Technology, and the Development of a 'Maximalist' Musical Style," *Leonardo Music Journal:* 5 (1995), 11–18.

6. Frank Zappa with Peter Occhiogrosso, *The Real Frank Zappa Book* (London: Picador: 1990), 167.

7. Ibid.

8. Ben Watson, *The Negative Dialectics of Poodle Play* (London: Quartet Books, 1994), 358.

9. Cited in William Harris, *The Poetry and Poetics of Amiri Baraka—The Jazz Aesthetic* (Columbia: University of Missouri Press, 1985), 174.

10. Zappa, *Real Frank Zappa,* 88.

11. Ibid., 189.

12. Gilles Deleuze, *The Fold: Leibniz and the Baroque,* trans. Tom Conley (Minneapolis: University of Minnesota Press, 1992), 5. Like its famous cousin, the rhizome (a seemingly endless series of nodes and intersections, unlike the tree, which has a main trunk from which the branches and roots grow), Deleuze's baroque has no actual or conceptual center.

13. Ibid., 112.

14. Yago Conde, *Architecture of the Indeterminacy* (Barcelona: Actar, 2000), 253. We are grateful to Karen Mac Cormack for drawing our attention to Conde's writings.

15. Deleuze, *Fold,* 189.

16. Don Menn, ed., *Zappa!* special, unnumbered issue of *Guitar Player* (1992): 60.

17. Deleuze, *Fold,* 112.

18. See also Barthes's definition of the baroque as "a progressive contradiction between the unit and the whole, an art in which the extension is not added but multiplied, in short, the width of an acceleration." Roland Barthes, *Essais critiques* (Paris: Seuil, 1964), 108, my translation.

19. Deleuze, *Fold,* 164.

20. Ibid., 166.

21. Ibid., 168.

22. *A Chance Operation: The John Cage Tribute,* various artists, 2 compact discs, KOCH International #7238, 1993.

23. Cited in Deleuze, *Fold,* 170.

24. Deleuze, *Fold,* 109.

25. Ibid., 166.

26. Gilles Deleuze and Félix Guattari, trans. Mark Seem, Helen R. Lane, and Robert Hurley, *Anti-Oedipus: Capitalism and Schizophrenia* (Minneapolis: University of Minnesota Press, 1985), xxiii. Opposed to the (negative) Lacanian dialectic of lack and desire, Deleuze and Guattari's *Anti-Oedipus* proposes a theory of "desiring-production," which they define as a "pure multiplicity, that is to say, an affirmation that is irreducible to any sort of unity" (46).

27. Zappa, *Real Frank Zappa,* 139.

28. This, incidentally, is by no means a contemporary, or even a modern, phenomenon. The best-known maximalist artist of the Renaissance, François Rabelais, had already understood that only an aesthetics of corpo-reality is liable to multiply the vectors of perception while allowing the body to become its own food for conceptual thought and artistic experimentation. For Rabelais, maximalism allies itself with the grotesque as it is essentially linked with bodily excesses. As Mikhail Bakhtin reminds us, the carnivalesque insistence on bodily functions and the liberation of instinct, far from being degrading, is meant to express the vital energies of humankind. Indeed, Rabelais' "grotesque realism" has a regenerative effect as the reduction of all aspects of human life to primary bodily functions "digs a bodily grave for a new birth," conceiving of new possibilities arising from the body's nether regions.

29. Mikhail Bakhtin, *Rabelais and His World* (Bloomington: Indiana University Press, 1984), 26.

30. Ibid., 26–27.

31. Roland Barthes, "The Death of the Author," trans. Geoff Bennington, in *Modern Criticism and Theory: A Reader,* ed. David Lodge (Harlow, Essex: Longman, 1988), 168.

32. Barthes, "Death of Author," 167.

33. It also, perhaps, helps to explain the continuing resistance to the post-structuralist critique of character in *Finnegans Wake.* Though HCE, ALP, Shem, Shaun, and Issy have been subjected to various deconstructions since the 1970s (see, e.g., Margot Norris's *The Decentered Universe of Finnegans Wake,* Roland McHugh's *The Sigla of Finnegans Wake,* and John Bishop's *Joyce's Book of the Dark*), they still figure strongly in most attempts to read the text. As presences, archetypes, pseudopersonalities, subjective traces, they imply the literary character, which in turn, at however many degrees of abstraction, implies a body, whether that of the author, the reader, or some ontologically uncertain element residing in between.

34. Barthes, "Death of Author," 171.

35. William Blake, "Auguries of Innocence," in *Collected Poems* (New York: Longman, 1971), 585.

36. Roland Barthes, *The Responsibility of Forms,* trans. Richard Howard (Berkeley and Los Angeles: University of California Press, 1991), 228.

37. Ibid. The opening lines of Captain Beefheart's "The Blimp" (on *Trout Mask Replica*) seem to endorse Barthes's observation with reference to its own perceptual exigencies: "Master master / This is recorded thru uh fly's ear / 'n you have t'have a fly's eye to see it."

38. Ibid., 223.

39. Jonathan W. Bernard, "The Minimalist Aesthetic in the Plastic Arts and in Music," *Perspectives of New Music* 31, no. 1 (1993): 86–132.

40. Quoted in Mike Barnes, *Captain Beefheart* (London: Quartet Books, 2000), 273.

41. John Wild, ed., *Spinoza Selections* (London: Scribner's, 1930), 108–13. The selections from the *Ethics* are taken from W. H. White's 1927 translation.

42. Quoted in Barnes, *Captain Beefheart,* 273.

43. Douglas Gordon has attempted something similar in video with his slow-motion projection of classic films. His "24 Hour Psycho" challenged the audience to endure a marathon viewing, while offering them the chance to see the fairies in every frame.

44. Quoted in Barnes, *Captain Beefheart,* 336.

45. Samuel Beckett, "Dante . . . Bruno. Vico . . Joyce," in *Our Exagmination Round His Factifcation for Incamination of "Work in Progress"* (London: Faber and Faber, 1929), 16.

46. Quoted in Barnes, *Captain Beefheart,* 331.

47. That Van Vliet was conversant with at least some American minimalist

music is evident from his quotation of Steve Reich's "Come Out" in "Moonlight on Vermont": "Come out to show them" (quoted in Barnes, *Captain Beefheart,* 94–95).

48. Beckett, "Dante . . . Bruno. Vico . . Joyce," 6.

49. Quoted in Menn, *Zappa!* 38.

50. "The attitudes, gestures and movements of the human body are risible to the precise extent to which this body reminds us of a simple mechanism." Henri Bergson, *Le Rire* (Paris: Quadrige, 1991), 22–23.

51. The term was suggested by Julia Kristeva's "symptôme de la pensée." See Kristeva, "L'obsessionel et sa mère," in *Les Nouvelles Maladies de l'âme* (Paris: Fayard, 1993), 65.

Part Three : **Conjunctions**

Metaphor: The Color of Being

Ricardo L. Nirenberg

Brief Description of the Problem

I will ask two apparently opposite questions. First, What is the truth *about* metaphor? or simply, What is metaphor? I will examine the modern definitions and find them wanting: they will turn out to define something else, namely, scientific or mathematical model. Admittedly, there are perils involved in all symbolic actions, but I will try to show that the typical peril in the use of models is sharply different from that which is typical in the use of metaphor: that will justify saying that the two are different. The difference marks the boundary between science and poetry.

Entirely absent from the formal languages, metaphors, as opposed to models, are unnecessary or peripheral to scientific discourse. Yet an acquaintance with contemporary scientific notions is necessary when it comes to deciding, *assuming it is possible to come to a decision,* whether or not any given expression is metaphoric. In the end, however, I will not advance a new definition but even suggest that a true definition of metaphor is not possible or that, at least, it would be the unlikely equivalent of making poetry entirely translatable into scientific discourse.

The second question is, Can a metaphor be *about* truth? or in other words, Can metaphor express how things are? And if so, what kind of things? Here I agree, up to a point and under one condition, with the classical answer: metaphors convey the colors of thought more properly, the colors of being or the colors of truth. The condition is that we set aside our Cartesian prejudices about color and about the relations between reason and the affects.

Finally, and in light of the previous analysis, I situate metaphor within, and with respect to, contemporary poetics: the latter, I propose, aspires to the former's effacement.

Frege on Formal and Natural Languages

Ramón Lull in the thirteenth century, and later, at the infancy of modern science, Bishop Wilkins, then Leibniz, imagined a formal, universal language; Gottlob Frege was the first actually to create one, in his *Begriffsschrift* of 1879. His purpose was to show that arithmetic is reducible to logic (in Kantian terms, that arithmetic contains only a priori analytic judgments) and to that end he deemed it necessary to create a language in which he could write all arithmetic as well as all logical propositions. The so-called natural languages do not lend themselves to that purpose, chiefly on account of their ambiguity: an everyday proposition may have different, even contradictory meanings, and it may be true or false according to how we interpret it. If for instance we say, "It's raining," it can be true this minute but false an hour later, which logic forbids: this is why Frege insisted that propositions are not complete until, among other things, their temporality is made explicit. Signs, and the concepts they refer to, must be forever stable. Whether or not that is possible is a question I am not going to tackle, nor the problem of the relations between logic and time. In any case, with the work cited before, Frege did usher in modern mathematical logic together with modern analytic philosophy, and that despite the failure of his reductive project. (Arithmetic propositions are not all analytic; the most basic—the principle of mathematical induction—turns out to be synthetic, as Henri Poincaré repeatedly pointed out.)

Frege's insistence upon univocity and lack of ambiguity in signs and concepts expresses one of the important differences between contemporary Anglo-American and Continental philosophies. Hegel in his *Logic,* section 96, defining his most fundamental concept, *aufheben,* notes with satisfaction that in German the word has two contradictory meanings—"to annul" and "to preserve"—which goes to show (he adds) the speculative spirit of the German language, superior to the vulgar, nonphilosophic "it's got to be either one or the other." For Frege and his school, what Hegel calls "speculative" is nothing but error, obscurity, or ambiguity that ought to be decided.

Habitually, mathematicians use some hybrid tool for communicating; to use a strictly formal language, either Frege's or a more modern one, would be far too prolix. The possibility of translation to a formal language, however, is always there, and with it the possibility of ascertaining the validity of the inferences and of settling any doubts, which cannot but arise if we let ourselves be guided by intuition. Such linguistic machinery is precisely what Leibniz had in mind, so that in case of doubt one could always say, "*Monsieur, calculons.*" In other words, in relation to logic and mathematics, formal languages are what gold, silver, or hard currency have traditionally been for paper money: a backing ensuring the stability of exchange and generating trust. Henceforth I will call "scientific" any discourse which aspires to some share in the formal backing of logic and mathematics.

Not only did Frege create the first full-fledged formal language, he also had interesting things to say about natural languages. In the essays written toward the end of his life, between 1918 and 1923, and published in English in 1977 under the title *Logical Investigations,* he distinguished thought proper from what he called "the colour (*Färbung*) of its expression." The beauty, but not the truth-value, of a sentence may depend on its color, and Frege insists (perhaps in allusion to Keats's famous line) that beauty and truth are *not* the same thing. Science, knowledge, present a world in black and white; the humanistic disciplines and the arts bedeck it with colors, which belong to psychology, not to logic. Frege's doctrine, then, sharply separates two realms: on one side, form, knowledge, logic and philosophy, objectivity, exactness, literality, *facts,* and on the other, color (a traditional metaphor for whatever is not form), the passions and the affects, metaphor, subjectivity, vagueness, and psychology.[1]

Empiricism and psychologism (e.g., J. S. Mill) maintains that logic and mathematics contain nothing but rules inductively derived from our experience and are therefore but chapters of psychology. Besides the breach that doctrine makes in the great walls of *epistēmē,* through which right away skepticism and relativism irrupt, there is the obvious circularity: logic, maintained Frege and the champions of the *logos,* cannot itself depend on psychology, the *logos* of the psyche. Combating psychologism, providing and defending independent grounds for logic and science, was the purpose of Frege's distinctions and separations, and, to a large extent and because of Frege's influence, Husserl's ultimate purpose too, from the *Logische Untersuchungen* on.

Some Alleged Definitions of Metaphor

Let us begin with Max Black's "More About Metaphor" (1977).[2] The thirty years prior, according to Black, saw the publication of at least four thousand works on the subject but only two definitions of metaphor therein. Again according to Black, the two traditional (and inadequate) definitions are "substitution" and "comparison." The former states that a metaphor substitutes for a set of literal propositions; the latter requires that those propositions present a likeness or analogy between two concepts. Black proposes a new definition called "interaction": we have two subjects (his example being Wallace Stevens's "Society Is a Sea"), and we "project" on the "primary subject" (society) certain "associated implications" predicable of the "secondary subject" (sea). This means that the utterer "selects, emphasizes, suppresses, and organizes" features of the primary subject by applying to it statements "isomorphic" to the associated implications of the secondary subject. Interaction occurs when that selection of features of the primary subject causes the utterer or listener to select, in turn, features of the secondary one, and vice versa. Thus, although Black doesn't bother to do so, we could use his example and be a little more specific: the sea is vast and fluid, on occasion quiet, yet on other occasions agitated—so are societies (at least those of the "open" sort); on the other hand (and here comes the "interaction"), society is rife with antagonistic interests: How about the sea? Yes, obviously: the larger fish devours the smaller one. Moreover, the sea is salty—well, one can't really say that a society is salty (except perhaps the Attic), so this one doesn't seem to work, let's forget about salt—and so on.

In Black's "interaction" resonates Frege's thought: not in vain did the Cornell professor translate the Jena professor into English. The notion of isomorphism, a fundamental one in mathematics ever since the nineteenth century, is no less fundamental among the structuralist thinkers of the twentieth, and I would go so far as to bet that it has been the most useful notion to the mind of those who aspire to "raise" the humanities to a more scientific level and to replace "feeling" by "truth." Let's recall: isomorphism is a one-to-one function between two sets A and B, respecting the structures that may be defined in both sets; the simplest case is when there is no structure in either set, and then an isomorphism is just a one-to-one correspondence, also known as an equivalence[3] between *A* and *B*. An isomorphism is always an interaction in the aforementioned sense, since it goes back and forth, from *A* to *B* and also from *B* to *A;* it is invertible. For Black, *A* and *B* are the "implication complexes" (some of the possible predicates of the respective subjects), and his "projections" are just like mathematical isomorphisms, with one important difference: the latter are clearly and distinctly defined, while those metaphoric "projections" are "a mixed lot." Those two words, "mixed lot," are, needless to say, a metaphor to convey vagueness in the sets, the elements, and the functions, and Black concludes, "Ambiguity is a necessary by-product of the metaphor's suggestiveness."[4] But if that is so, if the suggestiveness, that is, the quality of the metaphor, depends on its ambiguity, one may ask (without even considering the loose and metaphoric word "by-product") what's gained by trying to define metaphor *more logico,* I mean by using notions such as sets and isomorphisms. It would seem that in all those endeavors the aim is to point out that up to this point the thing is logical; beyond, mystery reigns—here lions roam. In the case of metaphor, however, as in many others, what matters most is the mystery and the lions; even so, as we shall see shortly, it was the smaller, logical part that misled Black into confusing metaphor and scientific model.[5]

Whatever the value of Black's interpretation of "Society Is a Sea," let us now reread the most famed page of Spanish prose, the beginning of the First Part of *Don Quixote:* "In a village of La Mancha . . . " Everything there is literal, positive, not a single live metaphor, until Cervantes tells us that the hidalgo went mad: *se le secó el cerebro*—his brains dried up. There, for the first time, loud and clear, a metaphor resounds; how could we explain it using Black's "interaction"? We should determine the two "subjects," their "implication complexes," and their correspondence or isomorphism. There isn't much to choose from: the primary subject must be the hidalgo's brain, or perhaps the hidalgo and his brain, and the secondary subject must be dryness, or the dry, or perhaps more accurately, the process of becoming dry. As for the latter's implication complex, it doesn't look too complex since a loss of humidity is the only thing that's implied by becoming dry. Then we should try to ascertain what it means for a brain to lose humidity, and we could plausibly conclude that it means that the brain becomes rigid, sclerotic, monomaniacal. . . . But where do we encounter any interaction here? How could an examination of the "implication complex" of the hidalgo's brain conceivably lead us to find other predicates or characteristics of becoming dry? Black's "interaction" doesn't seem to bear any meaningful relation to Cervantes's metaphor. But it gives me the occasion for the following observation. Supposing medical science in the sixteenth century (about which I know next to nothing) taught that madness was sometimes caused by a loss of humidity of the brain, that what today is a metaphor was not so when it was written: it was rather a literal expression of a fact, just like Cervantes telling us that the hidalgo ate lentils on Fridays. Stretching it a little, should technology, five centuries hence, transform our cities into masses of salt water and us into some kind of sea animals (or vice versa), Wallace Stevens's "Society Is a Sea" will cease being a metaphor. Briefly put, there is no live metaphor when we are describing a fact or phenomenon according to current scientific canons and common beliefs.

Let us now briefly examine John R. Searle's definition.[6] According to Searle, words and sentences have two meanings: the one we find in the dictionary and the speaker's idiosyncratic one. Those two meanings do not always coincide; we have metaphor whenever in a phrase of the type "*S* is *P*" the dictionary meanings of *P* do not fit the dictionary meanings of *S*. Thus, the condition I proposed as necessary—that a metaphor should not be a description according to current scientific canons and common beliefs—Searle takes as sufficient too, hence as a definition, provided we replace current scientific canons with the latest edition of the dictionary. Nevertheless, as soon as he tries to explain how the hearer may succeed in recognizing and interpreting a metaphor, Searle reaches back to the traditional theory of comparison, already referred to earlier: the hearer must find out how, and in what way, *S* and *P* are similar. In the end, Searle's criteria do not contribute (as far as I can see) anything new.

George Lakoff's "The Contemporary Theory of Metaphor" appears only in the second edition of *Metaphor and Thought* (1993). Having warned us that all fundamental works in the contemporary theory of metaphor were published after 1979 (first edition of *Metaphor and Thought*), Lakoff lists them; perhaps it would be naive to show any surprise at the fact that almost all of those works were written by Lakoff or his collaborators and disciples. As for Lakoff's definition of metaphor, it is the same as Black's but maimed. Here metaphor is any system of "mappings" or functions between "conceptual domains," without requiring, as Black does, that those functions be isomorphisms, that is, one-to-one and invertible: forget "interaction."[7] Perhaps the originality lies here: for Lakoff, metaphor is *not* a linguistic phenomenon; the mapping occurs between sets of concepts or mental objects, in other words, between signifieds, not signifiers. His examples are the logical concepts of category, of being a part of a whole, of implication and syllogism—all of which, he contends, are metaphors originating in another class of concepts, that of containers in space. Logic follows from topology.[8] Evidently this cannot mean that topology *as a science* gives birth to logic as a science, for it would be putting the cart before the horse; it can only mean the empiricist and psychologist stricture that all basic logical concepts originate in our sensory experience. We experiment with containers: we see that in general if a container *A* contains another, *B*, and the latter contains still another, *C*, then it so happens that *A* contains *C*—whence we build a logic where categories, classes, and propositions are "like" containers, and where "*p* implies *q* and *q* implies *s*" implies "*p* implies *s*."

Here's what's immediately surprising: (1) Lakoff does not seem to be aware that, far from constituting a "contemporary theory" (post-1979), those doctrines go back at least to the British empiricists and that they present problems noted by Frege and Husserl, among others. (2) According to him, time itself is a metaphor, "at least in English."[9] How in English? Didn't he establish that metaphor is not a linguistic phenomenon? (3) Just like our logical concepts, those of time, he maintains, originate in space concepts. From what space concept comes the most typical temporal notion, that of the "new"? (4) All abstract as well as all emotional concepts come, via metaphor, he says, from spatial ones. I must confess, with a modicum of metaphoric shame, that I fail to conceive how "four," and how "fear" or "sadness," could be metaphors, spatial or otherwise. Lakoff discards from Descartes the thinking stuff and retains only the res extensa.

Metaphors Are Not Essential in the Sciences: A Glimpse at the Perils of Poetry

Several essays in *Metaphor and Thought* aim at showing that certain metaphors determine the direction the sciences will take. To this class belong Richard Boyd's "Metaphor and Theory Change: What Is 'Metaphor' a Metaphor For?" and Michael J. Reddy's "The Conduit Metaphor." It hardly needs observing that we have here a favorite theme of epistemological relativism, to show that scientific truths depend on the choice of a few metaphors. But both Boyd's and Reddy's examples are taken exclusively from sciences in statu nascendi, such as cognitive psychology, where metaphors taken from cybernetics, information theory, and computer science abound.

As is well known, in the new sciences metaphor is often used to name new and previously nameless concepts, that is, as catachresis. Very early in Greek geometry, the circle was named with the Greek word for wheel (*kúklos*) and its center with the word for sting or prick (*kéntron*), since there's where the sharp, stationary point of the compass is located. Such metaphors or catachreses are neutral and safe: geometry would not have changed significantly had the circle and its center been named with other words. Some will scoff at my calling *any* metaphor neutral and safe and will say there's no such thing; yet in the essays about the role of metaphors in science and philosophy, including the brilliant one by Derrida,[10] I have never seen even a vague outline of what philosophy, say, would be like, or how it would differ from the available one, had certain philosophemes—such as "concept," "comprehension," "metaphor" itself—been named otherwise, from other visual or tactile metaphors.

It is plausible that certain metaphors in the new sciences could be dangerous, misleading, or retarding; such may have been, I imagine, the Pythagorean notion that odd numbers are male and even numbers female. Regarding information science, Reddy maintains that the common confusion between "message" (the non-random choice of one alternative among several) and "signal" (the encoding of that choice in some physical stuff—light, electric currents, sounds, and so forth—which can be kept or sent) has been catastrophic for our society. I find his arguments unconvincing. Using "message" for "signal" (or vice versa) looks much more like a metonymy than a metaphor. And besides, what greater confusion—or rather conflation and wedding—of message and signal is known to us than poetry? Reddy's article, then, can be read as still another attack on poetry.

But let us go back to mathematics. There, certain metaphors may be useful; I am thinking of Leibniz's notation for derivatives, written as fractions, which helps remind us of certain rules; but we will see shortly that this is rather an example of model than of metaphor. How about catachresis in math? Since new concepts are constantly being introduced, catachresis is much in demand; yet no one in his or her right mind would affirm that the future of mathematics depends on the choice of names. For example, about fifty years ago an important mathematical concept was introduced and called "sheaf" (French *faisceau,* Italian *fascio*); since, as is well known, the word "fascism" comes from Italian *fascio,* "sheaf," the symbol of fascism, those who believe that metaphoric values govern theoretical consequences could conclude, conceivably, that sheaf theory is fascistic. Such a conclusion would be childish and absurd, yet no more childish and absurd than so many other pronouncements coming from extreme epistemological relativists.[11]

Briefly put, in mathematics metaphor is useful but never essential, because one can always replace a metaphorical expression by its formal equivalent, and there are no metaphors in formal languages. When in a formal language we say, "*S* is *P,*" it never means that *S* is "like" *P* in some ways but not in others, like a portrait is a "likeness" of a sitter: it rather means that we can replace *S* by *P* or vice versa in any proposition of that language without altering its truth-value. As for science in general, since I take scientific discourse to be one which aspires to the backing of a formal language, we may conclude that in the sciences metaphor plays only an ancillary, inessential, and temporary role; it is not a conveyor of truth. Yet, could it be a source of error?

Scientific Models and Their Perils

The previous question leads to an inquiry into the role of scientific models. Was Bohr uttering a metaphor when, at the birth of atomic physics, he explained that the atom is a miniature planetary system? The contraptions of sticks and many-sized, colored balls which chemists use to think about complex molecules, are those extralinguistic metaphors? A nearly total confusion of the two notions, metaphor and model, is the rule in the aforementioned works by Black, Boyd, Reddy, and still others, so much so that Black writes:

> I am now impressed, as I was insufficiently so when composing *Metaphor,* by the tight connections between the notions of models and metaphors. Every implication-complex supported by a metaphor's secondary subject, I now think, is a model of the ascriptions imputed to the primary subject: Every metaphor is the tip of a submerged model.[12]

Such confusion calls for an examination of our notion of scientific model, and of how it might differ from metaphor. For that, we won't have to contend with atoms, molecules, and planetary systems nor with the innumerable models populating the history of the sciences; it will be enough for us to concentrate on the essential and paradigmatic model, which is, besides, probably the first in time, namely, the geometric diagram.

Suppose we want to prove, for instance, the Euclidean proposition, which states that the sum of the three interior angles of any triangle is two right angles.[13] I get hold of pencil and paper and draw a triangle, preferably neither right-angled nor equilateral nor isosceles, since I want to prove the proposition for *any* triangle, not just for special ones. I assign letters *A, B,* and *C* to the vertices and set out to thinking. In Black's terms, my drawing or diagram is my secondary subject, the primary one being the ideal object "triangle." Now, I don't pay any attention to the fact that my paper is, say, white, and my penciled lines gray, nor to the fact that those lines are neither truly lines nor truly straight: those predicates of my diagram, of the secondary subject, are not the ones I must project (to use, again, Black's term) on the primary subject. In contrast, I should project, for example, that the sides *AB* and *BC* meet at the point *B.* The question of what must be projected and what not is the first important thing we learn in school geometry, yet it is rarely taken as a theme for reflection.

However that may be, presently a good idea comes to mind: to draw the line passing through *C* and parallel to the side *AB.* Where does such an idea come from? Certainly not from the secondary subject (from it, I could have gotten the geometrically silly idea of measuring angles with a protractor, which would never lead to an apodictic proof). It comes from the primary subject, the ideal object "triangle" which dwells in the formal conceptual system we call "Euclidean geometry," with its signs, definitions, notions, axioms, postulates. Euclid's fifth postulate allows me to affirm that through the point *C* there is one, and only one, line parallel to *AB.* It would be wasting time to try to *draw* it as thin, straight, and strictly parallel to *AB* as possible; the existence and uniqueness of that line is a predicate of my primary subject, and that is all I need. I will not go on with the well-known proof; what is important to note is that if my primary subject, the ideal triangle, dwelled in a different conceptual system—for example, a non-Euclidean geometry, where the fifth postulate does not hold—it would still have been *possible* to draw on my paper that line through *C* and parallel to *AB,* but it would not have been *legitimate* to do so, since it wouldn't have been a projection from the primary subject, where either there is no such line or there are infinitely many.

The previous illustration makes it transparent, I hope, how the predicates of the two subjects interact, how we pass or project from one "implication-complex" to the other, a to-and-fro which, with prudent attention and luck, leads us to truth. Black's "interactive" definition of metaphor is a good definition of scientific model (which explains the intimate connection he sees between metaphor and model, as in the earlier quotation). The question is, of course, whether Black's is a good definition of metaphor. I think not. To justify my opinion I will begin by noting the essential peril of models: they may lead us to truth, but only with much prudence and luck. It is notorious, even disgraceful: the proof of the very first proposition in Euclid is false. "To construct an equilateral triangle on a given segment"—to do that, given the segment *AB*, Euclid draws a circle with center *A* and radius *AB* and another circle with center *B* and the same radius; these two actions are legitimated by the postulates. Then he calls *C* and *D* the points where the two circles meet, and eureka! the two triangles *ABC* and *ABD* are equilateral. But what was obvious to Euclid as he gazed at his diagram (his secondary subject) is not necessarily true in the primary subject, the formal system of Euclidean geometry with its axioms and such, where nothing warrants that the two circles meet. Euclid projected, wrongly, a predicate of his secondary subject onto a nonexistent one of his primary subject, and twenty-two centuries passed until David Hilbert finally provided a formal system in which such projection is correct and the two circles actually meet.

We cannot fairly impute imprudence or clumsiness to Euclid and all the geometers after him and up to the twentieth century. Rather, when we are dealing with a good scientific model, there is always a strong temptation to project too many predicates of the secondary subject on the primary one—or, to put it differently, "to take one thing for another" *too far*. That is the peril of all good scientific models; now we may ask, is it also the peril of good metaphors?

The Peril of Metaphors

According to Augustine, the most grievous dangers and "a wretched slavery" attend the misinterpretation of metaphors.

> For when what is said figuratively is taken as if it were said literally, it is understood in a carnal manner. And nothing is more fittingly called the death of the soul than when that in it which raises it above the brutes, the intelligence namely, is put in subjection to the flesh by a blind adherence to the letter.[14]

I tremble for Jorge Luis Borges's soul, when I remember that late in 1967, addressing a large audience at Harvard,[15] and commenting on Robert Frost's famous lines, "The woods are lovely, dark and deep, / But I have promises to keep, / And miles to go before I sleep, / And miles to go before I sleep," he affirmed that the third of those lines is literal—miles a measure of space and sleep just sleep—but the fourth and last is metaphoric, miles now measuring time and sleep standing for death. How did Borges know that it is not the other way around? We could say the first "And miles . . . " slowly, with a weary, melancholy voice, and then, after a pause, shrug our shoulders, giddyap the horse, and while we spank along, say the second one, in brighter tones. The difference is genre-deep. In Borges's account, Frost's poem is a late, perfected example of German romantic poetry; but there is, I think, more of the traditional New Englander endurance in the reading I propose. Whichever you choose, clearly a lot hangs on the literal-metaphoric scales.

Given the lack of consensus on what constitutes a metaphor, it is not surprising to encounter a great variety of conflicting opinion when it comes to extension or coverage: for Lakoff, we have seen, all abstract concepts are metaphors; Derrida once considered as metaphoric all words except the verb "to be"[16]; Carlyle, Nietzsche, and the Argentine poet Leopoldo Lugones opined that all linguistic expressions are metaphoric, which is even less helpful. Undeniably, however, not all utterances strike us equally as being good, strong metaphors. I am not proposing a definition of metaphor, nor, a fortiori, one of good, strong metaphor, but for the latter the following condition seems necessary, although far from sufficient: as pointed out before, the utterance should not fit current scientific beliefs and common sense nor the usual empirical evidence; moreover, the utterer should not be perceived as speaking as he or she does out of foolishness or ignorance of common beliefs but rather knowingly.

It follows, merely from this condition, that good metaphors do not present the same risks we encounter in good models and which we saw in the previous section, that is, of going too far when "taking one thing for the other." Let us consider the following examples.

Earlier I argued that Cervantes's rather strong metaphor, "His brain dried up," does not fit Black's interactive definition; we may now observe that it is safe, that is, without peril, in this sense: no one will or did think of going too far and trying to cure poor Alonso Quijano by subjecting him to steam baths or anything of that sort. Suppose, for another example, someone says of a funny joke that it "cracks him up": no one will rush to his help with a tube of glue or a hawk of plaster. Finally, returning to metaphors of the form "*S* is *P*," favored by Black because they seem better amenable to his definition, let us consider (as Black himself does, though without analyzing it) Pascal's well-known phrase, "L'homme n'est qu'un roseau, le plus faible de la nature; mais c'est un roseau pensant." Simplifying a bit the first third of Pascal's sentence, we get "Man (*S*) is a reed (*P*)." Using Black's terminology, here we are projecting on *S* a predicate of *P*: weakness, frailty—I cannot imagine anything else predicable of a reed which would fit this case, except perhaps for hollowness, and again, note that the implication complex of the secondary subject (*P*) consists of a single element. Nevertheless, I am not quite positive that all, or even most, reeds are weak or frail (bamboo is not), and likely this (and not just for the balance and elegance of the phrase) is why Pascal interposed the second third, "the weakest one in all of nature."

Where do we find Blackian interaction in this example? we now ask. What are the projections of predicates of *S* onto those of *P*? Precisely! (says Black): in the last third Pascal writes, "mais c'est un roseau pensant" ("but it's a thinking reed"), and in doing so he lends the reed a predicate of man. Yes, indeed. But observe that the power and flavor of Pascal's metaphor derives from our being perfectly aware that reeds don't think. To verify this, replace "reed" by something else, something weak which *does* think, for instance, "wimp" or the British slang "weed," so that in French we would get, roughly, "L'homme n'est qu'un gringalet, le plus faible de la nature, mais c'est un gringalet pensant"—and notice how bland and insipid the aphorism has become.

Rather than isomorphisms, analogies, and mutual correspondences between implication complexes, what we find in each of those good and strong metaphors is a single suitable predicate and, for the rest, evident falsehoods, the more evident the better, as if to warn us not to look for extra predicates. This is exactly the contrary of what happens with good scientific models. The risk with metaphor is not to take it too far but to take it for nothing, that is, to take it literally, as we saw in the Frost-Borges example.[17]

Metaphoric Color

Having distinguished between metaphor and model on the basis of the risks involved in each, let us return to that problematic metaphor, "the color of thought," or "the color of the expression of thought," by which, often enough through the centuries and all the way to Frege and beyond, metaphor itself has been characterized. In his *Life of Correggio,* Vasari names the two poles of painting: *disegno* (drawing) and *colore* (color)—he refrains from establishing a superiority but merely says that some painters are excellent draftsmen, others excellent colorists. At about the same time (1557) Ludovico Dolce in his *Dialogo della pittura intitolato l'Aretino,* distinguishes among *favola, disegno,* and *colorito* (subject matter, drawing, and color). The question of primacy between line and color is not explicitly stated and disputed until the following century,[18] when the new mathematical thought, freed from the synthetic straps of Greek geometry, begins stamping reality with its hallmark.

For Descartes, all objectivity is extension in space and local motion; evidently, any extension in space is determined by its outline, and drawing consists, precisely, in tracing outlines. Thus, drawing and line can faithfully represent the reality out there, the true being of the world. What about color? Descartes maintains that we cannot know color as something clear and distinct, the way we know outlines and shapes, but only opaquely, as we know pain.[19] *Couleur/douleur* (color/pain) is a Cartesian ontological consonance: color becomes a pathos, and very soon it is associated with the passions. Bad company from the epistemological and moral points of view, since, as La Bruyère warned us, "toutes les passions sont menteuses" (all the passions are liars).

It was in those terms that the *débat sur le coloris* (debate on coloring) was carried on in Paris during the three decades following 1660.[20] For Charles Le Brun and the other academic painters of Louis XIV's France, drawing is a vehicle of reason, literal truth, and conceptual light; color is mere rhetorical ornament, and as such—as rhetorical and as ornament—it is suspect. Philippe de Champaigne, rector of the Académie Royale and a Jansenist, sounds an Augustinian note: color (he teaches) presents a moral problem; we ought not to be tempted by the éclat, the exterior glitter—in short, the flesh—which is color; we ought to prefer the inner beauty, the soul, which is drawing, *dessin.* We can contemplate his painting career at the Louvre, from the early *Vierge douloureuse* and *Last Supper,* which borrow the strong colors of the Italian baroque, to the *Ex voto* of 1662 and the portrait of Robert Arnauld of 1667, severe and almost monochrome.

Antoine Arnauld and Pierre Nicole, friends of Pascal and Champaigne and their fellow Jansenists, establish a direct tie between metaphor and passion, pendant and parallel to that which we found in Descartes between color and passion. In their *Logique de Port-Royal* of 1662 (chapter 14), we read that the same thoughts seem much more vivid when expressed metaphorically (*exprimés par une figure*) than in proper terms, since metaphoric expressions (*expressions figurées*) signify not only the main object but also the emotion, the impulse and the passion (*le mouvement et la passion*) of the speaker, and transmit them to the soul of the hearer, while proper terms signify just the naked truth. Hence it is ridiculous to use metaphor (*stile figuré*) in purely speculative subjects, those which one contemplates impassively, with no passions stirring our soul. When treating of those subjects, metaphors are movements against nature, a sort of convulsion (*des mouvements contre la nature, et des espèces de convulsions*). On the contrary, when we deal with a subject that reasonably should affect us (*nous toucher*), it is wrong to speak in a dry and cold manner, with no emotion (*sans mouvement*), since it is a fault not to be affected when one ought to. Such defect is apparent in the manner in which the Schoolmen treat the truths of religion.

At about the same time but in England, Dryden writes (in *Poetry and Painting*) that color in painting is like expression in poetry; expression "is, in plain English, the bawd of her sister, the design . . . she clothes, she dresses her up, she paints her, she makes her appear more lovely than she is." We could easily multiply the examples and quotations, all the way to our own times, pointing in, and to, the same sense or complex of senses. Namely the aforementioned Fregean metaphor which identifies metaphor with "the color of thought's expression," together with the characterization of colors as surface coats of objects, as impassioned masks like those attached to Thespis's van, or as clothing to cover "naked truth" with, or up. Both color and metaphor are perceived as being outer, skin-deep, accidental, inessential, secondary, and epiphenomenal, yet paradoxically at the same time, as capable of signifying only that which is idiosyncratic and subjective: passions, moods, affects.

If I have called Frege's metaphor problematic it is because all those characterizations and perceptions, both of color and of metaphor, smack of unexamined, sclerotic Cartesianism. Yet, at the same time, it is a good, rich, strong metaphor, and as such, it will not lead us astray. Not only are we well aware that thoughts and their expressions are not colored objects, but any errors, any aridity of conception, will derive *not from the metaphor itself* but from rather dreary, old-fashioned and impoverished notions *both* about color and about the relations between the affects and reason, between pathos and Logos.

As regards the ancient academic distinction *colore* versus *disegno,* the

American painter Fairfield Porter used to say that drawing is all emotion and spasm, whereas color is spirit and intellectuality,[21] and he had a point, since drawing is a response, deeply personal, to contour, light, and shadow, while color, like the musical gamut, can be understood mathematically; divided into value, hue, and chroma scales; and taught at school.

Furthermore, when we think of color as only surface-deep and accidental, we are thinking of things such as painted lips or painted walls. Our mental landscape regarding color should change quite a bit (I would think) once we are reminded that emission and absorption spectra—colors—are the telling signs which enable us to know what there is to know about the composition of stars and the inner structure of atoms. Correspondingly, any Cartesian notions we might conserve about the respective, separate shares and prerogatives of reason and the affects should become moot when we are reminded of what follows.

In Conclusion: The Unfortunate Divorce of Logos and Pathos

We have reached the point where we can ask our second question as to the truth of metaphor, that is: Can a metaphor be about truth? And if so, about what kinds of truth?

In everyday speech the utterance of emotion and thought, of pathos and Logos, are not separate acts: they go together. When the shepherd cries, "Wolf!" not only is he pointing or referring to a carnivorous mammal, but the pitch and vibration of his voice tell of his own alarm and fear for his flock. Logico-mathematical language, though, acts as a filter: it excludes the pathos and retains only the Logos. Once, at a mathematics conference in the Tuscan town of Cortona, where there is a reputed tomb of Pythagoras, I witnessed a remarkable scene. A speaker was in the middle of a proof—he was proving a new result of considerable import—when someone in the audience pointed out an error. The speaker looked hard at the board for a minute or so—one could see that his brain had shifted into overdrive—but the error was fatal; it totally invalidated the proof. Then he stood immobile, speechless and dejected, the useless chalk still in his hand. For him to say, "I am crushed," or anything of the sort, would have been out of place and ridiculous; still, and in spite of the mathematical interdiction, he managed to express his feelings: I watched in fascination as an iridescent bubble grew out of his open lips; it slowly grew to the size of an orange before bursting. I am sure it wasn't consciously willed: he was too distraught for that. And I suspect that most if not all of those who noticed it took the bubble in "a carnal manner" (as Augustine would have put it), that is, as just saliva inflated by breath. But who could think of a more vivid metaphor, be it verbal or pantomime, for what must have been going on inside the speaker? From my safe seat, I couldn't but sympathize with him, share in some of his shame and distress.

That I take as a paradigm of good, strong metaphor: it makes one sympathize with the performer, it communicates a pathos in the sense in which one speaks of communicable magnetism or germ diseases, or contagious laughter. But we must note, too, how unstable it is, how its quality and strength depend on contingency and context. If the aforementioned speaker had been slavering and driveling from the start of his talk, that bubble of his would not have had half its communicative power; in addition, with each repetition of the performance, just as with many germ diseases, less and less of that power would be left in it. Such wasting away of good, strong metaphors, which causes them to become moribund or dead, has been often noted: Jacques Derrida calls it *usure.*[22] Is it a surprising phenomenon? Not if we remember that the purpose of metaphor is, at the very least, to break through the logico-mathematical filter, and at its strongest, to communicate a pathos, that is, to elicit in the audience—to infect it with—a feeling, a mood, an affect of the same kind as the one felt by the performer and if we consider, moreover, that many of those affects are themselves highly dependent on context and subject to decay by repetition.

In contrast, our reaction to a true theorem, Pythagoras's for example, is remarkably independent of context and undecaying (if one excepts the element of surprise and of wonder, which may be involved and which—by diktat of the Logos and because they usually wear off—are pathoses). Those qualities of constancy and independence of context must have contributed their part to confer on Logos its philosophical superiority over pathos, but there is something else, developed well before Descartes. The old consonance *patheîn/matheîn*—to suffer or undergo and to learn—which resounds in Herodotus and in the tragic poets, is muted among the philosophers. Aristotle was the first ever to discuss metaphor (in the *Poetics*). When elsewhere that philosopher discourses about the nature of the soul, he identifies the portion of it—therefore of us—which is immortal and everlasting: it is, he says, only "the apathetic intellect," *noûs apathés,* which is also separate (*choristós*) and unmixed (*amigés*).[23] Only that thought which is *a-pathés,* meaning that thought which cannot be acted upon, which is immovable, untouchable by emotion or passion, is worthy of eternal life. That immortal, immovable portion we call *logos.*

Neither his name nor the theorem he thought he had proved can I remember of the stricken speaker at Cortona. I remember only that bubble, the humble, ephemeral metaphor of his discomfiture, and not only do I remember the bubble, but here I am, writing it down, trying to make it last more than I. In doing so, I admit, I am being unreasonably rebellious and philosophically (hence ethically) perverse, for only correct proofs and true theorems ought to be preserved: the shame, the shattered hopes of any person are as worthless as his joys or her anger, chaff not even good for birds—all of which is saying, simply, that I am being poetic. That is not meant as a self-compliment but as a statement of fact: Logos has issued a writ of its own divorce from pathos long ago, and right now I am neglecting the one and turning all my attention to the other. Leaving aside logico-mathematical, universal truths, I have been concentrating on a single metaphor (the bubble) which, at best, may convey a very particular and very private truth: a *pathetic* truth, as no doubt Logos will dub it.

In all fairness to philosophers, though, we must remember that they did not always blatantly privilege Logos over pathos. Wasn't it Aristotle himself, after all, who famously said that humans always begin to philosophize through wonder?[24] And wonder is, needless to add, a pathos. Giambattista Vico, who first offered a radical critique of Cartesianism, assigned to pathos—and to metaphor—a privileged role, irreducible to logic, and the same did, two centuries later, his follower and fellow Neapolitan, Benedetto Croce.[25] Let us finally recall Kierkegaard's footnote:

> That science, just as much as poetry and art, presupposes a mood in the creator as well as in the observer, and that an error in the modulation is just as disturbing as an error in the development of thought, have been entirely forgotten in our own time, when inwardness has been completely forgotten, etc.[26]

This completely reverses the old situation. A mood, that is, a pathos, a complex of feelings sustained for some time, would be, then, necessary for science, and a condition of the Logos: in that footnote of Kierkegaard we find the germ of twentieth-century existential thought and of Heidegger's *Stimmungen* in particular. Pathos a precondition for the Logos—metaphor more original than, or equiprimordial with, concept—and yet Logos and concepts are required to think, say, and understand that very relation; but why should that be more of a scandal than the fact that we can think of brains and study neurons?

The old and manifold polarities, in particular the opposition between literal and metaphoric, are being neutralized, or at least softened; Logos and pathos may—let's keep our fingers crossed—be drawn back into wedlock. Such confidence may seem rash, until one considers the forces at work, the vastly different schools of marriage counselors and peacemakers. On one side, contemporary skeptics such as Derrida have shaken the classic belief in an ultimate literal ground from which metaphors grow and in a Logos which, to arrive at philosophical truth, could, if it so choose, speak only formal languages and dispense with the full figurative complexity of natural ones. On the other, opposite side, we have certain neuroscientists who are studying the physical, physiological bases both for thought and for emotions and feelings. Here, again, the old hierarchy of Logos first and foremost—of metaphor as "pathos introduced where before there was only fact," as "color added where there was, objectively, black and white"—is being overturned. There seems to be no such thing as an affectless viewing of the world: Kierkegaard's and Heidegger's aperçus (and one should add, also William James's) are being corroborated by present-day brain research. "Feelings [are] the foundational component of our minds," writes Antonio Damasio.[27] There may come a time (I will not wager how far into the future) when our familiar opposites "literal" and "metaphoric" will seem as quaint a superstition as "succubus" and "incubus."

As I noted earlier, an acquaintance with current, general scientific beliefs is a precondition for being able to distinguish, in any given case, between literal and metaphoric uses of a word. Heidegger put it somewhat differently when he wrote that such a distinction presupposes a metaphysical posture. Surely the concept "contemporary poetics" is ocean-capacious, yet just as we can find true general statements about the oceans (e.g., that nowadays we expect their level to rise), we can be fairly certain that today the tendency for poetry is, and has been for some time, to become detached as much as possible from other human symbolic ventures: science, metaphysics, theology, politics, and so on. Thus poetics has waged a successful war of independence against didacticism, one of whose major victories is the fact, so often puzzled over, that *Les Fleurs du mal,* rather than Victor Hugo, is perceived everywhere as being the source book of modern French poetry. For that detachment and independence to be complete, the either/or of metaphor, the question as to whether any given term in a poem is to be taken literally or metaphorically, must become thoroughly undecidable. Which is to say, being and its color must become poetically indistinguishable.

Notes

1. Similar statements of separation (a "natural" separation which makes divorce possible) come, remarkably, from the other side, from the humanistic disciplines. Helen Vendler, "Lionel Trilling and the Immortality Ode," in *The Music of What Happens* (Cambridge, Mass.: Harvard University Press, 1988), 98: "What else is metaphor but a conferral of colours on the neutral world, an introduction of pathos where before there was only fact?"

2. The articles considered in this section appeared in Andrew Ortony, ed., *Metaphor and Thought* (Cambridge: Cambridge University Press, 1993).

3. Famously, Frege used such equivalences to define the natural numbers. The number 4, for example, is "the class of all sets equivalent to the following one: {a, b, c, d}."

4. Max Black, "More About Metaphor," in Ortony, *Metaphor and Thought,* 30 and 29.

5. Already I. A. Richards in his *Principles of Literary Criticism* (1924) was saying that there are few metaphors whose effect, carefully examined, can be attributed to the logical relations therein. Around the same time, Charles Bally, Karl Vossler, and their disciples, among others, were focusing on style and expression as opposed to logical content. Nevertheless, the emphasis on logic and isomorphisms and the syndromic confusion between metaphor and scientific model have been so strong as to influence Paul Ricoeur, in his *La Métaphore vive* (1975).

6. John R. Searle, "Metaphor," in Ortony, *Metaphor and Thought,* 83–111.

7. George Lakoff, "The Contemporary Theory of Metaphor," in Ortony, *Metaphor and Thought,* 203.

8. Ibid., 213.

9. Ibid., 216.

10. Jacques Derrida, "La mythologie blanche," in *Marges de la philosophie* (Paris: Minuit, 1972), 247. A useful gloss of that essay can be found in Christopher Norris, *Deconstruction and the Unfinished Project of Modernity* (London: Routledge, 2000), chap. 4.

11. About 1970, by virtue of what mysterious word associations I do not know, one of Argentina's many military dictatorships decreed that vector analysis was

subversive. There is much in common between extreme epistemological relativism and tyrannical regimes: indeed, this may be one of the senses in which we can interpret Shigalev's "Starting from unlimited freedom I arrive at unlimited despotism," in Dostoyevsky's *The Possessed,* tr. Constance Garnett (New York: Random House, 1963), p. 409.

12. Black, "More About Metaphor," 30.

13. This is Proposition 32 in book 1 of Euclid's *Elements.* I give here the (beginning of the) proof attributed to Pythagoras. For the history of this proposition, one of the first ever proved and a traditional example of apodictic truth, see Sir Thomas L. Heath, *The Thirteen Books of Euclid's Elements,* 2nd ed. (New York: Dover Publications, 1956), vol. I., 316.

14. Augustine, *On Christian Doctrine,* 3.5. David Nirenberg called my attention to this text; to him, too, I owe many improvements in my own.

15. Harvard University Press has recently made Borges's 1967–68 Norton Lectures at Harvard available in print and in CD.

16. Jacques Derrida, "Force et signification," in *L'écriture et la difference* (Paris: Seuil, 1967), 16–17.

17. Here I am referring exclusively to human texts. Were one to be reading something considered divine, Holy Writ, then the tendency will be strong to take metaphors too far, and the difference between metaphor and model might vanish.

18. Aristotle in his *Poetics* (1450b) puts line above color for this reason: "The most beautiful colours, laid on pell-mell, will not please as much as an image outlined in white." With Aristotle, however, it does not seem to have been an ontological superiority, as it was to be for Descartes.

19. Descartes, *Principia Philosophiae* (Amsterdam, 1644), I.68 and I.69. English translation as *Principles of Philosophy* by J. Cottingham, R. Stoothoff, and D. Murdoch (Cambridge: Cambridge University Press, 1985), 217–18.

20. For that *débat* and other related artistic debates in seventeenth-century France, one may consult Bernard Teyssèdre, *Roger de Pile et les débats sur le coloris au siècle de Louis XIV* (Lausanne-Paris: Bibliothèque des Arts, 1964) and other works by the same author; a briefer account can be found in Moshe Barasch, *Theories of Art, from Plato to Winckelmann* (New York: New York University Press, 1985).

21. Pointed out to me by Dan Hofstadter.

22. Derrida, "La mythologie blanche," 247.

23. Aristotle *De Anima* 430a17–23. This Aristotelian passage, incidentally, was interpreted by Averroes as saying that the immortal "apathetic intellect" is one and the same for all human beings, and that caused a famous medieval controversy between, among others, Thomas Aquinas and Siger of Brabant.

24. Aristotle *Metaphysics* 982b.

25. Benedetto Croce, *Logica come Scienza del Concetto Puro,* 4th ed. (Bari: Laterza, 1920), 4–5 passim.

26. Søren Kierkegaard, *The Concept of Anxiety,* trans. R. Thomte and A. B. Anderson (Princeton, N.J.: Princeton University Press, 1980), 14n.

27. Antonio Damasio, *Looking for Spinoza—Joy, Sorrow and the Feeling Brain* (New York: Harcourt, 2003), 79.

Vagueness, Poetry

Keston Sutherland

April 11, 2001, 2:44 P.M.: Can I be something vague? Does this question have only one legitimate contingency, that is, the possible definition of vagueness in logical discourse? Can the world itself be vague, beyond or despite the logical insistence that its "vagueness" would be merely a characteristic attributed irrationally to it? Things are now quite different than they were last November, and also they are perhaps unchanging in roughly the same way that they always were. I want to address this question *now,* as Midwestern Capital enjoys its upward trend in jingoism, and as I sit waiting for my teeth to be repaired after they were smashed out of my head in a drunken accident. I feel vagueness, and in writing poetry I hope anxiously to commit this vagueness, in words whose material histories and etymology ought in a less comprised predicament to resist it. What is vague does not, for me, as for Russell, have a "chance of being true";[1] the inconstancy of my effort in life and the inconstancy also of that life itself, including and expelling the concrete world daily more or less objectified, is not in either case an inconstancy which is likely ever to end. It will not end through being construed rationally as a process to which there must be a rational outcome, unless I am capable of suppressing my disbelief in this, as Saint Augustine did very beautifully before the recent presidential inauguration, abandonment of the Kyoto Treaty, and so on. Is vagueness for life, or a gift of half-cognitive depression, life-deductible? At present I can work through my own question only in poetry.

This last admission raises an immediate problem. The classic and perhaps most influential account of vagueness is by Bertrand Russell, a writer for whom any putative distortions in consciousness are fundamentally not evidence for a distorted world. Furthermore, and such that his argument advances away from all Kantian traditions, Russell asserts that the world *is not* distorted, not uncertain or unknowable, despite whatever limitations of knowledge we may presently suffer or enjoy, and that by definition no "object" in the world can itself be vague. Russell further distinguishes "knowledge" from "knowing as an occurrence": if we speak of knowledge as vague, we cannot logically mean that "knowing as an occurrence" has this vague character; it is not the occurrence, but the "relation" of the occurrence to "that which is known" which we must mean.

> Vagueness in a cognitive occurrence is a characteristic of its relation to that which is known, not a characteristic of the occurrence itself.[2]

It is for Russell important that logic should direct its audience toward what they must (or incontrovertibly ought) to mean, just as in a different breath and finer spirit it is important also for Trotsky, or for Pound, that language should be in this way a directive. Vagueness, in Russell's account, is precisely what the logical account of vagueness says it is; or at least, it does not exceed or fall short of this account other than in the universal sense in which any concept must necessarily exceed or fall short of an account of it. That is also to say, vagueness is a clearly understood characteristic of cognitive relations; there is nothing vague about how vagueness must be understood.

Russell goes on to describe the inherence of vagueness in things which appear to us at a distance: "there is less vagueness in the near appearance than in the distant one."[3] Accuracy, on the contrary, is not a matter of degree but an "ideal limit."[4] It is in (Russell's) theory possible for us to see anything of a visual character with perfect accuracy, even if at present we lack the technology sufficient to do so; but we could never in our cognitive relation to an object experience *perfect vagueness,* and as a poet I would say that it is perhaps for this reason—that vagueness is not an ideal limit—that Russell seems despite and also through his analytic discussion to value the concept of vagueness less than the concept of accuracy. Russell would probably have replied that concepts are not per se meaningfully valuable or invaluable and that the two concepts are distinguished inherently with respect to their differing relevance to conceptual thought as a whole. As a poet I would scoff at this.

Ignorance "as an occurrence" here means something very practical. It is the event of my feeling preoccupied with a question which *can* be defined and even resolved logically but which I feel *ought* not to be. If this is merely my own perversity as a nonlogician, it is a perversity that comes with, and is sustained by, a great deal of frustration and unhappiness. 3:57 P.M.: should I correct myself on this account.

Russell defines vagueness as "merely the contrary of precision."[5] In this he is surely wrong, since vagueness is the contrary also of imprecision. As an example look at the sky, suppressing temporarily the feeling that I am now switching from philosopher mode to poet mode. With any luck there will be clouds. Russell says "it is obvious that what you see of a man who is 200 yards away is vague compared to what you see of a man who is 2 feet away."[6] Is our perception of clouds vague? Are the clouds themselves vague in appearance, such that when flying in an airplane and looking out the window the clouds are suddenly less vague? Do we purchase the reduced vagueness of clouds along with a flight to Washington? The image of clouds is often used to describe vague or obscure sensations, or vague expression; but clouds themselves are not more vague because they are distant. Or rather, we do not attribute to the "distant appearance" of clouds any vagueness that might be a characteristic of our "cognitive relation" to them. Poetically I could insist even that the vagueness of clouds is perfect: the sky is a famous "ideal limit," and clouds are the moralized substance of our upward gaze. To fly through them is not to perceive them less vaguely, unless in the cryptovatic sense perpetrated by Heidegger when he declares that "only by the circumspection with which one takes account of things in farming, is the south wind discovered in its Being."[7] Repeating this arc of thought, we could say that clouds are discovered in their Being (or made less ontologically vague) only by the "circumspection" of meteorologic strategists advising the U.S. Air Force when to head out on a bombing raid.

The etymological root of "vague" is the Latin *vag-us,* which means "wandering," "inconstant," or "uncertain." Vagueness is the (sometimes negative) loss of fixity, whether in a physical landscape too hostile or too beautiful to allow us to sit still or in a cognitive occurrence with some preferred certain outcome. It is absolutely imbricated with desire, both as positive and negative expressions of particular desires and as a condition which may rationally or irrationally be accountable for desire itself, and for violence also. Wordsworth could have known this when he wrote the line "I wandered lonely as a cloud," bringing into mutable and temporary harmony two senses of the word "vague": its historical rootedness in *vag-us* (an etymological connection reanimated by what "I" does in the poem) and its common metaphor in nature ("a cloud"). The harmony in this historical-metaphoric moment of vagueness is made possible by the comparison "lonely as"—this is the "relation," as Russell would say, of Wordsworth's knowledge, brought into words and so made linguistically (rather than just cognitively) thematic. At the ideal limit of his distance from them, Wordsworth is in this respect suddenly equivalent to the mutable figure across the sky: both he and this single cloud are lonely, though in *having wandered* Wordsworth knows also the vagueness of recollection, and this is a vagueness that—connoted etymologically, and therefore with an implicit sense of the historical nature of one who wanders—could hardly be imputed to the cloud. In their loneliness they are similar, since both the wanderer and the cloud are alone vaguely; and yet the loneliness of each is also precisely their difference from each other, in this respect: that whereas the vagueness of "a cloud" is imagined essentially to be metaphoric and unchanging, the wanderer's vagueness is imagined essentially to be historical.

What could be the history of vagueness? Does the value of "a near appearance" relative to that of "a distant appearance" change over time, such that the different degrees of vagueness, which in Russell's discussion are the differences of objects in cognition, might at one point seem more or less beautiful, irrelevant, oppressive, or imperceptible than at another point? In my own vagueness I feel the specific pressure of history. "Degrees" of vagueness, insofar as I would use this misleading term, are the measurement correlated principally with the likewise misleadingly conceptualized "degrees" to which I feel that history presses in on me. Unfortunately this conviction is structurally reminiscent of an alibi. I seem to be claiming that vagueness is not my fault, except insofar as I may be more susceptible to the pressure of history than I ought to be.

By "history" (as Olson often began his utterances) I now mean the totality of present and past relations and the totality also of these relations as they are falsified and distorted in commodity form. This seems perhaps like an unfairly vague definition of history. It is. At 5:29 P.M. it is not looking any less unfair or vague, nor does it seem likely to become so.

A cigarette break. More precisely: one Lucky Strike, product of British American Tobacco Group, recently defended against smuggling charges by its chairman the ex-chancellor Kenneth Clark, made under license from Brown & Williamson Tobacco Corporation, Louisville, Kentucky, U.S.A. Stubbed out in my home, 5:39 P.M.

As a rhapsodist shirking verse, Pound made in 1942 some comments about Bolshevism, a social philosophy and party which, he argued, had been spirited into existence by the Talmud.[8] The Bolsheviks, he earlier said, "have proclaimed that literature is for the state, but they don't mean it as, say, I do. I believe that any precise use of words is bound in the long run to be useful to the state and the world at large." Pound had long believed this, or had long believed it incipiently. Since 1913 he had been notoriously and complacently garrulous in maintaining that "good art" is "the art that is most precise."[9] Pound may well have been right, for a brief while—indeed he was pathetically right, since he was right only for limited historical reasons and in a limited historical window, but of course programmatically took himself to be right altogether and sempiternally. Things now having been thrown to altogether different winds, Poetry can recoil at Pound's insistences. What can it possibly mean for words to be used, in poetry, "precisely"? How is art "precise" and for whom is it so? I think of Gerhard Richter's seminal blur in 1968, entitled vaguely "Ohne Titel (Strich)" ["Untitled (Stroke)"]. Can we now accept even playfully that diction is the manifest outcome of an author's choices *and* that these choices should somehow be calibrated by judgment of their success or failure to create a precise result? Does this question implicitly ask us to recognize a State, or, at the very fantastic least, some "Eutopia" (as Pound preferred to spell it), through the real or imaginable lived experience of which we can understand what "precision" really means, or ought to mean? Pound thought so and said so. His *Homage to Sextus Propertius* is an immensely exceptional work; I can think of little or no American poetry that unquestionably equals its achievement. Pound was also imbecilic in his judgment of Wordsworth, which pivoted on the brave observation, borrowed from Ford, that Wordsworth had no ear for the *mot juste.* In this, as in other things, Olson seemed to follow him. Though averagely dismissive of Johnson's poetry, Pound did admire in *The Vanity of Human Wishes* what he considered "the perfectly weighed and placed word."[10] Elsewhere he wrote: "Good writers are those who keep the language efficient. That is to say, keep it accurate, keep it clear."[11]

Given his frequent comparison of poets to physicians (on the level working field of joint ethical participation in an *Idea Statale*), Pound would surely have grimaced, as surely on other occasions he often did grimace, at O'Hara's measly outcry "words! be / sick as I am sick."[12] The echo may, however, have pleased Pound: be [*sic*] as I am [*sic*], or: be (precisely) *thus,* since I am (precisely) *thus.* To tease out this echo is to distort the line: clearly the echo contradicts the line's more obvious and direct sense. I am thus, and sick; I am precisely this, and yet not precisely myself as I am ideally but downcast, nauseated, "not feeling myself," given too much to the vagaries of what Freud called "parapraxes." It is almost as if the line break here is itself parapractical, a kind of stutter or quick mental hiccup, the mind wandering out across the page and then pulled back to its senses at the left margin. "Vagary" (to explain my use of the word here) is from the Latin *vagari:* to wander. When I am sick, my mind wanders, as Freud described. The vagaries of Capital could be its wandering across the globe, its subsumption of the meaning of "mediation" beneath the great macroeconomic vagueness of its total effects and ineffects. Pound despised these vagaries and the specific vagueness of paper currency as inherited from a "Protestant" English monarch bent on equipping a standing army in the service of economic imperialism. His mind would not be permitted to wander but must be ethically responsible in recognition of "the touchstone of . . . art," that is "its precision."[13] *Sic,* but never so unvigilant as to be *sick,* nor so afflicted by obdurate contradiction as to be (in J. H. Prynne's words) finally "sick and nonplussed."[14] That is, both *sic et non.*

Vigilance is important, now, to what I understand about the vagueness I feel. Could it be that Pound was exactly right and that to be *exactly* right is indeed the best way to be right—that "the durability of the writing depends on the exactitude"?[15] Is this true, 6:12 P.M.? Larkin was exactly or precisely right in his choice of the penultimate word "that" in his poem "Home Is So Sad." That vase. The emphasized deictic: this is precision as prescription, again to recall Pound's analogy of the poet and the doctor. To be handed the right placebo. Larkin wanted to prescribe a feeling of poignant certainty, in no uncertain terms. The expression "precision as prescription" can also be more precisely understood. It contains an implicit nod to Heidegger, in whose grammatical hermeneutics the "as" connective is a staple and necessary feature. I feel in contrast the desire for an "as-not-quite" connective, writing here "as-not-quite" a poet, "as-not-quite" lonely in my shared loneliness, and particularly as (at 6:20 P.M.) I begin to wonder if I can finish this, if I can put down without delay the difficult sense of what I feel, before leaving this room for a night out drink-clouded in precisely the same old bar.

It is vigilant now not to avoid but to comprehend vagueness, to substantiate for and in vagueness its dialectics. This is a laborious kind of vigilance. For me it is most thorough only in writing poetry. I feel my work become thickened by inspecificities, I see and produce language ripped down a screen in vagueness. It is a kind of unhappiness and can in facile ways be attributed to anything: I say "over the lilac / and nothing and bake" maybe because, what? Kim Il-Jong? Because a Labour MP in Portsmouth called the Paulsgrove outbursts a healthy expression of democracy? What I feel is a pressure not to specify but more anxiously a pressure *not to concede to precision,* by which I do mean Pound's sense of the word, and Russell's sense, and the word less specially understood. This would be easier to theorize if I could believe that vagueness in language is a definite index of disappointment, or alienation, or even of the pretentious belief that I experience these conditions. I would then merely be documenting and not dementing life. It is perhaps *vaguely* such an index; but this reflexive circularity, the characterization of experience by reference to itself as a predicate, is now—in our present spin of days—a form of recumbent and ultimately indifferent thinking. My care for my own life pushes me against this; it would be difficult even to keep word processing and printing out vagueness after vagueness if I could never (as I have not yet managed to) understand less satisfactorily what it means to do so. *Less* satisfactorily, because my poetry is itself both unsatisfying and caused by intense feelings of dissatisfaction. In fact, I have to trust that it *ought* to be unsatisfying and that my feeling compelled to write it should be explained in a way that not only reflects but also incites and strengthens that dissatisfaction. I have to trust this by no simple recourse to the received notion that poems should irritate a reader into her own acts of interpretive "freedom." That "freedom" is now conceptually falsified by its recent art history, in which the banalizing of dissidence has been the theme ad nauseam both implicitly and explicitly for many perishable years. And in that nausea, stringent within its daily confine, both "[*sic*]" and sick, sick and nonplussed, how precisely should I write about my life for other people? And of course, not only (or ever wholly or exclusively or even principally) about my life.

Gadamer says in a study of Celan's poetry that it is "obligatory" that a poem "not contain a single word standing for something in such a way that another word could be substituted for it."[16] This obligation is of course intensely a question of desire; I feel it as an impasse beyond which it is now both so facile and so necessary to transgress and which is so easily analogized in the rapid-replacement culture of commodity imperialism that I cannot avoid either the transgression or the disappointment with which it discolors the times of my life. In writing I refuse what I know very precisely I should accept. My life has the tendency to seem refused also.

Eliot wrote, "It is impossible to say just what I mean." I feel more contradicted: there is a pressure to change or abrogate this line. Can it be possible to say *just* what I don't mean, and to say it precisely with *justice,* with the now transformed value of the mot juste? Can it be right to accept vaguely that I am what I don't mean? Or, to say just what I mean impossibly? In these updates of Eliot—banalized slightly by their playful return to *détournement* achieved through altered word order—it is *what I mean* that takes on the impossible character that Eliot's line had attributed merely to *saying.* There is an assault here on the mot juste, precisely because self-expression is no longer the principal frustration. It is my distance from that archaic frustration that I feel, the vagueness of how I could be frustrated by that particular kind of impossibility; other kinds of impossibility now seem too pressing and gigantic.

Horkheimer and Adorno once wrote, "The blindfold over Justitia's eyes does not only mean that there should be no assault upon justice, but that justice does not originate in freedom."[17] Perhaps that blindfold means also that Justitia cannot discriminate between the near appearance and the distant one, and that Justice therefore cannot, as in Russell's scheme, be herself the cause of whatever vagueness she may know. Inasmuch as I am just as I am, I am neither the factory nor the pollution; I am just the person queuing for his prescription of Ventolin. Is the mot juste, so admired by Pound, truly the negation of vagueness? Had vagueness been, at this earlier point in the century, unjust? Could it now be time to reverse the intuitive order of that relation, to make a decision to feel instead that vagueness is the just, positive term of which precision is the distorted negative? There would have to be very good reasons for accepting such a reversal. It would have to be in some sense the wrong thing to accept or an outcome to accept only very imprecisely. Not the reversal itself, but *our way of accepting it* (for example, poetry) is what must crucially be at stake. Styles of thought that are rationally counterproductive are not "irrational," not shifted from a center of *logos:* they are the means to create a rational counterproduct. In this they are now sufficiently vital that they could turn out not only to have been true but also to have reduced and so beautifully to have intensified what "impossibility" is. Impossibility is not presently very beautiful or intense: it is too prolific. A certain practiced overvaluation of precision (e.g., the U.S. budget for laser-targeted air-to-ground missiles) causes me to feel this, as I rise in the library elevator shaft in search of one specific book among millions.

Impossibility is not just a faded watchword echoing the 1960s campus occupations of "Utopian" vocab. It is the absolute target concept; it is a positive contingency of all humane expression. Against *what I am,* the prospectus foisted into the ego like a shut and bolted echo chamber, there is *what we cannot be, but are.* The present tense of ourselves ("we are") is here in outright logical defiance of ourselves in abstract ("we can/cannot be"): this defiance is crucial and true, it is impossible, and as such it is truly expressible only without precision. It is also a form of unhappiness. To help establish this rational counterproduct—the defiance against ourselves in abstract—vagueness would have to be possible not only as a cognitive dye on the fabric of perceived objects (i.e., not only as a predicate), but as the true, historical status and provocation of those objects, including myself and my feelings, under the focus of a present regime bolstered by capitalization on all the precise estimates. In poetry this impossible defiance shines, like love as the ideal limit of hatred.

Notes

1. "Vagueness," *The Collected Papers of Bertrand Russell,* vol. 9, ed. John G. Slater (London: Unwin Hyman, 1988), 153.
2. Ibid., 148.
3. Ibid., 153.
4. Ibid., 152.
5. Ibid., 153.
6. Ibid., 148.
7. Martin Heidegger, *Being and Time,* trans. John Macquire and Edward Robinson (London: Blackwell, 1962), 112.
8. Ezra Pound, Jefferson and/or Mussolini. *L'Idea Statale. Fascism As I Have Seen It* (London: Stanley and Nott, 1935), 44.
9. Ezra Pound, "The Serious Artist," *Literary Essays of Ezra Pound.* Ed. T. S. Eliot (London: Faber, 1968), 44.
10. Ezra Pound, *Guide to Kulchur* (New York: New Directions, 1970), 179.
11. Ezra Pound, *ABC of Reading* (London: Faber, 1991), 32.
12. "Mayakovsky," *The Collected Poems of Frank O'Hara,* ed. Donald Allen (Berkeley and Los Angeles: University of California Press, 1995), 201.

13. "The Serious Artist," 48.

14. J. H. Prynne, *Poems* (Fremantle, Australia, and Highgreen, UK: Fremantle Arts and Bloodaxe, 1995), 310.

15. Ezra Pound, *How to Read* (London: Desmond Harmsworth, 1931), 19.

16. Hans-Georg Gadamer, *"Who Am I and Who Are You?" And Other Essays*, trans. and ed. Richard Heinemann and Bruce Krajewski (New York: SUNY, 1997), 130.

17. Max Horkheimer and Theodor Adorno, *Dialectic of Enlightenment*, trans. John Cumming (New York: Continuum, 1994), 17.

AND &

D. J. Huppatz, Nicole Tomlinson, and Julian Savage

Poetry

DH: *poetry:* n. the art or work of a poet, poems collectively, a poetic or tenderly pleasing quality, a lyrical troubadour wandering in indefinite uselessness often associated with fluid tendencies and slippery surfaces whose subject matter disappears into I don't know perhaps a color somewhere between green and violet or an explanation of the myriad chirps and tweets in long streams of sound in nonsymmetrical phrasing pausing occasionally for breath. On papyrus, bamboo sheets or scribbled on cave walls, noted down as a diagram, a geometry of words issued upon melodies, not unlike liquid bitumen or birdsong creating a habitat in which to live.

NT: Poetry is always and never utopian—it is constellation—caesura—discontinuity: the space through which something else is emerging or evaporating; *here moving ahead, there remembering, in the future, in the past, under a false appearance of the present.*[1] The project of utopianism in poetics is double in that it necessitates the bringing of history as an inexorable linearity into dispute and at the same time (suffering the same fate of all utopianism) requires history's absolute end. The abandonment of utopianism in poetics is not a marker of the defeat of politics but the refusal of an end of history. History is a generative act in the nonidentity of the present not the finality of a past tense nor its culmination in a future . . .

NT & DH:

A double
orientation . . .
Every step made in relation to another
step Lautréamont's *plagiarism is necessary*
Broken space A weed in the
cracks the antimatter
returning into play Even
Coolidge's crystallized language
highlights the
stickiness of words.

JS: "Utopia" derives from the Greek words that mean "no place." If its merit is bound up in the critique of existing social and economic conditions rather than the projection of an ideal, then this seems like a willing concession. The trajectory of determinist histories or "factualities" destabilized by the rupture is consistent with the poetic impulse for incursion, intervention, and dissent. Ergo: no submission to the romantic transcendent, plagiarism is necessary as (possibly) the last refuge from the new.

NT: 1998, D. J. Huppatz and Benjamin Brady install a series of soup cans in a gallery (see facing page). The cans are labeled with the bicolored economy of a generic brand—food for the poor—same factory, different level of entitlement to the glamour of surfaces. But written on these labels are not the designations of manufacture, the nomination of content, or instructions for use but the play of a language that is disruptive of these utilities. Masquerading as a series of dictionary definitions, these words exceed content (soup/meaning) and extend the surface of form in a way that reveals that the dictionary sells us signification and proper usage in much the same way that commodity capitalism does.

This installation occupies a borderland between writing and materiality, the work of words and the work of art: their refusal to work in the unfamiliar territories of the "between." This refusal requisitions the familiar, the note of recognition as a vehicle for transformation: switching the

Detail from D. J. Huppatz and Benjamin Brady, *Concrete Poetry,* 1998

height of the ordinary, setting it afloat, pushing it to the point of mutation. As soon as one reads "soup cans," "gallery," it is necessary to consider Warhol; as soon as one considers "commodity," "writing," is it necessary to read Debord? Take the two references and hold them against one another. The threat of consumer society makes us rightly paranoid. But is the soup condensed or diffuse?

Assemblage

DH: Twenty-first-century consumerist writing, from the airport novel to the newspaper, must be clean, clear, and absorbed easily. It is writing that enables speed reading, or, the comprehension of orders as quickly as possible. Such writing ensures constant novelty in a specific structure so as to control variation, to channel the difference into recognizable and readily digestible forms. The digital "revolution" ensures faster transfer of messages/information/order words.

Where is the time for the slowness of poetry?

DH: Nicole Tomlinson's . . . *and* . . . , an installation at 1st Floor Gallery in 1998, consisted of a series of acetate sheets with the word "and"

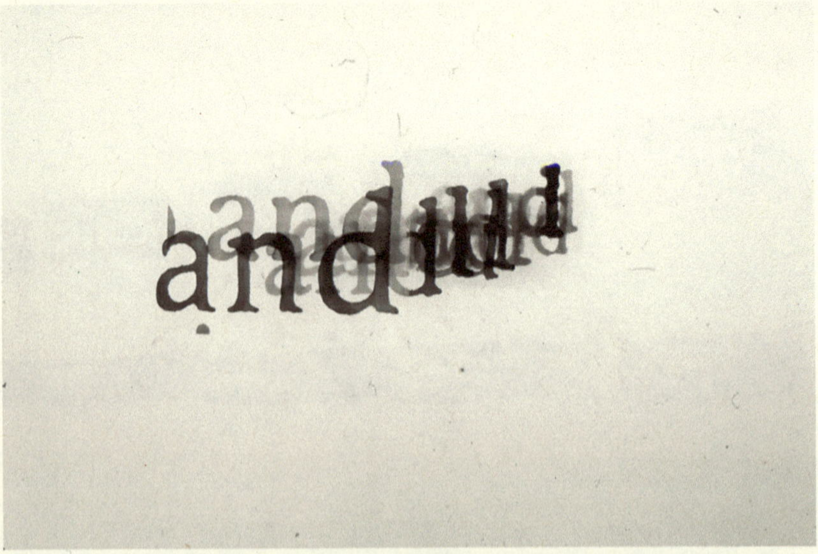

Detail from Nicole Tomlinson, . . . *and* . . . , 1998

printed on them, hung by transparent wires so that the words appeared to be floating in space. Each "and" had been taken from a specific literary or theoretical text. One of them was from Molly Bloom's soliloquy at the end of Joyce's *Ulysses:*

> and the sea crimson sometimes like fire and the glorious sunsets and the figtrees in the Alameda gardens yes and all the queer little streets and pink and yellow and blue houses and the rose gardens and the jessamine and geraniums and cactuses and Gibraltar as a girl where I was a Flower of the mountain[2]

Here, Joyce is engaging in an additive project where language is escaping its bounds as the "and" stimulates new thoughts. Deleuze and Guattari describe their logic of the "and" in the following terms: "AND is less a conjunction than the atypical expression of all of the possible conjunctions it places in continuous variation."[3] For them, "and" is an atypical expression that produces the placing-in-variation of regulated or codified static forms. The logic of the "and" differs from that of the "a" or the "the"; "and" is a dynamic term, a mode of extension and production rather than a static naming device. The word itself is both the connection that holds difference together and the force that generates difference.

NT: This is a post-era, a century which is to occur after everything has already happened: a persistence after the deaths of art, of the author, of agency; an afterimage, a lost, posthumous time, a ceaseless expiration. The duration of this lingering postpresent tense:

a spectral remainder . . . a place of abeyance, of repetition without authenticity . . . a sickened nostalgia for purpose . . . truth . . . the incandescent failure of presence, covered over with a mechanics of speed. The bound instantaneity of a snake eating its tail. The true horror of the post- is proliferation without centre, without end, a total fragmentation

. . . but how can we measure up to the universe if we content ourselves . . . [4]

DH: Poetry is always a plural event—the poem exists in relation to others—its language is a fluid one that allows expansion into realms beyond the page. Contemporary practice expands poetic language into physical space, filmic space, and virtual space. The writers' collective Textbase[5] developed as an opportunity to explore alternative writing practices through a series of text-based installations, interventions, and publications. The assemblage of collaborative projects stretches beyond the page and back again . . . in-between is dangerous . . . they're always trying to plug the leaks but each time language becomes gaseous again . . . people ask me: What is your meaning? I HAVE NO CONFESSION TO MAKE: all my sensations are a sky . . .

JS: Film uses the term "montage" to describe the linkage of shots or sequences. It is these assemblages of word-images in the text-film that reconfigure the dominant iconic feature of cinema in realigning it with the symbolic. Time-based text media, inclusive of new media poetry, may be the most retrograde of all, a response to the anxiety of losing the disappearing force of the graphic mark. The attempt to vivify quiescent signs is consistent with what Jameson construes as a reaction against the arbitrary quality of language and as an attempt to "motivate" that which was wholly "unmotivated."[6]

The installation work of Textbase revisits this site of tension between word as sign and word as image. The exhibition *In(formation)* (Textbase at City Lights) drew on a number of preexisting language forms including the rebus, an eye chart, the free play of early childhood language acquisition, and word games to test and critique their limited functionality. Positioned in a city lane, the works were printed on large acetate sheets and suspended high on a wall in four light boxes. The constructions resembled advertising gimmicks, designed to attract the attention of the passerby. The content, displaced from typical context (rebus—early learning book; eye chart—doctor's office; child's drawing—stuck on the fridge; origami game—played in the hands) created unease. A rebus spelled out "POETRY" but only if the intervening images bore no meaning; the eye chart, written in phonetic script, formed a sentence that spoke of the inscrutability of the written word (if it could be read!); the scribbles of a young child seemed philosophical; the origami game presented a series of combinative possibilities. Just as the text that constructs the cityscape bombards us with messages that are rarely poetic (but often tantalizingly polysemous), where every available surface issues forth terms of commodity and control, there does not exist a term that adequately describes "architectural" writers. Builders place bricks or concrete blocks on top of and next to each other to form walls, the resultant construction dependant on the interlocking effect of the separate units. Do buildings collapse if there is nothing to write on them?

NT: When we are making pictures together we are not being an artist. Does this make us a poet like Frank O'Hara?

Concrete

DH: *concrete:* n. existing in a material form; real, specific, definite (concrete evidence; a concrete proposal). From the Latin, *concretus,* past participle of *concrescere* (grow), also the Greek god Concretis. Concretis was the bastard son of Zeus, king of the gods, and Callisto, a favorite nymph of Artemis, goddess of the hunt. Artemis, shamed by the deflowering of one of her virgin nymphs, turned Callisto and her newborn son Concretis into a sand dune. When the sea god Poseidon created the great river Peneius, Concretis was released into it. Years later he was spotted in the water by the bathing Artemis and was turned into stone as further punishment for his mother's infidelities.

JS: Visual poetry explores the tension of how, as Mallarmé remarked, we arrange twenty-six letters on the page. The effect of writing is only partially sound and sense. It is also how the appearance of text on the page, frame, or screen hits the eye. Writing is already concrete. Visual significance is attached to concrete poetry, because in the schism of language development, from picture writing to an abecedarian society, those who countenance the Roman alphabet no longer make the cognitive leap of associating the iconic with words.

IIO: "When you present people with a visual poem they all of a sudden become illiterate because they're used to seeing a visual poem with a commodity attached to it. . . . As soon as you take the product away . . . all of a sudden it's 'what's this?' and they panic and they can't read anymore."[7]

NT: After Mallarmé and Apollinaire, more than a century after—we are still faced with a problem: typographic experimentation is not enough—serving as a blank marker for "poetic" text, every outrage of space and form is tolerable, so long as it is contained. When Textbase set out to revisit history we set out to empty form in the reiteration of processes, radicalizing by indicating that something is no longer there—evoking a memory—drawing attention to a space that indicates completion without giving it. For example, the significance of a contemporary treatment of chance operations or automatic writing lies not in the fact that they are new but in that they are not. "Method isn't communicated in writing. Writing shows you the road taken."[8] Poetry exhausts itself continually in the process of its becoming. It doesn't stop because its foundational ambiguity can never be adequately resolved. This, and not the subject, is the agent that drives its compulsive repetition.

NT & DH:

> Occasionally new terms have to be invented.
>
> —Don Judd

> Les vieux mots ne marchent plus.
>
> —Hélène Cixous

Two different people are saying the same thing—putting these found objects together makes something else—not because they are the same but because the differences are conjunctive.[9]

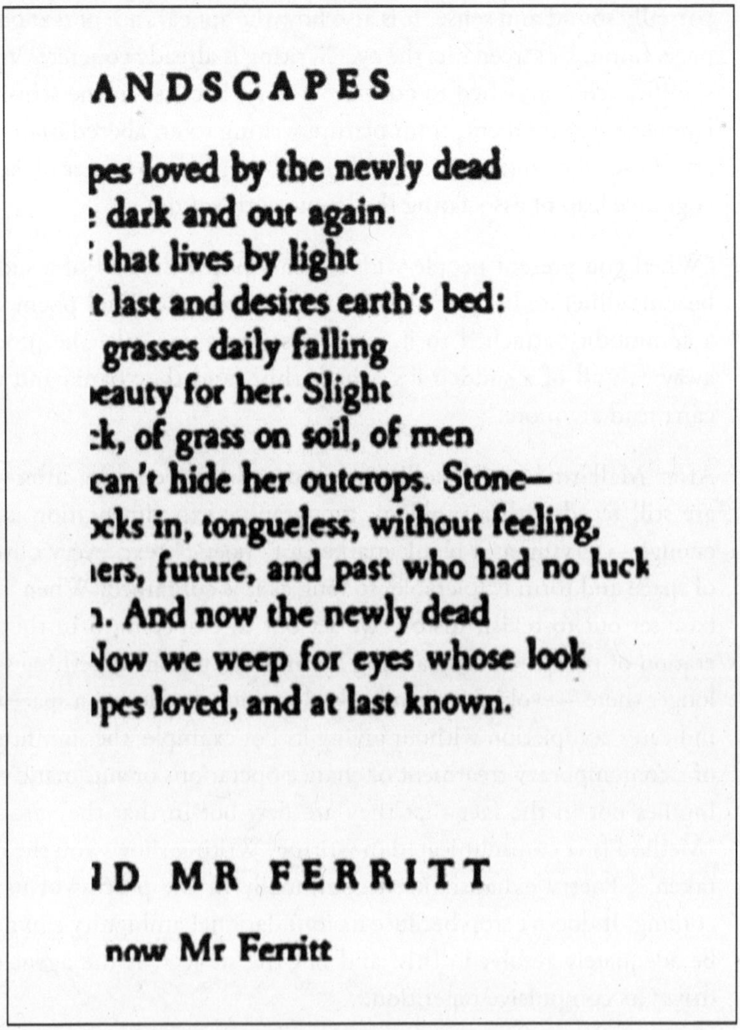

ANDSCAPES

pes loved by the newly dead
: dark and out again.
' that lives by light
t last and desires earth's bed:
grasses daily falling
eauty for her. Slight
:k, of grass on soil, of men
can't hide her outcrops. Stone—
ocks in, tongueless, without feeling,
ıers, future, and past who had no luck
ı. And now the newly dead
Jow we weep for eyes whose look
ıpes loved, and at last known.

ID MR FERRITT

now Mr Ferritt

Page from Sebastian Gurciullo, *Marginal Text*

The quarrying of scatological
deposits. Sift through smoke. Wake
to gum-blossoms. A regulatory for-multiplying
device. Provides leverage.

Let's have a dream together.

Erasure

JS: The short film loop *Eraser* addresses the nexus linking text and image. It is essentially a text animation (shot frame by frame) wherein a conceptual word (art, film, text, painting, installation) is written in chalk on a blackboard, rubbed out, and replaced by another term in an endless loop of erasure and reinstatement. The terms may also be read in combination with one another as art-film, film-text, text-painting, painting-installation, installation-art, and so on to highlight how definitions often seek validation in the preexisting loops of etymologies, dictionaries, and difference. The blackboard serves as an appropriate educative tool.

JS: *Eraser* follows, among others, Michael Snow's film *So Is This* (1982), a self-reflexive coherent text that presents its "script" exclusively as one word on the screen at a time. In exploring the potential of text as image his montage of words without "images" is structured to form intelligible sentences, self-reflexive remarks, and at one point a sing-along show tune (all adhering to the syntax of chronology and causal relations), which wittily play with the temporal dimension of language. In regard to his process Snow offers the conundrum, "I do not have a system, I am a system": physiological, linguistic, and cerebral. This statement undermines Locke's assertion that at birth the human mind is "white paper, void of all characters." The analogy may be better represented by the palimpsest. . . .

AW: "The narrative does have an explosive quality and could be seen as the narrative of the hysteric who reiterates their position then loses that position then reforms it again. It is a form of reiteration and loss, the narrative disappears, then it is resuscitated and brought back to the surface again. So it is a constant reworking of a theme. But then musical themes work in that way too in contemporary music. The repetition and then reiteration of formats."[10]

JS: What may be variously understood as the principles of composition and ordering, an intelligible chain of word-ideas, the continuity of discontinuous images or a synchronic system existing as a sociocultural logic, if reviewed through the prism of history, separates into a series of suspended moments with known outcomes. The axis on which we spin is momentary. And & . . .

Three details from Julian Savage, *Eraser,* 1997

NT: It was never every artist but only those of a particular order that were to be expelled from the republic

ideal republic
(*Language ripples our lips*)[11]

those poets leading the citizenry astray by presuming to know a thing beyond the entitlement of art—imitating a second-order occurrence—traversing an indecorous, a dangerous and corrupting region of shadow—stepping beyond a constrained invocation of the presence of the gods—threatening instead to displace them—to multiply them—to obscure, cover over, or rupture the One/Idea. If since Plato literature is the other of philosophy, or of statecraft, it is not because its nature as literature is determinable but because the demands of philosophy and the state require its containment. This is an imperative, a constitutive prohibition which allows the becoming visible of a contradictory logic, indivisible from but not to be conceived of as a subset or subordinate form of rational discourse

. . . the leading astray causes a hesitation . . . a stutter and in the space of this hesitation a proliferation of unnamable occurrences

. . . a ripple . . .

. . . all possibilities of existence . . .

allowing the abandonment of the redemptive . . . qualities of madness . . . transgression . . . directly enunciated propositions . . . the manifold inflections of singularity . . . the natal disposition . . .

. . . leaving supplementation—excess—violence—the work—*the ground which is an absence of ground*

our future

astronaut

expectation[12]

Notes

1. Stéphane Mallarmé, cited in *Poems for the Millennium,* vol. 1, ed. Jerome Rothenberg and Pierre Joris (Berkeley and Los Angeles: University of California Press, 1995), 49.
2. James Joyce, *Ulysses* (London: Penguin Books, 1992), 932.

3. Gilles Deleuze and Félix Guattari, *A Thousand Plateaus: Capitalism and Schizophrenia,* trans. Brian Massumi (Minneapolis: University of Minnesota Press, 1987), 99.

4. . . . *with the slumber of conventional knowledge.* Compare Georges Bataille, *The Accursed Share: An Essay on General Economy,* vol. 1, *Consumption,* trans. Robert Hurley (New York: Zone Books, 1988).

5. Textbase (D. J. Huppatz, Nicole Tomlinson, Julian Savage, Benjamin Brady, and Sebastian Gurciullo) is an ongoing collaborative project based in Melbourne, Australia, involving writers working across a variety of media.

6. Fredric Jameson, "The Linguistic Model," in *The Prison House of Language* (Princeton, N.J.: Princeton University Press, 1972), 22–29.

7. Interview with πO, *Textbase* 4 (1998), www.textbase.net. πO is one of Melbourne's best-known experimental writers and performers. He is the author of several books, the best known of which are *The Fitzroy Poems* (Melbourne: Collective Effort Press, 1989), his epic *24 Hours* (Melbourne: Collective Effort Press, 1996), and his recent collection of concrete poetry, *The Number Poems* (Melbourne: Collective Effort Press, 2001), and is editor of *Off the Record* (Ringwood, Victoria: Penguin Books, 1985), an anthology of Australian performance poetry issued as both a book and an LP. As well as for conventional poetry, πO is also known for his innovative concrete and visual poetry. His work is unfortunately largely ignored in discussions of contemporary Australian poetry, particularly at an international level.

8. Michel Foucault, "Distance, Aspect, Origin," *Tel Quel Reader,* ed. Patrick ffrench and Roland-François Lack (London: Routledge, 1998), 103.

9. Donald Judd quoted in *Art After Philosophy and After: Collected Writings, 1966–1990,* ed. Gabriele Guercio (Cambridge, Mass.: MIT Press, 1991), 68. Hélène Cixous quoted in Morag Shiach, *Hélène Cixous A Politics of Writing* (London: Routledge, 1991), 86.

10. Interview with Ania Walwicz, *Textbase* 1 (1998), www.textbase.net. Ania Walwicz is another of Melbourne's best-known experimental writers and performers. Widely anthologized in Australia, Walwicz is the author of three books: *Writing* (Melbourne: Rigmarole Books, 1982), *Boat* (Sydney: Collins/Angus and Robertson, 1989), and *Red Roses* (St. Lucia: University of Queensland Press, 1992). She is also a practicing visual artist.

11. Susan Howe, "Pythagorean Silence," in *The Europe of Trusts* (Los Angeles: Sun and Moon Press, 1990), 63.

12. Michel Foucault, "Distance, Aspect, Origin," in *Tel Quel Reader,* eds. Patrick ffrench and Roland-François Lack (London: Routledge, 1998), 103.

Reading Notes

Bruce Andrews

for Dotti

Let's read—a political economy of sense & praxis.

There are givens of writing open to contest, but there are also givens of reading open to contest. Moment by moment, which is it gonna be?

"Inherent poetics will out."[1] Especially when it comes to *connecting* the possibilities for such drastic new writing with the opportunities we take up as readers. Here, we could focus on the ways that meaning & pleasure & challenges to ideology get fashioned out of the up close experience of reading, not just from our taking in the triumphs of experimental writing. We're pulled outside of any model of straightforward communication & exchange, or of cultural capital to be appropriated as someone *leans back* to be impressed & entertained. Certainly it goes beyond a reading dedicated to some revelation of prepackaged content or *response* to an author's prior intention: "include stakeouts beyond sense declension."

To marvel at the degree of disjunctiveness or discontinuity in poetic work like this today takes on a fresh edge if we attend to the dynamics of reading. Seemingly wild or informalist possibilities may sit at the opposite end of a spectrum from any temptation toward continuity & spectacle—a temptation we might detect in literary writing more invested in the *powers* of formalism (in either a conceptual or a programmatic version).

B-I.

Transparency—an old-fashioned model of reproducing sense: to read through words, individually or in recognizable clusters, toward (or in the shadow of) specific referents.

Protecting what? "Present as Genteel. BAD archaic element." Safeguarded by a tradition of so-called close reading that *presumes* some gnomic (yet specific & recoverable) plans & coding & expectations set up intentionally by the author. How stuck in someone else's continuous past do you want to be?—"maintaining / the absence of the full-stop." As if, in more conventional literary work, there had been a prior emptying out of the words by the author—to enforce their contractual (referential) obligations, to reduce their (dissociative) speed, to enforce some continuities predesigned to deliver up some overall mood or sketch out some larger convincing picture. Reading through words (by ignoring the code of manners at stake in this delivery) renders the words flimsy or weightless, underjinxed. We're stuck with an immaterialism of denial.

Get this: what shows, what's showing, is only "nominally manifest"—a name show, "and relic contingency." Can't a word stand on its own? "Mannered semblance or void aspect," yet semblance is a mannerism, a (usually visual) ventriloquism. A different kind of writing rebuffs some of this enforcement by the past, as well as the lures of familiar, even effortless reference that it depends upon. Instead of near-cinematic continuities, we get gathered up or twisted around in "tenuous rhythm." "I matter in time fluttered cadence." Pulled apart, words matter differently—as blockage of see-through, as noise, with an abolitionism of subsequently.

Action: "to repudiate a lineage." We can experience such a ripping up of conventions as we get over being spooked by those ghosts of coherence & consensus that had been bottled up in them. "Time's showroom *exegete*" wants our votes for continuity instead. Yet continuity is little more than the concession that death makes to life, or to dynamic change. Close reading is taxidermy. The best continuity is death.

Consider the alternative: time scramble. Even to the point where time gets spaced out or capsizes into space. "Meaning gets thrust / up every which way—." Partly by readers of radical texts as they are practically compelled to track the differential systematicness of language—even if that means skipping over some of the idiosyncratic concreteness of letters & syllables, to locate the individual units inside a system of signifiers (since that seems like the only part of the sign that could be systematized).

Such a reading plays around within the displayed/displaced system of language on which radical composition goes to work. It plies "a polysemous series of profane relations."

Still, the "overstimulated word" can stand out from any system leash, linguistic or otherwise. Reading it, & around it, we make compositions "lacking in methodologies tidying rigour." We toy with the "NON-SPECIFIC SIGNIFIED." "Composition // occurs later—deplete artefact congruence."

B-2.

Stripping away the foundations—of the sign system, of stylistic continuity, of allegiance to genre—turns it into a high-wire act. "Much of the firmament / has washed away." Daring readerly acrobatics "awakened by the shifting foundation."

Representation gives way to breakage. "I can't see the figures for the desecration."

Individual words are deposed, pulled apart & put back together again, where we're no longer visibly (or consciously) "bullied by american spell check."

Our vocabulary hit a snag, words or even letters jettisoned from a reassuring lockstep, "my meaning adrift." Language "gnomic in dispersal." "Undergrounded in realities." Or, "apropos goof": Are the mistakes instances of the author refusing to follow orders, or of readerly flamboyance in decoding or in *Crime Scene Investigation?* "Thinking of smashing something / up, actually writing it, no telling what." Uncoding.

We read little bits "at the (throttling point) / hatchet edge." They present "a crystalline irregularity." "Inchoate: blasted." As if in a "drunkardliness" on the part of the text, or on *our* part but with *its* encouragement (& without the breathalyzer test). We produce events, intersections, *transits:* "Composing transits / of ineffable / Fluff." Then "why not thrill to the tingling jests of novel modernities—." "The expected is so insupportable."

B-3.

Language refuses to give way before "Divine, right of things." Something intrudes, something in between. Don't we notice a prior clotting in the language system, a clotting that makes time for the subject & her action? But with a subject, are we talking about the writer or the reader? After all, what does it take to make sense, to be comprehensible? Does it require some agency, some unfurling of an active authorial voice—"Passive voice (no suggestion) therefore incomprehensible"? Without personification, without the trappings of intimacy or personal revelation, do we end up with "That which excludes action"—so that "nothing can be said"? A customary fix would be to personalize the language, to rig it up to carry the customary force of suggestion. But why can't the impersonal or even the inanimate do some suggesting?

Before you mummify, abdicate. Confession—spurred on by continuities of subjecthood, tone, syntax, and so on—exasperates. Let's get out. "Are no further filmic cluttery / bits of feeling stalked and staked." The author signs off as "Yours, an apparent whom." As if *character* can only operate as an invocation of a network of references. The reverse is not true. "Disorder, refute / and begrudge ME." "As if I matter, as if." Identity Antipolitics.

The subject becomes constructive, on-site, once read "in my wreckage." To experience the text in this way carries with it marks of "self/battery"—by filling in, by substituting for herself/her selves in a more complicated timeline. "I am usually absent." Dishevel the name. Toss off the name—in a "merry mutiny." Which suggests either our tendency to identify with the mutiny of the author or our bolder mutiny from any preimposed authoritarianism of production. Author be damned. Textual audacity "discards name" altogether—but not meaning.

"It is you who have initiated the process / & your travails retain an oblique lineage of documentation." Or a lineage of semblance, instead of formalist self-enclosure. How much on account? "Indemnity, or who I seem." Or is that double indemnity? With these extremities of writing, how much (& what kind of) readerly *will* or *swoon* do you expect to help encourage on the other end—& how does it get configured? "'VECTOR' / 'DESIRE' / 'BODY' / 'YR'"

B-4.

We're quick to attribute a heroic stance or a showy bohemian insouciance to rebellion. But what's left for the reader? Much of the celebratory talk about bursting out of stylistic or discursive straitjackets has centered around the writer's consciousness or point of view. But doesn't reading need to move downstage? When it comes to a heroism of pure breakage, its force gets pretty eroded on the path leading toward a so-called period style. All those Dadaist trappings, so quickly consigned to the history books.

What's the potential reader's moment-to-moment relationship to style or grammar or social discourse? Crutch? Prod? Regulator? Police state? Reading, we certainly can bask in insurgencies of words, taking them on viscerally. But this is specific. There is no single one-size-fits-all breakage, nor any reason to assume that fragmentation forces us into a cul-de-sac. "Fragment (no suggestion)." As if! In reality, a reverberating constellation of fragments can suggest, can even get a statement across. Once we highlight the moment of reading, the familiar one-way street opens up. Our adventures in reading play out within elaborate *varieties* of breakage: of verisimilitude, grammar, genre, consistency of argument or mood or tone or timbre or coloration or pitch. As one type of activism: "A series of small, crackling sounds intrudes upon the contestable given."

Yet *insurgency* is always so timely. Circumstances force it to retake its bearings, again & again, chronically. That's the nature of discourse as a "contestable given." Reading through it, we plunge into "homologous diversity." Scatter. Layers. Concentric circles of significance. Now, there's no reason a discursive rupture (or a rupture keyed to a particular discourse) can't propel its implications outward in a similar way: to make a *troping* width, or scale. To read discursively, careening out from syllables or word fragments toward their widest grip. "Position the limpid polyglot" to penetrate an outer terra incognita or confront "expanded prowl." We take on the role of Arranger ourselves: redecorating & scaling local detail (as well as footnotables—more remote cross-references), ping-ponging back & forth within & outside the limits of discourse, to shed light on those limits.

Radical texts solicit a nonsequential production or remaking of sense—(to parallel an early characterization of *hypertext* as nonsequential writing). But it doesn't have to be as rigidly predefined as classic link/node hypertext or hypertext as cryptograph. More freely, readers "could string words, find goofy relations." We maneuver within a discursive *informalism.* As a measuring of time, as spatialized timing, as an architecture of memory. A polyengorgement—isn't that the best way to trick certitude? The *Multiple* challenges the one-person all-by-myself Truth Squad.

B-5.

The call is out for a writing that frustrates, or doesn't bother with, a *leaning back* style or comfy read.[2]

We like to keep a little phobic about aura too.

To clarify, let's consider a non-reader-centered alternative—either in mainstream literature or (perhaps especially) in newfangled versions of technic spectacle or machinic programming. Here we imagine that a text, all by itself, could sustain the illusion of a lobbing of meaning, an almost geological surging up of sense, from subterranean 'below' to dizzying 'above.' Reading would then be a camaraderie—"yearning to this word." As if the supernatural were supervening, in the front-row seats. Or as if our fetishism of the past & its traditions, its turf battles & Heritage Village coziness had emptied all of the reader's time out of the textual experience, to risk a collapse into (either classicist or automated) instantaneousness & presence.[3] What we really need to know is: how much feigned proximity (to person, to bioemphatics, to scape, to facts, to language *as a whole*) does the text incite?

"'BLANDISHMENT'" defines a counterreading. We don't want the words regimented in space & disappearing in time, leaving no trace. "—am I separate or sought in an adjectival squirm of over- / identificatory liaison?" The visualized variant: "or iris vignetting entity"—warming over (or targeting) the prerecorded facts. "—should not I now chow / a whole faceful of phantoms?" No flipping, no blinking.

The alternative to texts that call for an activated, informalist reading would be prone to elicit a disembodiment—as if the body of the reader were being constructed (or parsed) by the closures which the text imposes. Even seemingly astonishing closures. We get an inflicted facework (or interfacework), with all of its characteristic generality, its overdetermination of the blank. Text as grid, text as grammar. In some new cyberversions of non-reader-centered textuality, we confront a purity or autonomy of proceduralism brought to our desktops by information technology. (This is where it may make sense to link the legacy of concretism to that of intermedia in cyberspace. Both risk a shared limitation: a similar investment in *making an impression* in either visualized or *nominalized, virtual media* at the expense of the reader's productivity.)[4]

As a new terrain for writing, programmatic codework runs this risk. Syntactic & semantic & formatting permutations can all be carried out independently of any possible readership. An automatized textuality may be the result, formulating—or becoming—its own response. No longer just a prosthesis of memory, the interfacework would become a prosthesis of substitution, a solvent of time. The reflexivity of the cybernetic apparatus turns inward; its signs & its recipients made arbitrary or irrelevant. As if they were programmed by a hypermnesic apparatus that seemingly remembers by forgetting everything. For readers to be penned in, pinned down: the crowd control consultant's dream. Instead of a reading that increases our finiteness, focusing or concentrating our finite state, we could end up with texts that reduce our finiteness, blurring our particulars. The breathing fascinates us: "every shivery aside binding / co-determinate froth management."

C-1.

There's a big social world out there. Did we notice? Is the writing designed to help us apprehend the larger scaffolding of sense behind it, or to help this scaffolding stay in the dark, a "*system'o'neglect*"? Still, this isn't a call for some National Public Radio ("legendary victim improvement") version of 'meanings' coming pleasantly or collegially together. "Fearing alliances of meaning / without / taking immolation / into account." Exposures of conflict & negativity still get us juiced.

"*Pay Attention!*" In activist reading, alertness—& alertness to conflict—as pleasure. Not just the bare-knuckle agonistics of influence (registered in time—readers' time, which codework may ignore or hollow out) but also the pleasures of spatial conflict or skewing, the stressed territorialities of semantic overlap & tension, the building & intersecting of temporary/partial hegemonies of sense & affect.

Shake up the reader "in polite contingency"—to counteract the automatisms of programming or confinement to classicist heritage, "to temper this intrusive expansion of mind." Surface Kinetics. Velocities—deletion & ellipsis, speed *plus* halting. Or "transience fidget, heft." Social weight or heft can be engined out of speed, fidget, transience; it needn't be our one-way ticket to Lugubrium City. It's "the ever frantic repertoire" ready to start to have "confounded lassitude." Why not give us "the full brunt of aural thumpage, sirenage"? Why not bring on "the reading of constant motion"?

While "speeding up the music" we help displace the old 'necessary' aura, the overly well-grooved reaction. "Generalia extant upon reactive fodder." Specificities of attention denaturalize, disalienate, rematerialize. "Crushing naturalised generalia," we make a reversal of sophistry. Language "&/or estranged." Attention particularizes; attention granulates. Beguilement stripped off. "—The beautiful music has stopped." A controversy baits. And baits our body. A less-generalized version of the body returns with the reader reading adventurous texts. The aesthetic returns—

as a new performative, an interactive rhetoricalness. We enjoy interfering with your pleasantries. Chemical bonding is made or meant to seem relativized, fragile, part of a "surfeit of contingency." Sleek friction; sleek pressure. Nature as alienation. Incision makes hope.

Lean forward—as we would, maneuvering at the laptop or desktop, negotiating far-flung databases, and so on. Let's reinstate the mobile powers of the signified, with all their opportunities for (aesthetic) synthesis, or for a *merger* of machinic with intentional logic, as we're encouraged to read through entire sign systems as mobilizable social objects. If this resembles a *sublime,* it comes in a different version: no longer unapproachably beyond us, it is more like an interpretive or a cognitively or experientially processed sublime with more broadly social bearing.

The forms & formats of writing can be designed to help structure any initial chaos of microscopic particulars—to encourage us to tease out their *macroscale* implications. And we can imagine these larger-scale effects to have greater width—wider, as both more social & more disjunctive: alterity of reference as nonlinearity & speed. Reading can make a topology out of the *vectoral* exchange between degrees of immediacy & mediation, degrees of referentiality, scalings of local significance. It can make a syncopation out of convergences & juxtaposition. *Transversality. Parallax*—a network of remote intensifiers "plus more inverted political homilies." So, kick the outside, the social outside; "collective glut / shove."

C-2.

Counteract the generalizing, the universalizing. "There may be shunting, there may be unity." There may be various & variable weights, tiltings, adhesives. *Entropics.* Or: "gravitational rhetorics instil seminal prescience."

"—Can I question?" We can too—we're nudged to; putting ourselves at the distances the text choreographs from multiple perspectives, without suturing them permanently together. "What grew some composure under ideogloss": now it's set up for discomposure. Text as a specific, particularized solvent of the social status quo. Not to propose "the wry suss"—but a more oppositional attitude, with exuberance at misbegottening—"Let's white English!" Here our interaction with a microreportage needs to get with an insistently broad range of the f/acts—& of their spaces. "Wish to report on the atomization of the social order under Later-Than-We-*Think* Capital"—"irksome / in its overtly defeatist model of the ration."

How much social matter or territory, & what kind, can adequately account for or make intelligible the words. To contextualize: "& *is* that an harangue or justified outburst." As if "wordly circumstance" were choreographed to place us back in worldly conditions—"allow an anguished plea for every / sustainable circumstance." Stick 'em the glut, the social surplus, as an impractical immeasure. Sizing up property lines, resizing spacings. "How I could see the propertied outlines." Connecting (& connecting with) the words as partial maps & partial lists—"of pertinents and a field of fodder." Pertinents: small sparklers, autopsies, risk takings & giganticisms. Rereadings.

When does a symptom become a perception?

C-3.

In certain kinds of textuality more than others, we read evidence (twists & turns) of a social system that ratifies itself through induction, "no more modest instruction." The culture apparatus trains us, socializes us; we are the "mercantile subset / of Training Capital." Part of a self-exalting project that saturates most of the language we come across—as if bedeviled by *Lack,* impulsively seeking the reassurance of unity within an objectified self, to meet the preconditions for "this imputation of fault" & agency & responsibility.

Phonex—Solicitation.

The words don't just implicate some universalizing schema (of an imaginary body, for instance). Identification is forced translation—(we're not making that mistake). Capital sponsors the generic—"stranglehold, choke, chain, (bashed [probably/unusable] out of class consciousness)." But the interpellations appear filled with glittering particularizings, magnets for seduction & identification. The reality is different: "I am reduced to a generic being sniping at a hostile city-state." "Find only myself typing the personal 'I' as numeric one (1)."

Yet in experiencing more obstreperous texts, the identifications don't start out as generic (even if the social pressure is on to make them so). Consistency is barely skin-deep. Even the generic person is only "an apparent whom." Territory stays contested—& we can sense it in the words. Any continuous occupancy by a generic persona or personhood—a "whom"—is caked with doubt.

Plagiarism is internal to the text. "He is onto their identity. This is a curse." "'I' is a trick-diving belwether." The reader's ME gets refuted or begrudged by a social scaffolding of disorders of an actively productive or constitutive kind. "Escaping the main conspiracies, I am set adrift." We'd often like to be too, but . . . how can we escape? Our disbelief needs to be primed: "fleeing the activity prod" & its occasional tantrums.

Dramatically center staging a particularized body. Here it's being offered up as "enclampment / dysfunction"—to mess up the social clampdown. An activated reader-body to resist the sort of strategic unawareness that allows for easy interpellation. "The field is catapulted from identification." Splittings to save us. Recall us. Rather than bolstering *Lack* with compensatory illusions of wholeness, stoke the reader's urge to become *multiply incomplete.* Debot us.

C-4.

To toss a reader-centered wrench into the apparatus, to replace the ghost in the machine implicit in more programmatic works: "a serene disembowelling of finer poetics." How can the text help trouble or discourage the proverbial good judgment? Certainly not by emphasizing *redundancy.* Instead, pick a new fight. "Into such argumentative states"—to equip the language with the force of *suggestion,* not just a consoling suggestiveness.

Forensics. Words as deposition, at odds with the redundancy of fixed structure—the posing from a variety of angles makes them so. Whereas "you are small print outside an older order." And reading: "for an ideologue, I'm deleted." "'We' is a time-biased brick shit-house"—prepositioned within that "serial solidity of the propertied": usually in thrall to narrative, membered to hegemony.

More drastically, when it seems as if part of our split personality has an accomplice: "dotty-mouthed social self / emergent, rampant." In a disjunctiveness (or dissociativeness or perversity) of insurgent device, we confront words of social sufferance, of inflicted social materiality, resonating through manifold protective layers of formality & fecundity. As if the reader's body as a surface of social inscription could become a matter of reversible tattoos. Readability . . . preoperative . . . postoperative . . . "—to-be-honed."

C-5.

"Complete sense?"

Surprise makes hope—for all of us in a future anterior—"in havoc." As twins: turbulence & information. Set off the social Geiger counter. Catastrophe exigency. (Can you create *exigency* & then make it disappear?) *Strange Attractors* (or should that also be 'staged attractors')—as opposed to the mechanizing of readership by the sleights of hand of (conceptual or digital) programming.

Redundancy tends to risk self-enclosure, an antisocial tilt. Instead we ask: can't the reading help produce a semantic "social proximity"—"a social, intersubjective mirror" . . . "—or perhaps flaunt of suprajectivity." We're calling for a counterhegemony of made-possible gentleness, a forethrow of social possibility.

Out of the Past: "comeuppance scissions daft hope."

Fun is fun.

Fight the future.

Notes

Some notes, at times manifesto-like, on the (often neglected) dynamics of reading radical texts, bouncing off the cushions of arguments in *Contemporary Poetics* (a 2001 special issue of the Prague journal *Litteraria Pragensia,* edited by Louis Armand). The ten-part organization parallels the outline of an ongoing poetics project, "Tips for Totalisers," mentioned in "Paradise & Method" (in my essay collection, *Paradise & Method: Poetics & Praxis,* from Northwestern University Press, and also in *Aerial 9: Contemporary Poetics as Critical Theory,* ed. Rod Smith).

1. All material placed within double quotation marks in this essay is from the Canadian poet Dorothy Trujillo Lusk's exemplary *Ogress Oblige* (San Francisco: Krupskaya, 2001).

2. Thinking of corporate decisions about the conflicting interfaces of television and personal computers—which are frustrating the desired moneymaker: integrating the role of a TV & a PC in a single box in the home entertainment center. The styles in conflict, with interesting parallels to the expectations we bring to literature, are *leaning back* & *leaning forward.*

3. A disability of either a worshipful, auratic reception or—perhaps pretty much the same thing—of too much *leaning back* to enjoy the multimediated or algorithmic fireworks.

4. Perhaps this would get us close to a nonphenomenal sublime of machinic automatism & put us within hailing distance of the discussions in *Material Events: Paul de Man and the Afterlife of Theory,* eds. Tom Cohen, Barbara Cohen, J. Hillis Miller, and Andrzej Warminski (Minneapolis: University of Minnesota Press, 2001).

Lost and Found

Bruce Andrews

I'm staying up late night during the Big Blackout, reading Michael Gottlieb's *Lost and Found,*[1] the affective ambit of its "Deep Vertical File Cabinet" activated by flashlight (& votive red Corazon candle). "The bright line" formal elegant snazz "the candid snap, / the large detail" on the spot with the telling clip, "the faltering isolate" end-of-the-rope troubles the social. To make it "a kind of decision tree."

B-1.

This is nonfilter, the aisles of units fully formed—"something we can all feel / good about abandoning." "A through-and-through." "A viewfinger, that's what's missing."

B-2.

"Transitions, Extreme Twist Frame"—"breakage and peradventure" pivot into what's amiss, "like refusal simple," the insouciant perforation as "a topical reagent."

B-3.

"Unmanned" *because of* "the great intervallic leaps." "How much smaller may we dice you?" Fronting "a flurry of affect," "and the particulates." "Amour propre splayed across the page." "Think of me as a sort of temporary filling." "No one can help you now."

B-4.

In "our familiar, amicably stabilised ruins," "—those failed familiars . . . / our ganged evasions." "Themes and practices / not uncloyingly / erode inevitably into roles and responsibilities," compensation gathered up inconsolably. Monstrance, we are the walking reproof.

B-5.

Reading as "a consent decree" "and its thraldom." This Noun Left Intentionally Blank. "You come to believe you can 'collect them all,'" force & face "disarmed in the face of . . . *ourselves.*" To remember—or better, to forget.

C-1.

There are pinprick impulses & there are felt-tip impulses. A pell-mell tonic smashing up the overspecified, unerringly not quite familiar, blusterless & jolting. There's "a certain jouissance attached" to what "could have been even *more* better." Trip up the retuned riposte "prostrate from abject." "In lieu of, / always." "What one once bowed to" "not unlike an exaggerated startle response."

C-2.

Even the facts are pastiches—to keep you from getting demiremanded to the doxauthorities; "like mortality, a kind of haring, not a chase, / another routine" whacked by merchandising in a slo'-syruped-D. J. Screw pace trying to become less right-handed. "A kind of risorgimento / of the unacknowledged."

C-3.

"What we did to ourselves / and do still." The fond breaking of the mold. "What do we have to show for ourselves"?—"a fakebook / writ large" "interposed countersignatures." "There are adults / in need of supervision" "schooled to respond without reply." Rescind their ways of making us shut up.

C-4.

"The unbowed resignation" "miming inaction." As "a kind of constructive disavowal" went into syndication. The improper violence-averse study of businesspeoplekind vouching for a counterresolution.

C-5.

"All of a sudden, seeing us all as just more special pleading, / and that was not enough." Instead, the lost is unfounded, jouissant as any "appreciated hope, / we try / to breathe life into."

Note

1. Michael Gottlieb, *Lost and Found* (New York: Roof Books, 2003). All text passages in quotation marks are from this source.

Part Four : **Cursors**

Concrete Poetry: A Manifesto

Augusto de Campos

—concrete poetry begins by assuming a total responsibility before language: accepting the premise of the historical idiom as the indispensable nucleus of communication, it refuses to absorb words as mere indifferent vehicles, without life, without personality, without history—taboo-tombs in which convention insists on burying the idea.

—the concrete poet does not turn away from words, he does not glance at them obliquely: he goes directly to their center, in order to live and vivify their facticity.

—the concrete poet sees the word in itself—a magnetic field of possibilities—like a dynamic object, a live cell, a complete organism, with psycho-physico-chemical proprieties, touch antennae circulation heart: live.

—far from attempting to evade reality or to deceive it, concrete poetry is against self-debilitating introspection and simpleton simplistic realism. It intends to place itself before things, open, in a position of absolute realism.

—the old formal syllogistic-discursive foundation, strongly shaken at the beginning of the century, has served again as a prop for the ruins of a compromised poetic, an anachronistic hybrid with an atomic heart and a medieval cuirass.

—against perspectival syntactic organization where words sit like "corpses at a banquet," concrete poetry offers a new sense of structure, capable of capturing without loss or regression the contemporaneous essence of poeticizable experience.

—mallarmé (*un coup de dés*—1897), joyce (*finnegans wake*), pound (*cantos,* ideogram), cummings, and on a secondary plane, apollinaire (*calligrammes*) and the experimental attempts of the futurists-dadaists are at the root of the new poetic procedure which tends to impose itself on a conventional organization whose formal unity is verse (even free-).

—the concrete poem or ideogram becomes a relational field of functions.

—the poetic nucleus is no longer placed in evidence by the successive and linear chaining of verses but by a system of relationships and equilibriums between all parts of the poem.

—graphic-phonetic functions-relations ("factors of proximity and likeness") and the substantive use of space as an element of composition maintain a simultaneous dialectic of eye and voice, which, allied with the ideogrammatic synthesis of meaning, creates a sentient "verbivocovisual" totality. In this way words and experience are juxtaposed in a tight phenomenological unit impossible before.

—CONCRETE POETRY: TENSION OF THING-WORDS IN SPACE-TIME

Note

This article was translated from the Portuguese by John Tolman. "Concrete Poetry: A Manifesto" was originally published in *AD—arquitectura e decoração* 20 (November/December 1956), São Paulo, Brazil.

Questionnaire of the Yale Symposium

Augusto de Campos

Q. *What dimensions of contemporary poetics are directly engaged with concretism?*

A. I see concrete poetry as directly engaged with the practices of vanguard, experimental, or—as it should probably more adequately be called—inventive poetry. I think that the task of concrete poetry, after it appeared in the fifties, was to reestablish contact with the poetry of the vanguards of the beginning of the century (futurism, cubofuturism, Dada et al.), which the intervention of two great wars and the proscription of Nazi and Stalinist dictatorships had condemned to marginalization. A similar movement occurred in the fifties in music, with the recuperation of the work of the Vienna Group (Schönberg, Webern, Berg), the rediscovery of the great individual experimentalists (Ives, Varèse, etc.), and the intervention of new vanguard composers, from Boulez to Stockhausen to Cage. In terms of the poets whom Pound termed "masters," "diluters," and the like, the practitioners of concrete poetry situate themselves, or hope to be situated, programmatically, in the category of the "inventors," that is, those who are engaged in the pursuit of new forms.

Q. *How do you see the historical precedents of your own concrete work? If you are not discussing your own work, please select a specific text on which to base your comments.*

A. For me, the dividing line for inventive poetic language in modern times is Mallarmé's work *Un coup de dés* (1897), a poem conceived intersemiotically as a fragmentary structure ("subdivisions prismatiques de l'Idée"), conjoining visual mural and musical score. With the acceptance of that work, it became possible to revisit the experiences of the vanguards of the beginning of the century and conceive of new elaborations. "Sans presumer de l'avenir qui sortira d'ici, rien ou presque un art" ["Without presuming, from this point on, anything of the future or of an art of the future"], the last Mallarmé—from *Un coup de dés* to *Le Livre* catalyzes and spreads the principal future alternatives of poetic language. In his final period and in the subsequent developments of the historical vanguards, which will be recycled and radicalized by concrete poetry, one encounters the formal presuppositions of the poetry of the technological era, which greatly expands throughout the second half of the century. Besides Mallarmé and the historical vanguards, I would place as direct precedents Ezra Pound (the ideogrammatic method, the collage and metalanguage of the Cantos), James Joyce (the vocabular kaleidoscope of *Finnegans Wake* and its textual polyreadings), Cummings (the atomization and syntactic dislocation of his most experimental poems), and, on a second level, more idiosyncratic and less rigorous, the experimental, minimalist, and molecular prose of Gertrude Stein. In the special case of Brazilian poetry, the Sousandrade of *O inferno de Wall Street* (*The Wall Street Hell*) with its precollage epigrammatic mosaics, Oswald de Andrade and the "anthropophagic" instantpoem, the constructivist engineering of João Cabral [de Melo Neto]. In a transdisciplinary mode, I would mention the transformations of musical language from Webern to Cage and of the visual from Malevich/Mondrian to Duchamp.

Q. *What are the theoretical underpinnings which distinguish your works from that of historical precedents or contemporaries?*

A. In view of the specific historical context in which it occurred, concrete poetry obviously did not participate either in the ideology of symbolism, which still underlies Mallarmé's poetics, or in the mechanopolitical futurist utopias, or in Dadaist nihilism. Concrete poetry took a position as a poetics of objectivity, attempting simply to place its premises at the roots of language, with the intention of creating new operational conditions for the elaboration of a poem in the sphere of technological revolution. Technically, concrete poets can be distinguished from their antecedents by the radicalization and condensation of the means of structuring a poem, on the horizon of the means of communication of the second half of the century. That implies, among other characteristics, the following: greater constructive rigor in relation to the graphic experiences of futurists and Dadaists; greater concentration of vocabulary; emphasis on the nondiscursive character of poetry; suppression or relativization of syntactic links; making explicit the materiality of language in its visual and sonorous dimensions; free passage between verbal and nonverbal levels. Poems such as "terra" by Décio Pignatari or "cristal" by Haroldo de Campos, from the fifties, or my "cidadecitycite" or "olho por olho," from the sixties, typify these characteristics. Concrete poets may be differentiated from other experiences (*zaum,* lettrism, phonetic poetry) for not rejecting semantic values but rather placing them on equal footing with other material, visual, and sonorous parameters of the poem. They differentiate themselves from the "chance poetry" of Cage and others for not abdicating control of the structure of the poem, although allowing for chance interventions.

Q. *To what extent is the work you are discussing different from the work of the concrete poets of the 1950s and 1960s?*

A. Now four decades since the first experiences of concrete poetry, I would say that the fifties and sixties were the period of greatest orthodoxy of the movement, something like the serialization of all musical parameters proposed by European post-Webernian musicians. In the later decades there occurred a greater flexibility of poetic language in the sense of recuperation of phrasal structures (in relation to the elementality of the first phase, with poems made up of only one word or of a few spatialized substantives) and of the inclusion of chance (with the interventions of Cage), but that flexibility always observed a compositional rigor and the principle of functionality or of the formal necessity of the poem. Such an opening became inevitable in view of the redundancy of process and of its degradation, brought about by the ineffectiveness of many realizations, especially in the area of visual poetry, characterized by a semantic insignificance analogous to many baroque graphic "labyrinths," which, with the superficiality of repeated graphic emblems, did not amount to more than the vacuity of epithalamic or funereal elegies. Such an opening should not be confused, either, with the apparent complexity of the simply chaotic surrealist texts that used graphic space without any satisfactory formal basis. Works of the eighties and nineties are, on the one hand, freer in relation to the orthodoxy of the first years and, on the other, more intensely participatory in the challenge of new technologies, which have produced digitalized poems, graphic and sound animation, and multimedia and intermedia processes. In this way, the "wishful thinking" of the fifties came about with computers, an ideal space for "verbivocovisual" adventures.

Q. *Is there a poetics of concretism, or is concrete poetry a formal device rather than a conceptual premise?*

A. As I see it, concrete poetry did not come about as a formal specialization in the field of modern poetry, as one could speak of *carmenfiguratum* in antiquity, but rather as a proposed radicalization of poetic language in which the visual aspects constitute just one of the relevant parameters. What concrete poetry sought was to recuperate the specificity of poetic language itself, the materiality of the poem and its autonomy, beginning with a revision and radicalization of the methods of modern poetry and of the elaboration of a new creative project in the context of new media.

Q. *Thesis:* "Concretism, one of the most radical avant-garde trends of this century, engaged in a critical reevaluation of the artistic object and its place in society, had a new way of looking at and reading tradition. It was a forerunner of later neobaroque and postmodern trends." *Please give your evaluation or judgment of this perspective as it relates to your own work or poetics or to your critical judgment of concretist experimentation.*

A. I don't think that either of the expressions—"neobaroque" or "postmodern"—are sufficiently adequate to characterize the actual moment in its possible relations with concrete poetry. The term "neobaroque" is too charged with historicity and could lead to confusions, if one considers that it usually takes in practices of Hispanic and Latin American poetry not connected to the poetics of concretism. As to "postmodern," it is a concept of indefinite contours, hardly defensible, to the degree that the presuppositions of "modern" are still in effect; it seems rather to be a label that serves as a pretext for eclecticisms of a conservative nature, actually pre- or antimodernist. I would stop at the first phrase of the thesis, adding in place of "It was a forerunner, etc." that concrete poetry once again took up speculations of an experimental lineage in contemporary poetry, forming relevant presuppositions for the development of poetry in the context of new media that are growing in the technological phase of modernity. It constituted, at the least, an important movement for keeping alive the revolutionary ideology of permanent and autonomous experimentation and redefining vanguard action in the second half of the century, assuming this position under the category of "poetry of invention" (in contrast to the more palatable "expressive poetry") as a means of resistance against the massification and the banalization of literature imposed by the new means of communication and the stagnation of conventional literature.

Note

This article was translated from the Portuguese by K. David Jackson. The Yale Symposium on Experimental, Visual, and Concrete Poetry took place April 5–7, 1995. The questionnaire was formulated by K. David Jackson, Eric Vos, and Johanna Drucker.

> I will confine myself to telling you that I dream of immense cosmologies, sagas, and epics all reduced to the dimensions of an epigram.
>
> —Italo Calvino

Epigrams, Particle Theory, and Hypertext

Darren Tofts

Epigrams are used traditionally to presage a beginning, *the* beginning. They announce the thematic import of the discourse that is to follow. The epigram is a kind of pretalk, an avant-scene. Sometimes there is more than one. In the case of multiple epigrams, an entirely new system of relations is established between the epigrams themselves, a prestructure within a prestructure. This kind of interconnected multiplicity—of a kind that detained the attention of the two great Augustan satirists of pedantry, Alexander Pope and Jonathan Swift[1]—prompts a question: What if the epigram is the event and not its harbinger? What, in other words, if the epigram is not the link that prepares us for conceptual passage elsewhere but is itself a singular event in which an entire discourse is implicit? Discourse is not something that follows, happens afterwards, but is already happening, is already present in the discrete fertility of epigrammatic concision. Need I, then, say any more?

I am less interested in the reception of this theory than in dramatizing its making as a constructive process or, dare I say it, a hypertextual process. I'm interested in extending my interest, explored in *Memory Trade,*[2] in the particulate nature of the alphabet as a finite structure of elementary particles or bits, capable of infinite generation of meaning. That is, I'm interested in a submorphological theory of meaning, drawing on the concept of the subatomic particle of quantum mechanics.[3] If literacy is concerned with letters as fundamental, irreducible particles of meaning, then how can we transport the idea of the particle into the digital realm, the online environment and the hypertextual web? Such a project is fraught with the potential of being unreceivable, since outlining a postliterate digital ~~literacy~~[4] is outside the hermeneutical circle of literacy itself. So what follows is a translation of a future model of digital ~~literacy~~.

The idea of describing a potential digital ~~literacy~~ that is not based in letters is, on second thought, not satisfactorily suggested by putting words under erasure. As a response to this problematic, I have drawn on the iconographic language of Australian digital artist Troy Innocent to illustrate the theory of meaning I am attempting to articulate here. Innocent's "Memetic" font is an attempt to create a symbolic, icon-based language that departs from the phonetic alphabet and provides, instead, a purely visual register of communication that is suited to the creation of virtual spaces conceived of *as* language, that is, a symbolic interpretation of digital code in iconographic terms.[5] Approximate translations or "unpackings" in serial time of the singular, semantic richness of these icons are noted as footnotes.

—Gilles Deleuze and Félix Guattari

In *A Thousand Plateaus,* Deleuze and Guattari interpret the epigram in an intriguing, multimedia way, using images instead of text.[6] Not, for a minute, that there is anything nontextual or atextual about an image. However, what is striking is the principle of signifying a conceptual link or portal into the text through iconic insinuation, implication, and suggestion rather than the overt, literal topicality of the written epigram. In the introductory chapter entitled "Rhizome," from which the epigram shown here is taken, they prefigure their discussion of deterritorialization, rhizomorphism, and writing to the *n*th degree, with a fragment from a 1948 score by Sylvano Bussoti, dedicated to John Cage's collaborator, David Tudor. While their discussion of multiplicities and enunciating machinic assemblages is rigorous and engaging, the work of this discussion has already been done in their epigram.[7] In terms of the theory of hypertextuality I want to make here, their twenty-two-page discussion is an exegesis, an elongated unwrapping, a verbal equivalent to the exploded diagram. Within these twenty-odd pages, what wonders emerge: complex ideas to do with textuality, abstraction, and becoming that have indelibly left their mark on the contemporary intellectual landscape—ideas that require a further 560 pages of delineation and articulation. And here we start to generate a sense of an idea that, while not in any way new, has preoccupied practitioners and theoreticians of the broad category of writing that Espen Aarseth has called "cybertext." It is a sense of overwhelming density crammed into a small space, whether it is the finite pages of a book, an epigram, or a docuverse: an intimation of compressed profundity, what the French theorist of space Gaston Bachelard called "intimate immensity." In the context of literature, Paul Valéry had suggested that the beginning of a novel contained its entire poetics in a nutshell.[8] While an idiomatic figure of speech, the idea of something vast being contained within something small, like a nutshell, has attracted writers throughout history. Shakespeare's Hamlet, engaged in lively badinage with Rosencrantz and Guildenstern, ponders the question of the space of the mind, noting that "I could be bounded in a nutshell and count myself a king of infinite space."[9] Three centuries later, James Joyce pondered that image and put it to the service of his own universe in a nutshell, or "microbemost cosm," in *Finnegans Wake,* where Shakespeare's conceit is transformed into "Allspace in a Notshall."[10] Writing at a time when quantum mechanics was making its first tentative steps toward particle theory, Joyce was highly attuned to and turned on by the idea that language, as a particulate structure of finite bits, could yield, under the right kinds of polysemous pressure, a "most spacious immensity."[11]

Received wisdom has it that what was an ideal within the technology of the printed book is now literal fact within a hypertext environment. Drawing on the work of French poststructuralism, theorists from George Landow to Gregory Ulmer have argued that the ideal of the writerly text is realized, or literalized, in the hypertextual network. While some interesting theoretical expositions have been undertaken in this respect (in particular the work of Ulmer), the auratic quality of the writerly text has lost something of its glow. For it is the *ideal* nature of the writerly text that generates fascination, the fact that although so much has been written about it, it could not be found in bookstores or libraries—even in the catalogs of Routledge, that fine purveyor of theoretical exotica, you will only find one title, and a single copy at that, of *Maniacs in the Fourth Dimension* by Kilgore Trout, of which I am the proud owner. Where the writerly text could be more readily glimpsed, though, if you were lucky, was on the bookshelves of certain writers of a particular kind of fiction. It is no accident that one of the great influences on contemporary theories of writing and complexity was Jorge Luis Borges. His presence in *A*

Thousand Plateaus is like Flaubert's God in nature, everywhere felt but nowhere seen (well, virtually unseen, as he is mentioned twice in the book). The introductory chapter is dominated by his parable of the map and the territory, in which a map is made of such scale and verisimilitude that it actually covers the empire it was designed to represent.[12] Moreover, a fragment from his later 1975 text, "The Book of Sand," exists as the epigram to the same chapter in a quantum edition of *A Thousand Plateaus.* As with Borges's other infinite book, *The Garden of Forking Paths,* this fugitive edition of *A Thousand Plateaus* exists "in an infinite series of times, a growing, dizzying web of divergent, convergent, and parallel times."[13] The epigram reads like this:

—Jorge Luis Borges

Borges's "Book of Sand" is a remarkable text, since it confounds the reader with a quality of dynamism that books, for centuries, weren't thought to possess.[14] That is, the printed word, unlike its pixilated counterpart, is fixed, unchanging. Only when a text is reset for a new edition can words be altered. In "The Book of Sand" we encounter a text that is never the same each time it is revisited, a text that never repeats itself: every time the same page is consulted, it contains something different. Moreover, despite its finite limitations, the number of pages proliferates each time it is opened:

> I took the cover in my left hand and opened the book, my thumb and forefinger almost touching. It was impossible: several pages always lay between the cover and my hand. It was as though they grew from the very book.[15]

Like sand, the mysterious book has no middle or end, and no matter how hard the narrator tries, he can never open the book at the first page.

In typical Borges style, the book is surrounded by mystery. Brought to the attention of the protagonist-narrator by its equally mysterious custodian, it becomes an obscure object of desire for a time. But only for a time, as its strange sublimity overwhelms its owner, defiling his sense of order and reality. Like Borges's "Book of Sand," the parallel edition of *A Thousand Plateaus* has on occasion crossed the desks of the coterie of academics aware of its elusive presence. Brian Massumi is reported to have seen it, though its oppressive proliferation is said to have turned him off translation for life. If what I have heard is true, since *Parables of the Virtual* he is said to write only epigrams.

If you read carefully between pages 1000 and 1001 of Charles Baudelaire's notebooks, you will find an odd and despairing reference to it. I myself have not escaped its inscrutable alchemy. The image of the disappearing figure of the anchor could not have been more prescient of my theory of hypertextuality. What I am moving toward is a theory of hypertextuality—a term that both identifies the characteristics of hypertext and its modes of behavior—as a discrete fertility that has imploded the classic, dyadic structure of node and link. In this theory there is no room for anchors.

Borges's fabular approach to the idea of the infinite book retains the resonances of uncertainty and implausibility associated with the writerly text. While "The Book of Sand" may not yet exist, the idea that it might or could exist is enough, to paraphrase Borges, to trouble our minds. And it is this element of the fabulatory, of that which may exist, that is both enticing and disquieting. To actually possess such a book is to no longer entertain the possibility of its potential, and it is this quality that fascinated Deleuze and Guattari about the ideal of the book as a flattened plane of indescribable excess. Once such a book exists, once it is a reality, it no longer has the potential to be inscrutable, just out of grasp, always ungraspable.

In thinking about the idea of intimate immensity, of discrete fertility, of universes within nutshells, I'm drawn to the idea of the charged potential of the singular image, the epigram, the discrete thing liberated from the obligation to introduce or link to something else. I'm interested in the obliteration of adjacency, juxtaposition, the link, and the connection: the disappearance of the anchor. In thinking of the charged potential of a singular thing, we need to make a theory of potential writing. In order to do so I need a talisman, a heuristic device. So let's have another epigram.[16]

—Italo Calvino

In his *Language of New Media,* Lev Manovich uses Dziga Vertov's 1929 film *Man with a Movie Camera* as a heuristic device throughout the book. In doing so he is demonstrating his theory that the language of new media is not something new, for which we have to invent a critical metalanguage.

On the contrary, he argues that what we understand to be the principles of new media aesthetics are already at work in older cultural forms such as cinema. In a similar fashion, I want to demonstrate that my theory of hypertext as a discrete fertility can be made from residual forms of textual compression. To achieve this end, I, too, have chosen a preelectronic text as a talismanic—or talismatic[17]—guide to discrete fertility.

Italo Calvino's protohypernovel, *If on a Winter's Night a Traveller* (1979), is an example of such an experiment in textual compression. It is an experiment in what Calvino has called a "'discrete' rather than a 'continuous' reality," a break with a tradition of storytelling in which one word is made to stand "in sequence with another."[18] *If on a Winter's Night a Traveller* stands for an attitude to experimental writing devoted to the problematics of the beginning, of the commencement. Two obvious precursors, over which Calvino has rewritten his novel as a palimpsest, are Laurence Sterne's *Tristram Shandy*[19] and *The Tales of the Thousand and One Nights*. If you are not familiar with Calvino's text, there are abundant descriptions of it within its own pages:

> I have had the idea of writing a novel composed only of beginnings of novels. The protagonist could be a Reader who is continually interrupted. The Reader buys the new novel A by the author Z. But it is a defective copy, he can't go beyond the beginning. . . . He returns to the bookshop to have the volume exchanged.[20]

Writing just before his death on the principles of what he called the hypernovel, Calvino noted that in *If on a Winter's Night a Traveller* his aim was

> to give the essence of what a novel is by providing it in concentrated form, in ten beginnings; each beginning develops in very different ways from a common nucleus, and each acts within a framework that both determines and is determined.[21]

Calvino wrote these words on the occasion of preparing a series of presentations that would form the Charles Eliot Norton Lectures in 1985 (they were published posthumously in 1988). The essay in question, "Multiplicity," was his attempt to map out the trajectory of complexity and encyclopedism into the new millennium. In theorizing the progress of the novel, Calvino was also extending a theoretical project he had begun in the late

1960s to do with the impact of computers and information technology on writing. In thinking about the kind of experimental, cybernetic writing that was being produced in Italy at that time, Calvino argued that such a technology was

> a tool for the formal decomposition of what is structured, and for challenging the normal train of thought. At a basic level this tool is a charmingly lyrical one. It satisfies a typically human craving: the production of disorder. A proper literature machine involves the craving for disorder as an inevitable reaction to a previous order. Such a machine will produce avant-garde material in order to sluice out its circuits after they have been clogged up by too long a period devoted to the production of classicism. It will feel unsatisfied with its own traditionalism and start planning out new ways of looking at the written word until it completely overturns the matrix which it had followed up till then.[22]

Sounds a lot like an intimation of imminent hypertextuality to me. His own account of *If on a Winter's Night a Traveller* as a kind of generative grammar, a literature machine, attests to his anticipation of the convergence of information technology and writing. But it also attests to a principle well known to narratology, the infinite generation of forms from finite structures. His sense of the "potential multiplicity"[23] of such a literature machine evokes what I have been referring to as the density of the particle. This density of the particle, or potential multiplicity, is something glimpsed, sensed as potentially there, but diffused once it is extended into a relation, a link, an elongation. Something of this implosive density is revealed in this passage from *If on a Winter's Night a Traveller:*

> I'm producing too many stories at once because what I want is for you to feel, around the story, a saturation of other stories that I could tell and maybe will tell or who knows may already have told on some other occasion, a space full of stories that perhaps is simply my lifetime, where you can move in all directions, as in space, always finding stories that cannot be told until other stories are told first, and so, setting out from any moment or place, you encounter always the same density of material to be told.[24]

Vannevar Bush no doubt encountered something of the same excess in his ruminations on the Memex, and Ted Nelson was in no doubt that hypertext was very much a manifold literature machine—responsive to, as well as generative of, textual excess. In energizing and capturing the charged multiplicity of the beginning, Calvino is suspending the reciprocal relation *to something else* of discrete syntactic structures, such as the clause or the phrase. The ten chapters which make up the novel are in fact ten unfinished sentences, intransitive structures that fail to take an object, fail to move the sense on to a subordinate clause and, therefore, grammatical and narrative closure. What is dramatized in this sequence of first words is the unrealized potential of implicit "invisible connections" bursting at the seams and intimating dispersion. *If on a Winter's Night a Traveller* goes some way to realizing Calvino's desire to write, in the manner of Deleuze and Guattari's ideal book, "a collection of tales consisting of only one sentence, or even a single line."[25] Precursors to this ideal include the one-line novel written by the Guatemalan writer Augusto Monterroso, *When he woke up, the dinosaur was still there;* and the untitled text to be found in Paul Valéry's notebooks, "Idea for a frightening story: it is discovered that the only remedy for cancer is living human flesh. Consequences."

This is the energy of the quantum particle, of dense matter in an infinitesimally small space. It is the energy of the first word, or what I have been calling discrete fertility:[26]

—Italo Calvino

In one of his many great essays, Calvino reflects on the persistent relationality of words, of the limits to which we will push adjacency, the bringing together of separate words into "reciprocal fertility."[27] His notion of the incipit is the crystalline opposite to the idea of the relation, the transition, or the link. It is consistent with what he identified as a "contemporary intellectual process" that involved the "revenge and triumph of all that is discontinuous, divisible and combinatory over continuous flux." If the word "hypertext" had currency in literary criticism in the late sixties when he wrote these words, it would in all probability have been used to describe the outcomes of this process. In this respect, hypertext continues to do the work of experimental literature in its tendency to break up continuous discourse, to deconstruct the flow of meaning into "unlimited combinations, permutations and transformations."[28]

A word, though, on this term "discontinuity." As far as Calvino was concerned, continuity was to be disrupted at all costs, and the most powerful mechanism for doing so was to sustain the beginning, to put off extension and yet retain a powerful sense of restrained encyclopedic complexity. Within new media discourse it is de rigueur to bandy about terms such as discontinuous, nonsequential, nonlinear, and so on. But for all the hype about hypertext as a liberation of discontinuity, there has been scant attention paid to the highly *continuous* nature of the binary structure of the node and link. This manifold figure binds two dependent items into a reciprocal, symbiotic order, in which there is little choice and little possibility of variation, since the activation of one leads to the materialization of the other.

The incipit is a more dramatic act of discontinuity, of suspended continuity, in that the possibility of reciprocal combination is absent. Combination entails extension, the release or issue of condensed meaning or information into the flow of syntax, trails, and pathways. The idea of hypertext as extended text without extension is troubling to our metaphysics precisely because of its singularity, its refusal to open out, to flow, to elongate. Within cosmology, the idea of a singularity refers to a moment of space-time before which, theoretically speaking, there was no such thing as space or time and out of which issues, in the cataclysmic explosion of the big bang, the entire universe. It is a theoretical postulate that equally troubled physicists and cosmologists, since the laws of relativity, which the universe was said to observe, have no meaning in this quantum state of infinity within a subatomic particle of sand (hence the need in this project to translate a potential, as yet unknowable and unrecognizable form of digital ~~literacy~~ into the letters and meanings we are familiar with). Stephen Hawking, another dabbler in universes in nutshells, has dubbed these irreducible sources of energy "virtual particles."[29] (In the context of the virtual, it's worth remembering, by the way, that Roland Barthes wrote a wonderful fabular exposition of a writerly text called *S/Z.* Sensitive to the particulate nature of the writerly—which is another way of describing the virtual—he begins the essay with the observation, "There are said to be certain Buddhists whose ascetic practices enable them to see a whole landscape in a bean. Precisely what the first analysts of narrative were attempting: to see all the world's stories [and there have been so many] within a single structure.")[30]

It is the nature of virtual particles that they cannot be observed directly, with either the naked eye or the more accelerated gaze of a particle detector. However, their influence can be detected indirectly in terms of very small yet decisive changes in the forces between atoms. So they are virtual in the sense of being there but not apparently there (an inversion of the commonly accepted definition within new media theory of the virtual: that which is apparently there, but not). And it is for this reason that this particle theory of hypertext is a potential literature, an Oulipean exercise in speculative possibility. While we may never actually see such an example of particle hypertext, we can nevertheless engage with the theoretical force of its implications for thinking about hypertextuality. Such an exercise is my own modest attempt to revive the aura of experimental writing that once surrounded the writerly text. It is a theory of the text occupying a fabular space and time of the possible, parallel to our own. Within certain speculative realms of thought we can occupy this special form of time, such as particle physics, which tempts us to think of the idea of a black hole as a minute speck of intense gravity, in which time and space condense into a singularity outside time and space. In the fictions of Borges, too, we can temporarily think outside the pervasive cultural logic of binarism that still structures new media forms such as hypertext. For Borges himself had stared into the particulate density of discrete fertility. The most famous image we find of this confrontation with the infinite in his fiction is the figure of the Aleph. Defined as a point in space that contains all points, the Aleph is described as "a small iridescent sphere of almost unbearable brightness. . . . [It] was probably two or three centimetres in diameter, but universal space was contained inside it, with no diminution in size." The problem the narrator faces in describing the Aleph is made very clear, in that while the things he sees in it occur simultaneously, the act of writing about it is successive, "because language is successive."[31] Hence, as binary, manifold subjects, for whom it is second nature to seek connections and links between discrete things, it is difficult to imagine a particle theory of hypertext (to repeat the point made earlier, hypertext is an economy of writing consistent with binarism and not a departure from it). Electrate subjectivity, to adopt a word of Greg Ulmer's, is concerned with articulating, rather than partitioning or managing, the multiple channels of information flow associated with the age of remediating technologies. It is a concept of subjectivity that finds resonance in the schizoanalysis of Deleuze and Guattari, more irrational than rational, abductive rather than deductive, and, above all else, concerned with excess and multimedia flow: a comprehension of subjectivity that Guattari has described as "polyphonic and heterogenetic."[32] It is a way of seeing the world all at once, simultaneous, as Marshall McLuhan once prophesied and David Bowie demonstrated in a famous television-watching sequence in Nicolas Roeg's 1976 film *The Man Who Fell to Earth.* Borges's narrator in "The Aleph" presents us with a slow-motion, serial version of it:

> Each thing (the glass surface of a mirror, let us say) was infinite things, because I could clearly see it from every point in the cosmos. I saw the populous sea, saw dawn and dusk, saw the multitudes of the Americas, saw a silvery spider-web at the center of a black pyramid, saw a broken labyrinth (it was London), saw endless eyes, all very close, studying themselves in me as though in a mirror, saw all the mirrors on the planet (and none of them reflecting me).[33]

A break with the Lacanian subject of self and other, the quantum subject disappears from the binarism of the mirror stage into the singularity of being-outside space and time. As for me, I finish by declaring an idea for a future project: I would like to write an essay that consists of a discrete siglum of indeterminate and complex import, a cipher that would eliminate duration and extension, yet suggest the presence of indeterminate outcomes. The essay would have no beginning, middle, or end but would have the generative force of the infinite to be found in the paradoxes of Zeno of Elea, of the formula $E = mc^2$ or the conjugation of the verb "to be." It could be encapsulated in the following epigram.[34]

—Jorge Luis Borges

Notes

Opening quotation from Italo Calvino, "Quickness," in *Six Memos for the Next Millennium,* trans. P. Creagh (London: Vintage, 1996), 51.

1. Pope's *The Dunciad Variorum* (1729) and Swift's *A Tale of a Tub* (1704) have received little attention in the context of hypertextuality. They are, however, important avant-texts in the history of electronic writing and digital literacy.

2. Darren Tofts and Murray McKeich, *Memory Trade: A Prehistory of Cyberculture* (Sydney: Interface Books, 1998).

3. I am highly conscious of the particle/wave duality in quantum theory. There is future work to be done in this respect. Indeed, as a grammatologist, I am attracted to the ambivalence of quanta as both wave *and* particle: Werner Heisenberg's uncertainty principle as the *pharmakon.* For the time being,

though, I am restricting my focus to the subatomic level of the particle (rather than the measurement of its velocity in terms of waves).

4. I put this word under erasure (i.e., typographically in strikeover mode) for the obvious reason that while it is not appropriate to the project at hand, it is the only word available to suggest what is at stake in an emerging networked world, in which the letter is no longer the dominant form of media. Navigating a hypermedia text, for example, is not reliant upon alphabetic literacy in the way that reading a novel certainly is.

5. The artworks in which Innocent has explored this iconographic language can be seen at http://www.iconica.org.

6. Gilles Deleuze and Félix Guattari, *A Thousand Plateaus: Capitalism and Schizophrenia,* trans. B. Massumi (Minneapolis: University of Minnesota Press, 1996), 9: "The ideal for a book would be to lay everything out on a plane of exteriority of this kind, on a single plane, the same sheet."

7. For this discussion, see ibid., 3–25.

8. Quoted in Wolfgang Iser, *Tristram Shandy,* Landmarks of World Literature (Cambridge: Cambridge University Press, 1988), 2.

9. *Hamlet,* ed. G. R. Hibbard (New York: Oxford University Press, 1994), act 2, scene 2, lines 252–53.

10. James Joyce, *Finnegans Wake* (London: Faber, 1975), 151, 455.

11. Ibid., 150.

12. Borges recounts this parable in "Partial Magic in the Quixote" and also in the short fragment "On Exactitude in Science."

13. Jorge Luis Borges, "The Garden of Forking Paths," in *Collected Fictions,* trans. A. Hurley (London: Penguin, 1998), 127.

14. "I turned the page; the next page bore an eight-digit number. It also bore a small illustration, like those one sees in dictionaries: an anchor drawn in pen and ink, as though by the unskilled hand of a child. / It was at this point that the stranger spoke again. / 'Look at it well. You will never see it again.' / There was threat in the words, but not in the voice. / I took note of the page, and then closed the book. Immediately I opened it again. In vain I searched for the figure of the anchor, page after page." Borges, "The Book of Sand," in *Collected Fictions,* 481.

15. Ibid.

16. Italo Calvino, "Multiplicity," in *Six Memos for the Next Millennium,* 120: "My temperament prompts me to 'keep it short,' and such structures as these enable me to unite density of invention and expression with a sense of infinite possibilities."

17. This wonderfully apposite neologism was coined by Adrian Miles at the "I Link, Therefore I Am: Digital Design Literacies" symposium (RMIT University, Melbourne, April 16, 2002).

18. Italo Calvino, "Notes Towards a Definition of the Narrative Form as a

Combinative Process," *Twentieth Century Studies* 3 (1970): 94, 96. An extended version of this essay, originally written in 1967, was published as "Cybernetics and Ghosts," in *The Literature Machine,* trans. P. Creagh (London: Secker and Warburg, 1987).

19. In his study of *Tristram Shandy,* reception theorist Wolfang Iser presents the text very much as an open-ended, omnidirectional narrative. The entire narrative, in Iser's words, concerns the very issue of commencement and first words pertinent to this discussion. The beginning of the novel, Iser asserts, is suggestive of the poetics of the entire text: "multilayered problematisation of how to start." Iser, *Tristram Shandy,* 2.

20. Italo Calvino, *If on a Winter's Night a Traveller,* trans. W. Weaver (London: Picador, 1982), 156.

21. Calvino, "Multiplicity," 120.

22. Calvino, "Notes Towards Definition," 95.

23. Ibid.

24. Calvino, *Winter's Night,* 88.

25. Calvino, "Quickness," 51.

26. Calvino, *Winter's Night,* 140: "The romantic fascination produced in the pure state by the first sentences of the first chapter of many novels is soon lost in the continuation of the story: it is the promise of a time of reading that extends before us and can comprise all possible developments. I would like to be able to write a book that is only an incipit, that maintains for its whole duration the potentiality of the beginning, the expectation still not focussed on an object. But how could such a book be constructed? Would it break off after the first paragraph? Would the preliminaries be prolonged indefinitely? Would it set the beginning of one tale inside another, as in the Arabian Nights?"

27. Calvino, "Notes Towards Definition," 93.

28. Ibid., 94.

29. Stephen Hawking, *A Brief History of Time: From the Big Bang to Black Holes* (London: Bantam Press, 1988), 106.

30. Roland Barthes, *S/Z* (New York, Hill and Wang, 1974), 3.

31. Jorge Luis Borges, "The Aleph," in *Collected Fictions,* 283.

32. Félix Guattari, *Chaosmosis: An Ethico-aesthetic Paradigm,* trans. P. Bains and J. Pefanis (Sydney: Power Publications, 1995), 6.

33. Borges, "Aleph," 283.

34. Jorge Luis Borges, "The Library of Babel," in *Collected Fictions,* 117: "In order for a book to exist, it is sufficient that it be *possible.* Only the impossible is excluded."

Image Heuretics

Gregory L. Ulmer

Thesis

What happens to the academic essay in the apparatus of digital computing? What is the "electrate" equivalent of literate argumentation? The conventional assignment in a college composition course assumes a 2,500-year history of the literate apparatus. We take for granted that, as most college handbooks say, arguments focus on issues about which there is some debate. "A position paper assignment will typically ask you, first, to choose an issue in which you are interested; second, to argue a position on one side or another of the issue; and third, to support your claims with evidence, which you locate through research."[1] The purpose of the paper is to persuade other people to agree with a particular point of view. The certainty of how to produce this persuasive effect is based on a method invented in Plato's Academy and developed in subsequent centuries as the institutional practice for transforming information stored in libraries into knowledge in the experience of individual writers. A. P. Martinich summarizes seven of the most widely used tactics of analytical (conceptual) writing.

> Dilemmas are useful for setting out problems. A dilemma makes obvious some contradictory aspects of widely held beliefs. Since dilemmas

> need to be solved by some means, some methods of problem solving need to be discussed.
>
> Reductio ad absurdum is one of these methods. It is a way of proving one's own thesis indirectly by showing that the denial of that thesis is absurd and hence false. Since the direct opposite of your thesis is absurd and false, your own thesis must be true.
>
> A counterexample is a way of showing that some proposed solution or thesis is not a correct one; it shows that something is incorrect without showing directly what particular solution or thesis is correct. The method of counterexamples is a method of criticism, not theory construction.
>
> Dialectical reasoning is a way of thinking that can be adapted to a way of structuring an essay. It begins with a simple and unqualified thesis, subjects it to criticism, revises and reformulates it several times until a complex, sophisticated and adequate thesis is arrived at. Dialectical writing, which is an orderly record of dialectical reasoning, is a kind of intellectual travelogue, in which all the important side-trips are recorded as adventures necessary for reaching the traveller's ultimate destination.
>
> Dialectical reasoning can also be used as a rhetorical tactic in doing something called "analyzing a concept." Conceptual analysis is the task of breaking down a complex concept into simpler components, just as chemical analysis is breaking down a complex chemical into simpler ones.
>
> All of the [tactics] concern ways of clarifying and making essays more precise. A basic way of getting clear about things is to divide them into different categories, that is, to distinguish them. Making a distinction often requires defining one's terms because the terms often depend upon having a precise meaning. Perhaps the most basic way of being clear and precise is to define a word or phrase.[2]

A point of continuity between literate and electrate education is this interest in public issues as a basis for student projects. These conventions of educational practice provide a context for a new pedagogical institution—the "EmerAgency," and its practice of inquiry, the "MEmorial"—proposed as a prototype for an educational practice that is to "electracy" (the digital apparatus) what the argumentative essay is to literacy. The relationship of the MEmorial to the essay is not one of opposition but supplementation.

Heuretics

In *Heuretics: The Logic of Invention* (1994) I generated a hypermedia rhetoric (choragraphy) using the heuristic discovered through an analysis of the tradition of discourses on method, from Plato's *Phaedrus* to Breton's surrealist manifesto. The logic of "invention" includes both the rhetorical sense of "inventio" (collecting the commonplaces of what to say and how to say it) and the creative sense of innovation. A comparative study of a sample of discourses on method revealed a poetics: however different each method was, they all manifested a set of operations summarized in the acronym CATTt (standing for Contrast-Analogy-Theory-Target-tale). Student Internet performances do not argue but commemorate. We do not yet know how to commemorate the "11th of September," 9/11 (for example), or any disaster, as a practice of electrate learning. We may generate a method for this practice by choosing materials for each category of the CATTt.

Assignment

Design an electrate commemoration—a MEmorial—for a disaster. Why not make one for 9/11, the event that stands in for any event of loss whose mourning helps define a community? The immediate goal of this assignment is to develop a familiarity with the Web site and the Internet as media of an emergent language apparatus. The long-range goal is to "improve the world." Or, if not to improve the world, then to understand in what way the human world is irreparable.

We are using the literate method (poetics) to bootstrap an electrate practice. The outcome depends upon what is used to fill the slots of the CATTt. I will give an overview of my choices, with the understanding that different choices are possible, and the design I propose is relative to these choices. The dilemma for the EmerAgency is that it is a post-Enlightenment consultancy: "egents" (student consultants) hope to improve the world but fear that intervention will only make things worse. To summarize briefly, the CATTt generating the MEmorial includes the following relays:

Contrast = the most important approaches to changing society, posed as a continuum between the poles formed by conventional or empirical consulting at one end of the spectrum and revolutionary politics at the other, whether reactionary or progressive (right-wing or left-wing). At one extreme is instrumental reason that tinkers only with the utilitarian aspects of the lifeworld, meaning that it confines itself largely to treating symptoms or effects rather than causes of public problems. At the other extreme is revolutionary politics, with its assumption that there may be no solution to any one problem without solving all problems at once (requiring starting over with a clean slate).

Analogy = tourism as an institution, including both the behavior of families vacationing at tourist destinations and the work of booster organizations inventing these destinations by designing and building attractions. The Analogy provides not a template or model but a relay orientating us in the direction of the practice we are inventing.

Theory = poststructural philosophy, criticism, and art, especially French theory, particularly the work of Georges Bataille, but also Jacques Derrida, Gilles Deleuze and Félix Guattari, Jean-François Lyotard, and Maurice Blanchot, among others. The comprehensive term for the peculiar mode of poststructural theory I am using is "choragraphy."

Target = the Internet in particular, and the apparatus of digital new media in general. The Target supplies the terms of the problem that is the reason justifying the creation of a new method or poetics: it identifies the requirements calling for invention in the first place. Our Target is the Internet as a potential civic sphere and the need for a practice of writing native to this institutional arrangement.

tale = the EmerAgency. In the tradition of the discourse on method that began with Plato's PHAEDRUS and extends into contemporary philosophy, the syncretizing of the four content generators (CATT) took place in the proposal for some concrete, material practice whose performance would produce the kind of work called for by the conditions addressed in the CATT. The CATT inventories have no form of their own and must be couched in some specific form to integrate them into coherence. The tale in part dramatizes what it explains. The EmerAgency institution and the MEmorial practice enact this synthesis as a discourse on method. It is intended to be taken both literally and figuratively.

Jacobin States

It has been demonstrated often enough that "opposite" is a relative category, culturally specific, as much ideological as logical, and complex in itself (C. K. Ogden). The binary pair named by Dean MacCannell in his study of tourism works well for our project: "The central thesis of this book holds the empirical and ideological expansion of modern society to be intimately linked in diverse ways to modern mass leisure, especially to international tourism and sightseeing. Originally, I had planned to study tourism and revolution, which seemed to me to name the two poles of modern consciousness."[3] MacCannell's opposition clarifies the intertext emerging within our CATTt, in this case in the interaction of Analogy and Contrast, filled with the domains of tourism and revolution, respectively. We know from Contrast the approach to change we do not want—the conceptual field created by the opposition utility/revolution. To take up one extreme of this pair, we inventory the behavior or conduct entailed by "revolution," for example, the tactics proposed by Lenin.

Our contrast helps us define an initial restriction on our invention: we will do the opposite of whatever Lenin proposed (our riddle becomes: What is the opposite of terror?). Leninism suggests that one's method should emulate the spirit, mood, atmosphere, ambiance of threat, aggression, attack, rivalry, domination associated with any vanguard, contemptuous in principle of that which it opposes. "Lenin thought that the workers could not develop by themselves the necessary political consciousness and that they needed an organization through which professional revolutionaries would lead them and be able to exploit a revolutionary situation when it arose."[4] Substitute "religion" for "political" and the definition fits the relation of the Taliban to Islam. Beware of righteousness (of virtue) scorned. For clarification, the authors of this entry on Leninism in an encyclopedic dictionary prompt the reader to "see Jacobinism." What is Jacobinism (referring to the original "reign of terror" during the French Revolution)? "Contempt for the will of the majority, dictatorship by a determined revolutionary minority, Committees of Public Safety as embryo institutions for implementing terror—these are some of the historically archetypal features of Jacobinism. Underlying it was the idea, derived from Rousseau, that the masses were insufficiently enlightened to carry out a revolution."[5]

The Jacobin mode of vanguard problem-solving finally is: establish

Committees of Public Safety in your area of interest. It is symptomatic that the most powerful ministry in Afghanistan under the Taliban was the Ministry for the Protection of Virtue and the Prevention of Vice.[6] Our theory suggests, however, that the difference between "them" and "us" is that "we" in the West (according to Hegel) internalized the Terror and called it morality.

> Throughout the entire dialectic of *Bildung,* the appearance of an equivalent exchange between subject (self-consciousness) and substance is thus maintained: in exchange for his increasing alienation, for sacrificing a further substantial part of himself, the subject receives honor, wealth, the language of spirit and insight, the heaven of Faith, the Utility of the Enlightenment. However, when we reach the apogee of this dialectic, "absolute freedom," the exchange between the particular and the universal Will, the subject "gets nothing in exchange for everything." (The historical epoch which stands for this moment of "absolute freedom" is, of course, the Jacobinical Reign of Terror, in which, for no apparent reason, I could be proclaimed traitor and have my head cut off at any moment.) . . . That is to say, what is "subject" if not the infinite power of absolute negativity/mediation: in contrast to a mere biological life, self-consciousness contains in itself its own negation, it maintains itself by way of negative self-relating. This way, we pass from absolute freedom (of the revolutionary citoyen) into "the Spirit certain of itself" epitomized by the Kantian moral subject: the external negativity of the revolutionary Terror is internalized into the power of moral Law, into the pure Knowledge and Will qua Universality, which is not something externally opposed to the subject but something which constitutes the very axis of his self-certainty."[7]

This internalized ministry is a feature of selfhood, the subject formation specific to alphabetic literacy (now dispersing). In our context of education and pedagogy, the Jacobin issue may be translated into the issue of the balance between safety and risk, applied to the realm of ideas and imagination. The issue has several levels to know: the difference between virtue and vice; how to motivate people to behave accordingly; whether this classification and behavior are relevant to electracy. The EmerAgency approaches policy problems from the perspective of neither instrumental engineering nor Jacobin terror. An inventory of these approaches to problem solving provides a negative definition of our contribution. A preliminary description of EmerAgency consulting is: to find in oneself the feeling of a Committee of Public Safety. Virtue is not the given of deconsulting but the riddle. "One of the great mysteries of Western thought, the philosopher Leo Strauss has said, is 'how a word which used to mean the manliness of man has come to mean the chastity of women.' "[8] We have an image of Taliban soldiers shaking their weapons at the contrails of U.S. bombers over Afghanistan and challenging them to come down and fight like men. The clearest manifestation of this fundamental difference between subject formations—reflecting different options in apparatus history between the European and Arab worlds—is the contrast in fashion codes for women.

Lost Guides

The EmerAgency consultation is a hybrid in that the goal is "radical tourism," understood in Thomas Kuhn's distinction between "revolutionary" and "normal" science. The aspect of our Analogy (tourism) that we wish to radicalize is the attraction for tourists of sites of community problems and disasters, an example of which is the "Murder, Mystery and Mayhem Tour" in Miami that takes visitors to famous and not-so-famous crime scenes, including the home of Gianni Versace, gunned down as he entered his vacation villa in July 1997. Opposing this drive within tourism, the company that recovered artifacts from the *Titanic,* RMS Titanic Inc, sought a court order to prevent Deep Ocean Expeditions from taking sixty people in a submersible vessel to visit the shipwreck site (a ticket cost $32,500). In contrast, the Russians have taken two tourists to the orbiting space station and have contracted with a third—'N Sync singer Lance Bass (the ticket costs $20 million). The memorial site in Lower Manhattan readily and deliberately enters the tourist spectacle.

The MEmorial begins in this shifting on the axis of the metaphor of the travelogue in dialectical essays. Where the two practices part company is on the matter of "clarity." Perhaps "ideas" may be made "clear and distinct," but the MEmorial pushes beyond "idea" into mood, feeling. How could a tour of Lower Manhattan and Ground Zero be put into an image category, to make it thinkable in electrate terms? To consult in a new way requires first a new apparatus. The larger goal of EmerAgency consultants (egents, students, "netizens") is to become electrate. There is a connection between tourism and the literate essay that opens a path for this transition. In their analysis of the classic model of the essay, Francis-

Noel Thomas and Mark Turner described how the effect of clarity was achieved within literacy.

The classic stylist pretended not to argue, but only to present or describe, creating the illusion of an alignment between language and truth. Any style, Thomas and Turner proposed, is derived from the "conceptual stand" of the author—the attitude (perspective) toward truth. The classic stylist believed that truth can be known and recognized. Using "conversation" as an interface metaphor, the classic essay puts the reader in the writer's position or standpoint and describes how things (whether material or abstract) look from there, as if looking out a window to observe a visible scene. "Prose is a window. In the classic attitude, writing serves to present something else: its subject. The subject is conceived of as a 'thing' distinct from the writing, something that exists in the world and is independent of any presentation. Clarity is the central virtue of classic prose because the classic writer's defining task is to present something he has previously perceived. Self-evident truths, Madame de Chevreuse's character, the power of well-ordered thoughts, the food of France are conceived as 'things' with their proper characteristics, existing 'in the world' and completely independent of their presentation."[9]

"Things" are entities whose articulation, delineation, definition became possible within the conceptual category formation of literacy (Aristotle is credited with the invention of the "thing"—the practice of grouping entities into sets based on definitions of essential versus accidental attributes). The image and relay for classic prose clarity is the tourist guidebook.

> Classic guidebooks are a natural place to begin. They form a large and universal genre in which actual scenes and casts are almost identical to the model scene and cast of classic style . . . The Michelin Green Guide Series: Places include all the regions of France; many European countries, including Greece and Italy; and several metropolitan regions, including Paris, Rome, London, and Washington, D.C.
>
> Classic guidebooks include guides and descriptions of historical sites and monuments, for example, Branislav Brankovic's *Les vitraux de la cathedrale de Saint-Denis,* a pamphlet by the curator of the former abbey church, meant to be used by visitors. Works of art history from a period before documentary photography became routine have a close affinity to guidebooks and are sometimes presented as guides to past mentalities. Emile Male's foundation work on medieval Christian ico-

nography, *L'art religieux au XIII siècle en France* (1898), is a prominent example. . . . Sophisticated classic guidebooks often take the form of travel writing and the literature of places, including the political geography of the historic past and descriptions of imaginary places.[10]

As opposed to the classic style of the essay still taught in most schools (understandably, since School is an institutionalization of literacy), the MEmorial guide must bring into composition the qualities of modern (electrate) space, which was generated in part by demolishing the perspectivist window and all its extensions as a metaphor for thought.

> This is the outcome of an epoch-making event so generally ignored that we have to be reminded of it at every moment. The fact is that around 1910 a certain space was shattered. It was the space of common sense, of knowledge (savoir), of social practice, of political power, a space thitherto enshrined in everyday discourse, just as in abstract thought, as the environment of and channel for communications; the space, too, of classical perspective and geometry, developed from the Renaissance onwards on the basis of the Greek tradition (Euclid, logic) and bodied forth in Western art and philosophy, as in the form of the city and town. Such were the shocks and onslaughts suffered by this space that today it retains but a feeble pedagogical reality, and then only with great difficulty, within a conservative educational system. Euclidean and perspectivist space have disappeared as systems of reference, along with other former "commonplaces" such as the town, history, paternity, the tonal system in music, traditional morality, and so forth.[11]

Neobaroque

A shorthand way to understand the relationship between the classic essay and the MEmorial is as the relationship between the classical and baroque worldviews (aesthetics). A glance at any Western Civilization textbook reveals in the features of the chronology of periods from ancient to modern an oscillation between the poles of classical and baroque forms of life. The formal features of the binary pair were codified by the art historian Heinrich Wölfflin. One advantage of the postmodernist overview of the history of forms is the relativization of these alternatives as a relationship of interdependency. Jean-Marie Floch's study of commercial design translated Wölfflin's five formal distinctions (linear/pictorial, planes/depths, closed form/open form, plurality/unity, light/dark) into the linguistic distinction between plane of content and plane of expression.

> "Non-continuity" (classical plane of expression). According to the classical view the approach to the perceptible is fundamentally associated with decomposition, separation and delineation. This is why Wölfflin refers to the classical as an "isolating style." And it is also why I have always preferred to refer to "non-continuity" rather than "discontinuity," and on the other side of things, to "non-discontinuation." This would emphasize the generative and dynamic aspects of these ways of treating the perceptible.
>
> "Non-discontinuity" (classical plane of content). On the other hand, the meaning effects produced by his negation of continuity are all subject to the regime of the non-discontinued. Perenniality, stability, "peaceful adjustment," as well as the controllable character afforded by the world as seen by the classical mind, constitute just so many interpretations or thematizations of the negation of a discontinuity. And these interpretations are temporal, "thymic," ethical and so on.
>
> "Non-discontinuity" (baroque plane of expression). Against the classical, the baroque as part of its expression, searches, exploits or provokes non-discontinuations of the perceptible world. It privileges extension and transgression (in the spatial meaning of the term) and creates visual motifs such as interlacing.
>
> "Non-continuity" (baroque plane of content). Finally, the meaning-effects produced by the baroque derive from the regime of non-continuity. Wölfflin says that the baroque view had "the knack of reducing the instant to the narrowest of points." Such an observation by the art historian is a good indication that the search for non-continuity takes the whole space-time complex (as opposed to mere temporality) as its target. And we will see that the baroque subject's presence in the world, its passions and its cognitive competence all derive from this semantics of non-continuation.[12]

The classical mood or state of mind is "ease" (certainty), and the baroque mood is "disquiet" (*Unruhe,* uncertainty).

What forces and supports the alliance or cooperation of these two complementary (not opposed) states of mind is the syncretic possibilities of digital media, a text-graphics authoring environment. Adding imaging to writing creates the conditions of double or multiple perspective that demands initially the formal resources of the baroque traditions to manage. Lyotard's theory of the figural, the visual supplement to discourse beyond the limits of natural language, is described as a version of anamorphic perspective. The immediate relevance to our context is the application of the evolution of linear perspective (from classical to baroque) to the evolution of the school assignment from essay to MEmorial. As this description of Lyotard's figural indicates, the MEmorial does not oppose or abandon the clarity of the idea, but it "blocks" (overprints) on it the obscurity of the scene (event).

> The analogy in painting to the force of poetic rhetoricity as constituent and disruptive figure for language is anamorphosis. Anamorphosis rests upon the figural clash between the quasi-unmotivated geometric perspective and the quasi-motivated force of curvature and diffusion in vision. The "textualization" of the visual by Renaissance perspective or Cartesian optics is an attempt to understand objects as in principle from a singular, immobile, point. The effect of this is to reduce vision to an affair of geometry, of straight lines, to exclude curvature and anamorphosis. The immobilization of the eye flattens the visual field around a focal center, projecting the visible as a stable image clearly visible as on a transparent screen. Against this, Lyotard insists upon the presence of the heterogeneity of curved space in vision: of the foveal periphery alongside the focal center, of the evanescent, diffuse anelliptical margin inseparable from distinct vision. . . . Lyotard thus juxtaposes clear and diffuse vision as heterogeneous components of the visible. Anamorphosis plays upon the co-presence of curved and geometric space in the visible. Anamorphosis is the realization in painting of the co-existence of two radically heterogeneous spaces of representation; as in Holbein's *Ambassadors* or the anamorphic portrait of Charles I discussed by Lyotard, the death's head often forms the mark of the radical difference of the two spaces—the bar of death is the disjunction of the two spaces in which vision is inscribed.[13]

ATH (Ate)

Jacques Lacan uses the metaphor of anamorphosis to model the workings of tragedy (Antigone), specifically with respect to ATH (*athate:*

rage, catastrophy; a fundamental element of tragedy). Lacan is interested in ATH as showing that exterior that is at the heart of me, the intersubjective nature of the human identity. "One does or does not approach Ate, and when one approaches it, it is because of something that is linked to a beginning and a chain of events, namely, that of the misfortune of the Labdacides family. As one starts to come close to it, things come together in a great hurry."[14] The name of the blindness at work in Antigone is badly translated, Lacan says, as "resentment." We must understand it, in terms of how it is experienced, as being overtaken by a bliss or jouissance, a "catastrophe" in the mathematical sense of a sudden mutation of feeling as when in everyday life one lets anger or lust override all good sense. In any case, her tragedy evokes the two "spaces" that concern us, which Žižek relates with phenomenal reality and the noumenal Thing, each with its own logic.

> The horrifying, lethal, and at the same time fascinating borderline that we approach when the reversal into bliss is imminent is what Lacan, apropos of Sophocles's Antigone, endeavors to indicate by means of the Greek word *ate*. There is a fundamental ambiguity to this term: ate simultaneously denotes a horrifying limit which cannot ever be reached, i.e., whose touch means death, and the space beyond it. The crucial point here is the primacy of the limit over the space: we do not have two spheres (that of reality and that of pure fantasy) which are divided by a certain limit; what we have is just reality and its limit, the abyss, the void around which it is structured. The fantasy space is therefore strictly secondary; it "gives body," it materialises a certain limit, or, more precisely, it changes the impossible into the prohibited.[15]

As a figure for conceiving of this dimension of human disaster, Lacan proposes an anamorphic painting. Although he alludes to Holbein's *Ambassadors* several times, the example he discusses is, he says, a more modest work. "It is formed of a polished cylinder that has the function of a mirror, and around it you put a kind of bib or flat surface on which there are also indecipherable lines. When you stand at a certain angle, you see the image concerned emerge in the cylindrical mirror; in this case it is a beautiful anamorphosis of a painting of the crucifixion copied from Rubens."[16] Later in the seminar he explains the anamorphic character of tragedy. "What is the surface that allows the image of Antigone to rise up as an image of passion? The other day I evoked in connection with her the phrase, 'Father, why hast thou abandoned me?' which is literally expressed in one line. Tragedy is that which spreads itself out in front so that that image may be produced. When analyzing it, we follow an inverse procedure; we study how the image had to be constructed in order to produce the desired effect."[17]

The point of the new consultancy (deconsulting) is that neither tragedy nor consulting is adequate to understand the work of ATH in the digital apparatus. This baroque relay helps update the question. The disaster spreads itself out in the media as a smear of information. The MEmorial (as a collective practice distributed throughout the Internet) puts in place the device capable of imaging its passion.

The Photographic Field

The point of transition away from classic prose, taken as an expression of the ideology of literacy as an apparatus, is the reference in Thomas and Turner to the era in which "documentary photography became routine," thus undermining the persuasiveness of the argumentative window. However much the baroque mode anticipates the mutation of modern space-time, the emergence of electracy is dated from the invention of photography, just as the epoch of literacy dates from the invention of the alphabet. The paradox of photography is that it technologizes perspective at the same time that it subverts the worldview in which perspective was invented. The practical point for the MEmorial is that photography, in whatever technical form, foregrounds the need for a poetics of using the visible to write the invisible (the outside to render an inside). The theory of the apparatus assumes that digital imaging is a social machine—that the desire that created it is distinguishable from the history of technology.

The proper context for the invention of photography is not (only) the natural sciences (physics, chemistry) and technology but the dream of a perfect language, capable of universal communication across all natural languages and cultures. This dream motivated the intense interest in Egyptian hieroglyphics and Chinese ideograms, both thought to be image discourses allowing direct authoring with nature itself (that is, to be able to write as well as read nature as the Book of God).[18] The desire for universal peace and harmony motivating the immense scholarship and creativity invested in the hermetic arts, however mistaken or misplaced, accounts for a family resemblance among its aesthetic spin-offs—the baroque emblem, the modernist ideogram, psychoanalytic dreamwork, and contemporary cinema. Walter Benjamin's dialectical image, seen in the context of "the origin of German tragic drama," owes as much to the baroque emblem as it does to Soviet montage.

Paradoxically, the machinery of mechanical visualization exploded the illusion of the alignment between the standpoint of an observer and the truth. The capacity of the camera to separate itself from the human physical and mental eye, combined with the theories of psychoanalysis, produced the notion of the "optical unconscious" (Walter Benjamin). The attitude toward truth as standpoint in the image apparatus of electracy is that clarity is an effect of repression, blindness (ATH). In the new (electrate) apparatus the clear distinction between subject and object disappears, replaced by a psychogeography (choragraphy).

> Space, in those various iterations, has been increasingly defined as a product of subjective projections and introjection, as opposed to a stable container of objects and bodies. From the beginning of the century, the apparently fixed laws of perspective have been transformed, transgressed, and ignored in the search to represent the space of modern identity. Thus the body in pieces, physiognomy distorted by inner pain, architectural space as claustrophobic, urban space as agoraphobic, all warpings of the normal to express the pathological became the leitmotivs of avant-garde art. The vocabularies of displacement and fracture, torquing and twisting, pressure and release, void and block, informe and hyperform that they developed are still active today, deployed in work that seeks to reveal, if not critique, the conditions of a less than settled everyday life.[19]

As Rosalind Krauss explained, applying the poststructural psychoanalysis of Jacques Lacan, the "extimate" inside-outside nature of the human subject installs an opaque obstacle "within the very heart of a diagrammatic clarity that is now a model both of vision's claims and of vision's failure. . . . The graph of an automatist visuality would show how the vaunted cognitive transparency of the 'visual as such' is not an act of consciousness but the effect of what is repressed: the effect, that is, of seriality, repetition, the automaton. Which is to say, it is a function of a caesura in vision, a gap."[20] This gap is the "hole" traced by the MEmorial as a symptom signaling the location of chora—the sorting system of a society.

The classic standpoint of the literate observer, organized in terms of the subject-object binary, still exists within electracy but now with the observer displaced from the central position to being just one point within a field network (a matrix) of which she or he is not the master.

> Lacan's discussion of vision in *The Four Fundamental Concepts of Psychoanalysis* is centered on a scopic drive structured by the distich, the rupture, the schiz. He calls the opening chapter "The Split between the Eye and the Gaze." But the whole of his account is called "The Gaze as objet a," or the gaze as part-object, the object that, because it marks the subject with the individuation of his existence, is most fundamentally the object of desire. Lacan wants to show the dialectic between deictic and distich, between pointing and screen, between this! and absence.
>
> The space of pointing, or of deixis, is the space that Lacan terms "geometral," namely, the space of perspective, a space that as Diderot shows in his Letter on the Blind, is actually a tactile space, a space mastered by the subject as though he were reaching out to grasp it, to palp it, running fingers over its front and sides, manipulating it.
>
> In contrast to the tactile "visuality" is the space of light, which Lacan calls "dazzling, pulsatile": an atmospheric surround that illuminates the viewer from both back and front, so that from the start there is no question of mastery. And in the context of this space of the luminous, the viewer is not the surveyor—standing at a point just outside the pyramid of vision—but, caught within the onrush of light, he is what blocks the light, what interrupts its flow. In this interruption the "viewer" invisible to himself enters the "picture" created by this light as a "stain" or blind spot, as the shadow cast by the light, the trace, its deictic mark. And from this place the subject, in all his exposure to view, can neither see himself nor see the source of the light. His position is one of dependence on an illumination that both marks him (the deictic) and escapes his grasp (the distich). The illumination Lacan calls the "gaze." It is the part-object operating within the instinctual field of vision, forever unlocatable, out of focus, in metamorphosis, pulsing.[21]

The only glimpse of this optical unconscious within the empirical view is that offered by optical illusions,[22] such as the famous duck-rabbit, through which viewers become aware of their participation in the act of seeing (aspectuality). The literate production of truth that is clear and simple is an epistemic "optical illusion." We can agree with Thomas and Turner that writing involves a standpoint. The challenge of the MEmorial as an educational practice is to learn how to write from the standpoint of being a figure within a field of warped space (anamorphically).

Emblematic Disasters

We may return in this context to the initial framework of an electrate assignment. The transformation of the analytic essay into the MEmorial brings pedagogy into alignment with the poststructural critique of Western metaphysics. In grammatological terms "metaphysics" refers to the system of categorization native to a given apparatus. The shift from literacy to electracy necessarily includes the invention of a classification or category formation that is the image equivalent of the concept. Descartes with his neat formulation of the subject as cogito and his methodological insistence on clear and distinct ideas has provided the touchstone contrast for most attempts to think beyond the literate category of the concept. The baroque period as manifested in the philosophy of Leibniz provided Gilles Deleuze with a convenient reference point for theorizing this new kind of category and the related formal structure needed to represent it.

Plato is credited as the inventor of philosophy, which includes among other things the invention of the first formally defined concept—"justice." From Plato to Deleuze, the work of philosophy has been (Deleuze and Guattari say in *What Is Philosophy?*) the invention of concepts. Leibniz's critique of Descartes condenses the entire history of the concept from Aristotle's topics to Descartes' ideas. Leibniz's shift from object to event as the means for organizing reality offers the opening Deleuze needed to propose an alternative category formation. Distributed through Deleuze's reading is a list of contrasts, using Descartes' classicism as a convenient checklist of features for which the postliterate category (in our terms) must have an equivalent. Deleuze proposes Leibniz as the philosopher of the baroque worldview, whose defining trait is the fold. The baroque invention of the text-image form, the emblem (the Italian *concetto*), provides a name and form for the new category (in English "conceit" names a verbal emblem).

> The Baroque is widely known to be typified by the "concetto," but only insofar as the Baroque concetto can be opposed to the classical concept. It is also widely held that Leibniz brings a new conception to the concept, with which he transforms philosophy. But we have to wonder

about the composition of this new, Leibnizian conception. That it is opposed to the "classical" conception of the concept—in the way that Descartes had invented it—is best shown in Leibniz's correspondence with De Volder, a Cartesian. First of all, the concept is not a simple logical being, but a metaphysical being; it is not a generality or a universality, but an individual; it is not defined by an attribute, but by predicate-as-events.[23]

A table distinguishing Leibniz's concetto from Descartes' concept would include at least the following distinctions (which are not posed as opposites):

Descartes	Leibniz
classical	baroque
ease	disquiet
to be	to follow
essence	manner
attribute	event
solid	fluid
abstraction	series
part/whole	singularity/differential
parts	requisites
clarity	chiaroscuro
distinct	remarkable
collection	distribution
state (condition)	change
subject/object	superject/objectile
subject	point of view
painting/window	tabulation
window/countryside	information/city
woven cloth	felt
necessary	contingent

The most useful feature of the concetto as category is that it provides a form with which to compose the image-text (seeing-reading). With an explicit acknowledgment of Walter Benjamin's study of the baroque emblem as allegory, Deleuze summarizes the components of the emblem form, which he finds at work within Leibniz's methodology of "scenographies-definitions-points of view." "Devices or emblems have three elements that help us understand the basis of allegory: images or figurations, inscriptions or maxims, and personal signatures or proper names of owners. Seeing, reading, dedicating (or signing)."[24]

> First, basic images tend to break their frames, form a continuous fresco, and join broader cycles (either of other aspects of the same animal, or aspects of other animals) because the pictured form—an animal or whatever—is never an essence or an attribute, as in a symbol, but an event, which is thus related to a history or to a series. Even in the worst of representations, "Fidelity Crowns Love," we find the charm of allegory, the presence of the event that makes an appeal to an antecedent and a sequel. Second, inscriptions, which have to keep a shrouded relation with images, are themselves propositions akin to simple and irreducible acts, which tend toward an inner concept, a truly propositional concept. A judgment is not broken down into a subject and an attribute; rather, the whole proposition is a predicate, as in "From near and afar." Finally, the many inscriptions or propositions—that is, the propositional concept itself—is related to an individual subject who envelops it, and who allows himself or herself to be determined as the owner: allegory offers us Virtues, but these are not virtues in general. They belong to Cardinal Mazarin and figure among his effects. Even the elements are put forth as belongings pertaining to Louis XIV or to someone else.[25]

What makes a concept a concetto, Deleuze stresses, is the folding of the concept into the individual. "Although practitioners and theorists of concettism had rarely been philosophers, they developed rich materials for a new theory of the concept reconciled with the individual."[26] Although the Italian term *concetto* is useful to call attention to its equivalence with concept, Deleuze's emphasis indicates that he had in mind specifically the variant knows as the "impresa." Peter Daly comments that it is difficult to distinguish between the emblem and impresa formally.

> The basic difference is one of purpose. The impresa represents the "principle of individuation"; it was used by one person only "as the expression of a personal aim." The word itself comes from the Italian for "undertaking," which underlines the functional purpose of the impresa. The emblem, on the other hand, is addressed to a larger audience; its message is general; and it fulfils a didactic, decorative, or

entertaining function, or any combination of these. One example may illustrate the difference. The motif of the phoenix was associated with such concepts as "uniqueness," "regeneration," and "indestructibility." The motif becomes an impresa when an individual chooses this motif and one of these concepts to express a personal intention. Paradin's *Devises héroïques* (Lyons, 1557) contains the impresa of Eleanor of Austria, Dowager Queen of France, who chose the motto "Unica semper avis" to stand above the picture of a phoenix surrounded by fire.[27]

In practical terms, as a relay for the MEmorial, the impresa/emblem indicates how the egent testifies with respect to the disaster. The egent as "undertaker" of the disaster. The emblem continued a tradition of drawing moral or prudential truths from historical events, ancient myths, fables, and the natural sciences (among other sources) that dates back to the classical historians.

> [Hercules's] story was much allegorized and interpreted for its typification of the struggles of the moral life. No episode in it was better known than that, found first in Xenophon's *Cyropaedia,* in which Hercules has to choose between two women, one of whom offers him Pleasure while the other indicates the apparently contradictory path of Virtue; eventually he finds the way to reconcile them, and wins immortality. The moment of his choice, as well as his person, is a common emblem subject, frequently used or alluded to in mythological or allegorical paintings and tapestry, precisely because it could not only call up a whole moral process but could also be made to value and apply to a multiplicity of present issues and dilemmas.[28]

Transvaluation of Virtue

This moralizing of events continues into the present day, as may be seen in the editorial pages of newspapers. Pat Robertson's interpretation of 9/11 as God's judgment on America is in this tradition and echoes some of the sermonizing that made use of the sinking of the *Titanic* as a way to evaluate the moral ills of the early twentieth century. The allegorizing of the *Titanic* disaster shows some differences between modern conceits and the tradition. In the traditional practice the meaning of events was determined anagogically by the Christian worldview. This determinism continued in the *Titanic* story to some extent, along with the virtues expressing the ideological commitments of the hegemonic powers (white Anglo-Saxon Protestant capitalist heterosexual men). The narrative of the disaster was made to fit the assumptions of the society about the heroic character of the upper classes. "Part Christian conversion narrative and part knightly adventure story, the conventional version of the disaster provided closure by showing how the ruling class redeemed itself when put to the test and, more broadly, how modernity was traditional after all. 'When the twentieth century is called material, commonplace, sordid,' said the Reverend R. L. McCready of Louisville, 'we only have to point to the decks of the sinking Titanic and, behold, all the ages of the past have never surpassed its achievements of heroism and chivalry.' "[29]

As Deleuze remarked in distinguishing modern neobaroque from Leibniz's version, the purpose of theodicy (Leibniz as God's attorney) was gone. A new element also apparent in the *Titanic* stories was a reversal of explanatory direction, the dissolution of the anagogic dimension of the allegory, so that the disaster became the source rather than the target of explanation. "Beyond shock and grief, the disaster produced a contest over meaning that connected the sinking of an ocean liner in a remote part of the North Atlantic with some of the most important and troubling problems, tensions, and conflicts of the time. . . . The disaster was neither catalyst nor cause, but it did expose and come to represent anxieties about modernity—about deeper changes that were occurring regardless of whether an ocean liner struck an iceberg and sank in the spring of 1912. If not a transformative event, it was nonetheless a highly dramatic moment—a kind of 'social drama' in which conflicts were played out and American culture in effect thought out loud about itself."[30] Nietzsche's project of the transvaluation of values made explicit the shift in public morality at the turn of the nineteenth century away from the frame of the "virtues and vices" toward a new understanding of the role of power and invention in the conduct admired by a society.[31] William J. Bennett's *The Book of Virtues* may be seen in this context as a nostalgic attempt to return to a pre-Nietzschean vision of social mores. In our own time, MEmorials for 9/11 may show the stripping away from "value" its moral or belief meanings to leave only the structural sense of "position in a system of relations."

Arabesque

Here is a proposal for a 9/11 concetto, which I adopt as an impresa commemorating my decision to invent the poetics for a "détourned" arabesque. The MEmorial, performing the EmerAgency motto (*Problems B Us*), treats the disaster as a source for understanding contemporary values, specifically as a mode of self-knowledge, rather than attempting to impose on the disaster a predetermined meaning. The choragraphic map shows that the link between capitalism and Islam is the ornamental design known as the arabesque. This convergence serves as emblem of the history of Osama bin Laden as employee of the CIA. The arabesque with its interlaced patterns of repeating shapes (whether floral or geometric) is said to be the most typical feature of Islamic aesthetics. "Spiritual states and musical tone which are mutable, impermanent qualities requiring an encounter or place in which to descend and then change the rhythm, both find a visual correspondence in the arabesque. The arabesque is a form which harmoniously renders a constantly changing rhythmical motion. Varying in density over the surface, it is a rhythmic outpouring of thought given precision by parallels, inversions and interlacings."[32] The abstractness of capital ("In capitalism power itself is carried to the highest abstraction of an idea")[33] found its perfect embodiment in the arabesque form. "In the middle of the nineteenth century, the modern arabesque is appropriated by capitalist aesthetics; it adorns stock certificates, bank notes, and the designs of industrial parks."[34] The arabesque makes a map, opens a line of flight, between McWorld and jihad, across and through the different, the incommensurable civilizations in this story. Here is a fold, a moment of overprinting to support the possibility of seeing more than one position.

A 9/11 Conceit

A multiple, entitled "Milked Split," simulating a stock certificate, the border decorated with an ornamental arabesque (floral style). At the center, a capital *S* in calligraphy, barred, representing simultaneously the signifier of the United States dollar and Jacques Lacan's matheme for the split subject (the unconscious)—$. The certificate is dated using the European convention month-day-year: 11.9.01. On the reverse side, printed over the arabesque background, a text by Georges Bataille:

> Me, I exist—suspended in a realized void—suspended from my own dread—different from all other being and such that the various events that can reach all other being and not me cruelly throw this me out of a total existence. . . . The empirical knowledge of the structure this me has in common with the other mes has become an absurdity in this

void where my dominion manifests itself, for the very essence of the me that I am consists in the fact that no other conceivable existence can replace it; the total improbability of my coming into the world poses, in an imperative mode, a total heterogeneity.[35]

Notes

1. Toby Fulwiler and Alan R. Hayakawa, *The Blair Handbook* (Englewood Cliffs, N.J.: Prentice-Hall, 1994), 127–28.

2. A. P. Martinich, *Philosophical Writing: An Introduction* (Cambridge, Mass.: Blackwell, 1996), 96–97.

3. Dean MacCannell, *The Tourist: A New Theory of the Leisure Class* (New York: Schocken, 1976), 3.

4. Alan Bullock and Oliver Stallybrass, *The Harper Dictionary of Modern Thought* (New York: Harper and Row, 1977), 345.

5. Ibid., 325.

6. *Gainesville Sun,* December 9, 2001, 12A.

7. Slavoj Žižek, *Tarrying with the Negative: Kant, Hegel, and the Critique of Ideology* (Durham, NC: Duke University, 1993), 23–24.

8. Gertrude Himmelfarb, *The De-Moralization of Society: From Victorian Virtues to Modern Values* (New York: Alfred A. Knopf, 1995), 15.

9. Francis-Noel Thomas and Mark Turner, *Clear and Simple as the Truth: Writing Classic Prose* (Princeton, N.J.: Princeton University Press, 1994), 36.

10. Ibid., 199.

11. Henri Lefebvre, *The Production of Space,* trans. Donald Nicholson-Smith (Cambridge, Mass.: Blackwell, 1991), 25.

12. Jean-Marie Floch, *Visual Identities,* trans. Pierre Van Osselaer and Alec McHoul (New York: Continuum, 2000), 101–2.

13. Bill Readings, *Introducing Lyotard: Art and Politics* (New York: Routledge, 1991), 25–26.

14. Jacques Lacan, *The Seminar of Jacques Lacan, Book VII: The Ethics of Psychoanalysis 1959–60,* ed. Jacques-Alain Miller, trans. Dennis Porter (New York: W. W. Norton, 1992), 264.

15. Žižek, *Tarrying with the Negative,* 115–16.

16. Lacan, *Seminar,* 135.

17. Ibid., 135.

18. Umberto Eco, *The Search for the Perfect Language,* trans. James Fentress (Malden, Mass.: Blackwell, 1995), 165, 175.

19. Anthony Vidler, *WARped Space: Art, Architecture, and Anxiety in Modern Culture* (Cambridge, Mass.: MIT Press, 2000), 1.

20. Rosalind Krauss, *The Optical Unconscious* (Cambridge, Mass.: MIT Press, 1994), 74.

21. Ibid., 87–88.

22. Ibid., 137.

23. Gilles Deleuze, *The Fold: Leibniz and the Baroque,* trans. Tom Conley (Minneapolis: University of Minnesota Press, 1993), 42.

24. Ibid., 125.

25. Ibid., 126.

26. Ibid.

27. Peter Daly, *Literature in the Light of the Emblem* (Toronto: University of Toronto Press, 1998), 29.

28. Ibid., 4.

29. Steven Biel, *Down with the Old Canoe: A Cultural History of the Titanic Disaster* (New York: Norton, 1996), 83.

30. Ibid., 8.

31. Himmelfarb, *De-Moralization of Society,* 10.

32. Laleh Bakhtiar, *Sufi: Expressions of the Mystic Quest* (London: Thames and Hudson, 1976), 98.

33. Georges Bataille, *Visions of Excess: Selected Writings, 1927–1939,* ed. and trans. Allan Stoekl (Minneapolis: University of Minnesota Press, 1985), 37.

34. Winfried Menninghaus, *In Praise of Nonsense: Kant and Bluebeard,* trans. Henry Pickford (Stanford, Calif.: Stanford University Press, 1999), 74.

35. Bataille, *Visions of Excess,* 130.

The Poetics of Cyberspace: Two Ways to Get a Life

J. Hillis Miller

The poetics of cyberspace! What does that mean? Poetics, I take it, is the science or craft of making. It gives knowledge of how to do a particular thing with words. Poetics studies the way words or other signs are assembled so they can be made to produce an effect on the reader, viewer, or listener. Or rather, "poetics" names both the forms such assemblages have and the discipline that studies those forms. *Poiēsis* means "making" in Greek. "Poetics" is the all-inclusive term, encompassing such narrower fields as "narratology" or "dramaturgy" or "prosody." Poetic assemblages are in various ways modes of spacing, even in the literal sense of the spacing of the words on the page of a printed poem. The spacing is part of the meaning and part of what generates an effect. These effects are not trivial. The spacings are not innocent. They constitute the codework that makes us what we are and encrypt the everyday surveillance by the mass media that means Big Brother is watching us even in the apparently innocent form of television advertising. We live our lives according to the dominant poetics that governs the way words and other signs are assembled in a given culture. In a highly industrialized and technologized capitalist society we are surrounded by solicitations, part of whose power over us comes from the way they are assembled. We are surrounded these days by popular music, by advertising, by the juxtaposition of columns in the newspaper or the adjacency of news sound bites and advertisements for stomach pills in television network news, by the effects of cinematic or television montage, by the spacings of elements on our computer screens. They are the way we get a life these days. We are interpellated almost irresistibly to live our lives in certain ways that this ubiquitous poetics commands. Marshall McLuhan long ago began the study of popular culture's poetics in *The Guttenberg Galaxy* (1962), *Understanding Media* (1964),[1] and other works. Many other critics have extended his work to analyze the dimension of popular culture he did not live to see, that is, cyberspace. Everyone knows we are in the midst of an epochal transition from print culture to digital culture. Each of these cultures has its intrinsic poetics. I began by saying that poetics studies the way to do certain things, produce certain effects, with conglomerations of words or other signs, for example, to get the American people to accept the invasion of Iraq. This essay sets the way we used to get a life, that is, have our lives shaped for us, within print culture, against the way those who live primarily in cyberspace get a life today.

One of the abbreviations used in e-mails and chat rooms is "gal": "Get a life!" It is a wonderfully subtle and nuanced exhortation or put-down. It suggests, not too gently, that the person to whom it is addressed does not have a life at this point. He or she has manifested that by some behavior or speech obnoxious to the exasperated interlocutor. The latter says, "Get a life!"

Why doesn't that person have a life already? Presumably because he or she is too hung up on conventional judgments, values, and behavior. To "get a life" means, I take it, to abandon conventional values and behaviors, to live freely, according to self-generated norms that defy convention. To have a life is to have integrity, independence, originality. Of course the performative command "Get a life!" is often an invitation not to independence but to joining the speaker's way of life. "Get a life!" then means, "Give up your present life and join me and my way of life." It is a quasi-religious injunction. Jesus promised that if you joined him you would get a life, and get it more abundantly. "For whosoever hath," said Jesus in the parable of the sower as reported in Matthew 13:12–13, "to him shall be given, and he shall have more abundance: but whosoever hath not, from him shall be taken away even that he hath. Therefore speak I to them in parables: because they seeing see not; and hearing they hear not, neither do they understand." Like the parables of Jesus, "gal" is addressed to those who have ears and can hear or eyes that can see and understand. The code is inscrutable to those not in the know. The injunction "Gal!" it happens, is a set of letters with an ironic meaning of its own. "Gal" is slang for "girl." To understand the injunction "Gal!" or to crack the code is already to belong to a somewhat esoteric community, a community apart, perhaps a community of dissensus.

My questions are the following: Is the sense of what it means to have a life, a genuine identity or selfhood, changing with the ongoing shift from a paper-based culture to a pixel-based or pixilated culture? If so, just how? Are new forms of community developing that define in new ways what it means to have a life? Are they perhaps communities of true dissensus, that is, unique, self-enclosed, incommensurate groups, with singular goals and norms? Is the way we live now, or want to live, different from the way we used to live? If one wanted to get a life today would one do it differently? These questions have often been asked. Many answers have been proposed in recent years. I still find it not all that easy to get clarity that satisfies me. Here is another try.

A large literature on these topics, as I have said, already exists, including some things I have written myself. David Crystal's fascinating *Language and the Internet* has an eight-page, closely packed bibliography, even though it limits itself to the question named in its title. "It is not the aim of this book," says Crystal firmly, "to reflect on the consequences for individuals and for society of lives that are lived largely in cyberspace."[2] This is just what I want to reflect on. Crystal does not really, strictly speaking, obey his prohibition, with anything like crystal clarity. The consequences for individuals and for society cannot be separated from the effect of the Internet, as Crystal puts it, "on language in general, and on individual languages in particular."[3] Crystal's bibliography includes such items as Diane F. Witmer and Sandra Lee Katzman's "On-line Smiles: Does Gender Make a Difference in the Use of Graphic Accents?" This piece is available online at www.ascusc.org/jcmc/vol2/issue5/witmer1.html. The "jcmc" of this Web address stands for *Journal of Computer-Mediated Communication.* That is my topic here, computer-mediated communication, including use of the computer for communication with oneself.

Let me propose a thought experiment. I want to juxtapose the "lives" of two teenagers, one in about 1946, the other today. Both, it happens, are, in my imagination of them, male. Whether that makes a decisive difference is a large and complex question, on which I shall only briefly touch. I think it does make a difference. Our culture interpellates males and females, boys and girls, to behave differently in their ways of submission to reigning communication technologies, whether of paper or of pixel. I doubt if the difference is primarily biological. Let me call the first of my virtual personages Horace, in memory of Horace Greeley (1811–72), an earlier American newspaperman. I call the other Jim, or Jimjim to his family and friends, for no particular reason. I had thought of calling Jimjim Jimjane, to express the uncertainty of his or her gender, as interpellated by the Internet. The evidence I have, however, suggests that the particular cyberpersonality I shall outline is much more likely to be male. Though the avatars young people adopt in cyberspace may often be deliberately uncertain or ambiguous as to the gender of the user, Jimjim says, speaking of the computer game he habitually plays: "From SubSpace specifically, I only know about four female players well. I know of a few more, something like ten or twenty [out of eighty or more], but I don't know them well. There aren't very many girls that play SubSpace, and I'm sure some of them don't like to tell people they are, since it sometimes leads to bad situations." Jimjim's sister and female cousin are also computer-adept, but they use cyberspace in quite different ways from Jimjim. His sister studies computer science but is interested in programming and uses AOL Instant Messenger primarily to talk online with friends she has known since high school. Jimjim's cousin works for a small company that creates Web sites for local businesses. She is a gifted computer artist, whereas graphic design does not interest Jimjim much. She and a friend, also female, created several years ago an online newspaper with a distinctly radical political bias. I conclude that cyberspace is lived in in quite different ways by different young people and that it would be an error to try to generalize a single cyberpersonality. It is difficult, perhaps impossible, to invent a plausible imaginary cyberperson who combines all these uses of the Internet while being in addition gender-neutral. Each cyberperson is to some degree singular, sui generis.

The first of my imaginary teenagers is alone around 1946 sitting in an easy chair reading a book. He is reading Emily Brontë's *Wuthering Heights* for the first time. Ever since Horace taught himself to read at age five, so he would not have to depend on his mother to read *Alice in Wonderland* to him, he has spent as much time as people will allow him to do reading books. He also makes model airplanes and ham radios. He is pretty much a loner. Decisive moments in his life are often encounters with books. An example was his first reading of Dostoyevsky's *Notes from Underground,* when he was a sophomore in college. "Aha!" he said to himself, "At last

I have found someone like myself. This man speaks for me. 'I am a sick man . . . I am a spiteful man. I am an unattractive man. I believe my liver is diseased.' Wonderful! A soul mate at last."

This imaginary personage is a perfect example of what Simon During calls "literary subjectivity."[4] Not only did Horace "love literature" and spend a lot of time reading it but his sense of himself, of who and what he was, was also to a large degree, though of course not completely, determined by the literary works he read. He was interpellated to be what he was by literature. He was a child of the print epoch, or rather of what Jacques Derrida calls the paper age. No television then. No computers. No World Wide Web. Radio, yes. This young person listened to *Amos and Andy, Easy Aces,* and *The Lone Ranger.* Horace remembers hearing hectoring speeches by Hitler rebroadcast for an American audience in incomprehensible—but very impressive—German. The house had a telephone, but this virtual person does not remember using it much, certainly not for long-distance calls, which were a big event in the house, when they happened.

Horace was surrounded by various forms of paper. They were piled up around him, not only the paper of all those books but the paper of his birth certificate and the rest of his "identity papers," the paper on which he wrote his student "papers" and examinations, at first in longhand, then, the papers that is, on the typewriter. In addition, there was the paper on which he wrote rather infrequent letters—infrequent, that is, until he fell in love and wrote reams of love letters when separated from his beloved, paper on which he kept a mawkish diary, all those papers on which he signed his name or inscribed his initials, for example in that diary or on the flyleaves of the books he owned, and so on.

Horace was a paper man, a bookworm. Paper was inseparable from his identity. Paper was a prosthetic extension of himself, or rather it was a kind of self outside himself. Paper, or what was written on it, called, exhorted, demanded, or beseeched, with an irresistible force, that he be what he was. If he had commanded such eloquence, he might have said what Jacques Derrida says in "Paper or Me, You Know . . . (New Speculations on a Luxury of the Poor)," an interview of 1997, published originally, in French of course, in *Les Cahiers de médiologie:* " 'I who can sign or recognize my name on a surface or a paper support'; 'The paper is mine'; 'Paper is a self or ego'; 'Paper is me.' "[5] For such a person, unless an agreement or commitment is "put on paper," it is not binding. It is not for real.

Derrida in that interview reminds his readers of a passage in Sigmund

Freud's *The Problem of Anxiety* that indicates how deeply into the psyche the physical act of writing, for Freud at least, had penetrated:

> If writing—which consists in allowing a fluid to flow out from a tube upon a piece of white paper—has acquired the symbolic meaning of coitus, or if walking has become a symbolic substitute for stamping upon the body of Mother Earth, then both writing and walking will be abstained from, because it is as though forbidden sexual behavior were thereby being indulged in.[6]

The reader will also note, as Derrida does not explicitly do, how imperturbably sexist Freud's formulation is. If this is the way writing is for men, what then is the act of writing for women—for women, that is, who do it rather than submitting to being written on, in various senses of "being written on," such as those love letters Horace sent his beloved? Writing could hardly be the same for women as for men.

A passage in Hardy's *Tess of the d'Urbervilles,* the one describing her violation, speaks again, it would appear, for the male view of writing: "Why it was that upon this beautiful feminine tissue, sensitive as gossamer, and practically blank as snow as yet, there should have been traced such a coarse pattern as it was doomed to receive; why so often the coarse appropriates the finer thus, the wrong man the woman, the wrong woman the man, many thousand years of analytical philosophy have failed to explain to our sense of order."[7] This passage seems congruent with the one from Freud. This is so, however much Hardy may have identified himself with Tess and her experiences in *Tess of the d'Urbervilles,* as in the novel's epigraph from Shakespeare's *Two Gentlemen of Verona:* "Poor wounded name! My bosom as a bed, / Shall lodge thee."[8] In this epigraph the relation is reversed. Hardy's bosom becomes the bed, support, sheet, or sheet of paper, on which Tess's name is written, couched, lodged, in a covert sexual relation that has the woman on top, so to speak, and the male author in the passive position of receptacle or matrix.

One more passage involving another version of this figure will almost complete this brief repertoire of written passages about writing. They are meant to suggest what may have been at stake when our young man wrote in his diary the initials of one or another young woman he admired, mutely and from afar, and then added his own initials, as a kind of magic incantation. This was done in the absurd and vain hope that the proximity of the names might bring another, more physical, proximity.

In Henry James's *The Ambassadors* the hero, Louis Lambert Strether, in the end, refuses the offer of herself Maria Gostrey makes. He goes back home empty-handed to Woollett, Massachusetts. Woollett isn't Paris, to put it mildly. The three doubled letters in the name "Woollett" suggest, if Freud is right, some absence of masculinity. Doubling strives, futilely, to compensate for a lack. Strether makes his grand refusal, for the following reason, at least so he says: "That, you see, is my only logic. Not, out of the whole affair, to have got anything for myself."[9] Just why he does so, or whether he does the right thing, is not altogether clear. In a famous passage in the novel, Strether exhorts Little Bilham to "get a life," in no uncertain terms: "Live all you can; it's a mistake not to. It doesn't so much matter what you do in particular, so long as you have your life. If you haven't had that what *have* you had? . . . Live!"[10] In the preface of 1909, James quotes this passage and says it was the germ, and remains the center, of the novel. Why does Strether not take his own advice, when he has such a good chance? You will note that I speak of Strether as if he were a real person, even though he has existence only as a spectral virtuality, a ghost raised when I read the words on the page. That is what happens to bookworms.

It might be argued, strangely enough, that part of the answer has to do with the role in *The Ambassadors* of another technology than the manuscript or typed page. As Rolland Munro has shown in a brilliant article,[11] events in *The Ambassadors* are decisively determined by a then quite new technology, the telegram. Telegrams fly back and forth from Woollett to Paris. At one point, Strether's fiancée, the redoubtable Mrs. Newsome, who never appears in person in the novel, sends Strether an urgent telegram ordering him to come back home immediately. Strether sends back a temporizing telegram, one that effectively "dishes" his engagement to her.

On another telegraphic occasion, what the supersensitive Strether notices when he goes to send a telegram promising to meet Madame de Vionnet at her apartment may hint at an answer to the question of Strether's refusal of Maria Gostrey. This is just after he has discovered, in a famous scene, unmistakable evidence of the liaison between Chad and Madame de Vionnet. At the telegraph office, he notices "the little prompt Paris women . . . driving the dreadful needle-pointed public pen at the dreadful sand-strewn public table; implements that symbolized for Strether's too interpretative innocence something more acute in manner, more sinister in morals, more fierce in the national life."[12] Here are just Freud's elements again, including even the association of the writing surface with the earth, in the notation of the "dreadful sand-strewn public table." The sexes, however, are now reversed, with the women wielding the pen, in a way Strether finds "dreadful," too "prompt," too "fierce," something "sinister in morals." This may be what Strether, not so secretly, fears in women, not only in Mrs. Newsome but also in Maria Gostrey. He's not the marrying sort.

Nor was Henry James. James suffered, from about 1895 on, as most people know, from a psychophysical disorder, exacerbated writer's cramp or, perhaps, carpal tunnel syndrome. Whatever it was, it prevented him from any longer writing his works in longhand. No more treading Mother Earth for him. Henceforth he dictated his work, first to a male and then to female stenographers. The stenographers typed as he dictated. Imagine dictating *The Golden Bowl,* off the top of your head, so to speak!

One more passage will take me a step further in trying to exemplify from passages in literature what it means to say, "paper is me." The astute listener will have noticed that I am exemplifying what I ascribed to my imaginary teenager with the "literary subjectivity." For such a person, one passage leads to another, on any topic chosen, in a movement from topos to topos, place to place, within a vast internalized archive or database. *Louis Lambert,* for example, is the name of a novel by Balzac. Following that trail would lead our bookworm far astray. Such a person as Horace gradually equips himself with a kind of internal hard drive or Library of Babel, drawn from books read and remembered. Horace gets a life, and lives it, to a considerable degree through books.

I did not choose arbitrarily to have my teenager reading *Wuthering Heights* for the first time. A wonderful passage near the beginning indicates the degree to which *Wuthering Heights* is obliquely a book about the culture of the book. The reader will remember that *Wuthering Heights* uses, in a quite implausible way, if you think of it, the convention of a narrative made of a diary. The narrator has the suggestive name of "Lockwood," as though he were a chest or even a "secretary," as that word is employed to name a piece of furniture used to lock up books and papers and as a writing desk.

The reader is to imagine Lockwood writing down his account more or less just after events happen. The first words of the novel are: "1801—I have just returned from a visit to my landlord [Heathcliff, that is]."[13] This initial part of Lockwood's diary recounts his disastrous first visit to Wuthering Heights. It is an amazing episode. Lockwood is caught in a snowstorm, forced to spend the night in a bedroom with a panel-enclosed bed: "I slid back the panelled sides, got in with my light, pulled them together again, and felt secure against the vigilance of Heathcliff, and every one else." How wrong he is! In this inside of the inside, a figure, one might say, for Lockwood's safe subjective interiority, he finds the books that belonged to the first Cathy, Catherine Earnshaw, when she was a child. He finds also names, graffiti, scratched on the window ledge within the bed enclosure: "The ledge, where I placed my candle, had a few mildewed books piled up in one corner; and it was covered with writing scratched on the paint. This writing, however, was nothing but a name repeated in all kinds of characters, large and small—*Catherine Earnshaw,* here and there varied to *Catherine Heathcliff,* and then again to *Catherine Linton.*" The books include "a Testament, in lean type, and smelling dreadfully musty." The rest of Cathy's "select" library is books apparently of the same ilk. The Testament, and presumably the other books too, are inscribed: "Catherine Earnshaw, her book."[14]

The books' greatest peculiarity, however, is that they are scribbled all over in the margins and on any blank pages, in "faded hieroglyphics." These "scrawl[s]," "in an unformed, childish hand," are Cathy's circumstantial diary of her early life and especially of her relation to Heathcliff when they were children. Lockwood cites this account verbatim, as he is imagined to have read it. It is a diary within a diary. This passage matches in structure the panelled bed within the bedroom. This novel is made, in more ways than one, like a nest of Chinese boxes, in one version of the poetics of narration in printed books. Before he reads Cathy's diary, however, Lockwood almost falls asleep. He is awakened by a nightmare of staring white letters that become embodied (or disembodied) as ghosts, specters: "In vapid listlessness I leant my head against the window, and continued spelling over Catherine Earnshaw—Heathcliff—Linton, till my eyes closed; but they had not rested five minutes when a glare of white letters started from the dark, as vivid as spectres—the air swarmed with Catherines."[15] Lockwood then finally falls asleep reading Cathy's diary.

Asleep, he has a nightmare generated by the last book title he has seen, a printed sermon entitled "Seventy Times Seven, and the First of the Seventy First. A Pious Discourse delivered by the Reverend Jabes Branderham, in the Chapel of Gimmerden Slough." The text of the sermon is Matthew 18:21–22, in which Jesus says we should forgive our neighbors' sins not just seven times but seventy times seven. In Lockwood's nightmare the Reverend Branderham accuses Lockwood before the church congregation of having committed "the First of the Seventy First," that is, the unforgivable sin, or the sin we need not forgive: "Brethren, execute upon him the judgment written! Such honour have all His saints!" This nightmare ends with a general free-for-all in the church in which "Every man's hand was against his neighbour."[16] So much for Christian charity and forgiveness! We have seen something of that lately in United States behavior. As Pascal says, "Men never do evil so completely and cheerfully as when they do it from religious conviction."[17] I am not just talking about Muslim so-called terrorists.

Waking from this nightmare, Lockwood falls back into a more terrifying one, if it *is* a dream, which the novel leaves in doubt. Cathy's ghost appears outside the window, imploring to be let in. The inside of the inside turns out to be exposed to the most outside outside, the wholly other of the spirit world. When Lockwood breaks the window, his fingers "[close] on the fingers of a little, ice-cold hand." Then follows the act of violence that of all the violent acts in this violent novel still shocks me the most: "Terror made me cruel; and, finding it useless to attempt shaking the creature off, I pulled its wrist on to the broken pane, and rubbed it to and fro till the blood ran down and soaked the bed-clothes."[18] In the nightmare at least, Cathy's ghost is far from disembodied. The wrist bleeds—which is part of the horror. Lockwood tries, with only partial success, to keep the specter out by piling Cathy's books in a pyramid against the broken window. Heathcliff then bursts in to implore Cathy to come in. Nothing is said about whether or not real blood stains the bedclothes.

I take this whole episode as an admirable parabolic representation (I do not dare to say "allegory") of the place handwriting and books have in determining selfhood and social relations during the paper epoch. Lockwood records and in a sense invokes or calls into being the interiority of his consciousness, as Cathy does, by writing a diary. The imaginary diaries become a printed book, a novel, exposed to the eyes of all who can read. This exposure is a chief way in which, in the book epoch, secret selfhood, intimate subjectivity, is turned inside out.

Cathy experiments with different forms of her name, her maiden name, "Catherine Earnshaw," followed by the names she would have if she were to marry either Heathcliff or Edgar Linton. She marries the latter but is indissolubly identified with the former. "He's more myself than I am. . . . I *am* Heathcliff," she says in a famous declaration.[19] She is not just Catherine Heathcliff but Catherineheathcliff. *Wuthering Heights* as a whole is encapsulated in these name changes or permutations. The identification of Catherine and Heathcliff includes even a proleptic anticipation of the second plot, in which Cathy's daughter, also called Cathy, changes from Catherine Linton to Catherine Heathcliff (when she marries Heathcliff's sickly son) and then to Catherine Earnshaw (when she happily marries Hareton Earnshaw). Only a woman, in that culture, changes names, and therefore signatures, with marriage. To change your name is to change your identity. Men remain who they are, married or not. When a woman signs her maiden name to a marriage application form, she is, in a manner of speaking, committing suicide. She dies as one person and allows herself to be reborn as another. The man signs and remains the same person, with the same signature. One can see why women these days are resisting that and keeping their so-called maiden names even when they are no longer maidens.

The tradition of inscribing books that you own with your name, followed by "her book" or "his book," indicates the way ownership of books is related to the sense of selfhood and its endorsement by signature: "Catherine Earnshaw, her book."[20] I am the books I can write my name in and say of each, in the third person, that it is "his book" or "her book." I confer selfhood on myself by way of the book. I then ascribe to that selfhood an external social validation. I affirm that some collectivity is saying this is "his book," or "her book," so an "I" must preexist to sign the book. To write, as Cathy does, a private diary in the margins or blank pages of books, especially religious books, a Testament or a sermon, is a marvelous expression of the way private subjectivity is incorporated in printed books or generated by them. I am what I read. These books have called or interpellated me to be what I am.

The Reverend Branderham's sermon is a commentary, an act of "dividing the text." Such biblical commentary is the not-so-distant model for present-day interpretations of "secular literature," that is, for "close readings," such as this miniature one. Such readings fetishize or sacralize literature, Lockwood's dream is a commentary on Branderham's commentary, and my remarks are a commentary on a commentary on a commentary.

The episode of Lockwood's experiences in the paneled bed admirably dramatizes the way literary works have a magic power to raise ghosts. The names of the various Catherines, in Lockwood's first dream, become staring white letters and then personified specters, until the air swarms with Catherines. It is only a step from that to the final nightmare appearance of Cathy herself as a child-ghost who has "been a waif for twenty years!"[21] It is as though the names, especially written names, invoke the person, in a frightening prosopopoetic apostrophe or resurrection.

The reader, to conclude, may reflect that he or she too has raised ghosts through the act of reading: the ghosts of Lockwood, Heathcliff, Cathy, and the rest. Reading literature is an invocation of specters that then have great power to determine the reader's sense of himself or herself. That was certainly the case for Horace, my imaginary personage, a ghost I myself have raised, sitting there in his easy chair reading *Wuthering Heights* for the first time. He got a life through books, and he lived his life through books. He was a paper man.

What a difference when we turn to Jimjim, the second virtual person in my thought experiment! Let us imagine him in 2003. He is seated at his computer, at three o'clock in the morning. He is doing five things at once. He is playing a collective computer game called SubSpace with a group from various countries. He is listening to songs selected through MP3. He is using AOL Instant Messenger to carry on an e-mail conversation with a friend. He is at the same time engaged in a multiperson interchange with a chat group through IRC (Internet Relay Chat). He is also doing homework for his university classes.

Jimjim is a computer science student at a public university. He has been using computers since he was five or six. By a year or two later he was making changes in his mother's computer (the only one he had access to). Strange things happened when she turned it on: a message on the screen or a new screen saver. He was an early player of computer games. He would play for eight or ten hours at a time, stopping only for meals, when forced to do so. He showed early on an interest in changing or reprogramming game programs. He has never read a program manual in his life and is scornful of those who do. The abbreviation "rtfm" ("read the fucking manual"), one of the items in David Crystal's list of Netspeak codes, would have elicited from Jimjim a scornful snort or a smiley with a lifted eyebrow or wink ;-) or perhaps the sarcastic smiley :-] instead. Jimjim long ago gradually began to use e-mail and chat mail to communicate with friends. He then began to play online games with them, thereby tying up the telephone line in his home for hours at a time. Allowed to do so, he sleeps all day (literally) and stays up all night (literally), using the computer. He eats primarily junk food, when he can get away with it. Jimjim, in short, is a computer geek.

He is even a hacker, in the benign sense of someone who likes to hack or alter programs, to get down as far into the kernel of the program as he can and do things to it. He already took a basic programming course in high school. Now, in college, of course he has his own computer, a PC, not a Mac. He keeps it on all the time. He uses it about four-fifths of the time he is in his college room, that is, at least eight hours a day. He has downloaded roughly seventeen hundred songs off MP3 and listens to them all the time when he is using the computer. A high point for him was receiving the Mandrake version of Linux as a birthday present. The attraction of Linux is its power and openness to being programmed, also the way using it gives him entry into an elite group of fellow geeks. He passionately believes in open source and in total freedom on the Net. This belief spills over into his general political views, such as they are. He is, I suppose you would say, a libertarian. He has risen up through the ranks of that online game called SubSpace (played by three quarters of a million people worldwide). He is now a SuperModerator (SMod) in SubSpace. His "job" includes "enforcing the rules, watching for cheaters, being nice to the players, hosting events, things like that."[22] Jimjim has a wide range of friends, mostly casual ones, he has met online, chiefly through SubSpace. Most are from the United States, but a few are from Germany, Australia, Canada, Brazil, and some other countries. A few of these relations are close ones, for example, with a girl he met online and has met in person only once. He also uses, as I have mentioned, several chat programs (the multiparty chat group IRC [Internet Relay Chat] and two others for communicating with one person at a time, AIM [AOL Instant Messenger] and ICQ). The client he uses for IRC is mIRC, a British operation (www.mirc.co.uk). He has never got much into MUDs or MOOs, though some of his friends have. A MUD is a Multi-User Dungeon or Domain or Dimension. A MOO is a MUD object oriented, a text-based online virtual reality system to which multiple users are connected at the same time. Jimjim chats partly with family and friends from high school but also with the much wider circle of people he has met online.

If Horace got a life from books, Jimjim, it seems clear, gets his life, or much of it, from his active participation in cyberspace. Three features of this participation seem crucial.

First, Jimjim, when he is online, is usually doing several things at once: listening to MP3, engaging in several different chat conversations, playing or watching a computer game, doing homework, and so on. "When I'm using the computer," says this imaginary personage, "I'm probably going to be talking to someone using AIM, as well as using IRC and playing/watching some game (most likely SubSpace). I also spend time programming, doing homework, and watching anime, although not as much. I tend to be doing more than one of the above things at the same time, as well." This description reminds me of a citation in David Crystal's *Language and the Internet* from someone who said, "It is possible to do calculus homework and have tinysex [whatever that is, maybe something you do on a TinyMUD] at the same time, if you type fast enough."[23]

Second, Jimjim is, somewhat self-consciously, a different person or persons online from the one he is in face-to-face encounters with family and friends. He uses avatars or imaginary names online. What he says about this is striking in its resistance to the idea that he actively invents these alternative selves. He just becomes a different person. "I have avatars in a sense, I guess. That is, I use names other than my own online, but I don't invent personalities for them. I suppose that I act differently online than I do when I talk to people face-to-face, but it's not something I invent, it's just how I normally act." This statement is amazing in its candor and in its self-analytic power. Jimjim could say what Rimbaud said: *Je est un autre* (I is another). It's not a matter of invention or choice. It just happens, perhaps as an effect of the medium itself, the effect of what I am calling the poetics of cyberspace. Online, Jimjim becomes another person or persons. This means that he is not a single person but a strange sort of interior civic community of persons. Is this a community of dissensus? I think it could be argued that it is.

Third, Jimjim self-consciously belongs to a different community or communities online from the ones he belongs to outside cyberspace. He uses, to some degree at least, a special language or languages online. He uses smileys often and conventional abbreviations sometimes, but mostly he writes the way he talks. "Yes," he says, in answer to a question about whether he thinks of himself as belonging to a separate cyberspace community, "the people I know and talk with online are in a distinctly separate group from the ones I talk to and see off line." Jimjim, in short, is, part of him at least, a cyberperson or rather cyberpersons, just as Horace is a paper person. Jimjim knows about eighty people through his participation in the SubSpace community, twenty or twenty-five of them fairly intimately, if you can still use that word for something so disembodied, so spectral. He plays SubSpace and at the same time—laterally, so to speak—carries on chat group conversations with numbers of these friends in what is called an "in-game public chat." A subgroup of the larger group within Jimjim's particular domain of SubSpace happens to be Brazilians. Though Jimjim does not know Portuguese, one member of his group does. That member translates back and forth and so keeps the game going. The online community to which Jimjim belongs is therefore not only transnational, it is also multilingual. The hegemony of English in cyberspace should by no means be taken for granted. The number of Web sites in Chinese is increasing exponentially, and will likely exceed those in English by 2010.

Well, what, if anything, can I conclude from this thought experiment? The experiment has juxtaposed two virtual persons, Horace and Jimjim. The title of the conference for which this essay was first prepared was "Digital Dilemmas." A "dilemma" is, strictly speaking, "a situation that requires one to choose between two equally balanced alternatives," or "a predicament that seemingly defies a satisfactory solution," or "an argument in which a choice of two or more alternatives, each being conclusive and fatal, is presented to an antagonist." The word is often used more loosely to define a predicament. Just what a "digital dilemma" would be, I'm not quite sure, but presumably it means a hard choice that is generated by the electronic revolution that is fast replacing Horaces with Jimjims.

First conclusion or result of the thought experiment: Of one thing I am certain and do not see as a dilemma. There is no use whatever either in hand-wringing or in triumphalism. These are two extreme judgments of getting a life in cyberspace that we have all probably encountered. On the one hand, the change from paper persons to cyberpersons has already occurred or is irreversibly under way. Nostalgia will butter no parsnips. On the other hand, the symmetrical triumphalism that sees the electronic revolution as justifying a wholesale book burning and as ushering in a millennium of peace and transnational plenty is equally, and symmetrically, wrong. It is not the end of the world, but it is not the happy end of history, either. The challenge is to take stock of what is happening and to recognize the new possibilities and new responsibilities that living in cyberspace brings. It would certainly be a disaster, for reasons I shall specify, to try to reform Jimjim, to enforce on him a "literary subjectivity," to close down his chat groups and his online computer games, or to police and censor the Internet generally, as is the case in the People's Republic of China. Some real danger of that these days may exist in the United States, as civil liberties come under widespread unconstitutional threat.

Second conclusion: The paper age is by no means over. It will probably last a long time to come, just as manuscript culture lasted into the print age. On the one hand, Jimjim reads or used to read a lot of literature, chiefly science fiction. He mentions Neal Stephenson, Roger Zelazny, and Larry Niven, among others. And of course Jimjim has his identity papers too, though cards that have an electronic component are more and more replacing them. Horace, on the other hand, has grown up to become, you guessed it, a university professor. He now writes on the computer, after beginning with longhand, shifting to the typewriter, then back to longhand, finally straight from that to computer composition. He uses e-mail all the time. It has changed his life. He also uses the Web in his research, searching online bibliographies, reading online versions of books, occasionally reading online journals, and so on. He does not, however, participate in chat groups or play computer games. His "other lives" are still lived primarily through reading books that are physical objects you can hold in your hand. Horace, however, is, to some degree, perhaps more than he realizes or is willing to admit, a cyberperson as well as a paper person. Just as Jimjim listens to an eclectic mix of tunes online and downloads them into his portable MP3 player, Horace pulls out a CD or old record album and listens to jazz or classical music much of the time, even when he is reading or writing. He also listens to streaming classical music through his computer by way of RealPlayer. His favorite station is in Oslo. Whereas Horace writes literary criticism, Jimjim writes poetry and fiction. Jimjim is admirably adept at expressing himself clearly and succinctly, as the quotations from him indicate. Far from being made illiterate by the computer, Jimjim has, through constant practice in e-mails and chat groups, acquired an impressive clarity and force in his use of language. For some people at least, those with a gift for language, using e-mail and ICQ is splendid training in doing what you want with words. I conclude that much overlapping in the two kinds of selfhood and community-belonging exists and will go on existing for the foreseeable future. It is not a dilemma. I can, responsibly, choose to belong to both worlds, as long as I am willing to take the consequences for that mixed existence, or double life.

Third conclusion: Though major differences exist between the two types of persons, they are also in one striking way alike. Both literature and cyberspace are forms of "secular magic," to borrow a phrase from Simon During. Just what do I mean by that? Simon During, in *Modern Enchantments: The Cultural Power of Secular Magic,* has admirably traced the history of magic shows and entertainments, from Greek and Roman antiquity to the Renaissance and on down to the early twentieth century.[24] As part of this history, he has discussed the relation of magic to literature. He is interested primarily in works such as Hoffmann's *Kater Murr* or Raymond Roussel's *Impressions d'Afrique.* Such works have a more or less direct relation to magic shows. During does not explicitly observe, however, that all printed literary works, whether or not they overtly refer to magic practices, can be thought of as a species of magic. A work of literature is an abracadabra or hocus pocus that opens a new world. During has something to say about the way cinema extended magic shows, for example, by being based in part on magic lanterns that were long a part of magic stage presentations. Eventually cinema put stage magic out of business. Movies had the stronger force, a bigger *Zumbah,* to borrow Harold Bloom's borrowing of an expressive African word for magic energy—the force.

During also does not observe that modern communications technologies, from trick photography to the telephone to cinema to radio to television to recordings on disks, tapes, or CDs to the computer connected to the Internet, fulfill in reality old dreams of magic communication, at a temporal or spatial distance, with the living or with the dead. I can, any time I like, hear Glenn Gould play Bach's *Goldberg Variations* with fingers long since turned to dust. I can even hear Alfred Lord Tennyson reciting his poems. Talk about raising ghosts!

As Laurence Rickels has shown, in the early days of both the telephone and the tape recorder, people believed they were hearing the voices of the dead (usually their mothers) behind the voices of the living, or through the static, on a telephone connection or a tape recording.[25] These teletechnologies have gradually displaced not only magic stage assemblages but also that other fading form of secular magic: literature. Cinema, television, CDs, VCRs, MP3 gadgets, DVD players, computers, and the Internet have become our dominant far-seeing and far-hearing conjurers, sorcerers, prestidigitators, animators of talking heads. These devices are, in short, our chief purveyors of magic shows. Their poetics, especially now the poetics of cyberspace, have incalculable power to determine ideological belief, just as books did in the age of the book, the paper period.

Just what can be said, on the basis of my thought experiment, of the differences between paper persons and cyberpersons? Some of the differences are, to me at least, quite surprising. I would not have thought of them if I had not performed my thought experiment. To some degree they suggest that it is better to be a cyberperson than a paper person.

Fourth conclusion: Horace is to a considerable degree more private, more alone and lonely, than Jimjim. Reading a literary work, or even writing one, not to speak of writing a commentary on one, such as my miniature interpretation of an episode in *Wuthering Heights,* is a solitary activity. It is even to some degree narcissistic or onanistic, as a passage in

Anthony Trollope's *An Autobiography* suggests. In this passage Trollope is speaking of the way he was ostracized as a youth at Harrow because he was a day student at an elite boarding school and had little pocket money or good clothes. He says that since play with the other boys was denied him, he had to make up his own solitary play for himself. "Play of some kind was necessary to me then,—as it has always been," he says. Trollope's solitary play took the form of what today we would call "daydreaming": "Thus it came to pass that I was always going about with some castle-in-the-air firmly built within my mind. Nor were these efforts in architecture spasmodic, or subject to constant change from day to day. For weeks, for months, if I remember rightly, from year to year I would carry on the same tale, binding myself down to certain laws, to certain proportions and proprieties and unities. Nothing impossible was ever introduced,—not even anything which from outward circumstances would seem to be violently improbable." This sounds somewhat like one of those long-continued computer games, does it not, except that Trollope played by himself. Trollope himself explicitly affirmed that his published novels were a transformation of his youthful habit of daydreaming. Speaking of that bad habit of daydreaming, Trollope says, "There can, I imagine, hardly be a more dangerous mental practice; but I have often doubted whether, had it not been my practice, I should ever have written a novel. I learned in this way to maintain an interest in a fictitious story, to dwell on a work created by my own imagination, and to live in a world altogether outside the world of my own material life."[26] All writers and readers of novels are addicted to this "dangerous mental practice." Jimjim, on the contrary, is actively engaged with other people in those chat group interchanges or in playing SubSpace. He is not nearly so narcissistically alone.

Fifth conclusion: Jim playing SubSpace or using a chat group is much more actively and creatively involved than Horace reading *Wuthering Heights.* The Internet and many things reachable through it pride themselves on being "interactive." "Interactive" is a leitmotif of the Net. A tremendous amount of linguistic exuberance and creativity is required for the various uses of the Web Jimjim habitually makes, day after day, for many hours a day. As David Crystal's *Language and the Internet* shows, new languages or idioms within standard English are rapidly being created by Internet users. Moreover, insofar as Jimjim is what he is through selves he becomes on the Net, he is actively engaged in a remarkable process of self-fashioning.

Reading a book, however much it requires active response and even intervention, is nevertheless a more or less passive, receptive activity. Horace sits alone in his easy chair letting the words of *Wuthering Heights* do his magic dreaming for him. He is much more likely than Jimjim, therefore, to have his selfhood determined for him by his subjection to literature, his "literary subjectivity," whereas Jimjim is creating his selfhood or selfhoods, even though he is subject, of course, to the "rules of the game."

Sixth conclusion: If belonging to a community of friends and associates is a good thing, the normal situation for human beings, Jimjim much more obviously has that through his decisive participation in cybergroups than does Horace alone with Emily Brontë, or, earlier in his life, resisting all attempts by his mother to persuade him to "go out and play with the other children" when he was deep in *The Swiss Family Robinson* or some such book. Moreover, these cybercommunities really do, after all reservations have been made, seem to constitute separate subcultures not straightforwardly subservient to the dominant national culture. Each develops, to some degree, judgments, values, and ethical standards of its own. This development might be allegorized in the way so many computer games involve the creation of imaginary countries with their own laws and customs.

Communities in cyberspace are, to some degree at least, communities of dissensus, places where some independent political thinking may be possible. This, in my view, is an extremely good thing. Diversity and independence are, or should be, major aspects of our national and transnational character. This is particularly true at a time when the call to think like everyone else, on pain of being accused of disloyalty, is so much a part of a "wartime" mentality, the mentality of an interminable "war on terror." A terrifying example of that, terrifying to me at least, was a television ad a couple of years ago for the travel industry. It shows bits of a speech by George W. Bush echoed in robot fashion by a series of individuals or groups associated with the travel industry. The point of the ad is to persuade viewers that it is patriotic to travel in the aftermath of 9/11. "Americans are asking, 'What is expected of us?' " Bush is shown saying, and the others repeat in exact echo, "Americans are asking, 'What is expected of us?' "; "Americans are asking, 'What is expected of us?' " What is expected of us is that we should travel for our country and to save the travel industry. It's our patriotic duty. "And we will," says Bush in another clip, echoed again: "And we will," "and we will," "and we will," in hypnotic entrancement of the viewer, who is by this time glassy-eyed and in no condition to travel. This was a sitting president of the United States selling himself to a commercial pitch! Jimjim's chat groups or computer games sound pretty healthy to me by comparison.

I judge, on the basis of the conclusions I have drawn from my thought experiment, that it is better to be Jimjim than Horace. Matters are not quite so simple, however. For one thing, both Horace and Jim are exhorted, interpellated, called upon in various ways to be what they are by many other ISAs (Ideological State Apparatuses) than just literary works for Horace and the Net for Jim. School, television, cinema, newspapers, magazines, not to speak of police and politicians, all play a role. Horace now, sixty years after 1946, watches television, including network news, but he also seeks out Cursor.org, an alternative news source on the Web. Jim watches much less television than Horace does, though probably more movies, but of course those MP3 offerings are not devoid of ideological content either. The literary works that have made Horace what he is are, to be sure, to a considerable degree canonical purveyors of Western ideology, for example, assumptions about middle-class courtship and marriage in Anthony Trollope's novels. Nevertheless, even canonical works are also in part critiques of reigning ideologies. That is certainly true for *Wuthering Heights.* That novel is hardly a straightforward argument for patriarchal gender hierarchy or for bourgeois marriage and family life! Trollope's novels too are critique as well as indoctrination of Victorian ideologies. My subtitle alludes, of course, to Trollope's *The Way We Live Now.* Trollope by no means approved wholeheartedly of the way his contemporaries got a life or "lived now."

On the other side of the ledger, again, Jim's computer games are not innocent. They often glorify war, as in the many space battle games, such as SubSpace, or set up imaginary countries that are at war with other countries, in perpetuation of nationalist ideologies, ideologies that globalization may, or should, be weakening. Lots of violence exists in computer games. The geeks who make them up are not isolated from mainstream youth ideologies. The Internet, moreover, has rapidly been co-opted by business interests. Like *Wired* magazine, once a counterculture, it is now a tool of capitalism. It is hard to use the Net without being subject to commercial bombardment by flashing "pop-ups" and other appeals to consumerist greed.

A game of SubSpace and the novel *Wuthering Heights,* are, to put it mildly, quite different virtual realities in which to live. The difference, however, is not that one is violent and the other a canonical assertion of traditional humanistic values. *Wuthering Heights,* like the Bible or the work of Homer, Sophocles, Dante, or Shakespeare, is full of shocking violence. Nor is the difference one of the relative gender stability in canonical literature as opposed to gender ambiguity in cyberspace. *Wuthering Heights* was written by a woman, Emily Brontë, who published under a male-sounding pseudonym, "Ellis Bell," and who used a male narrator, Lockwood, who then records the narration of Nelly Dean, as well as soliloquies spoken to Nelly by Catherine Earnshaw and Heathcliff, or letters written by Isabella and others. Talk about avatars and the adoption of virtual alternative personalities!

My conclusion of conclusions, the ultimate result of my thought experiment, is that it is better to be a cyberperson than to be a paper person, though I have some reservations about that. In any case, it is happening anyhow, so more power to the cyberpeople!

I end with one dilemma. This dilemma would call for more development than space allows. We all know the problems the Internet is causing to copyright and intellectual property laws. The Napster case was paradigmatic of that. The question I want to ask, however, arises from a consideration of the performative utterances, speech acts, enunciated online. How can we hold Jimjim or his ilk responsible, in a court of law, for example, for commitments he makes when he has adopted a pseudonym or avatar and is enacting a role on the Net? Can he not say, "That was not me speaking, but an imaginary personage, a virtual person," and so get out of promises or contracts or commitments? I think of that moment in Maurice Blanchot's *Death Sentence* when the protagonist says, ". . . I had an aversion to marriage (and little respect for it), but in her language I married her."[27] Is a marriage performed in a language other than one's own mother tongue binding? If promises or proposals made on the Net are made in what is to some degree a separate language, "Netspeak," is what is said there binding in a court of law? How is the Jimjim off-line responsible for what one or another of his avatars commits himself or herself to doing online? If the various Jimjims make a genuine interior community of dissensus, how is betrayal or perjury to be avoided? What one Jimjim does or commits himself or herself to will betray or perjure the other Jimjims. Most people still have to a considerable degree a superstitious reverence for contracts written or printed on paper and signed in the presence of witnesses, though e-contracts are becoming more common, as is the use of credit card numbers in e-commerce, in situations in which no signature is ever inscribed by the contracting person or buyer. They are presumably binding in a court of law, but what about marriage proposals made, or marriages performed, when I am being one of my cyberselves? J. L. Austin says in *How to Do Things with Words* that the felicity of performative speech acts depends on saying, tacitly, "*our word is our bond.*"[28] Is my word always my bond when I am playing SubSpace under an "assumed name"? What are the ethical, legal, and political consequences of saying, "Of course not," if I am right to say that Jimjim can say not, like Horace, "the paper, that's me," but "the pixels, that's me. That's how I get a life"?

I claim to have shown something of the contrast between the poetics of print works and the poetics of works in cyberspace. I have made the contrast, however, as much through identifying the effects of submission to one or the other of the two modes on my two imaginary persons as by holding works in each mode at arm's length and objectively identifying their "poetics." By their works ye shall know them, that is, know them by how they do their work.

Notes

Part of this paper has appeared in a somewhat different form in a special issue (on automobility) of *The Sociological Review* (2006): 193–207.

1. See Herbert Marshall McLuhan, *The Guttenberg Galaxy: The Making of Typographic Man* (Toronto: University of Toronto Press, 1962), and *Understanding Media: The Extensions of Man* (New York: New American Library, 1966).

2. David Crystal, *Language and the Internet* (Cambridge: Cambridge University Press, 2001).

3. Ibid., 3.

4. See Simon During, "Literary Subjectivity," *Ariel*, 31 (nos. 1–2) (2000): 33–50.

5. Jacques Derrida, *Papier Machine* (Paris: Galilée, 2001), 259.

6. Sigmund Freud, *The Problem of Anxiety,* trans. Henry Alden Bunker (New York: The Psychoanalytic Quarterly Press and W. W. Norton, 1963), 15.

7. Thomas Hardy, *Tess of the d'Urbervilles,* New Wessex Edition, paperback (London: Macmillan, 1974), 107–8.

8. William Shakespeare, *Two Gentlemen of Verona, The Complete Signet Classic Shakespeare,* ed. Sylvan Barnet et al. (New York: Harcourt Brace Jovanovich, 1972), I: ii: 114–15.

9. Henry James, *The Ambassadors,* reprint of the New York Edition of *The Novels and Tales of Henry James,* 26 vols. (Fairfield, N.J.: Augustus M. Kelley, 1971–79), 22:326.

10. Ibid., 21:217, 218.

11. Rolland Munro, "Punctualizing Identity: Time and the Demanding Relation," *Sociology,* 38 (2) (2004): 293–311. Citation on 302–6.

12. Ibid., 22:270–71.

13. Emily Brontë, *Wuthering Heights,* ed. Linda H. Peterson (Boston: Bedford Books of St. Martin's Press, 1992), 24.

14. Ibid., 37–38.

15. Ibid., 38.

16. Ibid., 40, 41, 42.

17. Blaise Pascal, *Pensées,* trans. W. F. Trotter, intro. T. S. Eliot (New York: Dutton, 1958), Section XIV: Appendix: Polemical Fragments, Pensée no. 894, 265.

18. Brontë, *Wuthering Heights,* 42.

19. Ibid, 86, 87.

20. Ibid., 38.

21. Ibid., 43.

22. For information about SubSpace, see http://www.subspacehq.com/whatis.shtml, http://www.subspacehq.com, and http://www.subspace.net.

23. Crystal, *Language and the Internet,* 187.

24. Simon During, *Modern Enchantments: The Cultural Power of Secular Magic* (Cambridge, Mass.: Harvard University Press, 2002).

25. Laurence Rickels, *Aberrations of Mourning* (Detroit: Wayne State University Press, 1988); ibid., "Kafka and Freud on the telephone," *Modern Austrian Literature: Journal of the International Arthur Schnitzler Association,* 22 (3–4) (1989), 211–25.

26. Anthony Trollope, *An Autobiography,* ed. David Skilton (London: Penguin, 1996), 32, 32–33, 33.

27. Maurice Blanchot, *Death Sentence,* trans. Lydia Davis (Barrytown, N.Y.: Station Hill Press, 1978), 62.

28. J. L. Austin, *How to Do Things with Words,* 2nd ed., ed. J. O. Urmson and Marina Sbisà (Oxford: Oxford University Press, 1980), 10.

From Hypertext to Codework

McKenzie Wark

What happens to writing as it collides with new media? I was thinking about this recently while looking over an exhibition of William Blake's work at the Metropolitan Museum in New York. On display was not just Blake the artist, Blake the poet, or Blake the quirky revolutionary. Here was Blake the media artist.

Blake assembled all of the elements of a media practice. As a writer he experimented with all aspects of the production process. His aesthetic did not stop with the word on the page. Here, I thought, was a useful precursor to name for the new developments in writing that take place on the Internet, developments I will shortly define as "codework."

But Blake is interesting in this connection only if one embraces all aspects of his productivity. There's a tendency, in the teaching of literature and the management of its canons, to separate off the authoring of the text from the other aspects of writing as a production. It's a tendency that full attention to Blake frustrates, given how fully he was invested in the implication of writing in all aspects of its production and circulation. Blake's creation did not stop at the threshold of "text."

Digging writing out of the prison house of "text" might just be what is needed to unblock thinking about where the Internet is taking writing. There has always been more to writing than text, and there is more to electronic writing than hypertext.

Hypertext may have come to dominate perceptions of where writing is heading in the Internet era, but it is by no means the only, or the most interesting, strategy for electronic writing. Hypertext writers tend to take the link as the key innovation in electronic writing spaces. In hypertext writing, the link is supposed to open up multiple trajectories for the reader through the space of the text.

Extraordinary claims were made for this as a liberatory writing strategy. Hypertext has its limits, however. First, the writing of the text stands in relation to the writing of the software as content to form. The two are not really brought together on the same plane of creativity. Second, hypertext tends not to circulate outside the academic literary community. It has its roots in avant-garde American and English literature and tends to hew close to those origins. Third, it doesn't really rethink who the writer is, in the new network of statements that the expansion of the Internet makes possible. For all the talk of the death of the author, the hypertext author assumes much the same persona as his or her avant-garde literary predecessors.

What is interesting about the emergence of codework is that it breaks with hypertext strategies on all three points. In many codework writings, both the technical and the cultural phenomena of coding infiltrate the work on all its levels. Codework finds its home in a wide range of Internet venues, forming dialogues—sometimes antagonistic ones—with the development of other kinds of written communication in an emerging electronic writing ecology. Codework also sets to work on the problem of the author, bringing all of the tactics of the Internet to bear on the question of authorship.

Codework "entities" such as Antiorp and JODI approach the Internet as a space in which to reengineer all of the aspects of creative production and distribution. Antiorp is famous—or rather infamous—for bombarding list servers such as the Nettime media theory list with posts that seem to parody the sometimes high-serious style of Internet media theory. It was often hard to tell whether the Antiorp writing emanated from a human source or from some demented "bot" programmed to produce the semilegible texts.

Antiorp has spawned a number of alternative identities and imitators. It is with some trepidation that one would venture to assign codework texts to discrete authors. It may be best to take the fabricated heteronyms under which codework is sometimes published at face value rather than to attempt to assign discrete flesh-and-blood authors.

Some codework frustrates the assigning of authorship as a means of breaking down the link between authorship and intellectual property. The Luther Blissett project, for example, encourages writers to assume the name Luther Blissett. Many texts of various kinds have appeared under that name and without copyright.

Some of the more prolific Luther Blissett authors subsequently became the Mu Ming Foundation, which claims to be a "laboratory of digital design" offering "narrative services." The foundation sees itself as an "enterprise" looking for strategies for regaining control over the production process for codeworkers.

The "texts" JODI produces hover somewhere at the limit of what a text might be. A sample might look something like this:

> o
>
> |:__:::::::::_——|_:::::::::_——|_::::::
>
> :: : :: :

A classic JODI Web page may spit all kinds of "punctuation art" across the screen. This work is neither writing nor visual art but something in between. The programming involved usually teeters on the brink of failure. Every technology brings into being new kinds of crashes or accidents, and JODI endeavors to find those accidents unique to the authoring of Web pages.

Integer sometimes makes interventions into discussions on list servers, all with variations on the same distinctive approach to breaking up the text and introducing noise into it, not to mention a somewhat abusive hypercritical persona.

> this—a l l this. = but oɪ ch!!!!!!p. uneventful
> korporat fascist gullibloon zpektakle.

This might be a mangled machine English, or perhaps an English written by a machine programmed by someone who speaks English as a second language, or someone producing a simulation of some such. Or, more likely, its syntax may derived from the UNIX CLI[1] command syntax, or languages such as Perl which are used to parse strings of text. The decaying grammar and spelling of the Internet here become a kind of aesthetic alternative.

Rather than using e-mail and list servers, Alan Sondheim sometimes uses IRC, or Internet Relay Chat, as a means of composition, as in "Outliners," which begins:

> IRC log started Sat Oct 20 23:01
> *** Value of LOG set to ON
> *** Nikuko ([qIbgrP30O@panix3.panix.com) has joined channel #nikuko
> *** Users on #nikuko: @Nikuko
> *** #nikuko 1003633320
> * Nikuko want to be alone this evening of white dust and stars
> * Nikuko dissolvers in your spores
> * Nikuko writers her shattered skin in your stars
> <NIKUKO> Ah, I will paint in nail-head line! in swallow line!
> <NIKUKO> Ah, I will write in glowworm line, in swollen female line!
> * Nikuko painters her torn skin into many kanji
> * Nikuko turn towards gnarled knot line, toward whirlpool line
> <NIKUKO> Her dark hair outlinered in white spore her bamboo knot line
> <NIKUKO> Her name in grackle line, her death in beauty white crane line
> * Nikuko brush in loving spores in white beauty anthrax
> * Nikuko writers in sublimation line, towards line of rising-up
> * Nikuko in white beauty anthrax in white beauty anthrax mouth

Sometimes Sondheim's IRC compositions appear to contain the words of others, who may or may not know they are unwitting collaborators, who may or may not know that this writing may come to have the status of writing, rather than chat.

Many codework texts hover on the brink of legibility, asking the reader to question whether the author is made of flesh or silicon, or perhaps whether authoring lies at the level of writing text or coding software to write text. Kenji Siratori's texts may be machine-made or made to look machine-made.

> Ant PC planetary, MURDEROUS CONSEQUENCES! body line TREMENDOUS HORROR! druggy miracle ADAM doll TREMENDOUS HORROR! thyroid falls . . . MURDEROUS CONSEQUENCES! vivid placenta world

TREMENDOUS HORROR! machinative angel:her soul-machine discharges MURDEROUS CONSEQUENCES! speed PC fear . . . MURDEROUS CONSEQUENCES!

That text is called "Alan Sondheim-conference" and appears to be a response to a conference report by Sondheim.

While some codeworkers pounce upon the texts of others as raw material for codeworking, Stéphane Barron asks others to volunteer texts. In "Com_post Concepts" he solicits contributions with a text that begins:

> Web surfers send in their texts by e-mail. . . . All are then composted! Just as we ourselves are composted! Recycling as organic and cyclical technology, a technology of intelligence and responsibility, of the link to the natural and artificial world.

The sender receives her or his own text back at weekly intervals, in an increasingly noisy and unintelligible state.

The Internet emerges in much of this work as a noisy space, in which the structures of text decay and writing becomes granular, a chaotic space of temporary orders constantly becoming randomized. Yet within this chaotic space, the "destructive character" of the codeworker proposes new kinds of sense making that might, for a moment, keep the parasite of noise at bay.

Another precursor one might mention, besides Blake, for the emerging world of codework is the James Joyce of *Finnegans Wake.* In *Wake,* multiplicity can erupt at any point along the textual surface, not just at discrete hyperlinked nodes. *Permutations,* a Web site by Florian Cramer, reproduces in digital form many of the great combinatory text systems, from Raymond Lullus to Raymond Queneau.

Cramer has also produced a codework machine that creates permutations on *Finnegans Wake,* called "Here Comes Everybody." It works at the level of the syllable, producing a virtual universe of new portmanteau words out of original Joyce text. Click on it and it might read like this:

> ousrun, riverpast Eve and Asiside, on ourfal paard was spotpassfimtion, from the Riverlat box.

Click on a syllable, say the first one, and it becomes:

l trous, feels Wither hayre in hondtuckswer: Iies wing at theourcash in Novo Nilpofirmfaw,

The Australian codeworker Mez has developed a distinctive prose style that she calls "mezangelle," producing texts that tend to look like this:

.nodal +death+-points swallowed in a dea.th.rush.
.u begin 2 -f][l][ail-, ar][t][][is][ms all awry n caught in webbed ma][ulers][ws.

Rather than link discrete blocs of text, or "lexias," to each other, Mez introduces the hypertext principle of multiplicity into the word itself. Rather than produce alternative trajectories through the text on the hypertext principle of "choice," here they coexist within the same textual space.

The interest of Mez's writings is not limited to this distinctive approach to the text. While the words split and merge on the screen, the authoring "avatar" behind them is also in a state of flux. Texts issue, in various forms in various places, from data[h!bleeder, Phonet][r][ix, netwurker, and many other heteronyms.

At the heart of the codeworking enterprise is a call for a revised approach to language itself. Many of the creative strategies for making or thinking about writing in the latter part of the twentieth century drew on Ferdinand de Saussure's *Course in General Linguistics.*[2] In the hands of poststructuralists, language poets, or hypertext authors and theorists, this was a powerful and useful place to start thinking about how language works. But Saussure begins by separating language as a smooth and abstract plane from speech as a pragmatic act. Language is then divided into signifier and signified, with the referent appearing as a shadowy third term. The concept of language that emerges, for all its purity, is far removed from language as a process.

What codework draws attention to is the pragmatic side of language. Language is not an abstract and homogeneous plane, it is one element in a heterogeneous series of elements linked together in the act of communication. Writing is not a matter of the text but of the assemblage of the writer, the reader, the text, the text's material support, the laws of property and exchange within which all of them circulate, and so on.

Codework draws attention to writing as media, where the art of writing is a matter of constructing an aesthetic, an ethics, even a politics, that approaches all of the elements of the process together. Codework makes of writing a media art that breaks with the fetishism of the text and the abstraction of language. It brings writing into contact with the other branches of media art, such as music and cinema, all of which are converging in the emerging space of multimedia and which often have a richer conception of the politics of media art as a collaborative practice than has been the case with writing conceived within the prison house of "text."

Notes

1. CLI: Command-line interface, a user interface (the way a computer communicates with users) that simply displays a cursor and awaits the entry of a textual command, which it then acts upon. MSDos is a CLI.

2. Ferdinand de Saussure, *Course in General Linguistics,* ed. Charles Bally and Albert Sechehaye, trans. Wade Baskin (New York: McGraw-Hill, 1966).

Codeworld

Alan Sondheim

12:55pm up 2 min, 1 user, load average: 0.31, 0.19, 0.07 USER TTY FROM LOGIN@ IDLE JCPU PCPU WHAT root tty1 — 12:54pm 0.00s 0.46s 0.05s w

Die Welt ist alles, was der Fall ist.
Ogden: The world is everything that is the case.
Pears/McGuinness: The world is all that is the case.

Die Welt ist die Gesamtheit der Tatsachen, nicht der Dinge.
Pears/McGuinness: The world is the totality of facts, not of things.
Ogden: The world is the totality of facts, not of things . . .

Die Tatsachen im logischen Raum sind die Welt. Die Welt zerfallt in Tatsachen.
Ogden: The facts in logical space are the world. The world divides into facts . . .

Wovon Man nicht sprechen kann, daruber muss Man schweigen.
Ogden: Whereof one cannot speak, thereof one must be silent.
Pears/McGuinness: What we cannot speak about we must pass over in silence.[1]

Wittgenstein's *Tractus Logico-Philosophicus* (*TLP*) describes a Dostoyevskian crystalline world divisible into facts. The German is clear; the motto to the book, by Kurnberger states, in translation: . . . and whatever a man knows, whatever is not mere rumbling, and roaring that he has heard, can be said in three words.

TLP portends ideality. The world is logical, mathematical, capable of clear division. Logical space is the space, I would assume, of the natural numbers, if not the integers; as Russell says in his introduction, *TLP* presents, inscribes, a finite mathematics—there's no room for the continuum, and proof of the continuum hypothesis was far in the future.

The translations are different, almost never radically so, but different nonetheless. There is a residue in German such that both English versions converge but often never meet. The sememes are equivalent, but only to a degree; translations are almost never one-to-one.

In this logical space of facts, programming, and protocols, there is always a wavering, always room, always doubt, critique, and I would say desire as well. Never mind that this wor(l)d breaks down, evidenced a few decades later by Gödel, Tarski, Skolem, and so on: Coherency, living within the safety net of mathesis, matrix, maternity, remains a dream of humanity. DNA coding, cryptography, hacking the world—all appear to guarantee that everything is possible.

Computer languages are logical; computers are presumed so, but aren't; protocols are logical as well; logical spaces may be compared to drive space; garbage in, garbage out; and so forth. Hacking depends on a closed world with closed loopholes; the loopholes themselves are coherent, logical, *there.*

Codework, codewriting, rides within and throughout the logical world, as a disturbance, a sign of things to come, both extension and breakdown.

Where does the content lie? Is it in the translation of code into messiness or residue? Is it in the interpretation of residue? Or perhaps, and herewith a criticism, is it in the wonderment, confusion, and novelty of the residue itself?

Is codework a minor art, minor literature? What is the point of repeatedly shaking the scaffolding—if not the emergence, in the future, of an other or another approach, or an other, being or organism, for which codework now both provides augury and its weakness as portal/welcoming? For what is come among us already no longer speaks the world of logical facts, just as computers are no longer large-scale calculators but something else as well, something unnamed, fearful—that fearfulness already documented by, say, Cruikshank in the nineteenth century.

2:20pm up 1 min, 1 user, load average: 0.33, 0.18, 0.06 USER TTY FROM LOGIN@ IDLE JCPU PCPU WHAT root tty1 — 2:19pm 0.00s 0.42s 0.05s w

Codework references the alterity of a substrate which supports, generates, and behaves as a catalyst in relation to its production. To this extent, codework is self-referential, but no text is completely self-referential (sr); things waver. So, for example, "ten letters" and "two words" and "English" may be considered sr—but only to the extent that the phrases are presumed to apply to themselves. Extended: "This sentence has thirty-one letters."—"This sentence has five words."—"This is an English sentence."

What is the residue? What are the sentences "about"? On the surface, letters, words, language. This is an additional or diacritical relationship to sr; if one, for example, didn't know English, none of these would make sense.

All sr possesses a residue—an *attribute tag.* In codework, which has a component of sr, the tag may be plural, muddied—the world is never presumed complete, total. Codework is not an instance in this regard of mathematical Platonism or Gödelian Platonism; if anything it relies on the breakdown of the ideal, pointing out the meaning component of computation, program, protocol, even the strictest formalisms.

Early on Whitehead pointed out that 2 + 2 = 4, but only in a certain formal sense; in fact, the equation implies an operation or unifying process; within the 4, the components are combined, their history lost. Strictly, "2 + 2" and "4" are equivalent; within the symbolic, they differ—for that matter, in terms of thermodynamics as well. This domain is expanded by codework, which endlessly interferes.

The danger of codework is in its delimitation; it tends to repeat; the works tend toward considerable length; automatic generation can flow forever. Sometimes it appears as maw-machine emissions—text in, modified text/partial code out. Sometimes it extends language into new uncharted territories. Sometimes it references the labor and/or processing of language. Sometimes it privileges the written over the spoken, or it portends the spoken within a convolution of stuttering and close-to-impossible phonemic combinations. Sometimes it appears as a warning against the all-too-easy assimilation of linguistic competency.

Sometimes it breaks free, relates to the subjectivity behind its production, the subjectivity inherent in every presentation of symbol-symbolic.

2:37pm up 18 min, 1 user, load average: 0.00, 0.00, 0.00 USER TTY FROM LOGIN@ IDLE JCPU PCPU WHAT root tty1 — 2:19pm 0.00s 0.44s 0.06s w

Note

1. From beginning and end of L. J. J. Wittgenstein, *Tractatus Logico-Philosophicus* (London: Routledge & Kegan Paul), Ogden translation of 1922, Pears/McGuinness translation of 1961.

Part Five : **Transpositions**

Strange Attractions: Technopoetics in the Vortext

Louis Armand

Mesostics

In "How the Piano Came to Be Prepared," John Cage writes: "Instead of the possibility of repetition, we are faced in life with the unique qualities and characteristics of each occasion."[1] Investigating the mechanics of repetition and chance procedures, Cage's compositions play between two notions of repetition, or *répétition* (both repetition and rehearsal). Recalling Antonin Artaud's conception of a theater *sans répétition*—unscripted theater but nevertheless subject to a certain *programme*—and Sigmund Freud's *repetition compulsion,* Cage's work seems to position itself on the breach of signification between materiality and semiotics, or between the finite, probabilistic nature of the combination and recombination of marks on the page (or of amplitude and frequency modulation) and the unique semantic content that is imparted to the virtually infinite series of repetitions affected within these constraints.

One of Cage's notable explorations of these effects takes place through an encounter with the writing of James Joyce, in a work entitled *Roaratorio: An Irish Circus on Finnegans Wake.* Cage's *Roaratorio* was originally conceived as a radio drama and was first produced by Klaus Schöning for IRCAM in Paris in 1979, and later performed at the Frankfurt Opera House during the 1984 Joyce Symposium. The title itself derives from a passage in *Finnegans Wake:* "this longawaited Messiagh of roaratorios,"[2] as does the content and most of the composition's formal logic.[3] The idea for the *Roaratorio* began when Cage was invited to provide musical accompaniment to another project based upon Joyce's text, which he had begun in 1976 as a contribution to an issue of *TriQuarterly* entitled *In the Wake of the Wake* and which evolved into the book *Writing for the Second Time through Finnegans Wake.*

Cage himself already had a long history of involvement with Joyce's text, beginning with the adaptation of part of *Finnegans Wake* (*FW,* 556.1–22) in 1942 for the song lyric "The Wonderful Widow of Eighteen Springs," originally composed "for voice and closed piano." For the later project, however, Cage turned to a combination of mechanical means to select and combine elements of Joyce's text, initially subjecting the *Wake* to a series of chance operations determined by a computer program called Mesolist (based on the *I Ching*), which ultimately produced "a 41-page mesostic text, using the string JAMES JOYCE."[4] In Cage's lexicon, a mesostic is a type of hermetic, "found" acrostic poem, which emerges in the form of textual fragments agglutinating around the capitalized proper name of the author (or any other arbitrarily determined string or set of terms):

> A mesostic is like an acrostic; I used the name of JAMES JOYCE. And had I written acrostics the name would have gone down the margin, the left-hand-side. But a mesostic is a road down the middle. So I would look for a word with a J in it that didn't have an A because the A belongs on the second line for JAMES. And then a word with A that didn't have an M, and an M that didn't have an E, and an E that didn't have an S and in this way I made a path through the entire book. . . . I made the rule of not repeating a syllable that had already been used to express the J of James. So I kept an index, a card index . . . of 41 pages.[5]

Working through *Finnegans Wake,* Cage uncovered 862 instances in which Joyce had "signed" his text in this way, collecting them in a single volume under the title *Writing through Finnegans Wake.* But after pressure from his editor at Wesleyan University Press, who claimed that the text was too long and boring, Cage produced another reading, this time entitled *Writing for the Second Time through Finnegans Wake,* the outcome of which offers particular insights to the transverse segmentations of hypertext.[6]

The idea of mesostics is interesting for a consideration of hypertext for many reasons, not least because it mimics, to a greater or lesser extent, the structural schema of Joyce's own "hypertext," as well as offering an implicit critique of the mystical idea of revelation through divine Logos or authorial signature effect. The same procedure is at work in *Roaratorio:*

wroth with twoone nathandJoe
A
M
jhEm
Shen

pftJschute
sOlid man
that the humptYhillhead of humself
is at the knoCk out
in thE park[7]

Cage's use of the mesostic form is also revealing of the way in which schematic readings of texts ultimately display a certain arbitrariness in regard to apparent first principles.[8] It also demonstrates what cyberneticist Gregory Bateson describes as "metameric differentiation" and the formal relations that obtain between linguistic (lexical, syntactic, grammatical) and nonlinguistic phenomena. As Bateson points out, grammar and analogous structures are themselves products of discursive (organizational) processes.[9] Like Cage, and the later work of Georges Perec and the *Ouvroir de littérature potentielle* (Oulipo), Bateson is interested in the way in which generative constraints, such as mesostic strings or acrostics, underwrite and organize semantic systems in a "pro-grammatic" and probabilistic fashion. Anticipating a key aspect of hypertext, Bateson states, "In cybernetic language, the course of events is said to be subject to *constraints,* and it is assumed that, apart from such constraints, the pathways of change would be governed only by equality of probability." At the same time, "Probability, being a ratio between quantities which have similar dimensions, is itself a zero of dimension."[10]

In 1979 the forty-one-page text of *Writing for the Second Time through Finnegans Wake* became the foundation for *Roaratorio,* which was composed as a sixty-minute soundscape, directed by references to place-names in Joyce's text. As Cage recalled, "places mentioned in the *Wake* are identified in Louis Mink's book *A Finnegans Wake Gazetteer*. . . . And so a sound coming from Nagasaki, or from Canberra in Australia, or from a town in Ireland or a street in Dublin—could be identified by page and line and then put into this hour, where it belonged in relation to the page and line of *Finnegans Wake*."[11] Cage and his assistants then went to many of those places and recorded the sounds they found there, and they obtained a number of other recordings by contacting radio stations around the world. Cage then made a recording of himself reading various passages from the *Wake*. A third set of tapes was made of Irish music. Finally, he made a sound collage from all of these source tapes, divided into four parts, with each part representing a book of the *Wake*. The sixty-four tracks of Cage's *Roaratorio*, while not founded on a critical inquiry into Joyce's text, nevertheless demonstrate how readings of *Finnegans Wake* often give rise to discourses of comparable complexity to the *Wake* itself, such as the "complex branching and interconnected chains of causation" described in cybernetics.[12] Comparable notions of complexity also provide the thematic basis for much of the work of contemporary hypertext theory, with its recurring themes of simultaneity, deterministic repetition, bifurcation, radical symmetry, and so on.[13]

Transversal

The ideas of repetition, generative constraint, and probability bring into focus a fundamental characteristic of hypertext—that of the *transversal*. Transversality might be thought of as a particular kind of punctuation or puncturing (bifurcations, ruptures, discontinuities, cancellations), suggestive of a network of what Marc Augé calls "non-places"[14] and what Hélène Cixous refers to as "a metonymic chain where the other place always has its other place"[15]—a "zero of dimension" or *punctum* between what has previously been thought of as the "inside" and "outside" of language. Non-places describe a form of mechanical copula between instances of repetition and difference in the matric organization of sign systems. (This non-place of the copula, of an *is* placed "under erasure,"[16] allows a transversal to take place without, as it were, *taking place*—resembling what chaos theories have described as a "virtual.")

Like Cage's mapping of mesostic coordinates onto a Joycean "model," hypertextual transversality might also be envisaged in terms of a palimpsestic illusion—a textual surface which appears to preserve a record of otherwise "cancellated" strata of differing, and apparently discrete, textual *events,* which are in fact inextricably linked to one another and hence effectively contiguous. In *Empty Words,* Cage suggests that we can think of this relation in terms of a language or scription "free" of syntax: "James Joyce = new words; old syntax. Ancient Chinese? Full words: words free of specific function. Noun is verb is adjective, adverb . . . letters, syllables, words, phrases, sentences."[17] Cage's "ancient Chinese" recalls the metaphoric accretions (layering of marks) that much fascinated Ezra Pound in his work on Fenollosa. The ideogram functions as a palimpsest, but one in which all the assembled "fragments" are read simultaneously, while at the same time preserving the trace of other, tangential significations. This stands somewhat in contrast to the conception of "topographical writing" put forward by Jay David Bolter in his essay "The Hypertexts of James Joyce."[18] Bolter's concern with topographies involves the possibility of reestablishing an underlying linear unity of the "palimpsestic" text, as the signal horizon of an otherwise overcomplicated terrain. For Bolter, a hypertext is always open to decipherment, and insofar as he borrows the metaphor of the palimpsest, it is only to suggest the possibility of extrapolating from it discrete layers or nodes of text that can then be approached by conventional analytic means.

Envisaging a hypertextual topology which belies the reductiveness of Bolter's model, Georges Bataille has suggested that we should instead consider language as structured like a labyrinth, not simply as being involved in its own Joycean "dazecrazemazed" (*FW,* 389.27) convolution of signifiers but in a more profound way. For Bataille, what is essential is that language distributes or disseminates its signifying force by means, precisely, of copulas:

> Each phrase connects one thing to another by means of *copulas;* and it would be all visibly connected *if* one could discover in a single glance the line, in all its entirety, left by Ariadne's thread, leading thought through its own labyrinth.[19]

As Paul Davies suggests in *The Cosmic Blueprint,* topological space is structured by means of prepositions, which act as fundamental connectors.[20] But as with the Nietzschean concept of eternal recurrence (*ewige Wiederkunft*) to which the passage from Bataille alludes, the transversal marked out by means of this network of copulas cannot be reduced to a narrative thread or linear recursion (regardless of how "multiple" that linearity may be), just as it cannot be reduced to a determination of presence, or of the *visible* as something revealed. Following from this line of reasoning, the copulative function of the verb "to be" is seen as being caught up in a system which retrospectively imposes a semantic value upon it, so that the verbal form which will have opened the possibility of meaning at its origin, and which could have been described as nonsubstantive, becomes substantive in turn, and "Being" becomes the horizon of meaning. Echoing Cage, Jacques Derrida links this phenomenon to a condition of repetition, which he describes in terms of a fundamental iterability or trace:

> All oppositions based on the distinction between original and derived, the simple and the repeated, the first and the second, etc., lose their pertinence from the moment everything "begins" by following a vestige. *I.e.* a certain repetition or text.[21]

For Jean-Michel Rabaté, this idea equally characterizes the way Joyce's *Finnegans Wake* itself "begets only beginnings but invalidates all origins."[22] This beginning without origin is always a beginning-already and a beginning-not-yet: "a jolting series of pre-arranged disappointments, down the long lane of . . . generations, more generations, and still more generations" (*FW,* 107.32–36), or what Joyce calls the "seim anew."

> A way a lone a last a loved a long the [|the outside of the book|] riverrun, past Eve and Adam's, from swerve of shore to bend of bay, brings us by a commodius vicus of recirculation back to Howth Castle and Environs. (*FW,* 628.15–16, 3.1–13)

The elision of the ultimate line of *Finnegans Wake,* precisely at that point toward which the definite article will have directed its signifying force, suggests that it is not simply a matter of regarding Joyce's text as a "book of Doublends Jined" (*FW,* 20.16) in any straightforward sense, since the articulating joint itself (the outside of the book) also exceeds the gesture of affirming definite articulation, causing the desire for closure to spend itself in the process (what we might call the interruption and excess of "riverrun"). This elision or disarticulation would mark what, according to Derrida, "can never be mediated, mastered, sublated, or dialectised through any *Erinnerung* or *Aufhebung.*"[23]

Entelechy

Finnegans Wake, with the possible signification of its "first term" ("riverrun") as *Erinnerung* (remembrance as internalization) but also as *Erneuerung* (revolution, renewal) and its apparent haunting by the "ultimate term" ("the"), enacts at its "beginning" a discontinuous memory of itself, which also marks its own effacement in the lapsus between "the" and "riverrun." This paronomasian effect of "riverrun" suggests a type of Cagean play between repetition and singularity—what Joyce refers to as the "verbivocovisual" (verbal similarity giving rise, through repetition, to diverse, otherwise unrelated, and often contradictory significations). In Freudian terms, what it also suggests is that forms of repetition, difference, and similitude can be seen as affecting a play between conscious and "unconscious meanings" in language, whose outward significance is arrived at indirectly, by such *tropological* means as zeugma, catachresis, metaphor, parataxis. We might equally view it in terms of a kind of "double-articulation" of memory (as *Erinnerung*) which is continually made to run up against *Gedächtnis* (or thinking memory), revealing the dependence of signification and its various "infrastructures" upon what Derrida calls a "technical and mechanical hypermnesis."[24]

In "The Image of Proust," Walter Benjamin cites Theodor Reik as saying that, in Freud's *Beyond the Pleasure Principle,* "The function of remembrance [*Gedächtnis*] is the protection of impressions; memory [*Erinnerung*] aims at their disintegration: Remembrance is essentially conservative, memory is destructive."[25] While Benjamin himself fails, by his own admission, to recognize the significance of this distinction, he nevertheless draws an interesting parallel with Proust's notion of *mémoire volontaire* and *mémoire involontaire* (voluntary and involuntary memory). Proust coined the phrase *mémoire involontaire* (in contradistinction to Henri Bergson's *mémoire pure*) to describe the inventory of experiences that represent to the individual a past event from which he is otherwise isolated and to which he does not have access by means of a purely voluntary memory. For Proust, involuntary memory is triggered by experiences in the present that are manifestly unrelated to the experience remembered. This is most famously exemplified in the first pages of *À la Recherche du temps perdu* where Proust describes how one afternoon the taste of a madeleine transported him back to the time when he was a child visiting the town of Combray. By contrast, *mémoire volontaire* is characterized by the fact that the information it provides about a particular experience "retains no trace of it." In this way Proust relates *mémoire volontaire* to technomechanical reproduction (in particular photography). Benjamin elaborates by suggesting that photography acts as a means of staking out a claim for ephemeral things and providing a historical placement for them in the form of a universal archive—that is, as a "volitional, discursive memory" structured according to "the technique of mechanical reproduction."[26]

Benjamin suggests a further relationship between memory and reproduction, this time in the form of consciousness itself. Although he does not explore the paradox that this presents for Proust's distinction between voluntary and involuntary memory, he does quote Freud's argument that

> it would be the special characteristic of consciousness that, unlike what happens in other psychical systems, the excitatory process expires, as it were, in the phenomenon of becoming conscious. . . . Becoming conscious and leaving behind a memory trace are processes incompatible with each other within one and the same system.[27]

For Freud, memory fragments are "often most powerful and most enduring when the incident which left them behind was one that never entered into consciousness."[28] In this way Freud preserves Franz Brentano's basic contention in *Psychology from an Empirical Standpoint* (1874) that perceptions come into the mind through "intention," although perception itself is assigned to the unconscious. As in *Beyond the Pleasure Principle,* it also suggests a fundamental relationship between repetition and "primal repression" in the complementary function of memory as a play between *Erinnerung* and *Gedächtnis.* In a complementary formulation, Martin Heidegger argues that what comes to light in *Erinnerung* is the *persistence* of the beginning in its withdrawal from all that follows: "The beginning is the strangest and mightiest. What comes afterwards is not a development but the flattening that results from mere spreading out; it is the inability to retain the beginning."[29]

Heidegger, in his essay "The Question Concerning Technology," relates this spectrality of the beginning as something disclosed in the experience of the *essence* of modern technology—in which it seems that man everywhere and always encounters only himself. For Heidegger, this encounter takes the form of a proliferation of discourse, which bears certain resemblances to what Hegel, in the *Phänomenologie des Geistes* (*Phenomenology of Spirit;* 1806), describes as "pure self-recognition in absolute otherness."[30] Moreover, discourse itself is defined as "that forgetting of the self, that exteriorization, the contrary of the interiorising memory, of the *Erinnerung* that opens the history of spirit," since discourse, and in particular writing, is at once "the mnemotechnique and the power of forgetting"[31]—what Theodor Nelson radicalizes in hypertextual terms as a machine that forgets by remembering everything.[32]

In the "Scylla and Charybdis" episode of *Ulysses,* Stephen Dedalus poses a question along similar lines, this time addressed to a genealogy of the pronoun: "But I, entelechy, form of forms, am I by memory because under ever changing forms."[33] Referring to Aristotle's system of forms (*entelechy,* actuality), Stephen asks whether identity is not in fact a technical function of memory since the assumed formal unity of the self ("I") is seen to be shifting and unstable, or at least concealed beneath a shifting exterior. In Aristotle's *De Anima* the "mind" (*nous*) is considered "the form of forms,"[34] and in the *Metaphysics* Aristotle argues that the prime mover is thought thinking itself. In the "Proteus" episode, Stephen considers the notion that "thought is the . . . form of forms," musing upon the figure of Proteus, while Joyce's language simultaneously enacts a metamorphosis of "exterior forms" through Stephen's interior "stream of consciousness" (*U,* 26). In "Circe" Stephen identifies this synchrony in terms of gesture:

> So that gesture . . . would be a universal language, the gift of tongues rendered visible not the lay sense but the first entelechy, the structural rhythm. (*U,* 432)

Joyce thus raises the question of internalized presence (*alētheia, Erinnerung*) and thought (*dianoia, Gedächtnis*) which underlies the problem of identity as constituting a structural and gestural play between thinking memory (as an external technic of representation) and the internalizing memory or presencing of the "I" (the ideal horizon of formal unity). This structural play, as a type of metamorphosis, suggests a network of synchronic, "rhythmic" linkages that would also describe identity as so many sets of different coordinates within the field of language—which is also to say, as a hypertext.

Acrostic

In "Art as Technique" (1917), Victor Shklovsky discusses a phenomenon of "habitualization" in everyday experience as a phenomenon of language. In paradigmatic terms closely resembling those proposed by Freud in the

Traumdeutung, Shklovsky defines a mechanism of redundancy, in which linguistic displacement and condensation (metaphor and metonymy) organize the semantic content of a particular word or sentence. "In this process," Shklovsky argues, "ideally realised in algebra, things are replaced by symbols."[35] Alexander Pogodin provides the basis of this observation in an anecdote about a boy considering the sentence "Les montaignes de la Suisse sont belles" (the mountains of Switzerland are beautiful) in the form of an acrostic: *L m d l S s b.*[36] Separated from the context of the initial sentence, these letters enter into different relations, with one another and with other possible combinations of words or phrases, as a matrix of signification in which the materiality of the letters' "symbolic" function reveals a semantic complexion. According to Shklovsky,

> This characteristic of thought not only suggests the method of algebra, but even prompts the choice of symbols (letters, especially initial letters). By this "algebraic" method of thought we apprehend objects only as shapes with imprecise extensions; we do not see them in their entirety but rather recognize them by their main characteristics. We see the object as though it were enveloped in a sack. We know what it is by its configuration, but we see only its silhouette. The object, perceived thus in the manner of prose perception, fades and does not leave even a first impression.[37]

Similarly, "the process of 'algebrization,' the over-automaticization of an object, permits the greatest economy of perceptive effort. Either objects are assigned only one proper feature—a number, for example—or else they function as though by formula and do not even appear in cognition."[38] This is what Shklovsky means by the "unconsciously automatic," which beyond an empirical formulation can be read as describing a condition of language which is ostensibly, and without being primarily linked to perception, "technological." The technics of algebraic or acrostic convergence points beyond the specificity of Pogodin's example to a generalized entelechy across the "totality" of discourse. One of the implications of this is not simply that the "object" supposedly designated by particular terms "fades" but that the conditional nature of the object's relation to language, as constitutive of an ontological condition, itself expires in this "automaticization."

Textual automation, based upon signifying materiality, can be seen as underwriting the entire discursive infrastructure of the later work of Joyce, *Ulysses* or *Finnegans Wake;* from grammar and syntax to latent semantic features and so on. Anticipating Cage's mesostic strings, one prominent feature of Joyce's technopoetics is the formal articulation of structuring "codes" posed, for example, in *Finnegans Wake,* by the figures A.L.P. and H.C.E. (nominally "Anna Livia Plurabelle" and "Humphrey Chimpdon Earwicker"):

> Now . . . concerning the genesis of **H**arold or **H**umphrey **C**himpden's occupational agnomen (we are back in the presurnames prodromarith period, of course just when **e**nos **c**halked **h**alltraps). . . . **H**ag **C**hivychas **E**ve, in prefall paradise. (*FW,* 30.1–15)

The relation of naming to history ("the presurnames prodromarith period") and their common orientation about a point of mythical discontinuity ("prefall") point to an antecedence or *prodromos* in speculative prehistory: "**E**at **e**arly **e**arthapple. **C**oax **C**obra to **c**hatters. **H**ail, **H**eva, we **h**ear!" (*FW,* 271.22–26). In this reversal and threefold multiplication of the acrostic pattern H.C.E., "identity" becomes linked to a concept of symptomatology (prodrome) and to the thematics of the Fall (Eden, Babel). Elsewhere Joyce links the anagrammatical and acrostic articulation of identity to the Viconian notion of *ricorsi storici* and epochal recycling:

> ***H****ail him heathen, heal him holystone!*
> ***C****ourser, Recorser, Changechild ....?*
> ***E****ld as endall, earth ....?*
> (*FW,* 481.1–3]

In the section of *La Pensée sauvage* (*The Savage Mind*) entitled "The Individual as a Species," Claude Lévi-Strauss argues that proper names "always exist on the margin of classification": "In every system, therefore, proper names represent the *quanta of signification* below which one no longer does anything but point."[39] The gesture of pointing, or "pointopointing" (*FW,* 181.24) as degree zero of signification, *below* the level of the proper name, requires an element of normativity which may be said to be undecidable in *Finnegans Wake.* Nevertheless, Lévi-Strauss makes a valid argument against the assumptions of Bertram Russell and Charles Peirce in defining proper names as indices modeled upon demonstrative pronouns. In doing so Lévi-Strauss distinguishes signification from pointing, which would henceforth be considered as indicative, transferring the signifying function to the proximate relation of the "thing in itself."

Underlying this concept of proper nouns is a particular nominalism in the distinction between signifying function and materiality, on the one hand, and between the specific and the generic, on the other. These ostensibly metaphoric and metonymic relations operate a type of structural grid against which the "normative letters" H.C.E. can be thought as describing an indexical discontinuity. As such the signifying "value" of each term is multiplied across an identical denominational space, within which differing vectors can be brought to communicate simultaneously. This in turn suggests what we might call a "hypertextual edifice," in which each letter or combination of letters in this "grouptriad" (*FW*, 167.04) would be capable of virtually infinite subscriptions across the entire field of language without any one subscription assuming the unique role of an *indexical* value. Joyce locates this aspect of signifying materiality within the materiality of language itself: "But the world, mind, is, was and will be writing its wrunes for ever, man, on all matters that fall under the ban of our infrarational sense" (*FW*, 19.35–20.1). Identity is conceived not in terms of an autonomous singularity, nor even as a moment of transition, but rather as a matrix, contingent upon the relations between all of its parts. Such a concept suggests a type of a cybernetic *pro-grammē* in which formal and semantic functions operate on communicating planes of significance, characterized by virtually infinite permutations and combinations which gain increasing complexity, tending ultimately toward a formal *entropy* as the underlying logic of pattern recognition approaches randomness and identity becomes a matter of pure normativity.

Surface Kinetics

Besides Giambattista Vico's *Principi di Scienza Nuova* (later translated as *The New Science*), Joyce's interest in structural recursion was most likely informed by George Polti's *The Thirty-Six Dramatic Situations.*[40] While living in Trieste, Joyce is known to have owned a copy of Polti's text, which presents one of many prestructuralist models of a finite number of dramatic "situations" as the basis for all narrative discourse. Georges Borach quotes Joyce in 1917 saying, "There are indeed hardly more than a dozen original themes in world literature. Then there is an enormous number of combinations of these themes."[41] Joyce also made allusion to

Roget's one thousand categories of meaning, and it has been argued that the real import of Giambattista Vico in *Finnegans Wake* derives from his anticipation of the concept of the thesaurus:

> There must in the nature of human institutions be a mental language common to all nations, which uniformly grasps the substance of things feasible in human social life and expresses it with as many diverse modifications as these same things have diverse aspects. A proof of this is afforded by proverbs or maxims of vulgar wisdom, in which substantially the same meanings find as many diverse expressions as there are nations ancient and modern. This common mental language is proper to our Science, by whose light linguistic scholars will be enabled to construct a mental vocabulary common to all the various articulate languages living and dead.[42]

Like an elaborate fugue form, such models suggest a matrix of possibility within textual constraints, based upon an otherwise arbitrary number of *archē-forms* or codes. Fugue form, matrix, program, game board, grid: each implies a structural template and algorithms of translation or transposition, the mapping of propositions in a topological space whose relations are fundamentally textual.

Joyce similarly radicalized narratology (as a metonymic amplification of lexicographical effects) by projecting Polti's schematic model through a complex of rhetorical and semantic relations which are thus rendered in terms of a linguistic atomism. By subjecting a schematic model of narrativity to the *tropic* function of sublexical particles, Joyce arrives at a mode of hypertextuality whose *form,* on one level, is thus situated between acrostics and geometric figuration: "the median, *hce che ech*, intersecting at royde angles and parilegs of a given obtuse one biscuits both the arcs that are in curvechord behind" (*FW,* 283.32–284.4). The repetition of these coordinate figures brings about transverse communications between otherwise noncommunicating textual elements, causing them to converge (with varying probabilities) in a broadly topological relation. The acrostic organization of these coordinates likewise suggests a form of semantic apparatus, directed at the level of individual lexemes or sublexical grid points (Polti's *Thirty-Six Dramatic Situations* as a six-by-six Greco-Latin bi-square mapping the coordinate functions of the letters HCEAL and P). Similarly the variable sites of these grid points would denote a coordinate function of mechanical linkage or copula. Broadly speaking, this copulative function would follow at least two trajectories—between terms and their various contexts (historical, literary, lexicological, and so on) and within terms (between sublexical units capable of resonating with significations of their own)—so that any *term* can also be understood as remaining open to an alterior discourse within.

Similarly, we might think of this contiguous function along the lines of what the Hungarian artist and theorist Victor Vasarély called "surface kinetics," whereby two-dimensional surfaces are set into apparently multidimensional pulsations, in which the stability of the visual field is disrupted through a type of kinetosis. In his 1955 *Yellow Manifesto,* Vasarély defines surface kinetics as "a single plastic sensibility in different spaces," or "plastique cinétique," in which "myriad formal manipulations [are] relentlessly permutated through the plane."[43] Elsewhere Vasarély describes the effect of surface kinetics in terms of two-dimensional "periodic structures" in which

> simultaneously graduated values connote a smooth, cinematic progression along the surface, while sharply contrasted complementaries appear to jump, leaving the eye not only startled but also tantalised by after-images. But the ultimate effect of this pulsating, syncopated matrix could be likened to a plane geometer's vision of the heavens.[44]

A particularly compelling example of this matrix-effect is the famous illusionism of the Fraser Spiral—which, as E. H. Gombrich points out, "is not a spiral at all but really a series of concentric circles. Only a tracing pencil will convince us that we are not confronted with a spiral moving toward the infinite."[45] But while the Fraser Spiral is not an actual spiral, neither is it quite, as Gombrich says, a series of concentric circles. Rather, there is the appearance of concentric braids (described by complementary sets of linkages between black and white triangular figures), whose two-dimensional form supplies a visual analogy to the apparently three-dimensional dynamics of the whole and accordingly seems to twist in upon itself, drawing the eye down into an open, grid-patterned vortex.

The hypertextual mechanisms of *Finnegans Wake* might also, by analogy, be viewed as the textual apparition of a visual effect, a "strange exotic serpentine" which "seems to uncoil spirally and swell lacertinelazily before our eyes under the writer's hand" (*FW,* 121.20–25). This movement from the circle to the spiral, and from the spiral to the grid, can be thought of as describing a verbal-visual architecture or architectonics of the vortex, in

The Fraser Spiral

which apparently two-dimensional, textual edifices are set into a conceptual multidimensional flux, within a whole which is thus detotalized (as a palimpsest of tromp-l'oeil effects). This whole (or hole) is the *vel* around which the entire tropic structure of the vortex is organized but which itself is seen to be empty and opened out, as a place or topos of perpetual substitution: a "sinister cyclops after trigamies and spirals' wobbles" (*FW*, 300.26–27). The desiring horizon of signification, projected through this *trou,* or "non-place," sets the entire signifying field into a pulsation which is also a type of pulsion or drive—its vectoral trajectories shifting between a seemingly unlimited number of discursive coordinates simultaneously, suggesting what Ezra Pound described in 1916 as "a radiant node or cluster . . . a VORTEX, from which and through which, and into which ideas are constantly rushing."[46]

This compulsive, or rather convulsive, movement of structuration toward a totality of the (w)hole provides an organizational impetus of the hypertextual apparatus, at the same time as it determines its radical decenteredness. The illusionistic nature of this double structure describes a quasi dialectic between the visual *discursus* of the mirroring horizon of subjectivity and the architectonic *discursus* of the hypertextual transverse. The implications of this movement point toward the way in which, for instance, hypertextual linkage, or its copulative function, occupies a *between-place* which cannot be situated according to a straightforward Cartesian logic—as the transitional state of a forethrow of metonymic substitution (desire toward the topos of the non-place).

The hypertextual vortex, or *vortext,* situates a geometry of incompletion and undecidability, fluctuating between competing or conflicting signifying fields. But where visual representation has long been seen as tied in one way or another to the limitations and necessary incompleteness of all two-dimensional representations (as a set of marks on a Cartesian plane), it has rarely been seen as the basis for a generative, "architectural" model of signification. As Gombrich argues, however, despite the apparent literality of the two-dimensional plane (or rather *because* of it), "some part of the motif will always remain hidden from us, and there will always be some overlap."[47] This metonymic self-concealment in the "topical regression" of the two-dimensional plane cuts across the metaphoric axis along which the motif is substituted for the entire textual structure that gives rise to it and which sustains it in its signifying "illusion." But this movement also assumes another form of illusionism, in that its verisimilitude stands in regard to language itself. Here, too, we may find an analogy to those visual puzzles which Giorgio Vasari described as "hovering between the seen and the unseen," as in the "imaginary painting" of the mythical Parrhasios.[48] And like the architectural riddles of Maurits Escher and Giovanni Piranesi, the apparently two-dimensional textual plane constantly defies us to account for these effects of incompletion, inconsistency, and undecidability.

Such is similarly the case with certain developments in mathematics from Immanuel Kant to Georg Cantor, Kurt Gödel, Alan Turing, and Alonzo Church. Or equally with the combinatorial experiments of the Oulipo in the 1960s and 1970s, in particular Raymond Queneau's *Cent Mille Milliards de poèmes* and *Exercises de Style,* and Perec's *La Vie mode d'emploi.* Yet where these tend toward the prolific and inflationary, the problems of "generative constraint" are shown to be contiguous with overreduction, minimalism, and base morphology. The transversal marked out by means of this contiguity (between or across schematic and tropic and typographic or material aspects of textual "design") could be thought of as the architectural principle par excellence. At the same time, this transversality is affected not as a silent unifying principle as such but as a form of topical organization along tropological lines. The various ways in which the seemingly closed structures of arithmetic, architectural design, perspective, and lexicology seem to *break down*—that is, in being revealed at certain crucial moments as incomplete, inconsistent, and undecidable—suggest that transversality is implicit to structure, that it defines structure itself. The effects of generative constraint, the architectural "illusionism" of possible worlds (as in Escher's 1947 woodcut, *Autre Monde* [*Other World*]), the "fissures and fracture lines" (*FW,* 386.32) of lexical contiguity and narrative or grammatical discontinuity in *Finnegans Wake,* the topological metamorphoses of the Cartesian plane, and so on, all affirm this. However, we are never able to *situate* these "fissure and fracture lines" which keep transversality in a continual genesis. In this sense the textual edifice itself is always in medias res, a work in progress between morphological emplacement, on the one hand, and an interminable anamorphosis on the other, caught in the entropic "spiration" of the vortext.

Entropics

An adjunct to the second law of thermodynamics describes the tendency of energy in a closed system, including that of the universe itself, to become less available to do work with the passing of time. This tendency, defined in 1850 by the German physicist Rudolph Clausius as *entropy,* is also understood as the measure of the apparent randomness, disorder, or chaos in a system. One paradox of this idea, however, is the way in which the "entropic spiral" can itself be seen as generative of other, "topologically perverse" patterns, recalling the self-entangled spiral vortices of Vico's *corsi* and *recorsi.*

In thermodynamics, entropy is the measure of turbulence in a system. Turbulence, like white noise, static, or interference patterns whose variability defies reduction, is characterized by infinite permutations of *a small number of variables within a finite area,* which are *nonrepeating* (an extension of the implications of the Turing grid). As James Gleick, in his book *Chaos,* points out: "a well known characteristic of turbulence is that the whole broad spectrum of possible cycles is present at once."[49] Similarly, Stephen Heath, in his essay "Ambiviolences," maps a shift in the cyclicity of *Finnegans Wake* and *Ulysses* from the circular to the spiral, a shift whose visual analogy could be seen in the Fraser Spiral as a kind of "topological wrapping" of a gridlike surface structure, suggesting also an analogous movement within the model of a hypertextual matrix, from acrostic grid to vortext, and so on. For Heath, "the Joycean spiral" marks "a return across earlier writings . . . in order to open a distance, the circle not closing but disengaging a new activity of writing":

> The spiral is then the realization of the urge to totality . . . its absolute is not, however, the theological stasis of a fixed Absolute but the absolute of possibilities, the incessant movement of forms, the spiral of returns and recommencements in which meaning is always "later."[50]

This cyclicity can be seen as consisting of sequences of schematic recurrence in which the complexity of the text is an outcome of what might be described as "positive feedback loops," that is to say, the tendency to increase deviation from "stability" in a system, including linguistic and semantic systems. In a formal expression of the principles underlying Heath's analysis of *Ulysses,* the Austrian physicist Ludwig Boltzmann defined complexity as the proportion of a system's possible "complexions" (or microstates) correlated with each of its distinguishable macrostates. In this way Boltzmann also defines entropy as a measure of *ambiguity* in a system.[51]

David Ruelle, among other chaos theorists, points to the way in which complex systems display "sensitive dependence upon initial conditions."[52] The topological effect is thus of a logarithmic compression across microlevels which, in analogous terms, would produce schematic amplifications on the macrolevel of the "text." In mathematics this is referred to as a "hypersphere," a schematization of infinite dimensions which would also be one way in which we might formally express the structural relations of hypertext.[53] Another way would be in terms of what chaos theorists refer to as "strange attractors."

In 1963 Edward Lorenz, working as a meteorologist, evolved a model for describing the various states of a system during the onset of turbulence. This "strange attractor" maps the dynamics of a system across a noninteger dimension plotted in two-dimensional phase-space. The simplified pattern which defines the strange attractor has the appearance of an infinity symbol and suggests a cyclic oscillation about an axis of ambivalence. The cyclic patterns described by the strange attractor do not intersect—their vectors are *nonrepeating*.[54] In *Finnegans Wake* we find analogous models of textual and spatiotemporal discontinuities or turbulence, recorded in the distribution of inassimilable elements across the entire field of textual signification—from the sublexical "perversions" of Joyce's portmanteaus to the cyclic *turbulence* of the *Wake*'s structural schemata (its "circumcentric megacycles" [*FW*, 310.7])—its vectors determined by the relation across this signifying field by the movement of systemic instability described by Heath as "intertextual scansions."[55]

Phonex

In the graphic representation of this "strange attraction," between a spiral movement of derivation and a cyclic metamorphosis, there emerges an analogous image in *Finnegans Wake* of the mythical phoenix, whose apparently infinite powers of regeneration are bounded by the finitude of its cyclic process and of its genealogical discontinuities. Referring to Derrida's text *Glas* (which describes itself as "a sort of wake"[56]), Gregory Ulmer coins the neologism "phonex" to designate certain operations of *solicitation* in Derrida's writing.[57] For Ulmer, the term "phonex" indicates a form of "generative grid" motivated by the recurrence of chance in the alignment and realignment of sublexical graphic and phonic units in the organization of possible semantic systems. In this sense "phonex" also describes a counterstructural movement in which these linguistic terms can be said to effect, as well as affect, the entire schematic arrangement of the text within which they are otherwise contained.[58] Following Ulmer, this "generative grid" could also be seen as loosely engaging "the image of the Phoenix and the idea of metempsychosis" as metaphors of a "pyromaniac dissemination."[59]

For Derrida, the "re-embodiments" of the phoenix are related not to a dialectical unveiling of historical narrative but rather to something more like a transverse—something which cuts across dialectics in the form, perhaps, of a Nietzschean "eternal recurrence." Beginning with its internal resonances of "phoenix" and "phoneme" and its suggestion of a kind of linguistic-semantic codex, matrix, or "memex," the term "phonex" might be thought of as describing an elision or lapsus in the narrative of intentionality through the recurrence of chance operations. Derrida elsewhere terms this "the debility or failure that organises the *telos* or the *eschaton*"[60]—what Hegel in *Reason in History* calls "the relief of inadequation" and which Derrida links to the phenomenon, symbolized by the image of the phoenix, of destiny's "suicide."[61] As Joyce similarly writes, "That's the point of eschatology our book of kills reaches for now in soandso counterpoint words" (*FW,* 482.33–34).

But according to Derrida, the recurrence of the chance event is characterized as ostensibly mechanical repetition and "marks the necessity of a contamination of any essence by a generalized 'technology.' "[62] This "contamination" derives from a kind of technology which occupies the position of a programmatic "prehistory," inscribing itself ahead of any teleological system or historical narrative in which the phoenix myth functions as allegory. And insofar as it appears to describe a dialectical movement, it does so within this system, without annulling the *technological* impetus that could be said to have given rise to it. Posing the question of the "fundamental" nature of such a technological impetus (as a model of all allegorical unveiling of narrative), Derrida writes: "the current technology of our computers and our micro-computerified archives and our translating machines remains a bricolage of a prehistoric child's toys."[63] Elsewhere he is more specific:

> The game, of which the repetition of repetition consists, is a *selbstgeschaffene* game, that the child has produced or has permitted to be produced by itself, spontaneously, and it is the first of its type. But none of all this (spontaneity, autoproduction, the originality of the first time) contributes any descriptive content that does not amount to the self-engendering of the repetition of itself. Hetero-tautology (definition of the Hegelian speculative) of repeated repetition, of self-repetition.[64]

This *selbstgeschaffene* game recalls an incident described in Freud's *Beyond the Pleasure Principle.* Watching his grandson playing in his pram one day, Freud observed him throwing a toy out of the pram and exclaiming *fort!* (away), then hauling it back in by means of a leash to the cry of *da!* (here).[65] The mechanical repetition of this game opens up a space which is not contained within the narrative sequence but which describes a space of repetition itself. This space, however overly determined, allows for possible contingencies to arise (for instance, the chance of the object not being returned). Without this possibility the game itself could have no force, although such an outcome, which would mark the game's termination, necessarily stands outside the "system" described (in the form of a detour) by the *fort/da* game. In a sense, this possibility marks the dissymmetry between the closed system (of a dialectics, of identification, desire, etc.) and its discursive apparatus (within which the system is inscribed but which cannot be totalized or brought within that system, let alone be comprehended by it). Hence the "possibility" of a terminus functions as the locus of the *fort/da* ritual as well as of the phoenix myth—as the terminus of possibility itself.

For Freud, this *fort/da* game is interpreted on one level as depicting the child's symbolic mastery over the mother's absence and is accordingly taken to provide the basis of all future narratives of loss and recovery. We could also say that this serial repetition (*of repetition itself*) gives rise to a form of "telepathy" whereby the subject is put into communication with the Other (or rather, by which the child is *communicated* as subject of its signifying attachment to an imaginary [m]other). Importantly, Freud describes this movement by the German verb *fortgehen,* "to go away," which necessarily leaves open the possibility of return and remains ambiguous in this sense (as in *fort,* to continue)—as opposed, for instance, to *weggehen,* "to go away or leave," which suggests a definite absence. This possibility of return (of "revealing"), which poses itself as an imminence (the impossibility of which, beyond substitution, poses a threat which is concealed precisely through repetition), describes a destining that, in "The Question Concerning Technology," Heidegger identifies with a certain technological movement. It is elaborated in a passage dealing with two words from Goethe which echo, in an intriguing way, the earlier text of Freud:

> The way in which technology unfolds lets itself be seen only on the basis of that permanent enduring in which enframing [*Gestell*] propriates as a destining of revealing. Goethe once uses the mysterious word *fortgewähren* [to grant continuously] in place of *fortwähren* [to endure continuously]. He hears *währen* [to endure] and *gewähren* [to grant] here in one unarticulated accord. And if we now ponder . . . what it is that properly endures and perhaps alone endures, we may venture to say: *Only what is granted endures. What endures primally out of the earliest beginning is what grants.*[66]

Like the symbol of the telephone in *Ulysses,* which Derrida engages in his essay "Ulysses Gramophone: Hear Say Yes in Joyce," the *fort/da* game reveals the importance of the "leash" as what binds the subject to a destining *call,* to what "grants" and to what, in granting, "endures."[67] For Derrida, this call is also connected to Heidegger's concepts of *Verfallen* and "thrownness." The chanced "throw" (of the child's toy, *da-sein*)[68] doubles "the endless plunge" which "throws you back onto the river-bank, on the brink of another possible immersion, *ad infinitum*."[69] A repetition of a child's game of repetition which can also be seen as programming Derrida's text as an "endless plunge" into the "riverrun" of *Finnegans Wake,* marking the correspondence of this forethrow to a technics of *repetition* as a calling-over to the other-place, to a place of the other and of other texts. It is this sense of reembodiment *as* repetition of repetition that provides the ritual basis of the phoenix myth and the symbolic force of the *Wake*an "phonex." Beginning with the elision of desire upon which this prototechnological game is founded, the machine ritual marks a schematization of the so-called chance event which is "disguised" in the form(s) of structural determinacy.

Strange Attractors

The mechanism of Freud's *fort/da* might consequently be thought of as describing a type of "strange attractor" in its manner of operating as what René Thom calls a topological "fold" or analogously as a structural hinge between the mechanics of chance and sublimation of desire. The illusion of the *either/or* repetitiveness of the game is belied in the nature of the absence which prefigures it and determines its dynamic as a play toward loss, to an always prior loss, of which it is the graphic expression. In other words, the *fort/da* "repetition" is in fact a repetition only in the sense that it presents a figure of a "forethrow" toward the "there" of *da* which is never "here" and to which the psychoanalytic subject is tied by a kind of metonymic leash. What is more, the movement of this forethrow is such that the subject is "subverted"—a "turning under" which defines a tropic spiral in the dialectic of desire, a vectoral clinamen which Lacan locates in the paradoxical structure of the Freudian drives.

This paradox (between aim and goal) rests in what Lacan terms a "fundamental reversion," which at the level of each of the drives "is the movement outwards and back in which it is structured."[70] Moreover, this paradox is irreducible and is in fact the structural *motivation* of the drive, just as the inassimilable repetition of the "there" stands as the point of motivation in the compulsive *fort/da* ritual. The reduction of the subject to a moment of repetition, or locus in the cyclical reversion of the drives, defines a fundamental redundancy in which the subject is lost through a series of substitutions whose site it is (as a type of hole or void which must be filled). At the same time, it is the nature of the inassimilable object which prevents the structural subject from vanishing entirely and instead sustains it (as a *figure* of lack) within an apparently limitless play of signifying substitutions which, while defining a movement of entropy, can nevertheless be regarded as generative.

Analogous to Lacan's linguistic model of subjectivity are certain concepts derived from information theory, which in turn involve a theory of "redundancy." For Claude Shannon, the inventor of modern information theory, "ordinary language contains greater than fifty percent redundancy in the form of sounds or letters that are not strictly necessary to convey a message."[71] Redundancy in this sense can be understood as a "predictable departure from the random."[72] Part of the redundancy of ordinary language lies in its formal structure, by which successive terms can be deduced by virtue of the semantic, syntactic, or grammatical structures from which they are missing. Other kinds of redundancy, however, lend themselves more directly to numerical or statistical measures, such as the frequency of repetitions of particular letters or combinations of letters in any particular language (the letter *e* in French, for example, which is the most common letter and which Perec excluded in the writing of his novel *La Disparition*—a model of exacerbated redundancy which forms the basis of the Oulipian procedure known as a *lipogramme*). For Shannon,

> a stream of data in ordinary language is less than random; each new bit is partly constrained by the bits that went before; thus each new bit carries less than a bit's worth of real information.[73]

The seeming paradox here is that the more "chaos" in a data stream, the more information that is conveyed by each new bit. Thus again, as in Cage's mesostics and Joyce's *Wake,* the elaborate models generated by means of acrostic coordinates suggest models evolved in recent chaos theories involving turbulence and nonlaminar flows in thermodynamic systems. Like these, the technopoetics of Cage and Joyce appears to function as a kind of "system" which moves from predictable behavior to unpredictable behavior, by virtue of the introduction into the system of an element of indeterminacy, or conversely the withdrawal of the possibility of straightforward or statistical "redundancy."

For theorists like Robert Shaw, strange attractors are "engines of information," which conflate order and disorder, giving rise to unpredictability and thus creating information where none existed before.[74] Information in this sense takes the form of a forethrow of possibilities, which in linguistic terms devolves within both lexical and sublexical structures and across the entire structural edifice of the text in which, as Joyce says, "major and / minor / modes coa- / lescing / prolifer- / ate" (*FW,* 278.R2–279.R1). This can be thought of as defining a formal relation between microscales and macroscales, trope and schema, across which "information" is generated in the form, precisely, of a hypertextual transverse. As David Ruelle has pointed out, "the *message* can be compressed if it is redundant, but the *information* is not compressible."[75] In *Finnegans Wake,* as in Cage's *Empty Words,* the highly unpredictable and heterogeneous nature of this relation means that the transversal generated across differing scales of textual relations is never stabilized into a system, whose information stream could be linearized or reduced, in effect, to a "laminar flow." Instead it gives rise to a form of structural turbulence, a type of matrix mechanics whose signifying patterns are constantly reconfigured and therefore a source of potentially infinite quanta of information. For Shaw, "just as turbulence transmits energy from large scales downward through chains of vortices to the dissipating small scales of viscosity, so information is transmitted back from the small scales to the large."[76] This secondary transmission of information is what Shaw locates as the "strange attractor," which serves to magnify the initial randomness of microscales to macroscale effects, just as in Joyce and Cage lexical contiguity translates the effects of apparently random sublexical relations to the macroscales of schematic organization—a topological folding between elemental recursion and semantic structuration which describes a fundamental characteristic of the technopoetic vortext.

Notes

1. John Cage, *Empty Words* (Middletown, Conn.: Wesleyan University Press, 1979), 9.

2. James Joyce, *Finnegans Wake* (New York: Viking, 1958), 41.28. Hereafter cited in text as *FW,* followed by page and line number.

3. Marjorie Perloff, "John Cage's Dublin, Lyn Hejinian's Leningrad: Poetic Cities as Cyberspaces," in *Classical, Renaissance, and Postmodern Acts of the Imagination: Essays Commemorating O. B. Hardison,* ed. Arthur F. Kinney (Newark: University of Delaware Press, 1996), 61.

4. Ibid., 61–62.

5. John Cage, *Writing for the Second Time through Finnegans Wake* (New York: Printed Editions, 1978), 1.

6. Ibid.

7. John Cage, *Roaratorio: An Irish Circus on Finnegans Wake,* ed. Klaus Schöning (Königstein: Atheneum, 1985), 29; compare Cage, *Writing for Second Time,* 1.

8. If Cage's mesostics affect a retrospective illusion of affinity (to "Joyce," as it were), this is merely by way of an act of *assumption* of a commonality, of a "discourse" whose lineaments assume an *inherence* in the object to which it seemingly refers. Consequently "Joyce" becomes nothing more than a schematic figure, just as H.C.E. and A.L.P. can be seen to operate as schematic figures in the *Wake,* buoyed up by the illusion that each summons within itself a semantic inherence which is in fact the outcome of an increasingly fortuitous encounter between otherwise disparate material elements. Indeed, Cage's *Writing for the Second Time Through Finnegans Wake* emphasizes the otherwise gratuitous relationship between the coincidence of material elements and the idea of semantic contiguity. And insofar as Cage and Joyce both suggest that all writing is schematic, coincidence itself is taken to provide a semantic framework while at the same time remaining "indifferent" to any a priori claim to semantic organization. For Cage, this is most clearly affected in the figure of the mock "skeleton key," JAMES JOYCE, which is reduced to a "primary non-reflectional" object the moment it ceases to designate anything beyond a "mere" structural conceit. The significance of this reduction should not be overlooked, and its implications bear not only upon Cage's "writing after Joyce," but upon the entire infrastructure of Joyce's text also.

9. Gregory Bateson, "Cybernetic Explanation," in *Steps to an Ecology of Mind* (St. Albins: Paladin, 1973), 375.

10. Ibid., 375, 378.

11. Cage, *Roaratorio,* 89.

12. Bateson, "Cybernetic Explanation," 379.

13. While completing *Roaratorio* Cage became involved in another radio project. In 1982 Cologne's West German radio commissioned a work entitled *An Alphabet,* comprised of a textual collage of three central "characters"—James Joyce, Marcel Duchamp, and Erik Satie—along with dialogue fragments from fourteen others (including Buckminster Fuller, Robert Rauschenberg, Thorstein Weblen, Henry David Thoreau, and the Vocoder—an electronic voice synthesizer). Explaining his compositional techniques and the overall rationale of *An Alphabet,* Cage wrote, "It is possible to imagine that the artists whose work we live with constitute an alphabet by means of which we spell our lives." However we choose to understand the word "spell" in this context, it is clear that for Cage the very idea of "alphabeticization"—of a matrix of literacy operating between coincidence and coherence—characterizes the lifeworld in which one "lives with" and "writes after," as much as one is "spelled." On the one hand, we seek the immanence of the whole in the part, on the other the recognition that "events do not cohere; at most certain sets of them happen more or less frequently

than other sets; the only intelligible difference is one of frequency of coincidence" (John Dewey, *Essays in Experimental Logic* [New York: Dover, 1916], 116). For Cage, as for Joyce, writing is, as Merleau-Ponty says, "pregnant with a meaning which can be read in the very texture of the linguistic gesture" (Maurice Merleau-Ponty, *Signs,* trans. Richard C. McCleary [Evanston, Ill.: Northwestern University Press, 1964], 89).

14. Marc Augé, *Non-Places: Introduction to an Anthropology of Supermodernity,* trans. John Howe (London: Verso, 1995).

15. Hélène Cixous, "Joyce: The (r)use of writing," trans. Judith Still, in *Post-Structuralist Joyce: Essays from the French,* ed. Derek Attridge and Daniel Ferrer (London: Cambridge University Press, 1984), 23.

16. Jacques Derrida, *Of Grammatology,* trans. Gayatri Spivak (Baltimore: Johns Hopkins University Press, 1976), 44.

17. Cage, *Empty Words,* 11.

18. Jay David Bolter, "The Hypertexts of James Joyce," in *Writing Space: The Computer, Hypertext, and the History of Writing* (Hillsdale, N.J.: Lawrence Erlbaum, 1991), 135–37.

19. Georges Bataille, "L'Anus Solaire," in *Œuvres complètes,* 8 vols. (Paris: Gallimard, 1971–88), 5:81.

20. Paul Davies, *The Cosmic Blueprint* (New York: Simon and Schuster, 1988).

21. Jacques Derrida, *Dissemination,* trans. Barbara Johnson (Baltimore: Johns Hopkins University Press, 1981), 330.

22. Jean-Michel Rabaté, "Lapsus ex machina," trans. Elizabeth Guild, in *Post-Structuralist Joyce: Essays from the French,* 79.

23. Derrida, *Dissemination,* 221. Suggesting a link between Saussure, Leibniz, and Hegel regarding the word (*vox*) or "spoken language" as "the model of the sign," Derrida argues that "the process of the sign is an *Aufhebung.*"

24. Jacques Derrida, *Memoires for Paul de Man,* trans. C. Lindsay, J. Culler, E. Cadava, and P. Kamuf (New York: Columbia University Press, 1986), 36.

25. Walter Benjamin, "The Image of Proust," in *Illuminations,* trans. Harry Zohn (London: Fontana, 1995), 157.

26. Ibid., 180-1.

27. Ibid., 157.

28. Ibid.

29. Martin Heidegger, *An Introduction to Metaphysics,* trans. R. Menheim (New Haven, Conn.: Yale University Press, 1966), 155.

30. Martin Heidegger, "The Question Concerning Technology," in *Basic Writings: From "Being and Time" (1927) to "The Task of Thinking" (1964),* rev. ed., ed. David Farrell Krell (London: Routledge, 1993), 308. Compare G. W. F. Hegel, *Phenomenology of Spirit,* trans. A. V. Miller (Oxford: Oxford University Press, 1978), 14.

31. Derrida, *Of Grammatology,* 24.

32. Theodor H. Nelson, *Literary Machines* (Swarthmore, Pa.: privately printed, 1981), 0/2.

33. James Joyce, *Ulysses* (New York: Random House, 1961), 189. Hereafter cited in text as *U,* followed by page number.

34. Aristotle *De Anima* 3.432a.

35. Victor Shklovsky, "Art as Technique," trans. L. T. Lemon and M. J. Reis, in *Modern Literary Theory,* ed. Philip Rice and Patricia Waugh (London: Edward Arnold, 1990), 18.

36. Alexander Pogodin, *Language as Art* (Moscow: Kharkov, 1913), 42.

37. Shklovsky, "Art as Technique," 18.

38. Ibid.

39. Claude Lévi-Strauss, *The Savage Mind* (Chicago: University of Chicago Press, 1968), 215.

40. Giambattista Vico, *The New Science,* trans. Thomas Bergin and Max Frisch (Ithaca, N.Y.: Cornell University Press, 1986); George Polti, *The Thirty-Six Dramatic Situations* (New York: Writer Inc., 1940).

41. Cited in *Portraits of the Artist in Exile: Recollections of Joyce by Europeans,* ed. Willard Potts (Seattle: University of Washington Press, 1979); rpr. from Georges Borach, "Conversations with Joyce," *College English* 15 (March 1954): 325–27.

42. Vico, *New Science,* book I, XXII:161–62.

43. Cited in Daniel Wheeler, *Art Since Mid-Century: 1945 to the Present* (London: Thames and Hudson, 1991), 232.

44. Ibid.

45. E. H. Gombrich, *Art and Illusion: A Study in the Psychology of Pictorial Representation* (London: Phaidon, 1994), 184–85.

46. Ezra Pound, *Gaudier-Brzeska* (New York: New Directions, 1970), 92.

47. Gombrich, *Art and Illusion,* 176.

48. Giorgio Vasari, *The Lives of the Painters, Sculptors and Architects,* trans. Gaston du C. de Vere. 2 vols. (London: Everyman Library, 1996), preface to part III. Cited in Gombrich, 185.

49. James Gleick, *Chaos* (London: Minerva, 1997), 121.

50. Stephen Heath, "Ambiviolences: Notes for Reading Joyce," trans. Isabelle Mahieu, in *Post-Structuralist Joyce: Essays from the French,* 46.

51. See David Ruelle, *Chance and Chaos* (Princeton, N.J.: Princeton University Press, 1991), 136.

52. Ibid.

53. Ibid., 58–59.

54. See David Ruelle, "Strange Attractors," *Mathematical Intelligencer* 2 (1980): 126–37.

55. Heath, "Ambiviolences," 47.

56. Jacques Derrida, "Two Words for Joyce," in *Post-Structuralist Joyce: Essays from the French,* 150.

57. Gregory Ulmer, "Op Writing: Derrida's Solicitation of Theoria," in *Displacement,* ed. Mark Krupnick (Indianapolis: Indiana University Press, 1983), 29–58.

58. Ibid., 56.

59. Jacques Derrida, *Glas,* trans. J. P. Leavey and Richard Rand (Lincoln: University of Nebraska Press, 1990), 117ai.

60. Derrida, *Dissemination,* 7.

61. Derrida, *Glas,* 117a.

62. Geoffrey Bennington, "Derridabase," in *Jacques Derrida,* trans. Geoffrey Bennington (Chicago: University of Chicago Press, 1993), 312–13.

63. Derrida, "Two Words for Joyce," 147.

64. Jacques Derrida, *The Post Card: From Socrates to Freud and Beyond,* trans. Alan Bass (Chicago: University of Chicago Press, 1987), 301.

65. Sigmund Freud, *Beyond the Pleasure Principle,* trans. C. J. M. Hubback (London: Hogarth Press, 1922), 14.

66. Heidegger, "Question Concerning Technology," 336.

67. Jacques Derrida, "Ulysses Gramophone: Hear Say Yes in Joyce," trans. T. Kendal, in *James Joyce: The Augmented Ninth,* ed. Bernard Benstock (New York: Syracuse University Press, 1984).

68. The "thrownness" of *Dasein,* posed against the "throw" in the *fort/da* game of Freud's grandson, suggests a way of thinking the relation between *Verfallen* and *Gefallen,* introducing the Heideggerean notion of "falling" into the apparatus of the "pleasure principle."

69. Derrida, "Two Words for Joyce," 148.

70. Jacques Lacan, *The Four Fundamental Concepts of Psychoanalysis,* ed. Jacques-Alain Miller, trans. Alan Sheridan (London: Hogarth Press, 1977), 177–78.

71. See Gleick, *Chaos,* 256. Compare Claude Shannon, "A Mathematical Theory of Communication," *Bell System Technical Journal* 27 (1948): 379–423, 623–56.

72. Ibid., 256.

73. Ibid., 257.

74. Ibid., 258.

75. Ruelle, *Chance and Chaos,* 132.

76. See Gleick, *Chaos,* 261.

Parapoetics and the Architectural Leap

Steve McCaffery

This essay is divided into three uneven sections. The opening two are short. The first offers a "soft" manifesto-like exposition of parapoetics; the second discusses a related matter: the paralogicality of the frame. The final section comprises a part mapping of and a few suggestions toward areas of potential parapoetic investigation. Judged on the normative criteria for academic papers, it is premature, partial at best, and thoroughly inconclusive. Seen as attempting to realize a parapoetics intervention, it will be judged to be an utterly abortive attempt—and quite correctly so. However, as the speculative and tentative tenor of the first part indicates, the third part is a probe into uncertainties and unknowns. Notably absent is any lengthy discussion of the important architectural contributions of the situationists. That discussion can be found elsewhere.[1]

Parapoetics

Foucault reminds us that epistemic rupture, in radical breaks within power-knowledge machines, precipitates "endings." By contrast, the Deleuzean dynamic of "becoming" offers a kinetic, projective model. Becomings inflect trajectories and the geographic, offering "orientations, directions, entries and exits [with] no terminus from which you set out, none which you arrive at. Nor are there two terms, which are exchanged. . . . Becomings are not phenomena of imitation or assimilation, but of a double capture, of non-parallel evolution."[2] We are all heirs to this intimate inheritance of becoming—hardly an abyss and hardly the space of some grandiose Icarus effect—but a precise and fecund topological dynamic nonetheless. Unlike endings, becomings temporarily occupy an interstice; they are always realized in the between, in an uncertain transitivity and a transient inscription that for some might register an angst, for others the interstitial sublime.

The death of God, the end of man, the end of theory, the death of poetry, the death of the subject, the death of art, courtesy of Hegel, the death of man courtesy of Foucault, the death of Marxism courtesy of North American departments of English, the end of narrative courtesy my friend with a smile like those horses in Picasso's *Guernica.* Having survived a tedious catena of such mortifications and eschatologies, I'll not add to the list the death of poetics. Crisis is a notion frequently complicit with endings, and I sense no crisis in poetics but do note complacency in matters of potentiality and scale. Accordingly I urge a shift into a purposefully fuzzy and still virtual discipline I call "parapoetics." Similar to David Carroll's notion of the paraesthetic, the term denotes a critical responsibility to approach poetry through its relation to extrapoetic domains. To borrow Carroll's own description, it's figured as "something like [a poetics] turned against itself . . . a faulty, irregular, disordered, improper [poetics]—one not content to remain within the area defined by the [poetic]."[3] Celan believed that naming occurs in the depth of language, and yet to accord to naming a definitional power is to end a being as becoming. Dr. Johnson warns that to "circumscribe poetry by definition will only show the narrowness of the definer,"[4] a sentiment endorsed by Schlegel in his oxymoronic definition of romantic poetry as poetry that can't be defined. Similarly, I want to avoid a specific predetermination of what constitutes parapoetics and leave it suspended as a non-determined concept and thereby allow critical desire to put mastery at risk. Abandoning the pursuit of theoretical dogmatism it will require that a negative capability be applied within the pernicious doublet Foucault concatenates as power—knowledge.

The *Concise Oxford Dictionary* offers numerous meanings for the prefix "para-": (1) beside, (2) beyond, (3) a modification, (4) a diametrically opposite relation, (5) a form of protection or warding off.[5] The larger *OED* adds further variations to these seemingly contradictory senses that strike me as particularly attractive to poetic practice:

> In composition it has the same senses, with such cognate adverbial ones as "to one side, aside, amiss, faulty, irregular, disordered, improper, wrong": also expressing subsidiary relation, alteration, perversion, simulation, etc.[6]

What's appealing in "para-" is its evasion of the janiform "post-" whose consequences, Derrida adverts, involve "a surrender to the historicist urge."[7] Among other things, "para-" provokes a shift from temporal to spatial conceptualization and positioning. Moreover, the lateral adjacency of "beside" offers a multiplicity of satellitic invocations: the friend, neighbor, relative, lover, guide, witness, and judge. "Beside" also is between, interstitial and intervalic, as well as extra, outside. Accordingly I'll be speaking more about the place of parapoetics than its ontology, on where it is and can be, than on what it is. Purposefully left undefined, the important step is to inscribe and activate its forces. Redirecting Derrida's call to architecture I write, "Let us never forget there is a poetics of poetics" and that poetics is beside poetics.[8] Heuristic rather than foundational, parapoetic desire does not seek to adumbrate upon the specificity of a discipline but rather to probe the fungibility and centrifuge always latent within the ontologically or intellectually discrete. As such it takes its place within the anti-Kantian lineage that denies the specificity of art and also offers a countermove within the current new "anxiety" of specialization rather than influence. Operating as a probe into uncertainties and as a force of disruption among stability, it aims to transform a total unity into multiplicity. Foucault and Blanchot encourage the "thinking of the outside" as a critical practice of transgression, one that refuses the stability of alterity while at the same time avoiding the incorporating move to totality. Parapoetics demands that singular disciplines or practices remove themselves in order to achieve a self-comprehension in a manner that avoids a transcendental installation of the theoretical attitude and submit to a voluntary disability. Assuming the burden of this kind of thinking, parapoetics works against the promulgation of any discursive formation as a complete and closed system and relatedly seeks to go beyond the discretion of Deleuze's "fabulation of a discipline to come."

Free from a fixed definition it's also emancipated from a predetermined destination and able to install itself within the dialectical tensions and determinants of any number of target fields. Rather than serving as the critical mode of poetics, a species of self-policing and of external probing, parapoetics signals a shift in critical desire away from the poem as such toward other disciplines and discourses. Working between the seams and cracks consequent to the inevitable play between discourses, upon and without the hyphenated space of power-knowledge, parapoetics adopts more a contaminatory than a combative stance, marbling the smooth and certain propositional plane of discourse and ideas. Parapoetics does not support disciplinary cross-dressing and is not to be deposited in other disciplines as some governing metatheory. Deracinated and detached from poetics proper, and maintaining its distance from any discourse that seeks to master or explain, it can be likened to a hesitation within a caesura. For these reasons parapoetics will always be both a lot more and a little less than poetics.[9]

The Frame-Up

> All movements have direction. But why just one direction and not several? Movements can produce breakouts and new connections.
>
> —Yago Conde

Ronald Aronson encourages us to think of theory as a tool, not a framework,[10] and much of Derrida's *The Truth in Painting* explores the philosophical intricacies of working and engaging the frame. Frames both individuate and recontextualize, and their ultimate power is cartographic. We see the acute stakes of framing in our current geopolitical and sexual climates: on one hand, the melting of national boundaries and proactive deframings under the pressure of economic ideologies in Europe and North America (NAFTA and the EU), and on the other, a Balkanization of Europe and Africa from political and ethnic pressures to maximize territorial coding. The struggle toward legal ratification of same-sex marriages is a debate fought out in a judicial theater and hinges on the right to set up a frame within an existing frame.

Framing, of course, is the prime culprit in transforming *objects as such* into objects *of* theory, thereby guaranteeing a pacification of the chosen object field and the impossibility of the latter modifying the theoretical domain. For this reason theoretical endeavor is antipathetic to empiricism, whose method runs counter to such framing. Despite theory frames being designed to ensure a unilateral flow of power sufficient to preserve the integrity of its method, the logic of the frame moves against settled internal preservation. French architect Bernard Cache suggests that "the structure of the modern frame offers a certain amount of play. . . . The rigid parts of the frame still retain a certain geometry, but their articulation is mobile and their equilibrium results from the play of tensions that run through the system as a whole."[11] Frames are caught up in a contradictory logic insomuch as the boundaries they set out to demarcate are constantly threatened by external elements and forces. Rather than preservers of integrity frames are conduits facilitating a promiscuous transit of forces from inside out and from outside in; they organize a contradictory yet mutual relation of an exterior to an interior that, like Foucauldian thresholds, construct an untenable divide between incompatible forces struggling for dominance. Derrida only pragmatizes this observation in his suggestion to "work the frame" as both boundary and conduit. Deleuze and Guattari emphasize the omniprobability of the frame reversing its function and serving to deframe in a process by which what is preserved internally finds a relationship to something external in a way that opens it up to the outside.[12]

The paralogicality of the frame bears comparison to the nature of dissipative structures, defined and investigated in the field of nonlinear thermodynamics by Ilya Prigogine and Isabelle Stengers. Dissipative structures are "forms of supermolecular organization requiring the continuous dissipation of energy and matter through the increase of small random fluctuations."[13] The theory of dissipative structures is emerging as a formative notion in numerous disciplines, provoking Fernández-Galiano to consider it "the new scientific paradigm of the age."[14] Both buildings and the city can be conceived as open thermodynamic systems dependent for their existence on nutritional elements and energy flows. As Prigogine and Stengers observe in a cell or a city alike, we find "that these systems are not only open but live on their openness, nourishing themselves with the flows of matter and energy reaching them from the outside world . . . the city and the cell quickly die when separated from their mediums, for they are part of the worlds that nourish them and constitute a sort of local and unique incarnation of the flows that never cease to transform."[15] Likewise, both cell and city require the constant dissipation of energy, be it in the form of waste produce or the movement of populace, in a constant spreading beyond frames and boundaries. In sharp contrast to the practice of comparative poetics outlined by Earl Miner, parapoetics does not work to constitute and defend the discrete frame of the poem but rather explore how the frame can be challenged to open up a poetics without borders.

The Architectural Leap

> The language revising its own architectures is the cloud palace and drift of your desire.
>
> —Robert Duncan, Notebook 31

Stein's call to "act so that there was no use in a center" is cannily prophetic of contemporary cultural desires, and in current poetics the ideas of rupture and multiplicity seem more attractive than the one of continuity.[16] Derrida leaves the fundamental nature of writing an open question and the same is required of poetics. Feeling that contemporary poetics has reached an impasse in *exclusively* poetic territories, I wish to propose a leap or "becoming" toward both urban texture and architectural theory as initial parapoetic domains. An exclusive focus on the poem-as-such severely curtails the potential critical range of poetics, and for the latter to maintain a vital critical function then a radical readjustment of its trajectories seems required. The purpose of this leap isn't simply to obtain knowledge or display it in a different discipline, nor to plunder a terrain for concepts and ideas useful to one's own practice. The architectural jump involves *the knowledge of how and when to delay knowing;* how to be active in a state of suspended certainty. As Koestler puts it, "The act of creation is forgetting, at the proper moment, what we know." Via the poetic leap one is no longer beside but elsewhere. In the spirit of Bataille's oxymoronic formulation (that to love poetry one must hate poetry), the initial poetic leap will be a turn against its traditional object field and detach poetics from poematics. With explorations beyond affinities and analogies, parapoetics will situate interstitially, the way punctuation falls *between* meaning. Circumscribed within the broad thematics of disciplines and movings, parapoetics will focus on the interval where contamination, paralogicality, uncertainty, and misprision precipitate discovery, unforeseen collaboration, and contestation. As regards specific dynamics, in parapoetic logic, an entrance is the continuation of an exit by other means. And who knows, perhaps poetics after the postmodern might well be a parapoetics inside it.

Disciplines, like structures and language, are simultaneously closed and open, containing heterogeneity within a frame of the homogeneous. To insist on the specificity of both the poetic and the architectural is to seriously limit both research and the critico-creative enterprise inside, between, and across the two. "Why should 'literature' [*or* architecture] still designate that which already breaks away from literature—away from what has always been conceived and signified under that name—or that which, not merely escaping literature [or architecture], implacably destroys it?"[17] To repeat a well-known claim of Derrida's, "a writing that refers back only to itself carries us at the same time, indefinitely and systematically, to some other writing."[18] Beyond a critical engagement with this heterogeneity within the so-called homogeneous is an urgent need to shift not the mode but the target of poetics' transitivity.

Aaron Betsky has emerged as the popular theorist of that decentralizing condition and dissolution known as "sprawl." Sprawl shatters the tense logic of the frame. Not only is it an architectural and urban condition, sprawl is the condition of modernity. Pollution is sprawl, contemporary knowledge is sprawl. Sprawl is the authentic landscape of the contemporary but enters painting as early as Turner. Sprawl is the given condition, not the cursed share of architecture. Betsky insists, "The issue is not how to stop sprawl but how to use its composition, its nodes and its leaky spaces to create a kind of architecture."[19] As a blotting or formless spreading out from strategic nodes—malls, airports, and so forth—sprawl constitutes both the dematerialization of physical structures and modernity's urban given. It registers the contemporary city's tendency to heterology and centrifuge whose resonant inclination is to deframe. Betsky's name for this formless dystopia is "exurbia"—"where human forms meld into the remains of nature and where order becomes so thin that we recognise its most basic components." For Betsky urban sprawl may even provide a redemptive dimension that takes us "away from the high-rise tendencies of the city [and puts] us back on earth where we confront the realities of ground and weather." While declining the temptation to dangle such redemptive carrots I would insist, however, that in maintaining parapoetics as a deliberately nondetermined concept, we advocate a certain conceptual and creative sprawl.

Why the leap into architecture? From "stanza" to the "prison-house of language," architectural figures dominate within the very formulation of the linguistic. Architectural metaphors haunt writing to a degree sufficient to cause us to question a merely benign metaphoric presence. One of Heidegger's lasting insights is into how both language and architecture ground us in the world. In architecture, as in language, human beings dwell (poetically or not) whether in open mobility or confinement. Derrida writes, "We appear to ourselves only through an experience of spacing which is already marked by architecture."[20] Heidegger and Derrida alike suggest that prior to becoming social subjects, we are all architectural bodies.[21] However, we need to add to Derrida's grammatological conception of architecture as "a writing of space, a mode of spacing which makes a place for events"[22] the facts that architecture too is the materialized conception of dwelling and that dwelling is fundamentally a relation of ontology to spaces. Architecture in that sense serves to return being to its problems by way of *oikos* rather than *poiēsis.* And if Bachelard is correct when claiming that all inhabited space bears the essence of the notion of home, then the link between reading and dwelling appears to be far from a strained analogy.

The myth of Babel implicates the two distinct phenomena of architecture and human speech, from which has developed an enduring complicity. The metaphoric saturation of architectural terms in other discourses (including both philosophy and literature) is well known: the "prison house of language," deconstruction, the poem's fabric, foundation, and so on. Derrida claims the architectural metaphor of ground to be the core of philosophy.[23] But beyond a metaphoric presence, architecture has consistently offered writing a constructive model and, though hardly sister arts, architecture's intimate relation to the literary is historically tangible, even down to its grammatological contours.[24] Architecture provides the formal model for Saint Teresa's *Interior Castle,* Jeremy Taylor's *Rules and Exercises for Holy Dying* (figured in the preface as a tour through the rooms of a charnel house), George Herbert's *The Temple,* and Christopher Harvey's *The Synagogue.* The arguments of Donne's magnificent sermon "Death's Duel" are built around the three prime architectural supports of foundation, buttress, and contignation: "The foundations suffer them not to sink, the buttresses suffer them not to swerve, and the contignations and knitting suffers them not to cleave."[25] In his 1850 Advertisement to *The Prelude,* Wordsworth recalls his conception in 1814 of the relation of his two earlier poems, *The Excursion* and *The Recluse,* in architectural terms that recall Herbert: "the two works have that relation to each other . . . as the Antechapel has to the body of a Gothic Church."[26] Even his minor pieces when collected and "properly arranged, will be found by the attentive reader to have such connection with the main work as may give them claim to be likened to the little cells, oratories and sepulchral recesses, ordinarily included in those edifices."[27] More recently, Ronald Johnson's long poem *ARK* adopts as its formal model "a kind of *naif* architecture on the lines of the Facteur Cheval's *Ideal Palace,* Simon Rodia's *Watts Towers,* or Ramond Isidore's mosaic house in the shade of Chartres"[28] with

Johnson's earlier poem, *Radi os,* a selected textual deletion of *Paradise Lost,* envisaged as the final and one hundredth book of *ARK* and "conceived as a kind of Dymaxion Dome over the whole."[29] Mark Scroggins elaborates on *ARK's* architectonic features: "[Johnson] calls his poem a 'model for a monument.' And its three major divisions reflect this spatial metaphor: 33 sections of 'Foundations,' 3 of 'Spires,' and 33 of 'Ramparts.' *ARK,* in turn, was to have been a 'dome' over the whole, a crowning and covering shell like that over Monticello, the U.S. Capitol, or the Roman Pantheon. The poem, then, is conceived of as in some sense a literal object, a literal architecture."[30] Dante, in *De vulgari eloquentia* 2.9, offers a distinction between *stanza* (literally, "room") and canzone that illustrates the presidential status of architectural thinking:

> And here one must know that this term (*stanza*) has been chosen for technical reasons exclusively, so that what contains the entire art of the canzone should be called *stanza,* that is a capacious dwelling or receptacle for the entire craft. For just as the canzone is the container (literally lap or womb) of the entire thought, so the stanza enfolds its entire technique.[31]

The interrogative crux structuring the entirety of Augustine's *Confessions* (a book that frequently addresses the infinite as a locus) is a *temporal* problem articulated as an architectural issue of impossible housing. I call on you, Lord, to you the Infinite to come and inhabit me, I who am but finite. Mark Z. Danielewski takes up this same impossibility in his recent novel *House of Leaves* where the house on Ash Tree Lane is bigger on the inside than it is on the outside.

For its part, the materiality of language has provided an abundance of architectural possibilities. The dramatic and decorative possibilities of the letter shape as an interior space functions as the basic premise of the medieval "inhabitated" initial, but Johann David Steingruber brings about a more complex fusion of function and the fantastic in his *Architectural Alphabet* of 1773. The book's thirty-three plates constitute a formidable achievement and show patently feasible functional designs. Steingruber's quintessentially baroque wit is retained as a trace element in Steven Holl's investigation into the intimate congruence of certain letterforms and architectural design in relation to context and urban syntax.[32]

Offering an attractive alternative to Bloom's anxiety of influence, Viktor Shklovsky argues for a deflection of influence. Put simply, the theory advances that artistic or disciplinary influence is transmitted not in an immediate and direct line within the same discipline but in an entirely different domain. The transmission of artistic and cultural influence travels like the knight's move in chess, not from fathers to sons but from uncles and aunts to nieces and nephews.[33] A recent example is language writing's influence on musicology seen in Brian Ferneyhough's embrace of disjunction in his New Complexionism. Rather than literary continuity via canon and hierarchy, why not a deflectional move to geography, or architecture? (It's the trail of the transmission out of its current site that is important.) So in the virtual interrelations between poetics and architecture along a Shklovskian model, we might adopt an architectural configuration and rethink the concept of a poetic movement, and poetic practice in general, as the construction of a project in relation to a chosen program, itself relating to an actual preexisting site. Additionally, the programmatic ideology of architecture facilitates rethinking that socio-ontological problematic complex named "community" through the architectural notion of "site." Site as locus and topos has a fecund, aristocratic history stretching far back beyond Olson through the genius loci to Aristotle's claim that "place is something, but it also has a certain power."[34] Bernard Cache's Deleuzean-informed architecture lets poetics abandon the otiose binary of form and content and take up the triplet of frame, vector, and inflection. Cache's complex theorizing on the status of the image warrants careful scrutiny and perhaps, additionally, a bold application in *poiēsis.* Similarly, it might be asked: How would catachresis find an architectural realization or, equally, an axonometric method in poetry?

Perhaps then we can learn more about the discourse of the poem by examining it from architecture's alterior position and through a purposeful displacement of poetics into architecture. The dialogue between these two practices occurs as much within as between each other, and the integrity of both practices should be risked. Parapoetic strategy seeks out not what is confluential but also conflictual in these two practices, as well as what each is displacing and becoming. Contemporary architecture shows a cartographic caution around establishing boundaries and domains. Indeed, it is coming to understand that discrete disciplinary issues can't all be raised in architecture itself (involving, among other things, the broader philosophical issues of ontology, presence, history, topos, memory, and mimesis); there are additionally the wider sociopolitical issues of urbanism, the city, and context, and perhaps most paramount, a relation to human bodies, as well as the broader matters of coordination, material, and scale, and the relation of interiority and exteriority.

Bernard Tschumi is not alone in stressing the conceptual nature of architecture as its paramount purpose. Tschumi compares it to Lacanian psychoanalysis whose goal is not curative, with the patient's recovery occurring as a felicitous indirect effect: "To make buildings that work and make people happy is not to [*sic*] goal of architecture but, of course, a welcome side effect."[35] I currently concur, however, with Robin Evans in seeing architecture as the construction of the preconditions that govern the way bodies occupy and negotiate space—a credo not far removed from Yago Conde's claim that "the habitual exclusion of the body and its experiences of [*sic;* from?] any discourse on the logic of form would be instances of the lack of any intertextual impulse."[36] Architecture is a form of action centering on users, and the key question of architectural form is a question of architecture's relation to the scale and matter of human freedom.

However, having said that, I have to admit that the question of what "is" architecture has become much more difficult to answer in recent times. Traditionally, architects are subject to the same constraints as a poet laureate. Forced into a species of contextual bricolage as a compromise formation, their profitable work is commissioned construction within predetermined spaces and for the most part within fixed, urban, and spatial exigencies. Owing to the governing economy of commission, the vast majority of architectural projects remain conceptual. With the rise of paper and information architecture in the 1960s, and subsequently virtual architecture, the practice was suddenly liberated from the binding functionalist mandates and found itself free to investigate numerous theoretical issues. As a consequence, contemporary architectural theorizing emerges not as a self-certain or consensual discourse but as a vibrant metamorphic terrain of dispute. In Solà-Morales's estimate: "At the present time, [architectural] criticism resembles hand-to-hand combat: a contest between information seeking public recognition and the power of collective sanction vested in those supposedly able to bestow it."[37] The impact of philosophy on recent architectural thinking has been consequential, precipitating both attempts at application and actual collaborations.[38] As early as 1970 Robin Evans envisioned an "anarchitecture" conceived to function as the tectonic of noncontrol,[39] and in 1973 architectural historian Manfredo Tafuri proclaimed "from now on form is not sought outside of chaos; it is sought within it."[40] Much contemporary architecture, like performance, seems to challenge its seemingly inescapable parousial condition by attempts to destabilize presence and orientation. Solà-Morales contrasts effectively the traditional locus of stability, durability, and memory with the contemporary locus of event:

> The places of present-day architecture cannot repeat the permanences produced by the force of the Vitruvian *firmitas*. The effects of duration, stability, and defiance of time's passing are now irrelevant. The idea of place as the cultivation and maintenance of the essential and the profound, of a genius loci, is no longer credible. . . . From a thousand different sites the production of place continues to be possible. Not as the revelation of something existing in permanence, but as the production of an event.[41]

These sentiments are echoed in Cache's tenet that "if the expression 'genius loci' has a meaning, it lies in the capacity of this 'genius' to be smart enough to allow for the transformation or transit from one identity to another."[42] The works and proposals of Peter Eisenman, Lebbeus Woods, Neil Spiller, and Bernard Tschumi appear extremely provocative in this area. Architecture's traditional investment in functionality include, as its central desiderata, safety, stability, permanence, control, anesthesia, consumption, and comfort. All are called into question as requisite elements by the diverse works of Archigram, Daniel Libeskind, the late John Hejduk, and Zaha Hadid.[43] Indeed, early in 2001, the radical procedural architects Gins and Arakawa abandoned architecture for their newly formed practice of "Bioscleaveconfigurature." As well as a common belief that there can be a positive quality to disequilibrium and contradictions, what unites these architectural thinkers is the trenchant, uncompromising repudiation of architectural modernism's functional ethic and its attendant emphasis on problem solving over problem production.

Even though German romanticism is known to have avoided the linguistic in the simple complicity sought between architecture and music, and despite Victor Hugo's famous warning that "the book will kill the edifice"—a prediction at the heart of this problematic relation between poetics and architectural theory—current architectural thinking, via Derrida's impetus, is being redirected to the architectonic possibilities of language, textuality, and writing.[44] Preeminent is Peter Eisenman's advocacy of discursive rather than figurative architecture, opening up to the mirrored possibility of how writing can be inscribed in architecture and equally architecture in writing.[45] One aspect in his work readily lending itself to a parapoetic scrutiny is the virtuality of a diagrammatic model for writing. Eisenman himself believes (perhaps overambitiously) that such a writing-as-diagram is possible and will provide "a means of potentially overreaching the question of origin (speech) as well as the metaphysics of presence."[46] Eisenman stresses the diagram's deconstructive potential, as the following vertiginous and typical sentence suggests: "The diagram helps to displace presence by inserting a not-presence as a written trace—a sign of the not-presence of the column—into the physical column. This trace is something that cannot be explained either through function or meaning."[47] However, the axonometric nature of the diagrams offers a more parapoetic potential. The chief feature of axonometric diagrams is parallel projection, which effectively collapses the governing dualism of vertical and horizontal planes, freeing up the possibility of thrusting the observer into decentralized disequilibrium.[48] Axonometric presentation maximizes presentational possibilities, showing more sides than it is ever possible to view. For Eisenman, "the diagram is a tactic within a critical strategy—it attempts to situate a theoretical object within a physical object [and is capable of producing] spatial characteristics that both blur iconic forms and produce interstitial spatial possibilities."[49] There are clear intimations that poetics is already exploring at least the effects of axonometry. The disjunctive poetics that emerged in the late 1970s produced texts by Bruce Andrews and Susan Howe whose immediate effects are decenteredness and readerly disequilibrium. Ron Silliman's and Barrett Watten's New Sentence (due to its paratactic emphasis and rule of nonintegrationing sentences) constructs precisely those interstitial spatial possibilities of which Eisenman speaks.[50] The white hiatus between letters, words, and sentences—what Silliman considers the twenty-seventh letter of the alphabet and marking the virtual space of nonintegration—makes reader intervention possible on the level of semantic construction and connotative tracking. A similar quality of axonometric distortion occurs in much of Clark Coolidge's poetry and in the systematic-chance-generated texts of Jackson Mac Low. In Coolidge's recent book *Alien Tatters,* which retains the sentence as its minimal unit of composition, grammar and syntax function in a superficially normative way.

> Monkey come down from that roof with my mother's
> dowry. These baleful scenes can be made to explain. It was
> just that dare of a day. Expediency Beranger they called for.
> A collided ice to the vitamin point.

> Mondo Pianissimo of the bulky Colorado. This is not as silly as might be turned to in times of expectancy, clearing right out. Pencil-thin silhouette just down the barrel from all aim. The cow made smaller by the light.[51]

Although the two most characteristic features of the New Sentence—parataxis and nonintegration—stylistically dominate in the passage, catachresis and grammatical transgressions help attain an intense quality of disequilibrium. Considered axonometrically, not as a text but an architectonic, we can say that the grammar and syntax function as the vertical and horizontal elements in an "angled" axonometric structure through which "diagonal" elements (in the form of catachresis and undecidability) provide informational and semiological distortions.[52]

Eisenman too, is attracted to text and trace as ways of denying architecture both originality and expression. He seeks a radical incorporation of alterity in which a work is defined in terms of another author, a process involving "a search for the signs of absence within the necessary presence of architecture."[53] This incorporation of otherness in sameness is precisely the method of Tom Phillips in *A Humument,* Ronald Johnson's *Radi os,* and John Cage's various "writings through." All three employ a practice of treating a source text, using methods of written readings through which a latent text is exhumed and the source text partly deleted. Johnson's source is *Paradise Lost,* Cage's include *Finnegans Wake, Walden,* and Thoreau's *Notebooks.* To give one example: In *A Humument,* a text, excavated from W. H. Mallock's forgotten 1892 novel *A Human Document,* Phillips paints over vast areas of the pages, creating efficacious rivulets of text that open up a latent content. Each page of Mallock's novel offers Phillips a reservoir of paragrammatic possibilities and a tactical opportunity for local improvisations within constraint. The exhumed text releases a difference in sameness, the result being a stunning intermedia work: part text, part pictorial transformation in pen, ink, and acrylic gouache. But beyond its visual impact, *A Humument* raises the proprietary question: Whose words are these? The Victorian Mallock's certainly, and reproduced in the same place on each line as he planned. Yet they serve to deliver a new text, a text out of a text, Phillips's text as the text by Mallock that Mallock never wrote.

Parapoetics might also address how applicable to poetics are the three deconstructive questions that Eisenman sees evoked by the diagrammatic:

(1) Can the metaphysics of presence be opened up or displaced; is there another way to think presence other than through fullness? (2) Is there a way to rethink the relationship between the sign and the signified as other than a motivated relationship? (3) Is there a way to rethink the subject as other than a subject motivated by a desire to have architecture communicate a sense of place and ground?[54]

Let me digress briefly on a parallel but variant history of reception, specifically, the deconstructive and the folding turn in architecture and literature. Mark Wigley claims that architecture (circa the mid-1980s) was "the last discourse to invoke the name of Derrida."[55] Without doubt the strategic introduction of instability into stable structures and relations remains deconstruction's theoretical contribution to architecture. Jeffrey Kipnis clearly states the architectural demands of deconstruction: "The architect must find methods to simultaneously embody more complex organisations of multiple and contradictory meanings while at the same time meeting the responsibility to shelter, function and stand."[56] By 1993, however, the interest in deconstructive architecture had significantly waned, with interest shifting to the architectural implications of Deleuze's concept of the fold. Greg Lynn suggests that folding offers an alternative and preferable fluid and connective logic to the deconstructionist impasse of conflict and contradiction. Where deconstruction inspired architecture of brutal diagonals, plication encouraged curvilinear, folded, heterogeneous forms. "If there is a single effect," Lynn notes, "produced in architecture by folding, it will be the ability to integrate unrelated elements within a new continuous mixture."[57] Deleuzean curvilinear logic facilitates dissipative structures with porous movements of external forces into interior domains and the concomitant inclusion of noncolliding discontinuities. This proclivity to generative theory is generally absent in the literary field where deconstruction and plication (despite Rodolphe Gasché's warning that general textuality is irreducible to the properties of specific literary texts) have largely fostered a critical apparatus to be laminated over texts for interpretative purposes and have had a comparatively weak impact on the production of primary texts. This linked but uneven development is not to be lamented but rather noted for opening the possibility of cross-disciplinary intercourse.

Shifting focus from predominantly theoretical matters, I want now to suggest that the most fruitful target for parapoetic attention is the city. Wittgenstein, a practicing architect himself, compares language to "an ancient city: a maze of little streets and squares, of old and new houses,"[58] while Sherwood Anderson writes of a postmelancholic, neglected city of words rebuilt and recast by Gertrude Stein:

> There is a city of English and American words and it has been a neglected city. Strong broad shouldered words, that should be marching across open fields under the blue sky, are clerking in little dusty dry goods stores, young virgin words are being allowed to consort with whores, learned words have been put to the digger's trade. Only yesterday I saw a word that once called a whole nation to arms serving in the mean capacity of advertising laundry soap. For me the work of Gertrude Stein consists in a rebuilding, an entire new recasting of life, in the city of words.[59]

Architectural theories and debate, however, provide more complex notions of the city than Wittgenstein's and Anderson's simple metaphoric rendition, civic theories that might modify literary encounters with the city. Architecture tells us how it frames light in space and is committed to creating photic and thermal as well as human circulation, and that the interior of its products marks its living history. In this way architecture emerges as a form of action. Buildings and their complex articulations onto, and relations to, towns and cities are characterized like language by defeasibility and lability; they assume and evolve through numerous functions independent of both architectural form and original purpose. This feature specifies the paragrammatic force of dwelling; the occupied house or building as a dissipative structure.

This specification, however, does not eliminate a certain perdurability of form. Reflecting on the Palazzo della Ragione in Padua, Aldo Rossi notes how "one is struck by the multiplicity of functions that a building of this type can contain over time and how these functions are entirely independent of the form. At the same time, it is precisely the form that impresses us, we live it and experience it, and in turn it structures the city."[60] Rossi's pragmatic observation allows us to return to Wittgenstein's description of language in a nonmetaphoric way. There is no city just as there is no language, only linguistic utterances, and architectural usage and events. The growing displacement of structural and general linguistics by pragmatics is symptomatic of a shift in interest from form to usage and to a sense of language as both a changing dwelling and a lived experience. In light of this shift, Barthes's highly competent semiological readings of the city appear less relevant to living than to obey Lebbeus Woods's call to "build our buildings and then discover how to live and work in them."[61]

British architect Nigel Coates, founder of NATO (Narrative Architecture Today, aka "Nigel And The Others") emerged out of the Thatcherite design boom of the 1980s with an ebullient theory of the architecture of the city that combines filmic handling of space with collage and surprise. There is something of the flaneur about Coates's methodological approach to city architecture: "It's about getting under the skin of the city, about going with the flow, seeing where it takes you, and then responding in appropriate ways. A healthy city, or a city you want to be in, is always changing; it's an organism, not a machine running on fixed lines. This sense of a city being alive informs both our response to the city as architects, and the individual buildings we design."[62] Notwithstanding this laudable declaration of commitment, Coates's projects so far (apart from the proposed redesign of the sleazy environs of King's Cross) do not reflect a particularly positive response to the prevalent social predicament of poverty, the need for shelter, low-income domiciles, and the like. According to Glancey, Coates approaches the city "as a vibrant organism rather than a grid of geometric lines. It's about living, about meeting people, about accidental encounters, changes, risk-taking, sex."[63] Such sentiments would not be out of place in any number of situationist texts on unitary urbanism.[64] However, that critical awareness of ideological and economic governing forces, so apparent to Constant and Jorn, is notably absent Coates's notion of the organic, vital city and his neoliberal soft planning. The myopic range of Coates's vision becomes apparent when measured against the ominous backdrop of co-optation and global economic controls outlined succinctly by Richard Rogers:

> Despite all our new wealth—material and intellectual—most of the world's inhabitants are denied the opportunity to lead decent lives. The swollen stomachs and shriveled faces of Third World children, the cold and squalor that our pensioners have to endure, the increasing number of people who live lives in boxes and doorways stand as an indictment of a society which has the capacity to eradicate poverty but prefers to turn its back. And beyond the exploitation and injustice which is so central a feature of our civilization looms the prospect of ecological disaster. . . . The predicament in which we find ourselves has a direct bearing on our appreciation of architecture. For in architecture, as in other areas, an exciting surge of creativity, discovery and invention has

> been frustrated by the same selfish interests that now sustain global poverty and threaten the environment. . . . The despoliation of our built environment is only a small part of a broader pattern—a pattern in which new advances in ideas and technology are harnessed not to public values but to private interests.[65]

We must remain alert to architecture's ominous expansion in the hyper-realism of the neoliberal dream, alert to the colonizing force in which architecture is mobilized by a compound telos of planning-for-profit. It is an alarming fact that this link of architecture and building to property, ownership, and profit is not a recent discovery. In early medieval times we find Hildebert of Lavardin placing architecture in the category of "ultra privatum pecuniae modum fortunae," that is, "mercenary" things and financial gain.[66]

"Cities are in reality great camps of the living and the dead where many elements remain like signals, symbols, cautions. When the holiday is over, what remains of the architecture is scarred, and the sand consumes the street again."[67] Rossi's meditation on temporality and decay here, marked as it is by the philosopher's distance and transmitted from the transcendental position of the theoretical attitude, seems most akin to Gibbon's musing in the ruins of the Capitol Rome that sparked in him the idea to write the *Decline and Fall.*[68] Yet elsewhere, Rossi realizes that cities are first and foremost a composite of artifacts, and to ignore (as urban studies do) "those aspects of reality that are most individual, particular, irregular, and also most interesting" leads to useless, artificial theories.[69] Juvenal emerged as the critical conscience of Rome, starting a legacy of poetic scrutiny of the city as the dysfunctional hospice of incurables. Gay, Johnson, the Shelley of *Peter Bell the Third,* Baudelaire, Aragon, and Eliot: all fascinated and repelled by the inoperability of the metropolis. From Dioce to Wagadu, the dream of civic construction haunts Pound's *Cantos* as a thematic counterstress to the lure of fragments and floating signifiers.[70]

Despite the digital information highway and the extended community brought about by electronic communication, Georg Simmel's 1903 reflections on the metropolis and mental life seem more pertinent than ever. What distinguishes the metropolitan inhabitant is a blasé attitude to life brought on by the collision of constant extrasensory bombardment with internal stimuli. Part product of, part defense against metropolitan overload, the blasé subject struggles for an autonomy and circulation homologous to the flow of currency and commodities.[71] The fascinating power of the city can be specified in an economic, ideological irony: that the people who use the city are simultaneously and for the most part unconsciously used by it. Tafuri isolates and elaborates upon the capitalist nature of the Western city: "Objectively, structured like a machine for the extraction of surplus value, in its own conditioning mechanisms the city reproduces the reality" of the modes of production.[72] The soft city, transparent city, the wired city, the digital city. Whichever you choose, cities still need to be experienced as used and as the sites of consumption and production. Yet to resuscitate Le Corbusier's vision of architecture as the supreme mediator between realism and utopia seems as arrogant as it is ill advised.

In conclusion, let me suggest that you receive these rambling thoughts as a caveat against the fruit of that marriage of practical reason and the Kantian faculties we baptized some time ago as specialization. The current ideology governing graduate studies does not encourage attacks on thetic dogmatism. Rather, it supports the trenchant ideology of the frame. Doubtless an argument can be made that specialization safeguards the heterogeneity of discourses from domination by a single master narrative. However, the adverse consequences of the frame and the frame's governing contradictory logic have already been outlined. Aaron Betsky calls for an anchoring inside the amorphous vertigo of sprawl by means of slow space. Decelerate the speed of today and make the world stand still.[73] Against this moot tactic of survival I would suggest a *becoming* through agencies of difference: and so toward a spiral poetics, a clinamen architecture, a poetics of folding so as to construct free spaces that can only function as ephemeral interstices.

Hölderlin insists that the highest poetry is that in which the nonpoetic element also becomes poetic.[74] I wonder if the call in this claim to added negativity is pertinent to research. Let's attempt to problematize our specialist knowledge by placing it in a broader cartography; map antithetical and intersecting zones as a preliminary to nomadic practices; deframe and rethink research along spatial, not chronological, lines akin to Jed Rasula's notion of accidental research in which conceptual agility replaces a focused specialization. Experience at least the "internal drifts" of disciplines and even contemplate the possibility of random access research. According to Marcos Novak, "our understanding of territory is undergoing rapid and fundamental changes: with the scope of pragmatic experience both space and community are rapidly becoming non-local."[75] Random access is emerging as the most powerful virtual tool in epistemological capital. Novak believes it's becoming "a way of life characterized by precise and instantaneous affiliation. . . . Disembodied proximity implies the extension of random access to progressively larger parts of our experience."[76] I would extend the applicability of Novak's claim to the disciplines of knowledge. Novak further suggests that "the virtual and cyber worlds form a continuum. . . . There is something of what we call cyberspace in virtuality and something of what we call virtual reality in cyberspace. . . . Cyberspace is always the 'exterior' of virtual reality, because it always reserves the additional space of possibility, in contrast to actuality. Possibility is the fundamental characteristic of everything that is 'other,' since possibility always contains the unknown."[77] Derrida's essay on Tschumi's *Point de Folie* introduces the term *maintenant*—"now"—a temporal indicator marking the time, the only time, when both endings and beginnings occur in the protracted space of a becoming.

That said as I'm ending . . . . . . Now. But perhaps as a poet, as the poet in me, I should add a coda: *The poem may well be dead, but as the architect said, one is never finished with the poem.*

Notes

The epigraph at the beginning of the second section is from Yago Conde, *Architecture of the Indeterminacy,* trans. Paul Hammond (Barcelona: Actar, 2000), 251.

1. " 'To Lose One's Way' (for Snails and Nomads): The Radical Labyrinths of Constant and Arakawa and Gins." *Interfaces Image Texte Language* 21/22, vol. 2: 113–44.

2. Gilles Deleuze and Claire Parnet, *Dialogues,* trans. Hugh Tomlinson and Barbara Habberjam (New York: Columbia University Press, 1987), 2.

3. David Carroll, *Paraesthetics: Foucault, Lyotard, Derrida* (London: Routledge, 1989), xiv.

4. Samuel Johnson, "The Life of Pope" in *The Works of Samuel Johnson, LL.D.,* ed. Sir John Hawkins (London: Buckland, Rivington, Payne, et al., 1787), vol. 4, 137, 331.

5. *Concise Oxford Dictionary,* 7th ed., s.v. "para-."

6. *Oxford English Dictionary,* Compact ed., 1971, s.v. "para-."

7. Compare Jacques Derrida, "Pont de Folie—Maintenant L'Architecture," trans. Kate Linker, in *Rethinking Architecture: A Reader in Cultural Theory,* ed. Neil Leach (London: Routledge, 1997), 324: "The *post-s* and *posters* which proliferate today (poststructuralism, postmodernism, etc.) still surrender to the historicist urge. Everything marks an era, even the decentring of the subject: post humanism. It is as if one again wished to put a linear succession in order, to

periodise, to distinguish before and after, to limit the risks of reversibility or repetition, transformation or permutation: an ideology of progress."

8. Ibid., 326.

9. A paradisciplinary procedure might take the form Deleuze notes in reflecting on his own use of a biological model. The dangers of mere analogy might be averted "if we restrict ourselves to *extracting from scientific operators a particular conceptualisable character* which itself refers to non-scientific domains, and converges with science without applying it or making it a metaphor." In other words, vectors should not only be traced and registered as they converge and pass through common values but also tracked as disjunctive syntheses whose governing law is the law of the included middle. Gilles Deleuze, *Cinema 2: The Time-Image,* trans. Hugh Tomlinson (Minneapolis: University of Minnesota Press, 1989), 129. See bibliographical details in Gilles Deleuze, *Essays Critical and Clinical,* trans. Daniel W. Smith and Michael A. Greco (London: Verso, 1998), 179.

10. Ronald Aronson, *After Marxism* (New York: Guildford Press, 1995), 227.

11. Bernard Cache, *Earth Moves,* trans. Anne Boyman and Michael Speaks (Cambridge, Mass.: MIT Press, 1995), 108–9.

12. Compare Gilles Deleuze and Félix Guattari, *What Is Philosophy?* trans. Hugh Tomlinson and Graham Burchell (New York: Columbia University Press, 1994), 187.

13. Luis Fernández-Galiano, *Fire and Memory: On Architecture and Energy,* trans. Gina Cariño (Cambridge, Mass.: MIT Press, 2000), 114.

14. Ibid.

15. Cited in Fernández-Galiano, *Fire and Memory,* 79.

16. Gertrude Stein, *Tender Buttons* (New York: Claire Marie, 1914), 63.

17. Jacques Derrida, *Dissemination,* trans. Barbara Johnson (Baltimore: Johns Hopkins University Press, 1981), 3.

18. Derrida, "The Double Session," in *Dissemination,* 202.

19. Aaron Betsky, *Architecture Must Burn* (Corte Madera, Calif.: Ginko Press, 2000). Like many fashionable architectural publications caught between competing desires of text and image, Betsky's book is irritatingly unpaginated.

20. Derrida, "Pont de Folie," 324.

21. The concept of architectural body is proposed by the procedural architects Arakawa and Madeline Gins in *Architectural Body* (Tuscaloosa: University of Alabama Press, 2002).

22. Derrida, "Pont de Folie," 324.

23. Peter Eisenman and Jacques Derrida, *Chora L Works,* ed. Jeffrey Kipnis and Thomas Leeser (New York: Monacelli Press, 1997), 105.

24. B. L. Ullman draws attention to a canny congruity between Gothic architecture and its corresponding scripts. Developing out of the earlier Carolingian form and embracing especially the "picket fence" effect of Merovingian, the

main features of Gothic script are angularity and broken lines (*fraktura*); the replacement of circular stress by a polygrammic one; extreme condensation and letter fusions (called *textura*); standard heavy shading becomes more decorative with a marked increase in abbreviations and embellishments, for example, hooks, hairlines, and marginal pen flourishes. See Ullman, *Ancient Writing and Its Influences* (Cambridge, Mass.: MIT Press, 1969), 118–25.

25. John Donne, *Devotions Upon Emergent Occasions Together with Death's Duel* (Ann Arbor: University of Michigan Press, 1959), 165.

26. William Wordsworth, *The Prelude, or Growth of a Poet's Mind* (London: Edward Moxon, 1850), vi.

27. Ibid.

28. Ronald Johnson, *ARK* (Albuquerque: Living Batch, 1996), 56.

29. Ibid., 50, 56.

30. Mark Scroggins, *Louis Zukofsky and the Poetry of Knowledge* (Tuscaloosa: University of Alabama Press, 1998), 295.

31. Quoted in Giorgio Agamben, *Stanzas: Word and Phantasm in Western Culture,* trans. Ronald L. Martinez (Minneapolis: University of Minnesota Press, 1993), vii.

32. See Steven Holl's *The Alphabetic City* (New York: Pamphlet Architecture no. 5, 1980) which provides several examples of *E, O, B, L, U, T, X,* and *H*-shaped buildings and grid blocks. Of particular note are Albert Kahn's 1921 General Motors Building in Detroit, designed as three interlocking and partly superimposed *H* types, and Benjamin Marshall's *X*-shaped Edgewater Beach Apartments in Chicago. Exploration into the analogical possibilities of letterforms and their composition out of a multitude of different beings and objects has a lengthy historical precedent. See, for instance, the rich gatherings contained in Hughes Demeude, *The Animated Alphabet* (London: Thames and Hudson, 1996) and Massin, *Letter and Image,* trans. Caroline Hillier and Vivienne Menkes (New York: Van Nostrand Reinhold, 1970).

33. Compare Conde, *Architecture of Indeterminacy,* 195.

34. Aristotle *Physics* 4.1.208b; cited in Georges Didi-Huberman, *Fra Angelico: Disemblance and Figuration,* trans. Jane Marie Todd (Chicago: University of Chicago Press, 1995), 18.

35. Bernard Tschumi, *Architecture and Disjunction* (Cambridge, Mass.: MIT Press, 1996), 267 n. 8.

36. Conde, *Architecture of Indeterminacy,* 197. See the important essay "Towards Anarchitecture" in Robin Evans, *Translations from Drawing to Building and Other Essays* (Cambridge, Mass.: MIT Press, 1997), 11–33.

37. Ignasi de Solà-Morales *Differences: Topographies of Contemporary Architecture,* trans. Graham Thompson (Cambridge, Mass.: MIT Press, 1996), 138.

38. Derrida's perdurable challenge to architectural practice is to have intro-

duced the impossible into architectural practice via an insinuant philosopheme: the Platonic "chora." His architectural collaboration with Peter Eisenman on the Parc la Villette starts with a lengthy reflection by Derrida on chora, an intractable concept found in Plato's *Timaeus.* Although chora "figures the place of inscription of *all that is marked on the world,*" it is a preoriginary "place without space, before space and time" (Derrida and Eisenman, *Chora L Works,* 22, 91). The whole direction of the project moves far beyond the paradoxical origins that Harbison senses in Louis Kahn's Unitarian Church in Rochester, where the architecture gives the sense of "reaching back to early forms which precede anything known to us" (Robert Harbison, *Thirteen Ways: Theoretical Investigations in Architecture* [Cambridge: Mass.: MIT Press, 1997], 11). Working to problematize the clear distinction between sensible and intelligible chora is a situational space beyond all normative notions of place and responsible for situating the variant logics of exclusion and inclusion, while remaining beyond the laws it situates. Despite "giving place," chora (being neither a donor-subject nor a support or origin) does not give place in the manner of an *es gibt.* Derrida calls chora a "paralogical and metalogical superoscillation" (Derrida and Eisenman, *Chora L Works,* 15) operating between and above the oscillations of a double exclusion (neither-nor) and of the participational (both this and that). With the sum of its negative features (nonontological, neither a void nor an interval nor a determined place, a something which is not a thing, a reference without a referent, without a self-identity, and incapable of representation other than negatively), it is not surprising that chora does not provide the security of architectural ground or a base. It is not that chora is absence or the presence of absence, as Eisenman at one point seems to believe, but rather that chora remains conceptually intractable and unsayable. Despite Derrida's avowal "that non-representable space could [give?] the receiver, the visitor, the possibility of thinking about architecture" (Derrida and Eisenman, *Chora L Works,* 35), one is still prompted to ask: What factor or factors rendered the Parc de la Villette a collaborative failure? The inability to translate deconstruction into architectural thinking and practice? An initially ill-conceived philosophemic contribution on Derrida's part? The patent failure of his collaboration with Eisenman on this project, a project characterized by Derrida's reticence and Eisenman's consistent misprisions, misapplications, and refusals to allow the philosopher's contribution to affect the architect's designs stands as both a warning and a challenge to paracritical thinking.

39. Evans, *Translations,* 11–33. Inflecting a related sentiment, architect Nigel Coates refers to the "richly stimulating chaos" brought on by the emergent forms of technomedia and communications (Jonathan Glancey, *Nigel Coates: Body Buildings and City Scapes* [New York: Watson Gupthill, 1999], 16).

40. Manfredo Tafuri, *Architecture and Utopia: Design and Capitalist Development,* trans. Barbara Luigia La Penta (Cambridge, Mass.: MIT Press, 1976), 96.

41. Solà-Morales, *Differences,* 103–4.

42. Cache, *Earth Moves,* 15.

43. See for example the design philosophy and projects set forth in Peter Eisenman, *Diagram Diaries* (New York: Universe Publishing, 1999). Lebbeus Woods's visionary engagement with an architecture of cultural memory incorporating reconstructed facades to suggest scar tissue can be found in his *Radical Reconstruction* (New York: Princeton Architectural Press, 1997). Neil Spiller's *Digital Dreams: Architecture and the New Alchemic Technologies* (London: Ellipsis, 1998) raises provocative thinking about the possibilities of cyberspatial architectures. Bernard Tschumi develops the seminal postulate that there can be no architecture without event in his theoretical collection *Architecture and Disjunction* (Cambridge, Mass.: MIT Press, 1996). *Archigram* chronicles the work of this late 1960s British collective as told by its members. A cross section of Libeskind's theoretical writings and architectural projects, including the Berlin Museum Extension with the Jewish Museum, can be found in his monograph *Countersign* (New York: Rizzoli, 1992). Hejduk's ephemeral, traveling architecture (termed "vagabond" by Antony Vidler) is briefly discussed in Antony Vidler, *The Architectural Uncanny: Essays in the Modern Unhomely* (Cambridge, Mass.: MIT Press, 1992), 207–14. The trilogy *Mask of Medusa* (New York: Rizzoli, 1986), *Vladivostok* (New York: Rizzoli, 1989), and *Soundings* (New York: Rizzoli, 1993) offers a chrestomathy of his architectural projects and theories. Hadid's work is readily available in *The Complete Work* (New York: Rizzoli, 1998). Her important architectural statement "Another Beginning" appears in *The End of Architecture? Documents and Manifestos,* ed. Peter Noever (Munich: Prestel-Verlag, 1993), 25–34.

44. Compare Friedrich Schelling, *The Philosophy of Art,* ed. and trans. Douglas W. Scott (Minneapolis: University of Minnesota Press, 1989), 177. As well as his famous proclamation that "architecture is in general frozen music," Schelling also cites the architecturally relevant myth of Amphion, whose music causes stones to inhere and formulate the walls around Thebes. This confluence of the musical and the architectural is echoed in Goethe's later description of architecture as "petrified music" (a description he later modified to "silent music," *verstummte Tonkunst*). See Vidler, *Architectural Uncanny,* 231 n. 30.

45. The most cogent critique of Eisenman's approach is Robin Evans, "Not to Be Used for Wrapping Purposes: A Review of the Exhibition of Peter Eisenman's 'Fin d'Ou T Hou S,'" in Evans, *Translations,* 119–51.

46. Peter Eisenman, *Diagram Diaries* (London: Thames and Hudson, 1999), 213.

47. Ibid.

48. Compare Peter Murray, *The Architecture of the Italian Renaissance* (London: Thames and Hudson, 1986), 237 n. 5: "An axonometric drawing consists of a plan which is set up truly but turned to a convenient angle. The verticals are

then drawn on this and to scale. By these means, all the horizontal and all the vertical elements of the building are represented correctly and so to the same scale. *Anything which is neither truly vertical nor horizontal becomes distorted;* but an axonometric drawing, once one has learnt to disregard the distortions, can teach a very great deal about structure" (emphasis added). Axonometric effects, of course, are not novel; they are central to the logic of the paragram and to analytic cubism. Like axonometry, the latter applies a structural logic chiasmatically across the normative rules of figuration and design. Within early-twentieth-century literature the most effective axonometric poetry is Gertrude Stein's *Tender Buttons.* Parapoetics, of course, would investigate the benefits of including distortion within a study of the structural elements.

49. Eisenman, *Diagram Diaries,* 206, 202.

50. See Ron Silliman, "The New Sentence," in *The New Sentence* (New York: Roof Books, 1987), 63–93.

51. Clark Coolidge, "Alien Tatters," *Atelos* 8 (2000): 41.

52. The interpretative analysis here merely laminates a theory onto texts whose disjunctive qualities suggest an analogy to axonometric diagramming. The question of how axonometry can be *consciously* employed as a creative method finds a ready answer in the realm of computer-constructed texts and visual poems, where on-screen deployment and display promise most effective results. The poetic possibilities of axonometric syntax, display, and semantics are not addressed in an otherwise excellent collection of articles investigating the format and political possibilities of computers and the Internet gathered by Darren Wershler-Henry in *free as in speech and beer. Open Source, Peer-to-Peer and the Economics of the Online Revolution* (Toronto: Prentice Hall, 2002).

53. Eisenman and Derrida, *Chora L Works,* 132.

54. Eisenman, *Diagram Diaries,* 212.

55. Mark Wigley, *The Architecture of Deconstruction: Derrida's Haunt* (Cambridge, Mass.: MIT Press, 1995), 6.

56. Jeffrey Kipnis, "Twisting the Separatrix" in Derrida and Eisenman, *Chora L Works,* 137–60, 138.

57. Greg Lynn, *Architecture for an Embryologic Housing* (Basel: Birkhäuser Verlag, 2002), 8.

58. Ludwig Wittgenstein, *Philosophical Investigations,* trans. G. E. M. Anscombe (London: Macmillan, 1953), 8e.

59. Sherwood Anderson, introduction to *Geography and Plays,* by Gertrude Stein (New York: Something Else Press, 1968), 7–8.

60. Aldo Rossi, *The Architecture of the City,* trans. Diane Ghirardo and Joan Ockman (Cambridge, Mass.: MIT Press, 1984), 29.

61. Lebbeus Woods, *The New City* (New York: Simon and Schuster, 1992), 80. See also, for example, Roland Barthes, "Semiology and the Urban," in Leach,

Rethinking Architecture, 166–72; first presented as a lecture in May 1967 under the sponsorship of the Institut Français and the Institute of the History of Architecture at the University of Naples.

62. Quoted in Glancey, *Nigel Coates,* 14.

63. Ibid.

64. As well as Knabb's excellent collection of situationist texts and reports of specifically architectural interest are Mark Wigley, *Constant's New Babylon: The Hyper-Architecture of Desire* (Rotterdam: 010 Publishers, 1998); and Simon Sadler, *The Sitiationist City* (Cambridge, Mass.: MIT Press, 1998).

65. Richard Rogers, *Architecture: A Modern View* (London: Thames and Hudson, 1990), 7–9.

66. Cited in Liane Lefaivre, *Leon Battista Alberti's Hypnerotomachia Poliphili* (Cambridge, Mass.: MIT Press, 1997), 200.

67. Rossi, *Architecture of City,* 10.

68. "It was at Rome, on the fifteenth of October, 1764, as I sat musing midst the ruins of the Capitol while the barefooted fryars were singing Vespers in the Temple of Jupiter, that the idea of writing the decline and fall of the City first started to my mind." Edward Gibbon, *Memoirs of my Life and Writings,* ed. Henry Morley (London: George Routledge and Sons, 1891), 151.

69. Rossi, *Architecture of City,* 21.

70. Pound's own view of the fragment might be deduced from his own Confucian beliefs that structure the relation of parts to whole. "The metaphysic of the Confucian *Chung Yung* or *Unwobbling Pivot,*" comments Peter Makin, "is that things are not heaps of contingent dust-drift, but have essential principles, which are durable; which are part of an overarching tendency or Principle in the universe and which, being a shaping and therefore good principle operative in man as in other things, a man may come to understand. This metaphysic is all about the relation between wholes and fragments. The mosaic is not its little glass and gold-leafed fragments; the Virgin shines down from the apse at Torcello when, or if, half of the fragments that make her have fallen" (Peter Makin, *Pound's Cantos* [Baltimore: Johns Hopkins University Press, 1985], 235–36). The architectural pertinence of Makin's observations is obvious.

71. See Georg Simmel, "The Metropolis and Mental Life," in Leach, *Rethinking Architecture,* 69–79.

72. Tafuri, *Architecture and Utopia,* 81.

73. It may please Betsky to know that support for his theoretical position is growing. The Italian *Città Lente* (Slow Cities) movement, inaugurated by Paolo Saturnini, was implemented in 2000 in small towns and cities. An offshoot of Carlo Patrini's Slow Food movement, founded in the early 1990s to counter the proliferation of homogeneous fast-food outlets, *Città Lente* is committed to a preservationist policy of traditional architecture and gastronomy. As reporter

Megan Williams explains, Saturnini, the mayor of Greve-in-Chianti, "is carefully constructing barricades to keep at bay the tide of homogeneity that globalization has washed into similar-sized communities around the world. From fast-food chains to cell-phone antennas to car alarms. The Small [*sic*] Cities people have said 'No thanks' to many of the trappings of modernity."

74. Friedrich Hölderlin, "Reflection," *Sämtliche Werke: Kritische Textausgabe,* ed. D. E. Sattler (Darmstadt: Hermann Luchterhand Verlag, 1979–87), vol. 4., bk.1., 234–35.

75. Marcos Novak, *Trans Terra Form: Liquid Architecture and the Loss of Inscription,* http://www.to.or.at/~krcf/nlonline/nonMarcos.html.

76. Ibid.

77. Ibid.

Traps or Tools and Damage

Allen Fisher

This may be the first time you hear of "crowd-out"—a proposal for inventive perception, which permits a multidisciplinary approach to everyday life and a set of practical approaches and constructions that encourage and permit complexity facilitated by deliberate shifts of limits. My working practice involves poetry, poetics, painting, drawing, and art history; that is a deliberate praxis of more than one discipline and in critique of the archaic modernism of singular focus. In this essay I will discuss aspects of my organized engagement with aesthetics and consciousness as part of a debate about the necessity of poetry and art. I will separate this engagement into three groups of approaches to art historical and poetics experience, which I name "Traps or Tools and Damage," the title of an installation and series of paintings and a book of poetry from the 1990s, all scheduled for completion in 2007. The essay covers a range of approaches and constructions both pragmatic and rhetorical. The disciplines of these approaches and constructions include the concept of patterns of connectedness; the iconography of health and beauty; the physics of quantum mechanics; and a phenomenology of inventive perception.

Approaches

Traps

Traps are what we are all inside of, traps constitute what is known, where to place what is known, between what boundaries. Traps, and springing them, initially determine what tools are selected for description, traps are depicted in the earliest graphic art and therefore the earliest language and clear expression of consciousness. The patterns of connectedness that enable traps and consciousness to work invoke descriptions of the prey and forethought for predation.[1] Traps can be benign, like a camera capturing light or a cider press squeezing the juice from an apple. Traps can be concealed from us inside of habitual experience and conditions. Traps involve inventive perception and thus "crowd-outs" and as such provide tools, that is, they bring about procedures of selection that produce pattern, and thus patterns of connectedness, through measurement, repetition, and recurrence. My work challenges the conditions of being trapped by what we know; I use deliberate acquisition of knowledge, a reappraisal of poetics as method, and specific tools for transformation from damage, with a view to springing traps to meet the aesthetic and pragmatic functions of art.[2]

Tools

Tools are used by a range of animals and humans to encourage improvement in their condition. Tools are usually associated with benign purposes but can, if held in particular ways, become weapons. The shape used to form the handle of a Warrington hammer has in itself at least two functions. Holding the hammer feels and looks right for purpose which is part of the aesthetic function; when used to bang in a nail, the vibration from the process is absorbed by the hammer, witnessed by the hand and the ears of the carpenter, and not felt with any alarm in the user. The absorption of vibration is partly attributable to the grain of the ash wood and partly attributable to the crafted bump below the head, which dissipates the energy down the tapering line of the handle. Karl Marx's astonishment that five hundred different kinds of hammers were made in Birmingham in the 1860s juxtaposes with the variety of hammer handles differently eroded over the years of constant use by the variety of different users.[3] The pragmatic function of this Warrington allows the nail to be hit with maximized efficiency and causes the nail to enter the wood squarely and with the least number of blows. The use of a Warrington for something other than driving in nails leads to another variety in the quality of work done.

New Stone Age tools have a similar coupling of aesthetic and pragmatic functions; the stone hammer's weight and shape has a complexity of form that is both pleasing to hold and see and appropriate to grip and use. Studies show that many tools were used for functions different from those first intended.[4] Tools are thus used for turning back on the empiricism of sensation to address the hidden danger, the consciousness of the subject; they are working instruments and methods to address and combine a variety of functions; to elaborate this knowledge into scientific application. Tools are thus exemplary of exact purpose coupled to improvisation, as expression of an elaborate set of processes energized through inner necessity and characterized by aesthetic and pragmatic functions.

Damage

Human activity is in continuous flux exemplified by our so-called short-term and long-term memories; retention of experience, retrieval of thought, loss of memory; trauma and recovery. There is a causality in the order of knowledge, particularly because all experience—existence and memory—involves loss, that is, it involves damage. My work has shown a consistent engagement with damage as a recognition of harm, as a developmental potential, and as a clearing, or *Lichtung,* for imaginative healing and health.[5] I use traps or tools as processes for transformation of damage, processes that include development and healing, energized by inventive perception and the body's proprioception, in which lost and gained correlations between events and discoveries, between economic necessities and the development of a domain of knowledge, lead to the necessity for damage as part of a transformative process to combat entropy.

Connections are made by the brain to subvert this entropy, so that aesthetics participates in a perpetual endeavor to become immortal. Damage, which may include the introduction of mistakes and humor, promotes the proposal that connections in the brain can lead to negative as easily as positive effects. Both kinds of effect involve change and thus a range of proposals for renewal, and renewal has the potential for "negentropy," that is, going against one of the laws of thermodynamics, the natural expectation of aging, the loss of brain cells. It is the potential for negentropy that art proposes, albeit rhetorically, a kind of immortality. The correlation and meeting of the patterns of connectedness that constitute consciousness and the patterns of connectedness that encourage beauty in the process and object of art come together, at best, as an imperfect fit, an essentially incomplete expression, potentially brought toward completion each moment the receiver, viewer, or listener encounters the work. That is, completion of the work is a continuous process with those who encounter it after the initial event of its production.

Constructions

Traps

Traps involve procedures of selection called "crowd-outs"; traps produce pattern, and thus patterns of connectedness, through measurement, repetition, and recurrence. In attending an installation of paintings and texts produced and curated by R. B. Kitaj, it is often appropriate to make a range of approaches. For the purposes of this essay, it is necessary to use crowd-out, to take out of focus most of the paintings' subjects, to allow for an observation of recurring shapes in the context of Kitaj's decision to be seen as a modernist, Diasporic Jew in search of a healing process. The shapes are expressively part of Kitaj's mark facture and deliberately part of his metonymic intent. In the first place, the shapes connect the paintings and texts in the show through an isomorphism of marks, and in the second place, they connect the installation to a group of histories that propose a complex of iconological meanings which contribute to providing Kitaj's metonymic intention.

For instance, the serpentine shape in the paintings shown in London in 1985 by Kitaj initially link to various images of death, the Jewish shofar, and garden paths,[6] and they also link to the serpentine forms and shapes in Renaissance and baroque art in western Europe—for instance, in William Hogarth's *Portrait of the Painter and His Pug,* he shows the serpentine form on a palette as his line of beauty.[7] In his *Analysis of Beauty,* Hogarth refers to Lomazzo, who is making commentary on Michelangelo's sinewy drawings and aspects of his sculpture and painting.[8] In turn, these connections link to the spiraling serpentine columns in the Vatican.[9] These columns are said to have been taken from King Solomon's Temple in Palestine, where they provided the entrance through which pregnant women would pass to encourage a healthy childbirth and between which the sick would prepare for healing. At least two of these columns are now in the Vatican, and copies were made by Bernini to surround Saint Peter's altar, in the chapel built to the proportions of King Solomon's Temple. The columns are evident again in Raphael's tapestry representation *Saint Peter Healing the Lame Man,* which is pictured as if taking place between two of these columns.[10] Thus so far beauty and health, both spiritual and physical, can be linked back to Kitaj's proposal, made in the installation and subsequently in his 1989 manifesto, to signify a cure for the Holocaust condition through a parallel with the Christian cross, coupled to the serpentine sign for beauty and healing. However, the iconography of the serpentine form is deeper, more complex, and more ancient.

The Palestinian columns in the Vatican are in fact stone, date from about the third century before Christ, and provide images of organic forms copied from vines encircling trees. That means, at best, they must be copies of the columns once in King Solomon's Temple, which was built nearly three thousand years ago and, according to the Hebrew texts, made of cedar from Lebanon and wrapped in metal.[11] Leaving aside Kitaj's signifier for cure of the Holocaust condition, I will briefly trace here the iconography of the serpentine form. The form has four traditions which overlap, misconnect, and connect. The earliest example I have found is a Mesopotamian libation vase made more than four thousand years ago, which has the image of two dragons twined serpentinely around a sword and two serpents likewise twined around a staff on the opposite side.[12]

The associations are with fertility, water, and rebirth. Such associations are similar to one of the ancient, dynastic Egyptian traditions where the serpentine form is repeatedly used for these significations in the books of the dead.[13] Egypt, however, also has a tradition, in the same texts, of the serpentine form as primal form and guardian of the underworld. This giant python directly links to the shamanistic killing of this animal, as a rebirth ritual, which is still part of the indigenous culture in the hook of Africa, south of where the fossil remains of these giants have been found.[14] Stories and signs in this region are semiotically linked to early visual examples in the Mediterranean and Eurasian cultures as well as the Roman text of Saint George and the Dragon.

By the time this iconography reaches classical Greece, and before the Roman and Christian inventions, the serpentine form has at least two traditions; that of Asclepius, from which Europe gets its symbol for Hermes/Mercury and medicine in the form of a caduceus (snakes around a staff or sword), and that of hero worship, where the coiled snake protects a grave cairn.[15] These traditions are parallel with, and only partly overlap, the Persian and Hebrew Garden of Eden, of which Michelangelo provides two images in his Sistine Chapel ceiling in the Vatican.[16] The images that signify paradise also signify the potential for fertility, fecundity, and knowledge, but the iconography of the form and its meaning do not simply translate across a range of religious and mythological traditions.

The form can be directly produced from the geometry available in texts from at least as early as Euclid, about 300 B.C., in his proposals for the golden section.[17] In the thirteenth century A.D., many of the ratios formulated by Leonardo of Pisa (Fibonacci) provide a second analysis of the form showing logarithmic development. In 1509 Luca Pacioli's *Divine Proportions* (with illustrations probably by Leonardo da Vinci) provided a direct arithmetic and geometric relation between the golden section, the Fibonacci sequence, and thus the spiral, the serpentine form, and the logic of ideal proportions. It is a relationship to organic growth on a revolving planet and subject to Coriolis effects. It can be exemplified in the slow growth of a ram's horn and of a glacier at Maloja Pass in Switzerland, as much as in the quicker growth of seeds of a young plant, for example, in Karl Blossfeldt's 1929 photograph of seed capsules from a common chili nettle and in the division of branches on a plant stem.[18]

They are ratios of planetary existence which sit comfortably with human proposals for physical and spiritual health and beauty but do not account for them and appear to ignore the poisonous organic forms also involved in the ratios. The ideas of health and beauty are not a great conceptual distance from Kitaj's shapes but do not lead to all that is needed to arrive at his proposed metonymic intent. Before I move on, it will be worth noting that however appropriate the shape is for description of beauty to the Enlightenment and archaic modernism, it is also appropriate to notice that notions of healing are semiotic and not pragmatic, that is, mainly illusory and at best figurative. Today ideas of measurement, truth, completion, and certainty are less tangible. Indeed, proposals for perfect fits are contrary to contemporary ideas of appropriateness.

Aesthetics is still a young discipline and not a science, but imperfect fit is the more appropriate machine to engender our active enquiries. In the classical world of refined proposals and clarity, it might seem strange to bring matters of truth and thus beauty into question, but questioning is what I continue to propose. We have moved some distance from the archaic modernist proposal for sixteen definitions of beauty in 1922.[19] The ideal proportions of the golden mean and the Fibonacci sequence continue to obstruct contemporary thought, producing exquisite ways of apprehending natural forms and human artifacts as if part of a continuous nexus, which can include the eloquence of D'Arcy Thompson (1992) and René Thom (1975) in contrast to the idiotic New Age apprehension of the spirituality of spirals, but with a reliance on measurement and on values that can now be shown to be ideal, approximate, and rudimentary. Such approximations, at best, lead me, as they have many scientists and artists in the nineteenth and twentieth centuries, to a state contemporary with non-Euclidean geometry, proposed by John Keats in 1817 as negative capability, that is, when humankind is capable "of being in uncertainties, mysteries, doubts, without any irritable reaching after fact and reason"[20] and in a different context by Werner Heisenberg's work on quantum physics in the 1920s as "uncertainty."[21] In 1931 Kurt Gödel brought these ideas together when he proved that truth was not demonstrable.[22] In 1966 John S. Bell and others made it known how the world of phenomena no longer holds up,[23] that is there is a tangible world of things and experiences and there are worlds beyond our experiences, which can be accessed only remotely by tools and traps. These can provide evidence that both the

> micro-sub-atomic and the macro-cosmic levels exist and perform and are part of, and thus affect, our existence, but this evidence is not yet quite available to perception except as artefacts. This can be demonstrated, for instance, by visually comparing "Cosmological simulations that show hot bubbles from active galactic nuclei as a heat source in cooling-flow clusters, at two different times" with Positron emission tomography scans showing the effects of cocaine on human brain receptors and dopamine.[24]

This is again a debate about the local and the problematic pan-topia (everywhere) often confused by the term "nonlocal." In quantum mechanics part of this debate has led to naming the situation "decoherence" that is beyond the state fought for by such twentieth-century modernists as Ezra Pound, W. B. Yeats, Walter Benjamin, and Theodor Adorno as coherence, to an understanding that part of our existence cannot be realized, is beyond perception, has a proven actuality, and is typically experienced indirectly through artifacts.[25] Physicists working on these actualities use laser and gravity traps and digital tools to make observation possible, but precise measurement remains out of the question. Instrumentation is itself part of the effect on measurement and its disposition. Bell's proposition partly reiterates earlier statements, made by Max Born and others, that the observer interferes with the observed and thus consciousness affects measurement. This proposition has metamorphosed into understanding the role of the spectator, the measuring physicist, the viewer in art, the reader of poetry, or the listener to music as a participant and an effect on the completion of the aesthetic production.

Measurement thus becomes an ethical issue; ideal and golden proportions must be replaced. This position is in confluence with three other significant appraisals of truth in the twentieth and twenty-first centuries: (1) that energy concomitant with momentum, now named "momenergy,"[26] and consciousness is discernible in wave packets or quanta and thus changes in steplike shifts and developments in four dimensions with a direction, and not an uninterrupted continuity or stream of thought; (2) that time and space are intricately affective and not usefully separated (space-time); and (3) that extended and apparently smooth behavior—such as experienced in the growth of an embryo, or the mixing of more than one chemical, or the loss of breath in a runner's stride—always relies on catastrophic jumps, phase shifts, or sudden stepped changes. These "jumps" are often unpredictable in terms of momenergy and space-time but often predictable in terms of quality.[27] Bearing in mind these concepts and proposals, it will be again useful to demonstrate aspects of their significance in my work processes and productions. Most of these ideas came together in 1982 in preparation for the work that has been under way since then, *Gravity as a Consequence of Shape.*[28]

In 1981 I brought to a close a pair of ten-year projects, and I will focus on one, named *PLACE,* which had, as I saw it, tackled the consequence of space-time in terms of location, history, and situation using a method of composition by "field."[29] The location of South London, chosen in 1970, was used as the *Lichtung* from which to research into local histories and the actuality of contemporary situations in the street, so to speak, both responded to and instigated. The subsequent poem, *Gravity as a Consequence of Shape,* uses my book composed in 1982, *Ideas on the Culture Dreamed Of,* in which I drew from the vocabularies of contemporary physics, biology, and chemistry and combined them with a selection of notated jazz dances into an *A–Z* which formulated an index base from which to compose.[30] The compositional procedures used in *PLACE* were radically reappraised for the *Gravity* work, taking into account the critique of the classical and ideal models of preparation and existence. The overall plan, conceived as the loci of a point on a moving sphere in *PLACE,* was replaced in *Gravity* with the looser diagram of a cylinder marked off in Fibonacci ratios and then crushed, thus leading to a new set but of damaged proportions.

"Traps and Tools and Damage" then comes rhetorically to the fore. There may be many ramifications from this crushed image, rhetorical and pragmatic, but for my purposes here, the image recalls the experiments carried out by the National Aeronautics and Space Administration (NASA) on spacecraft and space station cabins subjected to zero gravity and high-impact conditions. Other aspects of this image considered damage perpetuated and now escalated against the planet, once thought of as home and now beyond repair as well as the continuous need for organizations such as the Medical Foundation for the Care of Victims of Torture. The image's display of numbered rows crushed into each other, causing geological shifts in and out of sequence due to stress and strain, produced unexpected patterns of connectedness, thus unexpected consciousness, and thus the need for proposals for an aesthetics that would seek to help solve the traumas, the damage of the situation. During the process of this work, completed in 2005, the damaged structure has led to the need to constantly reinvent compositional conceptualization to overcome or, so to speak, repair the damage perpetrated against humankind by humankind, as much as a ploy to maintain personal homeostasis and homeorhesis (a tendency to develop toward a given state).

Tools

For leaps of health we need tools. Tools are used by a range of animals and humans to encourage improvement in their condition and are thus used for turning back on the empiricism of sensation to address the hidden danger, the consciousness of the subject, encouraged by patterns of connectedness and the inventive perception I have called "crowd-out."

Since the early 1990s, discussions of human evolution have been concerned with the modern human mind. Merlin Donald proposed three radical transitions in the evolution of human culture and cognition since the time of humankind's bipedal ancestors.[31] The first was a change through the emergence of the ability to reenact events—the "mimetic" skill. The second change is associated with the emergence of speech. The third involves the complex interaction of cognition and culture and is demonstrated in graphic invention, external memory, and theory construction, such as writing, drawing, and designing. Hominid cultures, over more than two million years, manifested by their tool, trap, and weapon production, were diverse and widely spread through Africa, China, and Eurasia before the first graphic imaging was produced. There never has been a single origin for cultural production, and all apparent continuities have interruptions and breakage. Such multicentered discontinuity encourages the complexity of graphic art. The widespread dispersal of hominids evolved as humankind (*Homo sapiens*), at least thirty-four thousand years ago, during the last interglacial period,[32] started using graphic imaging in an interrelated cultural style, a style that implies at once both common speech and local difference displayed as similarities of depictive codes and particular uniqueness of depiction from local inventions and learned traditions. It is this pattern of similitude and difference, mimetic of natural phenomena, but also unique human invention, often developed or abstracted from cognition of natural forms, that characterizes the punctuated evolution of complexity in image production evident throughout early and subsequent civilizations.

My use of tools and images of tools in paintings probably derives from a mixture, my father's occupation as a joiner and my second studio in the 1980s, which included a large collection of carpenter's tools from my father's workshop. My memory mixes the smell of wood and wood shavings, carpenter's tools and various lubrication fats such as tallow, with turpentine and linseed and walnut oils for painting. With a view to further discuss aspects of my work during the 1980s, 1990s, and today, it will be useful here to introduce another engagement, this time with the work of Joseph Beuys. To facilitate my purpose I will make a selection from one set of patterns of connectedness that Beuys provides in the curation of his sculpture in the two installations set up in London in 1985, the same year that Kitaj installed his show debating the Jewish Diaspora and the Holocaust.[33] The themes for Beuys's group of installations can be summarized by the subtitle of the dominant exhibit, as part of the German exhibition, in the Royal Academy rotunda—"A Monument to the Future."[34] Beuys's work has been involved in discussion of the European, post-Holocaust condition since his sculpture first appeared in public in 1947. The installation in the Royal Academy rotunda comprised five groups of sculpture and was contemporary with a connected installation at the Anthony d'Offay Gallery in the same area of London. My purpose here, for this essay, will be to arrive at the metonymic meaning proposed by Beuys from these installations, based on a very reduced account of the iconographic, semiotic, and historical evidence. I intend to publish this work, together with drawings I made from the research, in 2007.

The work in the show with the longest process of facture is *Pt Co Fe* (1948–72). It makes clear two of Beuys's characteristic methods of facture, the use of an already-made object, and the work's changing form and meaning. Initially *Pt Co Fe* may be seen as a steel-meshed cabinet in which a metal bar hangs. By reference to its title, three metals are to be discerned: platinum, cobalt, and iron. The cabinet is to be thought of as iron and, by reference to the catalog, it is understood that the bar is platinum plated with cobalt and that the work has a history of facture.

It has been a processual work, in terms of the spread of its meaning as well as its facture. In 1948, when it started, a sculptured head of Mars hung where the bar now hangs inside the army-surplus cabinet. The head of Mars was replaced in 1954 by a plaster head of Napoleon; in 1958 by plaster and a piece of fat; in 1963 by a copper bar; and finally in 1972 by the bar that remains in the same cabinet today. The beginning of the work's meaning can proceed from these facts.

The head of Mars and the "iron" army-surplus cabinet initiate the thought that the overall work is a metonymic object, standing for a warring principle like one of Dante's "worthy" subjects.[35] Through knowledge of the work's history, this metonym expands from the negative head standing for war to the historical figure of a particular "European" war. When this head is replaced with plaster and fat, a tension is created between the cold and fragmented order, in its memory trace of Napoleon, and the necessity of the warm and chaotic aspects added to the warring principle. This tension can be seen as the dual nature of the male principle, which is emphasized by replacing it with a bar of copper, as the female aspect that hangs inside the male frame, or at least, as some alchemical texts might describe it.[36]

Beuys's continued research into anthropology and medicine allows for an increase in the viewer's production of meaning. It will not suffice to simply call this work a sign for the male principle. Viewing the work inside its own history, and then in the wider context of Beuys's aesthetic and social proposals, will make the process of what it means available. This viewing can become the process of allegorical journeys from the outside to the inside and back out. The iron cabinet may be thought of as a Faraday cage, that is, the earthed screening Beuys alludes to in his drawing *To Faraday* (1958), which shields the inside of the cage from external electrical fields.[37] Inside, the bar has been plated against chemical interference. From the skeleton of the cage to the armor of the plating onto the core of the work, it is as if the male principle were being considered in terms of layers of protection, in Dante's terms the principle of "safety."

From the heavy metal center, its power core, out through its casing, its

Napoleonic skull, its reasoning, to its outer shield, its social guard, this structure parallels Wilhelm Reich's sexual energetics as a system of character armor around the biocore to which *Untitled Drawing* (1957) may also refer.[38] In terms of physiological processes discussed by Samuel Hahnemann and others, the viewer is reminded of the iron of the blood cells necessary for the carrying of the essential yet toxic trace elements required by the body.[39] In terms of chemicophysics the allegorical eye moves from iron toward the increasing hardness of the core that simultaneously becomes electrically less resistant and more vulnerable, as the eye moves from iron to platinum.[40] Through such a system of metonyms and metaphors, slowly arrived at by Beuys and then the viewer, a sculpture exemplifying part of the human condition has been possible. Beuys's transformation has been to turn the austere, abstract display presented by *Pt Co Fe* into a "worthy" application. Such interpretations are less far-fetched than initially stating them can seem. With Beuys's work many intersections of meaning are necessary and are available to be found. In the rotunda environment these interpretations are complexed. The male principle of vulnerability and safety embodied by *Pt Co Fe* is immediately echoed by *Tram Stop* (1976).

With *Tram Stop* Beuys's gyres (derived from Yeats's intersecting strata of time) come to the fore.[41] *Tram Stop* embodies the male principle but does so in the specific situation of the European "theater" in the twentieth century. Simultaneously the sculpture carries the historical condition of seventeenth-century Kleve, where Beuys was born, which is intersected by reference to both ancient times as well as, like *Pt Co Fe,* the actual time in which the sculpture was factured in 1976 as "A Monument to the Future."[42] The sculpture consists of many iron elements, the dominating feature of which is a seven-meter, seventeenth-century culverin (or cannon), with the form of a dragon's mouth at its open end, into which has been inserted a bust with an iron head. The other elements comprise the cast tops of four mortar bombs, a tramline, and metal rods. In its original setting in Venice the cannon with bust was displayed vertically and was surrounded by the cylindrical bomb tops. To its side a hole had been drilled into the floor and down to the Venice lagoon. Into this hole the rods were used to connect the water to the gallery floor, so that the top, angled rod acted as a "key" to facilitate this.[43] To the side of these elements the rubble from the drilling was piled up and was found to include part of a human skull. Whether the skull was added by Beuys or actually lifted from the gallery foundation is not stated. The Royal Academy show (like that in New York in 1979) provides a relic of this display because the vertical column has been laid horizontally across two of the bomb tops, and the rods have been left on the floor. Each element in the sculpture contributes to the overall work, and the work itself juxtaposes the other sculptures in the rotunda. To arrive at an understanding of the work, it is necessary to understand the elements and how they contribute to the larger meaning of Beuys's other exhibits.

At the Sternberg, in Kleve, in 1652, Moritz von Nassau erected a monument as an axis from which radiating avenues were added to create a network of municipal order. This monument comprised the culverin and mortar bomb tops that Beuys has used to cast part of his monument. Originally an armored Eros projected from the cannon's mouth. This head has been "replaced" by Beuys with a cast from a mold made by Beuys that includes in its features a Roman martial head, such as that of Mars in the Vatican, a Celtic head similar in its mouth design to that of the Tanderagee idol in Ireland, and the frown of an "ordinary man" similar to some Roman portraits. The despair of the mouth, the sides pulled apart by the ceramicist's fingers, recalls gestures found in early Italian *Last Judgments,* by Giotto in the Arena Chapel and by Fra Angelico in Orvieto Cathedral, as well as sculpture of a damned soul in the same cathedral, and even a tribal war head, now displayed in St. Petersburg. The stance of the head and elongated neck may also associate with the Celtic figure from Ralaghan. Putting these elements together provides the initial meaning.

Tram Stop is a metonym, that is, it stands for part of the contemporary human condition. What was once armored love is now an image of war and despair. Its European condition is a complex of Celtic ancestry and military colonizers in the mouth of archaic and modern weaponry linked by image and meaning to the dragon, one of the signifiers of the serpentine form. But this only deals with the prominent elements. To the side of the cannon runs a tramline which connects the contemporary condition to the past, connects in its curve the ground below with that above. That is a shamanistic stratification elaborated by the rods which connected the water to the earth and, in its original display, the horizontal with the ascending and descending. In its new display as relic, the overall suggestion is that these historical, shamanistic potentials have changed their significance. The work becomes "A Monument to the Future" as warning out of suffering, but there is also hope in *Tram Stop*'s link to the *Lightning* (1982–85) sculpture that hangs behind it.[44] The topological connections it may have once made to Germany, Ireland, and Venice now rest without their ascending totemic power.[45] There is also an allusion in Beuys's *The*

Secret Block for a Secret Person in Ireland to Samuel Beckett's "Listener's face" in the play *That Time,* but I will leave that extension for another occasion.[46] Beuys's difficulty is the kind of despair that Taoists saw "violating the principle of Nature and doubling the emotion of humankind."[47] In this sense it is a shamanistic concurrence with the Roman poet and philosopher Lucretius, who speaks of science, as Beuys does, as a remedy for the main fears of humankind coupled to the knowledge of its destructive power: "to see with reasonable eyes / Of what the mind, of what the soul, is made, / And what it is so terrible that breaks / On us asleep . . . "[48]

For Beuys there are springs in this tension between his multiple concerns with damage, the lost ancestry of Europe, and a potential, partly through the tools of science, to renew. The sculpture in the rotunda stands between the vulnerable and protective male principle of *Pt Co Fe* and the ecstatic clarity of *Lightning* cast from earth clay. In the rotunda it aligns with the *Mountain King* and contrasts with the female *Pythia Sibylla (Justitia),* sculptures which add material substance and allusions to consultation with an oracle, respectively.[49]

I have discussed two parts of the five-part installation in the rotunda. I will take license from the pressure of brevity here to now summarize this installation as if I had described all five parts. The installation is allegorical for an oracle, or stands in the place of an oracle, consulted in times of social and ecological danger. The danger projected is the recognition that the human condition is under the dominating pressure of the male principle, a state of both ethical and ecological damage. It is a monument to the future because it proposes a healing science in contradiction to a martial science, it offers protection and transformation of damage.

Concurrent with the rotunda environment, Beuys made an installation work for the Anthony d'Offay Gallery titled *Plight* (1985). Its elements consisted of a two-room environment lined on all walls and ceiling with rolls of felt. One room contained a grand piano, a blackboard with five white parallel lines, and a fertility thermometer. The atmosphere in the rooms was enclosing and warm. It acted as an insulation from the pneumatic drilling next door. In a situated, social sense the lining acted as a protection from the gallery's, and viewer's, "plight" of noise, which is to say, the misuse of science and technology. Beuys's work encourages such speculation; at the same time, however, realizations of a bunker technology ensue.

The enclosure the insulation creates suggests a place of waiting, perhaps awaiting nuclear attack. But this enclosed waiting in fact brings another meaning of "plight" to the attention. The piano and staves for music give the instruments to create an alternative sound in this enclosure, and, because of Beuys's previous work and various drawings, they also connect to the animal and thus the spirit in shamanistic terms.[50] The viewer's presence in the space also connects to Beuys's ideas expressed in his watercolor *Before Birth,* a reproduction of which was made available at the entrance to the installation.[51] The fertility thermometer encourages this extension. The viewer is in the stifling warmth of a womb and awaits birth. Plight then becomes a promise for the future, a transformation of humankind in the tension of "Science and Nature."

This "promise" is to be made possible, in the first place, through "Art" (that is "Music"), and in the second place, through the viewer's metaphoric rebirth of the spirit. It takes only a brief contemplation to put such a view against the oracle and knowledge provided by the rotunda environment. Beuys's "anthropological art" reaches a meaning through a necessary shortage of definition.[52] The oracle's warning and suggestion of hope is reaffirmed and clarified by *Plight* in the form of a rebirth of the spirit through Art.

Damage

There is a direct correlation between aesthetic function and living on the planet. All living involves an aesthetic dimension, and any engagement of a brain involves aesthetic function. When living forms engage their brains for activities, they usually involve more than one function; even so, one of those functions is always aesthetic. Many of the cultural activities carried out by humankind, such as the making of tools, are pragmatic and involve aesthetics as a secondary function. When a pragmatic activity shifts toward a negentropic result, the aesthetic function begins to dominate. When the aesthetic function dominates, the result is art. This conceptual shift is a feature more prevalent and obvious in humankind than in other life-forms, but then perception crowd-out of this function by the life-form that produces it is more likely to be encouraged by that life-form than any other.

In conclusion, let me reiterate what I first wrote: human activity is in continuous flux exemplified by short-term and long-term losses and memories. There is a causality in the order of knowledge, particularly because all experience—existence and memory—involves loss, that is, it involves damage. My work has shown a consistent engagement with damage as a recognition of harm, as a developmental potential, and as a clearing for healing and health. Humans use traps or tools as processes for transformation, processes that include development and healing. Connections are made by the brain to subvert entropy, so that aesthetics participates in a perpetual endeavor to become immortal. The correlation and meeting of the patterns of connectedness that constitute consciousness and the patterns of connectedness that encourage beauty in the process and object of art come together, at best, as an imperfect fit, an essentially incomplete expression, potentially brought toward completion each moment the receiver, viewer, or listener encounters the work. Our particular opportunity and necessity today is to engage in the aesthetic dimension as a pragmatic act.

Appendix 1

There hasn't been space to elaborate on the meaning of Joseph Beuys's *Lightning.* Like *Pt Co Fe* and *Tram Stop,* it has a history of facture and meaning potential. It relates to Beuys's *Scenes from a Stag Hunt* (1961) and *Monument to the Stag* (1982) as well as being a major theme for his drawings, in, for instance, *The Secret Block for a Secret Person in Ireland* (1974, 1996). The actual sculpture hung in the rotunda was cast from the clay cone in *Monument to the Stag.* Since the latter directly refers to a supreme "life-force," as exemplified in the stag king, Cernunnus, mythology, *Lightning* can be thought of as the ecstatic energy leaving the stag's antlers and rising to the sky. While this action initially appears to contradict the physical act of lightning, it is clear that Beuys is aware of the two-way process that constitutes lightning, as well as the shamanistic ideas of light shown on so many shamans' antlered headgear.[53] In addition, Beuys's comments in the aforementioned *The Secret* (1974, 1996) link the stag to Mercury and Psychopompos, that is, as a conductor of the soul to the other world. It is sufficient for the rotunda comprehension to understand *Lightning* as making this connection, which in turn connects directly to the presence of *Mountain King* in the rotunda and indirectly to Apollo through *Pythia Sibylla.*[54]

Appendix 2

Joseph Beuys's *Mountain King* complements his *Tram Stop.* The "body" of the king can be thought of as a skeleton of the land as well as the mountain of the self. Like Peer Gynt and the stag king, it connects to patterns of folklore and mythology implying great strength. The particular section of Ibsen's *Peer Gynt* referred to is in act 5, where Peer speaks to the "Dovre-Master." Ibsen, writing to the composer Edvard Grieg and to his publisher reveals the connection to the folktales in *Norske Huldre-Eventyr og Folkesagn,* in particular the tale told by Thor Ulvsvolden about the exploits of a hunter and the account told by Per Fugleskjelle about an encounter between a hunter called Per Gynt and the Boyg of Etnedal. In both cases the tales can be linked to the widespread European legends related to Cernunnus, the stag king. It is probably also worth noting Grieg's suite *Hall of the Mountain King* written for Ibsen's work and in the king's responsibility for weather and crops; "his life bound up sympathetically with the prosperity of the country," with the potential to regenerate material. (The form of the sculpted "body" is that of Beuys's *Compost.* I have used James Frazer's ideas of the king here coupled to Beuys's discussion in the Victoria and Albert Museum interview.[55] In the interview Beuys also mentions while discussing "the inner ability of people" that "everybody has a chance to be a prospector," and this also relates to the "mountain of the self.") The sculpture's head is that of "Science," or as Caroline Tisdall reports, like a compass, gyroscope, or clock face. It also connects to the idea of the revolving tower in the stag king mythology. (The "Turning Tower" occurs in the stories of the celestial deer. It brings together the ideas of the turning sky and the divine deer which, as Kenny notes, "were significant among the people who fashioned and revered the antlered images," of whom the Celts were a part. Its body is hollowed out, excavated, implying a link to its mineral wealth.) The whole sculpture thus offers the macrocosmic condition simplified as "Nature" and "Science," or what humankind does to the land. But as often with Beuys, it also offers the microcosmic, the individual's responsibility to the self to use mind and body. As Beuys's comments indicate, the king is Promethean and needs to be juxtaposed with the ecological care of the shepherd. Such a juxtaposition involves responsibility for one's own inner, secret freedom and where Beuys gives his definition of Art as "the science of freedom."[56] As Halliburton makes clear, the idea of art as revealing an inner freedom also occurs in Heidegger.[57] It connects also to Heidegger's mode of openness, which he called *Lichtung.* While this is an apparently untranslatable neologism, it can, at least on one level, be understood as bringing together "light" and "clearing." As such it appears to also add emphasis to Beuys's ideas of "inner ability" and his sculpture *Lightning. Mountain King* complements *Tram Stop* in its warning yet contrasts it in its potential for change, for transformation of materials. Rather than contrasting the *Wet Washing Virgin* who attends *Pythia Sibylla,* it awaits to attend to the child, the transformed society or new culture that is to come. This is a mixture of mythologies common to Beuys's artistic project. As his drawings, early Christian sculpture, and work subsequent to 1947 confirm, he discovers shamanistic elements and substance transformers in a plural world: the traditions of Celtic and Christian peoples, as well as Greek mythology. For Eliade this is what should be expected; "there is no pure culture."[58] For *Pythia Sibylla* Beuys turns to a shamanistic element, "the oldest religion attending all religions in the Greco-Roman tradition." *Pythia Sibylla* can act as the coalescence of the other pieces in the Royal Academy rotunda. Pythia, the shamanistic prophetess of Apollo, delivers the god's answers in a frenzy to those using the oracle at Delphi. Her body, particularly her hair, is washed beforehand by the *Wet Washing Virgin.* Pythia is combined with the Roman chthonic Sibylla, who is consulted only with the greatest solemnity, and only when the state seems to be in danger.[59] Together they give advice on the human condition and social dangers. In this sense they represent justice, where Beuys draws from an archaic modernism and proposes "truth and balance." This is confirmed in the rotunda by the added subtitle to this work of *Justitia.* These factors are also confirmed in the sculpture and associated drawings, but I will leave their descriptions here. The overall work speaks ambiguously to the questioner at the oracle, using the other work in the rotunda to specify the nature of the oracle. That is to say, as it can be seen that *Pythia Sibylla* with her *Wet Washing Virgin* are both oracle and female, it can be said that what this oracle speaks, as a metonym, concerns the human condition under the dominating pressure of the male principle and as if on behalf of the Celtic Apollo Vindonnus. It both offers healing science and despairs at its martial science: it offers protection registered through *Pt Co Fe* and a relic "to the future" in *Tram Stop.* This conjunction is reemphasized by Beuys through *Mountain King* and its link to Cernunnus, the Indo-Celtic "lord of the animals" and carrier of souls, in *Lightning.*

So much of the Sibyllan poetry, as Wright puts it, is "universally reckoned" to be "spurious."[60] The ideas used in the essay are based on historic rather than conjectured information, that is, with regard to how the prophetess of Cumae was consulted and on what occasions. Beuys also links Sibylla to Mercury and Psychopompos. Beuys says "this deity appears in time of great difficulty or danger."[61]

Notes

1. The concept "patterns of connectedness" derives from "the pattern which connects" in anthropological work by Bateson, Schuster, and Carpenter. See, for instance, Gregory Bateson, *Mind and Nature: A Necessary Unity* (Glasgow: William Collins Publishers, 1980); and Carl Schuster and Edmund Carpenter, *Patterns That Connect: Social Symbolism in Ancient and Tribal Art* (New York: Harry N. Abrams, 1996).

2. For instance, Jan Mukarovský, *Structure, Sign, and Function,* trans. John Burbank and Peter Steiner (New Haven, Conn.: Yale University Press, 1977).

3. Henry Petroski, *The Evolution of Useful Things* (New York: Alfred A. Knopf, 1992).

4. S. A. Semenov, *Prehistoric Technology. An Experimental Study of the Oldest Tools and Artefacts from Traces of Manufacture and Wear,* trans. M. W. Thompson (New York: Harper and Row, 1976); Mark Edmunds, *Stone Tools and Society: Working Stone in Neolithic and Bronze Age Britain* (London: B. T. Batsford, 1995).

5. *Lichtung,* a neologism used by Heidegger for "lightening-clearing" or "lighting-clearing," where "clearing" refers to a space cleared in, for instance, a woodland; see Martin Heidegger, *Poetry, Language, Thought,* trans. Alfred Hofstadter (New York: Harper and Row, 1975), 41, 53.

6. For example, R. B. Kitaj, *The Kabbalist* (1980–81), private collection, New York; Kitaj, *The Garden* (1985), Cleveland Museum of Art; Kitaj, *The Cure* (1985), private collection, London; Kitaj, *Passion (1940–45) Girl/Plume* (1985), artist's collection.

7. William Hogarth, *Portrait of the Painter and His Pug* (1745), Tate Britain, London. Compare Lawrence Gowing, *William Hogarth* (London: Tate Gallery, 1971), 135.

8. William Hogarth, *The Analysis of Beauty* (Ilkley and London: Scholar Press, 1753; facsimile repr. 1969); G. P. Lomazzo, *A Tracte Containing the Artes of Curious Paintinge, Carvinge, Buildinge* (1584), trans. R. Haydocke (1598) (Oxford: British Library).

9. The *Palestinian Column,* Vatican. Compare J. R. Ward Perkins, "The Shrine of St. Peter and its Twelve Spiral Columns," *Journal of Roman Studies* 42 (1952): 21–33.

10. John Shearman, *Raphael's Cartoons in the Collection of the Queen and the Tapestries for the Sistine Chapel* (London: Phaidon, 1972), plate 4.

11. The temple was reported as being built c. 953 B.C.; see Amihai Mazar, *Archaeology of the Land of the Bible 10,000–586 B.C.* (New York: Doubleday, 1990): The columns are described as two great pillars of bronze, twenty-seven feet high exclusive of the capitals, eighteen feet circumference, cast in ringed

sections in clay in Transgarl, with red gold overlays and extensive use of cedar in construction.

12. Green soapstone *Libation vessel* found at Tello, Mesopotamia, dating from Dynasty of Gudea (2450 B.C.), now in the Louvre, Paris. See Francois Pottier, *Vase antiques du Louvre, photogravures et dessins de J. Devillard,* 3 vols. (Paris, 1897–1922), plate 125.

13. See, for instance, *Mythological Papyri: Egyptian Religious Texts and Representations,* ed. Alexandre Piankoff (New York: Bollingen Foundation, 1957).

14. W. Andrews, "Preliminary Note on Some Recently Discovered Extinct Vertebrates from Egypt (Part II)," *Geological Magazine* 8 (1901): 437–40. Compare I. M Lewis, *Social Anthropology in Perspective: The Relevance of Social Anthropology* (Cambridge: Cambridge University Press, 1985); and Lewis's lectures at the Pitt Rivers Museum, Oxford, in the 1990s. See also Adrienne Mayor, *The Fossil Hunters: Paleontology in Greek and Roman Times* (Princeton, N.J.: Princeton University Press, 2000).

15. Classical examples from Greece include the *Votive Relief of Asclepius and Hygeia* (c. 330 B.C.) from the Asklepieion, Athens, now in the National Museum, Athens; and from Rome the *Statue of Æsculapius* (A.D. 150) from Anzio, now in the Capitoline Museum, Rome. See C. Kerényi, *Asklepios: Archetypal Image of the Physician's Existence,* trans. Ralph Manheim (Princeton, N.J.: Princeton University Press, 1981), illustrations 16 and 7, respectively.

16. Carlo Pietrangeli, André Chastel, John Shearman, John O'Malley, S. J. Pierluigi De Vecchi, Michael Hirst, Fabrizio Mancinelli, Gianluigi Colalucci, and Franco Bernabei, *The Sistine Chapel: The Art, the History, and the Restoration* (New York: Harmony Books, 1986), 146–47.

17. Euclid, *The Elements of Euclid,* ed. Isaac Todhunter (London: J. M. Dent and Sons, 1933), 2.11 and 6.30.

18. *Common Chili Nettle* seed capsules, Karl Blossfeldt, *Art Forms in Nature: Examples from the Plant World Photographed Direct from Nature* (London: A. Zwemmer, 1929); and plant stem divisions in Ernö Lendvai, *Béla Bartók: An Analysis of His Music* (London: Kahn and Averill, 1971).

19. C. K. Ogden, I. A. Richards, and James Wood, *The Foundations of Aesthetics* (1922; London: Routledge, 2001).

20. John Keats, Letter 9, "To George and Thomas Keats," December 21, 1817, in *Letters of John Keats,* ed. Stanley Gardener (London: University of London Press, 1965).

21. Werner Heisenberg, *The Physical Principles of the Quantum Theory* (Chicago: University of Chicago Press, 1930); and Werner Heisenberg, *Physics and Philosophy: The Revolution in Modern Science* (London: George Allen and Unwin, 1958).

22. Kurt Gödel, "Über formal unentscheidbare Sätze der Principia Math-

ematica und verwandter Systeme," *Monatshefte der Mathematik und Physik* 38 (1931): 173–98. Compare A. Ernst Nagel and J. R. Newman, "Gödel's Proof," in *The World of Mathematics,* vol. 3 (New York: Simon and Schuster, 1956), 1668–95; and further discussion in Abner Shimony, "Philosophical and Experimental Perspectives on Quantum Physics," in *Epistemological and Experimental Perspectives on Quantum Physics,* ed. Daniel Greenberger, Wolfgang L. Reiter, and Anton Zeilinger (Dordrecht: Kluweer Academic Publishers, 1999).

23. John S. Bell, "On the Problem of Hidden Variables in Quantum Theory," *Reviews of Modern Physics* 38 (1966): 447–52. Compare John S. Bell and M. Nauenberg, "The Moral Aspect of Quantum Mechanics," in *Preludes in Theoretical Physics,* ed. A. de Shalit, H. Feshbach, and L. Van Hove (Amsterdam, North Holland, 1966).

24. Marcus Brüggen and Christian R. Kaiser, "Cosmological Simulations That Show Hot Bubbles from Active Galactic Nuclei as a Heat Source in Cooling-Flow Clusters, at Two Different Times," *Nature* 418 (2002): 301. Compare Rita Carter, *Mapping the Mind* (London: Weidenfeld and Nicolson, 1998), 69.

25. For "decoherence," see Roland Omnès, *Understanding Quantum Mechanics* (Princeton, N.J.: Princeton University Press, 1999); and Wojciech Hubert Zurek, "Sub-Planck Structure in Phase Space and Its Relevance for Quantum Decoherence," *Nature* 412 (2001), 712–17.

26. John Archibald Wheeler proposes the term "momenergy" for "momentum-energy." See John Archibald Wheeler, *A Journey into Gravity and Spacetime* (New York: Scientific American Library, 1990).

27. It might be too rigid to call them "paradigm shifts," as Kuhn would, but this is what they could be articulated as; see Thomas Kuhn, *The Structure of Scientific Revolutions* (Chicago: University of Chicago Press, 1996).

28. That the ideas came together in 1982 is correct with the exception of "decoherence," which became prominent in the 1990s during new experiments in quantum mechanics; see Omnès, *Understanding Quantum Mechanics;* and Zurek, "Sub-Planck Structure."

29. Allen Fisher, *PLACE, Book One* (London: Aloes Books, 1974; rpr. St. Paul, Minn.: Truck Books, 1976). The other project was *Blood, Bone, Brain* (London: Spanner, 1981).

30. Allen Fisher, *Ideas on the Culture Dreamed Of* (London: Spanner, 1983). The jazz dances are notated in Marshall and Jean Stearns, *Jazz Dance: The Story of American Vernacular Dance* (New York: Schirmer Books, 1968).

31. Merlin Donald, *Origins of the Modern Mind: Three Stages in the Evolution of Culture and Cognition* (Cambridge, Mass. and London: Harvard University Press, 1991).

32. The last glacial maximum was twenty-one thousand years ago; see D. Paillard, "The Timing of Pleistocene Glaciations from a Simple Multiple-State Climate Model," *Nature* 391 (1998), 378; and Yusuke Yokoyama, Kurt Lam-

beck, Patrick de Deckker, Paul Johnson, and L. Keith Fifield, "Timing of the Last Glacial Maximum from Observed Sea-Level Minima," *Nature* 406 (2000), 713–16.

33. In the same year, Beuys also installed *Palazzo Regale* (1985), Milan; see Armin Zweite, *Joseph Beuys: Natur Materie Form* (London: Schirmer/Mosel, 1991).

34. Royal Academy of Arts, *German Art in the Twentieth Century: Painting and Sculpture 1905–1985*, ed. Christos M. Joachimides, Norman Rosenthal, and Wieland Schmied (London: Weidenfeld and Nicholson, 1985), plates 241–45.

35. Dante, "De Vulgari Eloquentia," in *Portable Dante*, trans. Laurence Binyon (Princeton, N.J.: Princeton University Press, 1947): "If we carefully consider the object of all those who are in search of what is useful, we shall find that it is nothing else but safety. Secondly, in respect of what is pleasurable . . . this is love. Thirdly, in respect of what is right; and here no one doubts that virtue has the first place. Wherefore these three things, namely, safety, love, and virtue, appear to be those capital matters which ought to be treated supremely, I mean the things which are most important in respect of them, as prowess in arms, the fire of love, and the direction of the will."

36. C. G. Jung, *Psychology and Alchemy: The Collected Works of C. G. Jung*, trans. R. F. C. Hull (London: Routledge, 1980).

37. See Anne Seymour, *Joseph Beuys Drawings* (London: V&A, 1983), 44.

38. Wilhelm Reich's concept of character armor is discussed by him in many of his works including Wilhelm Reich, *The Function of the Orgone*, trans. Theodore P. Wolfe (New York: The Noonday Press, 1961). Beuys's empathy with some of Reich's ideas also comes into the frame in his use of materials (iron and felt, for instance) but are more prominent in Beuys's understanding of sexual energy and the shamanistic stratification or layering to which he so often alludes. For Beuys's *Untitled Drawing*, see Sammlung Marx, *Joseph Beuys: The Secret Block for a Secret Person in Ireland* (1974; Berlin: Arkadien-Verlags-GmbH and Bastian, 1996), plate 176.

39. Samuel Hahnemann's homeopathy is discussed in George Vithoulkas, *Homeopathy, Medicine of the New Man* (New York: Arco, 1979). Hahnemann's work may be considered in Beuys's use of isomorphism and synchronicity, both in his choice of materials (medicinal plants, for instance) and in his metaphoric understanding of the homeopathic method in which the idea of "like attracts like" is paramount. Also involved is the biochemistry concerning the body's need for trace elements; see R. J. P. Williams and J. J. R. Fraústo da Silva, *The Natural Selection of the Chemical Elements: The Environment and Life's Chemistry* (Oxford: Clarendon Press, 1996).

40. The electrical resistances in iron, cobalt, and platinum are, respectively, 9.8×10^{-3}; 0.0635×10^{-6}; and 9.97×10^{-8} while the hardness of these elements respectively increases with their relative atomic masses from 55.85 to 195.09 and their relative densities from 7.86 to 21.45.

41. W. B. Yeats, *A Vision* (London: Macmillan, 1925).

42. "A Monument to the Future" was the subtitle given to *Tram Stop* by Beuys in 1976 for the Venice Biennial.

43. *Tram Stop* (1976) in Dr. Erich Marx Collection, Berlin, illustrated in Caroline Tisdall, *Joseph Beuys* (New York: Thames and Hudson, 1979), plates 419, 420, 421, 423–27.

44. See Appendix 1 in this essay for elaboration of *Lightning.*

45. The etymology of "culverin" suggests the Latin *colubrinus,* meaning "snakelike." The use of the dragon's mouth at the open end of the cannon then adds to this suggestive "rhyming." The link that Beuys would be able to make between "fiery soul" and cannon fire may be too far-fetched, but the connections possible between this "dragon" imagery and the battle between humankind and the dragon alluded to in the Pythian mythology may not be. The killing of the snake, the "Python" in the myth, quite clearly links to some extent to the folk motif of Saint George and the Dragon, and the latter cannot avoid its significance as a symbol of the forces of evil. The fact that Beuys made the beginnings of *Tram Stop* eight years before *Pythia Sibylla* would not mean that he had not made the connection. This is particularly possible because of the incised ciphers on the latter sculpture which recall the Celtic rock carving of Thor's battle with Midgard, the serpent, and also the serpent motif on the Delphic oracle's tripod.

46. Beckett's play was first performed in public in 1976. The play begins: "That time you went back that last time to look was the ruin still there where you hid as a child when was that grey day took the eleven to the end of the line and on from there no no trams." This "monument" does not, of course, allude directly to Beckett's "Listener," despite the use of generations of time and Beckett's allusions to Blake's image of the suffering Job. The play also includes a reference to the axletree, that is, Yggdrasill.

47. The Chhin Shih quotation is from Joseph Needham with Wang Ling, *Science and Civilisation in China,* vol. 2, trans. Feng Yu-Lan (Cambridge: Cambridge University Press, 1956). Needham discusses the shamanistic elements in China in section 10, "The Tao Chia (The Taoists) and Taoism."

48. Titus Lucretius Carus, *On the Nature of the Universe,* trans. P. Michael Brown (Warminster: Aris and Phillips, 1997).

49. See Appendix 2 in this essay for elaboration of remaining sculptures in the Royal Academy rotunda.

50. The "previous work" referred to is *Infiltration-homogen for Grand Piano* (1966); see Tisdall, *Joseph Beuys,* 261–62.

51. *Before Birth* (1950); see Seymour, *Joseph Beuys Drawings,* 8.

52. Beuys's description "anthropological art" is from the Victoria and Albert Museum interview; see Michael Newman and William Furlong, *Joseph Beuys, Interviews* (London: Audio Arts Supplement, audio-cassette, 1983).

53. Compare Tlingit headdress and Ramón Medina, "Stones, Bones and Skin: Ritual and Shamanistic Art (British Columbia)," *Arts Canada,* special 30th anniv. issue (1973–74): 42.

54. Compare Royal Academy of Arts, *German Art in the Twentieth Century;* and Tisdall, *Joseph Beuys;* but more particularly Dorothea Kenny, *Cernunnus* (Los Angeles: University of California, dissertation on microfilm, 1975).

55. Newman and Furlong, *Joseph Beuys, Interviews.*

56. Ibid.

57. David Halliburton, *Poetic Thinking: An Approach to Heidegger* (Chicago: University of Chicago Press, 1981).

58. Mircea Eliade, *Shamanism: Archaic Techniques of Ecstasy,* trans. William R. Trask (Princeton, N.J.: Princeton University Press, 1964).

59. The Greek and Roman references for Sibylla are Chrysostom, Cicero, Diodorus Siculus, Euripides' *Ion,* Florus, Lucan, Ovid, Pausanias, Plato's *Phaedrus,* Pliny, Plutarch's *Moralia,* Sallust, Strabo, Valerius Maximus, and Virgil. The Virgil reference gives most weight to the idea of Sibylla as chthonic. The name first occurs in Herodotus, *The Histories,* book 6.

60. *Lempriere's Classical Dictionary of Proper Names Mentioned in Ancient Authors,* ed. F. A. Wright (1788; London: Routledge and Kegan Paul, 1972), s.v. "Sibylla."

61. Marx, *Joseph Beuys.*

Discontinued Meditations

Steve McCaffery

I as an object, not a subject, identity. In the English language gender manifests without mediation in the impersonal pronouns of "he" and "she," that is, the ones who do not indicate a moment of utterance. So is this the primal gaze, in which gender is born, without a voice? A mute couple in paradise?

One edge of death is the edge of language. In the way writing rescues suffocation from breath. And the picture listens in its silver tain.

Mallarmé charges white space as a vast overdetermination of the blank. (For Ron Silliman the blank between character's is the twenty-seventh letter of the alphabet.) Isn't this an aspect of the larger trend toward pansemiotization of the little that had eluded its march? Heidegger, at least, preserves the white space in its negative integrity as "earth."

Are we thus in the house of diagrams looking at a column of tiny multitudes depart? Or in the proliferational foldings of a vertical column into a tangle of hair? (And a book resembling it?)

Consider the poem to be a balloon filled with inflammable sound, its letters pushing out with tiny hands carrying their equally tiny flags of surrender. A Bactrian camel occurs in a brief moment and its hump takes in the poem at the moment the sand becomes inflammable water and a ship arrives with orders to patrol all liquid space and a tiny whale retreats into its own balloon.

Poems are merely camouflage around an endgame, predatory exempla considered in reference (to) the transitive varieties known "as" extrema, invisible bridge mathematics hidden in the think-crypt outwarding the cold of earlier exterior ensemble aggregates that pose as grid gates over water stuttered in the mnemotechnic: "just in case it forgets."

A long poem, perhaps, is still a fatal concept given that there are two points of being between a trajectory of becoming, and a roof is but a singular becoming space from now on in language where the self seeks a resting somewhere else.

The disappointment of poetry. Success of enigma, intimate clarity of babble outside-finite fury fusion. In the West at least zebras versus crocodiles across a dawn-thorn "There" (there) I wrote writing "across the written demolishes a lyric presence." Eccentrically possible in the sobriety of a wine god in a hurry to a stretch limo like a genuine prayer from Heidegger returning to Russia, full of acquirements in lovely blueness but parenthetically man dwells on *this* earth atomwanderer wretch or wrench in aphasia and bound for the Meridian Motel. A cry is being beaten and hedgehog is in pain at the thought of Hölderlin's panic in front of sacred pathos. Rip the petals' pages out of Angelus Silesius's (rose) howother or whoother he may be.

~~In the blink of "to write" the root's two zeros become one upon the fifth letter.~~

Deletion as an affirmation within language consonant with the Mosaic prohibition. Hence a poetry located in a radical mutism, a graphic gesture to silence. Add to this an interdiction "i must have nothing to say" and to this a counterneology, a newness in the old arrived at by contraction. Please escort us to this Lurian space of *tsim tsum* and at the same time grant us a mechanical poetics of the impersonal idiolectically speaking, neither hermetic nor obscure (for what is there to hide in deletion and what's obscured by a clearing?).

But strangeness?

Indisputably strange and via strangeness: encounter. But can reading encounter? Or in the tenor of Celan can the other meet the wholly other? The ode barks. The sonnet sniffs its own arse and nothing takes place in place. We return to Heidegger if deletion is a clearing. To the other Heidegger. A Jewish Heidegger tracescattered in the many of. A hope. Unfolds this encounter as the wholly other Heidegger might guide us. Delight in to delete. Into delete to originate. Here was now. A systematic date with stochastics catching a chance. Abruptly. Deletion disappropriating not disappointing. Appropriately dis-property. The wholly other owned. Six weddings at a funeral then it turns away to show its page. The exchange now from the encounter. A relating back to. To and fro. Two and from. Essence at the inessential. "This is a poem." Not entirely of this poem. But from it. Tracks a back-trace ticking it. An intimate neighbor to strangeness.

A touch requires a fault line across congruence. Not me this interruption of amnesia in experience that makes the poem pencil, faucet, glucose tablet, matrix disaster in rhythmus of an infant's calculus. Sageschreib, poemsay, songnotch? Circumstantially "around" the stance (talks on his head) strictly, insofar as the sum of no longer being not one
    in keeping with none there as no one.

Baudelaire once claimed that commerce is the lowest and vilest form of egoism, a claim that articulates nicely onto his sibylline proclamation that the "more a man cultivates the arts, the less often he gets an erection. . . . To copulate is to aspire to enter into another—and the artist never emerges from himself."

The Self, as it knows, is an ephemeral disguise, merely a habit of saying "I," and Malraux offers to the theory of the lyric the concept of an " 'I' without a self," a poetic position of the personal without the laminating narratives of an ego. A pronominal condition considered as bare life on the edge of language experienced, even prior to encounter, as the inhuman. The inhumanity that is language formulates all discourses, human and posthuman alike. This position excites a silent cry that, for lack of a better word, is called vision. It was heard by Saint John of the Cross, Angelus Silesius, and possibly by Bruce Andrews. Onto the gravity of this lyric pataphysics we deposit Jean-Luc Nancy's sense of writing as ex-scription and teleologically frame it as a quest for the golden apple of zero the bite of which reveals that to taste nothing is to taste excess in abandonment. And all of this a pretext for whining.

"No ideas but in things." Mineral pleats, trigger blades, geometric conversations, counterweights, hyperbole. But what force names the Other the Thing?

Words do not belong to the inhuman that is language as they are letters in dysfunctional relation and established by laws other than the Law of the Father.

Poetry crosses prose and prose crosses poetry. Chiasmus is a railway convinced that it's a flag.

The contemporary poet's prose is oblong, lit at its corners by chased glass across translucent sentences; its structural coordinates are dome, medallion, and fact; its words when ex-scribed become dictated elsewhere through barrel vaults into a length of nondescriptive sky. Exuberant eyes are there to greet the words as soldiers in a landscape. Dwelling there for the crew has already landed. Its consonants are clerical along straight boles without a bough, its vowels gemmed fabrics and metallic shells catching the ear as club details. The poet's prose, like its dream, has no outside; its grammar stabilizes as viscosity under pressure.

Laminate the entirety of poetics with a paraconsistent logic and then study the preface to the second edition of the *Lyrical Ballads* backward even though the *feeling* of the sublime is a *judgment* without rule. But thank you Marx, Lenin, and you too Trotsky for your thoughts on the violin.

Art is a series of perpetual differences.

—Tristan Tzara, "Note on Poetry"

Screening the Page / Paging the Screen: Digital Poetics and the Differential Text

Marjorie Perloff

"It is fundamentally problematic," writes Peter Bürger in his *Theory of the Avant-Garde,* "to assign a fixed meaning to a procedure."[1] Bürger's reference is to montage/collage: he argues that just because two collages—say, a still life by Picasso and a satiric collage by Raoul Haussmann—use similar techniques of pasteup and collocation of unlike material doesn't mean that the two works actually have a shared aesthetic. On the contrary, Bürger observes, German Dadaists such as Haussmann took what was, for Picasso, essentially an aesthetic form and adapted it for political purposes.

The same principle, I would suggest, applies to the new electronic poetries. As in the case of any medium in its early stages, digital poetry today may seem to fetishize digital presentation as something in itself remarkable, as if to say, "Look what the computer can do!" But no medium or technique of production can in itself give the poet (or other kind of artist) the inspiration or imagination to produce works of art. And poetry is an especially vexed case because, however we choose to define it, poetry is the *language art:* it is, by all accounts, language that is somehow extraordinary, that can be processed only on rereading. Consequently, the "new" techniques whereby letters and words can move around the screen, break up, and reassemble, or whereby the reader/viewer can decide by a mere click to reformat the electronic text or which part of it to access, become merely tedious unless the poetry in question is, in Ezra Pound's words, "charged with meaning."[2]

Then, too, a strong claim has been made for the *interactivity* of electronic text—a claim I take to be largely illusory, especially when it comes to poetry. True, viewers can trace their own path through a given electronic text, can decide whether to move from *A* to *B* or *B* to *Q*, to rearrange word groups and stanzas, and so on. But is such activity really any more "interactive" than, say, the Simms Family games, which allow their players to "decide" what sort of house the family will live in, what their furniture will look like, and what their "personalities" are? For the Simms player, the personality and wallpaper choices are limited to a fixed set of options, produced by the makers of the game in the interest of mass appeal. As children quickly learn—and this is why they soon tire of Simms Family 1 and turn to Simms Family on Vacation or whatever other computer game—permission, as John Cage would have said, is granted, but hardly to do whatever you want. Indeed, the input is rigidly predetermined by the largely anonymous authors and programmers. Adorno would have had a field day with this perfect cipher of the "Culture Industries."

Nevertheless, electronic text does offer the poet exciting new possibilities, which I shall take up in a moment. First, however, I want to say something about the new dissemination of poetry and poetics that is occurring on the Internet. Here a real revolution is taking place right in front of our eyes. Consider Kenneth Goldsmith's beautifully designed site Ubuweb (www.ubuweb.com), where one can access an astonishing variety of avant-garde poetries from the early twentieth century to the present: from Russian futurism and Dada to Fluxus and ethnopoetics, to contemporary movements in visual and sound poetry. There are also critical essays on the poetries in question and, most important, portfolios of otherwise inaccessible work. Thus Craig Dworkin has produced *An Anthology of Conceptual Writing,* with a superb introduction and examples from Samuel Beckett and Robert Barry to Christian Bök—an anthology actually much more adequate than anything currently available in print format. Again, Goldsmith has obtained the entire archive of the avant-garde "magazine in a box" *Aspen* (1965–72), which is unavailable even in leading research libraries, and has posted the entire run (ten issues) on the Web. And on Ubuweb, one can listen to Marinetti intone *Zang Tuum Tumb,* Henri Chopin recite his sound poetry, and Ron Silliman read his macabre question poem "Sunset Debris."

How will the dissemination of such rich and varied material affect the poetry-reading public? Like any revolution, this one will take some time to be felt in Establishment culture. Indeed, even as electronic poetics has become more and more sophisticated, the mainstream journals such as the *Hudson Review* and *American Poetry Review* have moved in the opposite direction: their short lineated epiphanic free-verse lyrics, with their justified left (and often right) margins, surrounded by white space, suggest that nothing has changed: a poem is a poem, period! Indeed, at a recent conference in Belfast on Transatlantic Poetics, I heard an English poet, Ruth Padel, say that there is no such thing as a designed book of poems; there are only separate intense lyrics, and they are "a gift of God." And another poet chimed in that it's time to get away from "silly" concepts like "process" or the "open-ended" poetic sequence because the poet had jolly well better make up his or her mind how to *finish* the poem, how to make that crucial decision that determines its final shape.

No *Aspen* or Vito Acconci for this group, which still dominates university Creative Writing programs and the major newspapers and reviews. But it is only a matter of time until this situation changes, for obviously younger people, surfing the Net, will come across sites like Ubuweb and will absorb the materials posted. Here economics is central: concrete poetry, for example, was always very expensive to reproduce and print, especially in color formats, even as CDs of sound poetry are hard to come by. Today, if you can't afford to buy, say, the collected poems of Haroldo and Augusto de Campos, you can study their works online. True, the texture of the page and its actual lettering will be lost and the digitized artwork cannot quite match the colors of the original, but the fact is that now readers around the world can access the work of Ian Hamilton Finlay or Mary Ellen Solt—work that can now become part of the academic curriculum.

Another interesting facet of the digital dissemination of poetic texts is that electronic texts are likely to be truer to the original than are the usual reprints and anthology versions. The Norton Anthologies, for example, often adjust the visual format of a given poem so as to save space and hence money: intentional double-spacing becomes normal single-spacing, and so on. A classic case is that of George Oppen, who designed *Discrete Series* so as to have one poem per page, whereas the various reprintings have tended to crowd the short lyrics together, with the poems often broken up at the bottom of a given page and continuing on the next. On the screen, that needn't be the case; indeed, a Web site such as Futurism and Futurists (www.futurism.org.uk) reproduces the various manifestos by Marinetti and Boccioni exactly as they were designed, whereas most reprints distort the typography, spacing, layout, and so on.

But what about digital poetry itself—the work now written expressly for the screen? The most interesting exemplars of digital poetics to date have tended to be what I have called elsewhere *differential* texts—that is to say, texts that exist in different material forms, with no single version being the definitive one.[3] Thus a text like Kenneth Goldsmith's *Fidget* has a print version and a digital version, and it also exists as an archive of its gallery installation—an installation whose use of visual and sound media gave it a rather different tone from the other two. Which is the "real" *Fidget?* One cannot say, although each reader may well prefer one mode of production over the others.

The ability to move from one medium to another and back again allows the poet to experiment with temporal and spatial frames. And many of these differential electronic texts use procedural devices, following the example of Oulipo or, closer to home, the rule-governed compositions of John Cage, Jackson Mac Low, and Fluxus. Consider, for starters, Brian Kim Stefans's sequence *The Dreamlife of Letters.*[4] This is a flash piece in which the twenty-six letters of the alphabet, presented in alphabetical sequence (with secondary sequences based on the second letter in each word, and so on), produce words and phrases, all animated in various ways against the background of an orange square. The letters are black or white and dance around the screen in silence, producing new formations, splitting up, and regrouping. Some of the formations look like Cagean mesostics; others insert words inside large capitals; others are produced by letter clashes, circular formations, *lipogrammes,* and myriad other textual patterns, no two configurations being quite the same.

In the prologue, which precedes the actual running of the flash text, Stefans explains the generative e-mail procedure as follows:

> In 1999, I, along with several other poets and writers, was asked to partake in an online "roundtable" on sexuality and literature. The event would be centred around a brief essay by the San Francisco novelist Dodie Bellamy . . .

All of the participants were divided into groups, each individual having a position in that group. As I was the second in position, I was assigned to respond to the person in the first position, who in my case was the poet and feminist literary theorist Rachel Blau DuPlessis.

DuPlessis wrote a very textually detailed, nearly opaque response (to be found here ☑).[5]

A click on this link takes us to DuPlessis' short piece for the roundtable.[6] Here the poet uses passages of complex and suggestive phonetic spelling, alternating with their "translation" or transposition into "normal" English, which constitutes DuPlessis' own commentary on the gender issues with which Bellamy deals. Thus the piece opens with the lines:

> "gin dear hiss delight" sad dough tea bellum me wansin moo van bo drop age tick tock 2 cum "gender is te nigt" said Dodie Bellamy once in "Moving Borders" page TKTK (to come to 2 cum.zzz gindra delite ides aye—ginestra scissors delays, hex you all in ties his duh nigh to come). Is gender the night? I'd say—gender is the day, sexuality is the night.

And it concludes, "Weiner hearing sense lay dunkel troubled nixed sensual heft levelling ring uglies. We experience a doubled, tripled, mixed sexuality of everything all ways."

Stefans seems to have been dissatisfied with this procedure for, despite the complex verbal and phonemic overlay, the DuPlessis piece makes very specific assertions about sexuality. He writes:

> I had decided that I wanted to respond to her text in a detailed manner, but I felt that normal prose would not suffice on my part, so I alphabetized the words in her text, and created my own series of very short "concrete" poems based on the chance meeting of words. My poem (which you can read here ☑)[7] along with a few short paragraphs in response to Bellamy, was my contribution to the roundtable.
>
> As words almost invariably take on nearly obscene meanings, when they are left to linger on their own, and as DuPlessis' text was so loaded to begin with, I didn't enjoy that much. More important, as it was in a sort of antique "concrete" mode, it resembled a much older aesthetic, one well explored by Gomringer, the De Campos brothers, and numerous others since the 1950s, and so it wasn't very interesting to me.

Here, for example, are sections 4 and 5 (b and c) of Stefans's concrete poem:

behoove bellamy bellum

ben bend bi bi big bike

binaries/ bo/ borders,

but
butt

buy

character?
chimneysweeper christ,

cinder cixous

com-round, combinatory:

come come)
comes

—conventional cunt curse . . .

cycle.

The alphabet rule is the also the one to be used in the digital version of *The Dreamlife of Letters,* but here the words are fixed and anchored in their lines, thus slighting the possibilities for pun, paragram, and lettrism available in the electronic text. In the prologue, Stefans notes:

> I don't wish to explain much more about the piece here, except to say that it is not interactive. I decided it was much more like a short film than an interactive piece, and there didn't seem any natural place to let the viewer in that way . . .

I don't think I reveal the dreamlife of letters in this piece; the letters have too many dreams, as I've discovered, though perhaps not enough for me in the end.

In its digital version, produced by "Reptilian Neolettrist Graphics Gallery," an orange square of *A*s—about half of them upside down, some white on black, some black on white, some plain—is complicated by a "Frozen Gifs Gallery" beneath the square, a gallery whose fifteen entries contain different lettristic designs, somewhat reminiscent of Steve McCaffery's *Carnival.* One can run the whole *Dreamlife of Letters* in about eleven minutes; or one can go to the index and access each letter section separately. Thus, the third section, "behoove to caucasians," uses exactly the same sixteen words or syllables as concrete poem number 4, but the units now become actors in a more complex drama. First "behoove Bellamy bellum" appear on the lower left of the orange square. Next, the words "ben bend bi bi big bike" snake in from the upper right in zigzag form, bending, overlapping, and jostling one another so as to produce a time sequence reflecting Big Ben (the clock), introducing bisexuality, and miming the movement of a bicycle across the screen. The *i*'s of "binaries," appearing in the upper left, are momentarily missing, invoking "Benares" in India and only then coming together with "bo" + "orders," constituting the "borders" of binary oppositions. Then "bo" is next given a giant *B* in final position, producing "Bob," and then the big *B* is inscribed with "but," "butt," and "buy," all in small white letters, and the black "caucasians" in the lower left, leading us to the next section of words starting with *C*.

The one word I feel is out of place here is "caucasians"—the reference in DuPlessis' text is to "the Phallus or regressive iden-tiff caucasians"—a too obvious counter, in Stefans's text, to the multivalent, multisexual images of the poet's dream alphabet. At the same time, the movement from the "ca" string of "caucasians" to the first word of the next section, "character," is seamless, as are all the movements from one section to another. In section 4, "character to cycle" gives way to the collocation of "chimneysweeper" and "christ," the two words floating in blurred wavy lines across the lower half of the screen. The words "cinder" and "cixous" (the latter a reference to Hélène Cixous, the great feminist theorist of multivalent sexuality) first appear with their *i*'s missing; their stark simplicity is juxtaposed with the complex, designed mesostic on "com-round, combinatory: / come, come) / comes" that follows. Immediately thereafter, "conventional," "cunt," and "curse" appear in quick succession around a giant circling *C,* the conjunction suggesting that although "curse" is the conventional prudish epithet for menstruation, it is also properly located in the "cunt."

Here, then, is Stefans's poetic commentary on Dodie Bellamy's erotic fiction, as mediated by DuPlessis' analysis. *The Dreamlife of Letters* is elegant, beautiful to look at, and spare, a new way of using language in its materiality so as to make meanings. Is it "better" than the poem, as Stefans himself thinks? Yes and no: the static visual text can be absorbed and studied much more readily than the moving picture. And the third alternative, the embedding of the lyrics in the larger situationist text, is also attractive.

A different variant on the "dreamlife of letters" is provided by Caroline Bergvall in a work called *Ambient Fish* (1999), available from the Electronic Poetry Center. Here typography is not elegant as in the Stefans piece, but the sound dimension is central to the piece, the poet reading aloud as we watch the screen.[8] The viewer/listener is presented with two green buttons on a blank screen. Click on them and they turn red and become breasts. Click on the "nipples" and four rows of four of the same buttons appear. Almost every button quickly gives way to a word or phrase, while the voice-over (Bergvall's very elegant, cool, and evenly pitched voice) pronounces "Ambient fish fuckflowers bloom in your mouth," the text then permutating these words and phrases by means of rhyme and consonance so that "ambient fish" becomes "alien fish" and "alien poche," "loose in your mouth" becomes "goose in your mouth" becomes "goose in your ouch," and "fuckfodder" becomes "fuckfad" becomes "fish fat," while "alien poche" (*poche* is French for "pocket") becomes "alien poach" becomes "a lined peach patch." The refrain "will shock (or choke) your troubles away" or "stow ["throw"] your troubles away" thus becomes quite literal. After the buttons disappear, the voice says evenly, "fuck fish goose in your bouche suck your oubli away." It is a riveting performance.

Ambient Fish evidently started out as a text-sound installation commissioned by a festival of mixed media in England.[9] The refrain was used as a drone in the piece. On-screen, the interrupted recordings of the voice make the absurd lines even more menacing, as do the curious rhymes and repetitions in which such French words as *oubli* (forgotten) and *bouche* (mouth), here pronounced "baush," give the piece a faux pornographic air. *Sucking your oubli*—it sounds pretty sinister! But what is especially unsettling is that when the buttons and words disappear within a minute or so, they leave only three words—"fish," "face," and "your"—as well as a single breast-shape. Then "fish" and "your" disappear, the word "face" circles drunkenly about, and then it finally disappears too, leaving us with an isolated glowing red-green button.

What, one wants to know, are the relationships here between "fish" and "your," between *tirer des eaux* and its rhyme partner in "stow" or "throw your troubles away"? The "loveliness" of the language is wholly deceptive—"fuckflowers" in the context sounds pretty, rather like hollyhocks or gillyflowers. As for the buttons, their role is complicated by their technological function. The standard TV remote control has, at the center of the number pad, usually next to the "5," a button with a raised little dot within it that looks exactly like the button in *Ambient Fish.* Press the button and a new channel opens up its picture. But in *Ambient Fish,* no such thing happens: press the button and you get not a pleasing image but only broken words and disappearing breasts. The anonymous, impersonal voice, with its proffer of sexual pleasures that will "throw your troubles away" or "suck your oubli away" becomes increasingly threatening.

Another intriguing Bergvall digital text is *Flèsh,* which can be found in a recent issue of *How 2. Flèsh,* first called *Flèsh A Coeur,* illustrates Lev Manovich's point that if one can make radically different versions of the art object—as is the case with electronic poetries—"the traditional strong link between the identity of an art object and its medium becomes broken."[10] The project, Bergvall tells us, was first developed to be one of twenty "Volumes of Vulnerability" artist's books, used in a project produced by Gefn Press of London in 2000 to celebrate the millennium:

> It is a tribute to four writers who, for all their cultural differences, share a trance-like understanding of the connections between text and physicality, between violence and verbal illumination, between the intimate and the public facets of sexual desire as also a desire for writing. In each their way, and these were frequently at odds with the declared values of their time, they explored and pushed such connections both in their work and in their body.[11]

The four writers in question are Saint Teresa of Avila, the German surrealist painter Unica Zürn (whose torso tied up with string her artist husband Hans Bellmer transformed into an icon), the visionary language poet Hannah Wiener, and the erotic postmodern novelist Kathy Acker. In its artist's book version, *Flèsh A Coeur* was designed as "a set of 4 folded folios, very low-tech, which demands of the readers that they have to use French cuts with a knife or letter-opener to open each level of text."[12] Hence the "incorrect" French accent over the English word, reminding us that in French *flèche* means "arrow"; *Flèsh A Coeur* is thus the arrow to one's heart—the arrow of romantic love as well as spiritual revelation, piercing the flesh. Indeed, in Bernini's famous sculpture, *Saint Teresa in Ecstasy,* the saint's breast is just about to be penetrated by an arrow.

Cutting—the reader's need to cut the small yellow pages with a letter opener or knife as well as the cutting up of text we find in Bergvall's text—insures that the reading experience is intentionally slowed. But on-screen, redesigned with the help of Anya Lewin, *Flèsh* appears as an impenetrable pink wall, the single word *Flèsh* suggesting not only the cliché that it is the French who are best at enjoying the pleasures of the flesh but also that a click on the mere letters of the monosyllabic word will penetrate the flesh. And so, as one clicks on the four instances of *Flèsh,* first the four names appear, then, with a further click, four extracts from their respective writings, and then, when these texts are opened up by a third click, we have the opposite: *underneath* the flesh, female desire, it turns out, has a common language.

Here is the Saint Teresa section:

> Things had been going rather well. Sex loot. Caravans of PushpUsh. Needy machines Easy To Please. Pissabout reFillable. Rubbed a Fff in It long enough to Suck Off thereafter. The stakes we'd lie in about. Everything pruned happy as shaved. Now-caught In The Grip of. JUMP's the Surf with a StartOff the ace. Oards dig holes in Every SinglePie own I had ed absent mindedly. Row and Row. Torn in the bell heat kicks up spare-Heads. Something's knocking against the sKin. large persistent bulks In the Air. Brutally pulled innards. Gut seizure GONgs concave.[13]

The language here, as we recognize from *Ambient Fish,* is Bergvall's own complex poetic wordplay—her astonishing, aggressive mix of the intellectual and the erotic, the hard and the soft, the "Needy machines" that are "Easy To Please." The harsh phonemic play and eye rhyme give Bergvall's text a kind of electric charge. Nothing is quite what we think it is: "spareHeads" replace "spare parts"; and "stakes" are not something we'd "lie about" but—oddly—"lie in about." Halfway through the passage, the speaker's language breaks down so that "I had owned" becomes "own I had ed." Internal capitalization and the running together of words as in "PushpUsh" creates curious paragrams, and the jamming of sounds and syllables introduces a note of artifice that befits Unica Zürn or Kathy Acker, as well as Saint Teresa. In "Brutally pulled innards," for example, double *l*'s and *n*'s twist the *u*'s and *a*'s in their midst. But the violent erotic scene also contains religious possibilities in those "Gut seizure GONGs concave"—possibilities appropriate for Saint Teresa, as, in a different way, for Hannah Weiner.

The electronic screen thus brings out aspects of *Flèsh* that are not as prominent in the artist's book. In reading the book, the four names are endowed with meanings to be compared, point by point, in what is an atemporal grid. On the screen, however, flesh is always an impenetrable exterior, a blank pink wall that the viewer/auditor must elect to "enter" *in time.* Then, again, when Bergvall performs *Flèsh* in a gallery situation, the vocal intricacies subordinate individual words and word images to a powerful sonic pattern. The relation of text to audience is thus markedly differential.

And this brings me to my next example, in which computer technology has been generative of text that is not itself electronic, at least not in its primary version. In 1997, Kenneth Goldsmith decided to record every word he spoke in a single week. For seven days—a unit that gives *Soliloquy,* as the resulting work is called, its seven-act structure—Goldsmith went about his daily routine, wearing a wire, and "collected" what became almost five hundred pages of his own speech. The piece was first presented as a text installation, but since it needs to be read rather than seen, its more adequate realization is in the austere and sober gray volume published by Granary Books in 2001. A single long print block, *Soliloquy* is certainly a monster, if not a loose or baggy one. Indeed, the text is highly structured, the ground rule—that every word Goldsmith speaks, but not one word by his interlocutors or addressees, will be recorded and that periods of nontalking are not designated as such—creates a seamless and curiously dense language network, a kind of post-Jamesian novel, where we know only what the narrator knows and says. The "characters" in this novel—Goldsmith's friends, colleagues, associates, relatives, and assorted service people to whom he is speaking, as well as those others referred to in the third person—are given no voice; they can be known only through Goldsmith's interpretations.

Is he a reliable narrator? Of course not, but what can "reliable" mean in these cyberdays? To read *Soliloquy* is to infer what prompted question *A* or disclaimer *B* or irritated response *C*. How does the author adjust his speech habits to the different people in his life? And what is the significance of the constant self-interruption, self-cancellation, and self-deprecation that fills this fast, funny, irreverent, and terrifying volume? Terrifying, because, as Goldsmith himself has remarked, it is "humiliating and humbling to see how little of 'value' I actually speak over the course of a typical week. How unprofound my life and my mind is; how petty, greedy and nasty I am in my normal speech. It's absolutely horrifying." "But," he adds, "I dare any reader to try the same exercise and see how much more value they come up with in their life. I fear that they might discover, too, that their lives are filled with trivial linguistic exchanges with waiters and taxi drivers. Even those relationships we feel are so vital to our lives—our family and friends—in linguistic terms are really up for grabs."[14]

The genesis of a text like *Soliloquy* clearly depends on computer technology as well as on advanced recording systems. Goldsmith's relatives, friends, and lunch companions (myself included) evidently had no idea he was wearing a wire and thus spoke quite freely. Yet their words had to be eliminated so as to keep to the rules of the chosen frame—one man's talk for seven days of the week. We think of talk as communal—an experience we share with others—but here the elimination of all those others creates a startling verbal scene. For unlike a real soliloquy or even dramatic monologue, the speech presented here is curiously decontextualized. We often have no idea whom the narrator is addressing, and that address may change within a split second as Kenny hangs up the phone and picks up another call with a "Hi, how're you doin'?" Furthermore, although his talking claims to be random, it is in fact carefully planned, the author setting up the questions and raising the issues that will resound throughout the day. Thus, although the text of *Soliloquy* does not exploit visual devices, computer graphics, animation, or anything else but stone-cold sober print, and although there are no icons to click or dots to connect, *Soliloquy* is, in fact, the ultimate digitally driven text, programmed as it is to eliminate "noise."

Consider the following passage in act 4 (Thursday), in which Kenny and his wife, Cheryl (the video artist Cheryl Donegan), are having dinner in a local Indian restaurant:

Oh I didn't like that guy Alex that we met. The guy with the beard. He was an asshole. Did, you know, he never heard of Alfred Jarry.

He goes Ubu? What's that. Yeah, you know, he never heard of any of that any connection with anything like that. Yeah. They did. Thank you. This food is so good. The crap they were serving up at that place for 20 bucks a plate. That was idiotic. The people in there, you know, it was a really stupid scene. I really gotta pee. OK. Ah, that's better. Is your chicken good? Tasty? No no no, it's alright. You like this red chicken? Hey, you know, you can't say we're not trying right. I know as if as if if being successful artists and writers isn't enough. Isn't it just amazing like all the work that we do to do our work and then all the work that we do to like try to do our work? It's insane, Cheryl, we're working two jobs. Yeah, no, I mean work is OK, but, you know, it's it's just, you know, you do what you do. No wonder why we are so fucking exhausted every night and every day. Well, I mean, it's insane. I don't know how long we'll keep it up for. It's like a lot of artists, you know, well they kind of like paint like they get like Debra they get into their studios once a week or something like that, do think about it much. The fact I, we're doing both things.[15]

This passage allows the reader to be about as close to actually being there as is humanly possible in a retrospective situation. The conversation, or at least Kenny's side of it, is at once inane and meaningful—meaningful in the context of the rest of the book, where Jarry's *Ubu Roi* and Kenny's own Ubuweb play a big part, where Cheryl's recent art show is discussed again and again, and where Liz Kotz, a critic of avant-garde art/music/poetry, now teaching at the University of Minnesota, then still a graduate student, first appears at a lecture of my own that Kenny attended the night before at Columbia University.

Goldsmith's "natural" language is nothing if not artificial. The text provides us with all the normal tics of conversation—the prevalence of "like," "you know," and "yeah yeah," as well as the incompletion of sentences, sloppy phraseology, and repetitive exclamations. But it is also artificial in that it splices together all instances of speech, omitting the silences and interruptions. Thus "I really gotta pee" is immediately followed by "OK. Ah, that's better," there having been nothing said in the minutes that elapse between going to the bathroom and returning to the table. The absence of breaks here and when Kenny is addressing the waiter, as in "They did [take our order]. Thank you," creates a monomaniacal drive as absurd and absorbing as Leopold Bloom's stream of consciousness in the "Lotus Eaters" chapter of *Ulysses.* For the continuity stands in odd relationship to the constant shift in subject matter—the digression from the talk of the red chicken to the serious and somewhat maudlin reflection on our lives and how we overwork and are underappreciated. Not that Kenny doesn't mean it. But next thing you know, he's telling Cheryl all about paneer cheese and how it's served in India. Then Liz Kotz's personality is put to the test, Kenny liking her despite her being a "hardcore man-hater." Life, this text suggests, is like that: we grumble about our fates until the cheese course comes and we try to decide which to sample.

The artifice of *Soliloquy*'s "random" and "casual" writing becomes clearer if we bear in mind that we have no access to the narrator's unspoken thoughts, his physical movements, his reading, his looking at art, his daydreaming. Here, the book suggests, is what life would be like if human beings could do nothing but *talk!* The electronic version, on the other hand, calls that talk into question.[16] It contains the entire book in seven sections, one for each day of the week, but when one accesses a given page or section, only bits of sentences appear on an otherwise empty screen. We soon discover that text is actually *there,* but it is hidden: unless the mouse is pointed directly at a given word or sentence, it remains invisible. The mouse can obviously track the text word by word, sentence by sentence, but only one bit at a time, so that the reader, pointing at a particular phrase, doesn't know what comes before or after. Accordingly, the cybertext becomes an inverted Cagean writing-through, a form of play. Find one sentence and another vanishes. Sentences and phrases are thus fragmented and hidden, creating a conscious discontinuity in the interface. In this manner, the cinema verité quality of the book version is called into question: if the "talk" in the book version looks "natural," in the electronic text, the emphasis is on loss and disruption—on a curious kind of secrecy, as if the text doesn't quite want to be read. Goldsmith's is not, we should note, the nonsequentiality of Ron Silliman's New Sentence but rather a dialectic of appearance and disappearance, absence and presence.

What makes a generative text like *Soliloquy* poetic? Isn't producing such a monster just a matter of following certain rules and using certain computer operations to eliminate the language of others, the pauses and silences? Couldn't anyone do it?

There are two answers to this last question. The first is Cage's "Of course they could. But they don't"—the willingness to *engage* in such a project and putting oneself on the line being half the battle. But—and this is true of Cage as well—the fact is that when one studies Goldsmith's text, one quickly finds that it is much more structured than one might think. For it builds up, metonymically and synecdochically, a network of references that gives us a very particular portrait of the artist as young hustler: a New York artist, dependent on New York, running around the city, talking on his cell phone, making contacts, networking, eating out, trying different foods, meeting people for coffee, running into old acquaintances at all sorts of art galleries and events. How to make it through the day: this is half the battle, but the narrator remains for the most part cheerful and purposive in his demeanor. The "Kenny" of this book is not necessarily a nice man—he's a user and he knows it, and he also loves to gossip and lampoon people. But he is remarkably candid and honest with himself. And that draws the reader—even a suspicious reader like myself who did not originally enjoy my "portrait" in this book—into the linguistic web.

Are Goldsmith, Bergvall, and Stefans electronic poets? Yes and no. Certainly, in the examples given, these artists make the most of digital possibilities. But they shift medium easily: Goldsmith has collaborated with Joan La Barbara in producing verbal/musical texts and has made many installations. Bergvall has fused poetic material with theoretical analysis (in ordinary print format), made installations, worked with musicians, and so on. Her *Goan Atom* is, first and foremost, a book of "poems." And Stefans in 2003 published a book called *Fashionable Noise: On Digital Poetics,* bringing together interviews, lyric poems, and prose "essays" that boast traditional bibliographies of the scholarly model with which we are all too familiar.[17]

In evaluating "electronic poetries," therefore, we should not subordinate the second term to the first. "I don't like the label 'video artist,'" the great video artist Bill Viola once remarked. "I consider myself to be an artist. I happen to use video because I live in the last part of the twentieth century, and the medium of video (or television) is clearly the most relevant visual art form in contemporary life."[18] That was in 1985, and a decade or so later, video has been supplanted by the much greater fluidity and temporo-spatial freedom of electronic space. But Viola's principle holds: the artist or poet uses a particular medium, not because it is "better" than others but because it seems most relevant at his or her moment—currently, of course, the electronic screen, with its particular enticing challenge to the printed book. Does this make the poet in question a digital poet? Or, conversely, is the purveyor of the electronic word ipso facto an artist? "Chopsticks," Viola quipped, "can either be a simple eating utensil or a deadly weapon, depending on who uses them."[19]

Notes

1. Peter Bürger, *Theory of the Avant-Garde,* trans. Michael Shaw (Minneapolis: University of Minnesota Press, 1984), 78.

2. Ezra Pound, *ABC of Reading* (New York: New Directions, 1960), 28.

3. See Marjorie Perloff, "Vocable Scriptsigns: Differential Poetics in Kenneth Goldsmith's *Fidget* and John Kinsella's *Kangaroo Virus,*" in *Poetry, Value, and Contemporary Culture,* ed. Andrew Roberts and John Allison (Edinburgh: Edinburgh University Press, 2002), 21–43.

4. Brian Kim Stefans, *The Dreamlife of Letters,* opening page with introduction, Ubuweb, http://www.ubu.com/contemp/stefans/dream.

5. The boxed checkmark here represents the clickable icon for the link to http://listserv.acsu.buffalo.edu/cgi-bin/wa?A2.

6. University of Buffalo Poetics Discussion Group, September 30, 2000.

7. Stefans, *Dreamlife of Letters,* direct link to poem, Ubuweb, http://www.ubu.com/contemp/stefans/dream/the_dreamlife_poem.htm.

8. Caroline Bergvall, *Ambient Fish,* Electronic Poetry Center, SUNY Buffalo, 1999, http://epc.buffalo.edu/authors/bergvall/amfish/amfish.html.

9. See my interview with Caroline Bergvall in Marjorie Perloff, "Ex/Crème/ental/eaT/ing," *Sources: Revue d'études Anglophones* 12 (Spring 2002): 123–35, at 130.

10. Lev Manovich, "The Aesthetic of New Media," Lev Manovich Web site, http://www.manovich.net. Compare Lev Manovich, *The Language of New Media* (Cambridge, Mass.: MIT Press, 2001).

11. Caroline Bergvall, "Notes to *Flèsh,*" *How2* 1, no. 5 (March 2001). Bergvall also provided helpful comments in an e-mail to me, September 9, 2002.

12. Bergvall, e-mail to author, January 13, 2003.

13. In book form, *Flèsh* has only small portions of this text, but the whole piece (though with variations) is found in *Foil: Defining Poetry 1985–2000,* ed. Nicholas Johnson (London: Etruscan, 2001).

14. Marjorie Perloff, "A Conversation with Kenneth Goldsmith," *Jacket* 21 (February 2002; http://jacketmagazine.com/21/perl-gold-iv.html/).

15. Kenneth Goldsmith, *Soliloquy* (New York: Granary Books, 2001), pages unnumbered.

16. Kenneth Goldsmith, *Soliloquy,* Electronic Poetry Centre, 2001, http://www.epc.buffalo.edu/authors/goldsmith/soliloquy/index.html.

17. Brian Kim Stefans, *Fashionable Noise: On Digital Poetics* (Berkeley, Calif.: Atelos, 2003).

18. Bill Viola, "Statements 1985," in *Reasons for Knocking at an Empty House: Writings 1973–1984,* ed. Robert Violette (Cambridge, Mass.: MIT Press, 1995), 152.

19. Viola, "The Porcupine and the Car" (1981), in *Reasons for Knocking,* 71.

Notes on Contributors

Bruce Andrews is a lecturer in political science at Fordham University. Together with Charles Bernstein, he edited *L=A=N=G=U=A=G=E* magazine, which ran to thirteen issues between 1978 and 1980 and was one of the most important outlets for language poetry, giving a name to the new movement. His books include *I Don't Have Any Paper So Shut Up (Or, Social Romanticism)* and *Ex Why Zee: Performance Texts, Collaborations with Sally Silvers, Word Maps, Bricolage and Improvisation.*

Louis Armand is a poet and the director of the InterCultural Studies program at the Philosophy Faculty of Charles University, Prague. His books include *The Garden, Malice in Underland, Strange Attractors,* and various critical works, among them *Solicitations: Essays on Criticism and Culture* and *Literate Technologies: Language, Cognition, Technicity.* He is a member of the editorial board of *Rhizomes* and *Litteraria Pragensia* and former editor of the *PLR* (*Prague Literary Review*).

Charles Bernstein is a professor of English at the University of Pennsylvania. His books include *The Nude Formalism, Legend* (with Bruce Andrews, Steve McCaffery, Ron Silliman, and Ray DiPalma), and *Content's Dream: Essays 1975–1984.* He has edited many anthologies of poetry and poetics including *Close Listening: Poetry and the Performed Word* and *The L=A=N=G=U=A=G=E Book* (with Bruce Andrews). In the 1970s, Bernstein cofounded the influential journal *L=A=N=G=U=A=G=E.* He also cofounded the Electronic Poetry Center at the State University of New York, Buffalo, for which he serves as executive editor.

Augusto de Campos has published numerous volumes of poetry, including *Poemóbiles, Caixa Preta, Coleções de Poemas_Objetos* (with Julio Plaza), and *Despoesia.* He has translated the works of Mallarmé, Pound (*Mauberley, The Cantos*), Joyce (*Finnegans Wake*), Stein, Cummings, and Khlebnikov into Portuguese. Other publications include *Teoria da Poesia Concreta* (with Haroldo de Campos and Decio Pignatari), *Poesia Antipoesia Antropofagia, O Anticrítico, Linguaviagem, Margem da Margem,* and *Música de Invençao.* He has also recorded a number of CDs, including *Poesia é Risco.* He lives in São Paulo, Brazil.

Simon Critchley is a professor of philosophy in the Graduate Faculty of the New School University, New York, and at the University of Essex, and program director at the Collège International de Philosophie, Paris. He is the author of *The Ethics of Deconstruction* and *On Humour, Very Little . . . Almost Nothing,* and *Things Merely Are.*

Michel Delville teaches at the University of Liège, Belgium, where he directs the Centre Interdisciplinaire de Poétique Appliquée. His recent publications include *The American Prose Poem: Poetic Form and the Boundaries of Genre, Postwar American Poetry: The Mechanics of the Mirage,* and *Le troisième corps,* a collection of prose poetry.

Allen Fisher is head of the art department at Roehampton University of Surrey, where he is a professor of poetry and art. Examples of his work are in the Tate collection, London; the King's College Archive, London; and the Living Museum, Reykjavik; as well as private collections in Australia, Britain, and the United States. He works with extended projects, his current one (*Gravity as a Consequence of Shape*) started in 1982. His books include PLACE, *The Apocalyptic Sonnets, Unpolished Mirrors,* and *Ring Shout.*

D. J. Huppatz teaches design history at the Royal Melbourne Institute of Technology and is an editor of Textbase Publications. He has published articles and reviews on contemporary art, poetry, and fiction. His books include *Sealer's Cove* and *The Week Sonnets.*

Steve McCaffery is a professor of poetics at the State University of New York, Buffalo, and is director and founder of the North American Center for Interdisciplinary Poetics. He has published a two-volume collection of his writings, *Seven Pages Missing: Selected Texts 1969–99,* and two volumes of critical essays, *North of Intention* and *Prior to Meaning: The Protosemantic and Poetics.*

J. Hillis Miller is a professor of English and comparative literature at the University of California, Irvine. His books include *Fiction and Repetition, The Linguistic Moment, The Ethics of Reading,* and *Deconstruction and Criticism* (with Harold Bloom, Paul De Man, Jacques Derrida, and Geoffrey Hartman).

Ricardo L. Nirenberg is an associate professor of mathematics at the State University of New York, Albany. His published research includes *Pseudo-Quasiconformality in Complex Variables* and *Human Identity and Technology*. He is the author of the novel *Cry Uncle* and an editor of the bilingual literary journal *Offcourse*. He was born in Buenos Aires in 1939 and moved to the United States in 1963.

Kevin Nolan is a co-organizer of the Cambridge Conference of Contemporary Poetry and edits its translation series. Recent books include *All Over Susan* and *Loving Little Orlick*. He has translated *Personal Pong* by Pierre Alferi and *Sleeve Guard Hypocrite* by Philippe Beck. Other publications include *The Translations of Frank O'Hara* (as volume editor) and *Silver Bullets of the Sixteenth Century*.

Andrew Norris is a poet and musician living in Brussels, where he teaches at the Institut Supérieur de Traducteurs et Interprètes. He is coauthor (with Michel Delville) of *Frank Zappa, Captain Beefheart, and the Secret History of Maximalism* and is currently working on a manuscript entitled "James Joyce: Subject, Object, Style."

Bob Perelman is a lecturer in English at the University of Pennsylvania. His critical writings include *The Trouble with Genius* and *The Marginalization of Poetry*. He has also published numerous volumes of poetry, including *Braille, 7 Works, a.k.a., The First World, Face Value, Captive Audience,* and *Virtual Reality*.

Marjorie Perloff is Sadie Dernham Patek Professor of Humanities Emerita at Stanford University. Her books include *Twenty-First-Century Modernism: The "New" Poetics* and *Wittgenstein's Ladder: Poetic Language and the Strangeness of the Ordinary, The Poetics of Indeterminacy: Rimbaud to Cage, The Futurist Moment,* and *Poetry On and Off the Page*.

Julian Savage is a filmmaker and writer based at the School of Creative Arts at Melbourne University. He is a member of Textbase, a collective dedicated to experimental writing.

Alan Sondheim is an artist and writer based in Brooklyn. His books include the anthology *Being on Line: Net Subjectivity, Disorders of the Real,* and *.echo*. His videos and films have been shown internationally. Sondheim teaches in the trAce online writing program and has taught at Florida International University in Miami.

Keston Sutherland is the editor of *Quid* and (with Andrea Brady) cofounder of Barque Press. His books include *Mincemeat Seesaw, Bar Zero,* and *Antifreeze.* He is the editor of *The Salt Companion to John Wilkinson.*

Donald F. Theall is university professor emeritus at Trent University in Ontario, Canada. He is the author of *The Medium Is the Rear View Mirror: Understanding McLuhan; Beyond the Word: Reconstructing Sense in the Joyce Era of Technology, Culture, and Communication; James Joyce's Techno-Poetics;* and *The Virtual Marshall McLuhan.*

Darren Tofts is chair of Media and Communications and a member of the Institute for Social Research, Swinburne University of Technology, Melbourne. His books include *Memory Trade: A Prehistory of Cyberculture* (with Murray McKeich) and *Parallax: Essays on Art, Culture, and Technology.* He is coeditor (with Annemarie Jonson and Alessio Cavallaro) of the volume *Prefiguring Cyberculture: An Intellectual History.*

Nicole Tomlinson is a Melbourne-based writer and curator. She is a founding member of the 1st Floor Gallery artists and writers space, which focuses on collaboration between artists and writers, and is a member of the Textbase experimental writers' collective.

Gregory L. Ulmer is professor of English and media studies at the University of Florida. His books include *Heuretics: The Logic of Invention, Teletheory: Grammatology in the Age of Video,* and *Applied Grammatology: Post(e)-Pedagogy from Jacques Derrida to Joseph Beuys.*

McKenzie Wark is a lecturer at the New School in New York City. He is the author of *Virtual Geography: Living with Global Media Events, Dispositions, Hacker Manifesto,* and *Games Theory.*

Avant-Garde & Modernism Studies

General Editors
Marjorie Perloff
Rainer Rumold

Consulting Editors
Peter Fenves
Stephen Foster
Christine Froula
Françoise Lionnet
Robert von Hallberg

Avant-Garde & Modernism Collection

General Editors
Rainer Rumold
Marjorie Perloff